Whelan
Dec 1966

PSYCHOLOGY

The Science of Behavior

PSYCHOLOGY

THE SCIENCE
OF BEHAVIOR

ROBERT L. ISAACSON, MAX L.
HUTT, AND MILTON L. BLUM

HARPER & ROW, PUBLISHERS
NEW YORK, EVANSTON, AND LONDON

CONTENTS

PREFACE

We believe that the introductory course in psychology is an experience to be shared by professor and student. The student's own experience can be enriched greatly through his professor's encouragement to pursue and to gain mastery of those areas of psychology which are of mutual interest to them. We recognize that students do not enter an introductory psychology course as "blank slates," but that, today, most students have good high school backgrounds in biology, chemistry, mathematics, and other sciences. Some even have had partial training in psychology or sociology during their high school years, and certainly every person has developed, at either an implicit or an explicit level, ideas about behavior in general, and about his own mental processes in particular. We recognize that a student's learning is an individual accomplishment, and that the classroom and the textbook, ultimately, can serve only as adjuncts to the learning process. Thus. if the individual student is to attain the objectives of the course, he must obtain an accurate orientation of his own, a perspective with which he can identify, and plenty of encouragement to think out for himself the problems that confront psychology. Too often the beginning student comes away from his course with merely a vocabulary, a few isolated facts, and disappointment.

With these considerations in mind, we have attempted a book which has certain special characteristics. To begin with, the present book is restricted in scope to less than the whole range of psychology in favor of a more concentrated treatment of the field as a "natural science" than is given in existing texts. We have reserved for another volume (in preparation) the social-science aspects of psychology. Perception, learning, motivation, and other topics are viewed herein from an essentially experimental and behavioristic perspective. Not only has this restriction in scope enabled us to probe in greater depth than is usually the case, but we believe such an orientation lays a concrete, scientific foundation in psychology for today's student, who has already been nurtured in an essentially scientific culture. Our own experience has shown that students not only can master this more extensive information, but, in fact, become motivated by it to a more critical understanding of, and interest in, psychology as a subject, himself, his social environment, and the world in which he lives.

Further, this book emphasizes the importance of theory in psychology and in science generally. We have tried to refer to experiments in their theoretical context. Without adequate awareness of the theoretical contexts in which they are rooted, the results of individual experiments can be misunderstood and often seem trivial or insignificant. Theories themselves evolve from the collection and integration of experimental studies. In turn, they provide the basis for suggesting further, more accurate studies. In addition to its fundamentally practical value, the development of the theoretical structure of psychology is most intriguing. Thus, we have, so to speak, invited students to come behind the scenes of experimental work to listen critically as the theoretical issues are debated.

In sampling the current psychological scene, we have, of course, stressed those areas of theory and research which seem to us—in light of present trends in the field (and, more broadly, in science as a whole)—to have the greatest value for understanding and predicting behavior. Naturally, the individual professor will have his own scientific preferences, which may not be in complete accord with those selected for this book. Yet one of the most important roles of the professor in the student-teacher relationship is to share with his student his own particular interests and enthusiasm. By sharing this enthusiasm and interest, the professor can evoke and encourage the student's curiosity and initiative.

The professor who directs his students to further reading along the various lines of particular concern to himself will surely find his teaching experience enriched and facilitated. Further, the extension of regular classwork through independent reading can greatly enhance the learning experience for the student, activating in him latent areas of interest. To assist both professor and student toward this end we have provided extensive bibliographies for each chapter.

There are many individuals who have been of great assistance to us in preparing this volume. First we should like to express our appreciation to the several colleagues who have been kind enough to offer helpful criticism of different parts of the text; while we have tried to incorporate all of their suggestions, we may not always have done so, and any inadequacies in the text we must claim for ourselves. So many secretaries and typists in New York and Ann Arbor have helped prepare the manuscript that to list all of them would be impossible; however, we gratefully acknowledge the significant contribution made by Miss Judith Plekker in her handling of many of the final, prepublication details.

Finally, we would like to express our deeply felt thanks to our wives, Susan, Anne, and Naomi for their forbearance and encouragement during the time this book was being written.

ROBERT L. ISAACSON
MAX L. HUTT
MILTON L. BLUM

December, 1964

ONE INTRODUCTION: THE FRAMEWORK

In constructing a framework for the scientific study of be-havior, we shall indicate how such a study differs from the layman's knowledge of behavior. In addition, psychology will be defined and differentiated from other scientific bodies of knowledge and from the layman's assumptions about it. We shall deal with hypotheses, theories, and facts, and with their use in the description and prediction of behavior. Two important tools of psychology will be introduced: descriptive and inferen-tial statistics.

Observing Behavior

Most people are interested in observing and analyzing their own behavior as well as the behavior of others. The boy who wants to impress a certain girl attempts to decide whether a box of candy will be the right kind of gift for her when he visits her home for their first date. He wonders whether he should ask her out for New Year's Eve at that time or later, and if they are in the same class, whether to ask her out for a cup of coffee. In a similar fashion, a girl might wonder how she can get *the* boy in her French class to notice her. A salesman also uses his knowledge of people's reactions when he makes a sale. Even professors must have a great deal of "know how" when interacting with their students, and this knowledge is based upon their previous observation of student behavior. All these people are using information they have acquired about the behavior of others. Although the success they sometimes have indicates that their information can be useful, in every case their activities are quite different from the professional activities of psychologists, who study behavior from a *scientific* viewpoint.

In order to understand how psychologists study behavior, let us look first at the layman's use of psychology. The salesman or the lover who successfully uses his own "psychological" knowledge often cannot express exactly *how* or *why* he is able to do it. He may have learned how to deal with some people in some situations, but he has not learned how to state his findings in terms of precise principles or techniques which are easily used in other situations by different people. Whereas scientific information must be communicable, the nonscientific, private information of the layman is useful only to its holder. Its privacy may often stem from the fact that it represents and depends on a highly individualized technique. For although one salesman can do wonderously well with a "soft sell" to customers, the same approach, by all observable measures, used by another may mean dismal failure.

One might wish to specify the personality characteristics that identify people who do well using certain techniques. A salesman may have ideas about why the soft sell works for him. He may attribute its success to his friendliness and capacity to establish warm relations with others. But before we accept his hypothesis that warm people like himself should use his particular selling technique, evidence must be submitted that the hypothesis is valid. The salesman might point to one or two cases where warm persons were found to improve their sales by learning to use the "soft-sell" method. What evidence should we accept that training in "soft-sell" really makes men more effective salesmen? Perhaps we might accept the number of sales during a given month, but this figure could result from many other factors and not merely from a special kind of sales training; for example, it might be the result simply of people having more money during this period and thus buying more in general. Another kind of evidence would be the verbal reports of salesmen after they had received such training. Would the statement "I am a better salesman—I know it," be a sufficient criterion of success? The answer to this question is "No," if one is interested in the *performance* of the salesmen.

None of the questions posed in our salesman example is simple to answer. For example, can one be sure that personality characteristics, such as warmth, can be effectively measured? And even if they could, how could we be sure that our measurements were not tapping other, more important personality dimensions capable of producing the observed effects? How can we measure increased selling effectiveness? It would be a good intellectual exercise for the student to design a study to determine the effects of a training program on sales performance for the simple reason that there is no single correct answer. A good design for a study depends on creativity and thoughtfulness, among other things. Science cannot be divorced from human ingenuity. Often a problem in any science must wait for its solution until the right person comes along with just the appropriate idea for an experimental design, but basically, any good experimental design results from the methodical and careful examination of the problem by a disciplined, creative mind.

Scientists depend upon information obtained from experiments that are controlled well enough to allow precise determination of causative factors which can be trusted to yield the same results every time the experimental conditions are repeated. Such information can be called *data.* As psychologists use this word, they mean observations which come from acceptable processes of collecting information. However, all data are not necessarily reliable. One of the values of psychology is that it hopes to teach people what data are reliable and what data are unreliable and even erroneous about behavior.

Facts of Behavior

The justification for the cliché—"psychologists seek the facts of life"—comes from the interpretation of the word *fact*. If we agree that reliable data are observations and records which come from well-controlled and repeatable experiments, then what is a *fact?* A fact is something more than data.

For example, suppose we held the hypothesis that girls with southern accents were more attractive to men than other girls. To test this hypothesis in a well-controlled and repeatable manner, we might ask every tenth girl in the student directory of a college to help us in an experiment. Let us assume that none of the girls has a southern accent. We train all the girls to speak in the manner of southern belles when instructed to do so. After completion of speech training, each girl is placed in a group situation with men. In half these situations the girls speak in their newly acquired accents and in the other half they speak in their normal manner. Ratings of the girls' attractiveness are made by the men in the groups. Suppose we find that the girls who use their southern accents are rated more favorably than the girls who speak naturally. We would have collected data that tend to confirm our hypothesis. But, would it be a *fact* that southern accents make girls seem more attractive?

To accept this statement as a fact would be to go beyond our data. All the experiment demonstrates is that in our specific circumstances girls who use southern accents are rated more favorably by men than girls who do not use them. Since the girls came from only one college and were observed by men in only one situation, our data are limited to this specially selected sample. Data are always limited to the situation from which they originate. If the southern-accent hypothesis were tested in many college, business, and professional circles, with subjects of different ages and from many kinds of social and economic classes, and if all experiments were well controlled and repeatable, then on the basis of these additional data we might be moved to accept the *generalization* that southern accents do make girls seem more attractive to men. Facts are general statements of relationships that have been supported by data from many kinds of tests. They are hypotheses about behavior that have been accepted as being generally useful and significant.

Facts and Theories

In modern science hypotheses become confirmed facts through repeated collection of data. Hypotheses are most often simple statements of relationships between variables. One way of viewing a *theory* is to think of it as a set of interrelated hypotheses. Psychological theories can also be defined as a collection of statements—verbal, mathematical, or symbolic—from which predictions of behavior can be made. When a theory has been supported by vast amounts of data it assumes the status of a fact. Newtonian theory in physics has come to be accepted as fact; synaptic transmission of impulses between the nerve cells in the brain—which only sixty years ago was a hotly debated hypothesis with which many well-known physiologists disagreed—is now a fact (see pp. 88–89).

One of the most important features of a theory is that the statements it contains act jointly to predict behavior. Since psychologists are interested in the prediction of behavior, their whole enterprise centers on the development of useful behavior theories. Their ultimate aim is to produce theories about human behavior that attain the same factual status as Newtonian theory has in its application to physical objects.

A simple theory of behavior might be something like this: As a response is repeated by an organism in a specific situation, a tendency builds up in the organism to make the same response in that type of situation in the future. Let us complicate our theory somewhat by assuming that the organism must be motivated to make any response in the situation. For the sake of simplicity, motivation in this case can be defined as the specified number of hours of food deprivation. Let us further assume that the longer the time without food, the greater will be the tendency to make the response. This is an inadequate theory of behavior, to be sure, but let us examine what we have.

The tendency to make a given response in a situation is determined by two factors: motivation and the frequency with which the response had been made in the situation in the past. The prediction of the response cannot be made knowing only one of these variables. Both the motivation and the number of past responses must be known. To test this theory, we would experimentally manipulate one or the other or both of these variables and note whether or not the predictions are borne out by the resulting data. If the theoretical predictions were fulfilled in all of the test situations, we would begin to have confidence that the theory was useful enough to be acceptable. Sometimes we talk of theories which are generally useful for predicting behavior as *laws*. Of course our simple theory model would not be supported by data, but it should serve to illustrate the idea of predicting behavior from a theory.

Most theories in psychology, as well as in any other sciences, have arisen as attempts to explain a great deal of *existing* data as well as to predict the discovery of new data. In this capacity they serve as summaries of accumulated information and provide sources for developing additional facts about behavior. The theories of color vision presented in Chapter 4 describe a great deal of what we know about the rules of color mixture, the effects of color upon perceived brightness, and certain kinds of color deficits found in humans. Results can be predicted on the basis of the theories because the theories were developed by men who had knowledge of pertinent data. Given the theory, one can accurately predict many color phenomena. Unfortunately, there are some data which cannot be explained (or predicted) by any existing color theory, but we hope that some day a better theory will be developed that will be more useful than the present ones.

Thus, psychologists attempt to predict behavior through the use of hypotheses and theories which may be more or less useful, but when they become generally useful in predicting behavior, they assume the status of facts. Facts, then, are those hypotheses about behavior which have been repeatedly confirmed through the collection of data in many situations at many different times. Theories which are effective in predicting behavior are sometimes called *laws*.

A Definition of Psychology

Many branches of science other than psychology attempt to explain behavior by formulating hypotheses and testing them; and many of the interests evidenced by psychologists in their theories and research are exactly like those of scientists in other areas. Physiologists study men and animals to understand their basic physiological mechanisms. Psychiatrists study behavior of individuals with the aim of alleviating mental disorders. Anthropologists study the behavior of men in different cultures. All seek to understand and predict behavior. Psychology is only one of many areas of science which are concerned with the study of behavior, and psychologists study many aspects of behavior that are also studied by other disciplines.

There have been many attempts to define psychology in ways which will differentiate it from other areas of science. These attempts have not been entirely successful. To understand why this is the case, let us examine some aspects of the study of psychology. Most psychologists tend to be more concerned with the entire individual than do most physiologists. The latter may study the function and activity of the liver without direct concern about the behavior of the entire organism. Although they would agree that to understand the functions of the liver one must take into account all the other operations of the body, they would focus their study upon the liver. A psychologist would rarely approach the study of behavior in such a specialized manner, but would tend to study a given function in terms of its effects on the behavior of the whole person. Thus, if there is one characteristic which acts to set psychology apart from the other scientific areas, it is the relative emphasis on understanding the individual as a total functioning unit. Looking at the kinds of things psychologists actually do, and assessing many of their professional activities, will give insight into the diversity that is psychology.

Some psychologists investigate the neural mechanisms underlying sensation and perception, studying the structure and function of the eye or the ear. Their methods and their background usually are similar to those of physiologists interested in the sensory processes. Some psychologists work with emotionally disturbed people or with patients in hospitals or in clinics. Psychologists also try to discover the best techniques for designing machines, and the most efficient ways of operating them, to take advantage of the characteristics of man. Others study the man at his job as an individual, a social, or a group phenomenon. They consider the effects on morale and attitude of joining unions and of participation in various kinds of company programs. Psychologists also work on the development of testing programs ranging from intelligence measurements, with which all of us have had experience, to the measurements of specific kinds of aptitudes or abilities. Although many psychologists are concerned with applied problems such as these, there are many others who are entirely involved with the development of theories of behavior, and who are quite removed from any immediate or practical considerations.

Theoretical psychology   Psychologists working in the theoretical areas attempt to understand the basic functions and organization of man. Some want to understand why individuals differ from one another, and there are many approaches to understanding individual differences. Some psychologists work to study the development of behavior from birth onward, and there are many who investigate the influence of genetic and prenatal environment factors. The assessment of individual differences, as basic research, is a field in itself, quite apart from any practical application. Other psychologists study how we perceive the world around us. Certain of these psychologists center their attention on the sensory organs (eyes, ears, etc.) while others study the perceptual characteristics of the human in more complex environments. Quite a number of basic scientists study the physiological mechanisms underlying behavior. They seek to establish the neural correlates of learning, memory, and the emotions. Other psychologists studying these basic attributes of behavior prefer to seek understanding in entirely behavioral terms, and thus we have specialists in theories of learning and memory. Even though many people are interested in the human as he exists in global perspective, as an entire individual or a unit in his culture, their field need not be *applied* psychology. Their emphasis is on the development of more adequate conceptualizations of man, not upon predicting his behavior in the *real world*.

Applied psychology   Yet, there are many competent scientists who are interested and concerned with man in the real world. They study man in his natural environments—at home, at his job, and in the marketplace. These psychologists are interested in the application of psychological knowledge to behavior. Increasingly, society is demanding psychologically trained people to work in industry, education, and government. Applied psychologists work with man and machine systems (sometimes called the general area of human engineering), as school psychologists and consultants in education, in industrial settings concerned with employer-employee relations, in clinical settings where they attempt to help emotionally disturbed people, and even in the marketplace to learn why people buy what they buy. Of course, many psychologists have found it possible and profitable to combine theoretical and applied psychology.

Historical Development of Psychology

The present-day activities of psychologists are derived historically from at least four different streams of influence: philosophy, clinical studies, physiology, and mental testing.

INHERITANCE FROM PHILOSOPHY Man has always been curious about himself. Where does he come from? Where is he going? What is his purpose in life? Is he born with inherent knowledge of right and wrong? Is the mind or the body more real? Does man exist, or is he merely an idea in the mind of God? Questions such as these have persisted since the beginning of recorded human life, yet their answers have not been found and are not likely to be found. At least you will not learn them from present-day psychology. Theories are intended to predict data which arise from well-controlled and repeatable experiments, nothing more. They are to reduce trial-and-error methods in dealing with behavior [1], but do not attempt to learn the eternal truths of life. Theories, the backbone of psychology, are not necessarily absolutely true or false. They tend to offer explanations, understanding, and predictions of behavioral phenomena.

Nonetheless, one the most prominent historical roots of psychology comes from the philosophers and their attempts to understand the nature of man through reason, logic, and argument. The most important philosophic roots of psychology come from the Greeks, especially Plato and Aristotle. The Eastern philosophies (Zen Buddhism, Hinduism, Confucianism, etc.) have contributed little to our modern view of behavior. More recently, the school of philosophy called British Associationism and some German philosophy, as developed by writers such as Leibnitz and Kant, have had some influence. More will be said of the contributions of the British Associationists in Chapter 6, on learning (see pp. 212–213). Those interested in the philosophic background of modern psychology have several excellent sources available to them [2, 3]. The greatest influence of these philosophic roots can be found in the areas of learning and perception. For example, when we speak of learning as an *as-*

sociation between a stimulus and a response we are using a concept of association not very different from that propounded by the British philosophers several hundred years ago.

CLINICAL INHERITANCE Differentiating normal behavior from mental illness and knowing the sometimes tenuous border-lines between them are some of the demands placed on psychologists. The antecedents for this are to be traced directly to Sigmund Freud (1856–1939). Freud was an Austrian physician who founded a new method of treating the mentally ill and developed a new theory of personality. Both the method of treatment and the personality theory are called *psychoanalysis*. Freud emphasized the role of unconscious impulses (wishes, desires, drives, or motives). The behavior of the individual, and especially of the emotionally disturbed individual, is thought to reflect his unconscious motives, which are always active although unknown to him. We shall take up the contributions of Freud relating to the development and organization of personality at great length in a companion volume to this book, touching on them only briefly here.

Freud's influence is far-reaching and pervasive throughout all of psychology. While crediting Sigmund Freud, we should note that the assumption of continually active unconscious impulses had been anticipated earlier many times by philosophers. In particular, the German philosopher Herbart (1776–1841) proposed a theory of unconscious impulses that was remarkably similar to Freud's. The latter's major contribution was to make explicit the sexual nature of the unconscious impulses.

We speak of Freud's contribution as *clinical* because it is based on the clinical study of persons with mental disorders, but clinical psychoanalysis should be distinguished from the more general clinical contributions of the health or medical sciences, since these have contributed in different ways to modern psychology. Scientists in basic medicine have contributed in great part to our understanding of the sensory, nervous, and other physiological systems underlying behavior.

INHERITANCE FROM PHYSIOLOGY For our present purposes, physiological investigations represent the most direct contribution to modern psychology. Our knowledge of the functions of the brain, its sensory systems, and the anatomical substrates of behavior comes almost wholly from physiology. The indirect effects of physiological investigations can be seen in theories of learning and motivation. For example, the work of the Russian physiologist Ivan P. Pavlov (1849–1936) is clearly reflected in our current theories of learning. The work of the modern physiologists is now effecting our theories of motivation and emotion. In short, there is a great deal of cross-fertilization between physiological and psychological investigations. In one sense the behavioral study of the organism defines the problems that may someday be solved through understanding the physiological functions of the body.

Probably the most important physiologist to contribute to modern psychology was Hermann von Helmholtz (1821–1894), whose work on the anatomy of the eye and the ear as well as on color vision remains classic. Experimental psychology started in the laboratory of Wilhelm Wundt (1832–1920), a German physiologist and former assistant of Helmholtz. Another German scientist, Gustav Fechner (1801–1887), was the first to study the relation between physical stimulation and perceived sensation (psychophysics).

MENTAL TESTING The fourth historical root of psychology comes from France, where Alfred Binet (1857–1911) developed the first standardized method of mental testing. He was commissioned to develop a method for identifying mentally retarded children so that they could be educated more economically and effectively in special programs. Binet developed the first mental test, and one of the contemporary tests of intelligence, the Stanford-Binet, still bears his name.

Mental tests have been successful in predicting success in school and in industrial and military programs. Some people have argued that there has been too great a reliance upon objective testing of mental capacities especially in the United States. If this is so, it comes from the undeniable efficacy of such tests in predicting many aspects of human behavior. The success of mental-testing methods has stimulated the development of many other kinds of specific techniques and methods which have been applied in all areas of psychology.

Today we find psychologists working directly along the lines of these four historical approaches to understanding man. Psychologists work toward understanding the physiological mechanisms supporting behavior, they work in mental testing, they work as learning theorists using many of the rules developed by the British Associationists, and they work toward helping those who are mentally disturbed. But each of these historical roots has extended beyond its own domains: The psychologists working to understand the basic laws of learning know and use concepts derived from mental testing; those working with mentally disturbed patients know the many facets of intelligence which have been reported from mental-measurement efforts, and this information helps them understand the potential abilities of their patients. There is a constant process of cross-fertilization among all of the areas of psychology.

Psychology, Other Sciences, and the Student

Psychology is a kind of bridge between certain of the pure and applied sciences. On the one hand, psychology stands in a close relationship to the pure sciences of neurophysiology, biochemistry, genetics, and others; on the other, the applied areas of clinical psychology, industrial psychology, human engineering, and educational psychology are closely connected with education, medicine, industry, and engineering. Somewhere between these basic and applied sciences can be located the subareas of psychology which aim at understanding how people learn, why people show greater or poorer retention of material already learned, what motivates people's behavior, how they perceive the world around them, their personality organization, and its interaction with their social environments.

How should psychology be categorized? Should it be classified as a biological science or a social science? Parts of the study of behavior could be included in either of these academic classifications. Not only does this present a problem to the administrator, who has to make decisions for the purposes of granting student credit, but it is also a problem for the student, who must learn about the recent developments in many areas of psychology to understand what it really is.

In the past twenty-five years we have witnessed an unprecedented growth in the sciences. All areas of psychology have produced knowledge and theory at rates almost impossible to exaggerate, and as a direct result it is hard for the professional psychologist to keep abreast even of the most recent developments in his own area of specialization. Now, if it is difficult for the psychologist to keep himself current because of this fantastic growth of knowledge, imagine the student's difficulties, in his introduction to the subject.

Each subdiscipline has been so active that the cross-fertilization of one area of psychology with another has probably seemed to diminish. Ideas developed in one area do cross over to another, but so many new facts and concepts arise in each subdiscipline that they seem almost to give rise to separate sciences. Contemporary psychology, as a result, is composed of many different and partially isolated approaches to understanding behavior.

The Need for Statistical Data in Psychology

Earlier in this chapter we suggested a difference between data and facts (hypotheses about behavior that have been repeatedly confirmed by experimentation). Investigators in the subareas of psychology classified as natural and social sciences are active in collecting more and more reliable information. All areas of psychology are experimental. The personality theoretician, the clinical investigator, the educational psychologist—all collect data from well-controlled experiments just as do psychologists in the physiological or learning areas. As the student will learn, the methods of experimenting and the control over experimental conditions differ among these areas. The amount of information that can be obtained from even one experiment is nearly overwhelming. There is a universal need to be able to summarize research results so that they can be more readily grasped and be more meaningful. To do this, we use descriptive statistics. Usually we wish to describe at least two characteristics of the data coming from an experiment: (1) the central tendency of the data and (2) the variability of the data.

MEASURES OF CENTRAL TENDENCY A measure of central tendency is a combined score, a numerically expressed figure, that tells us something about the characteristics or the level of performance of a group under observation. It is the best single measurement of the set of data collected from observing the group. The most commonly used measure of central tendency is called the *mean*, which is simply the numerical average of the scores obtained from each individual in the group. To obtain the mean, the *sum* of all the scores is divided by the *number* of scores involved.

Returning to our salesman who believes in soft-sell methods, let us assume we allow him to test his theory and we advance him to an executive position and place him in charge of the company's hiring and training program. He hires twenty new salesmen and assigns ten of them to the new soft-sell program he has developed and ten of them to the regular training program. He assigns the salesmen by flipping a coin to eliminate possible biases in his assignment. After completion of the two training programs, the ten soft-sell salesmen join the other

TABLE 1.1   UNIT SALES: SPECIALLY TRAINED GROUP (A) VS. REGULARLY TRAINED GROUP (B)

Group A		Group B	
Salesman	Units Sold	Salesman	Units Sold
1	23	A	22
2	25	B	20
3	17	C	14
4	13	D	18
5	19	E	22
6	27	F	24
7	16	G	22
8	21	H	23
9	21	I	16
10	15	J	16
Total	197		197
Mean	19.7		19.7

ten salesmen in the field. These latter, remember, have only had the benefit of the company's regular program. After three months of actual selling experience, the sales manager collects the sales records of the ten men in each group. His results are presented in Table 1.1. The total sales in terms of units of the company's product are identical for both groups of salesmen. Since the groups were composed of equal numbers of salesmen, the mean number of sales in each group is also identical. Remember, the mean is simply the total divided by the number of cases which make up the total.

Our new sales manager is downhearted at this result, since his specially trained group did no better than the salesmen completing only the regular training program. However, he argues, "Well, that's not unexpected, because you remember I predicted that my soft-sell methods would only work for those who were warm and friendly to begin with." Thereupon he determines which salesmen were rated as warm and friendly by their trainers in the training program. He finds that five of

TABLE 1.2. UNIT SALES OF SPECIALLY TRAINED GROUP, "WARM"-RATED VS. "COLD"-RATED SALESMEN

Salesmen Rated "Warm"	Units Sold	Salesmen Rated "Cold"	Units Sold
6	27	1	23
2	25	3	17
8	21	7	16
9	21	10	15
5	19	4	13
Total	113		84
Mean	22.6		16.8

the special group were rated warm by their trainers and he compares their sales with those of their colder associates. Table 1.2 presents the sales manager's new results. Now he finds that the mean sales of the warm salesmen who completed his soft-sell program were far above the colder personality types

TABLE 1.3. UNIT SALES OF REGULARLY TRAINED GROUP, "WARM"-RATED VS. "COLD"-RATED SALESMEN

Salesmen Rated "Warm"	Units Sold	Salesmen Rated "Cold"	Units Sold
F	24	G	22
H	23	D	18
A	22	I	16
E	22	J	16
B	20	C	14
Total	111		86
Mean	22.2		17.2

who were similarly trained. Here at last is evidence for his view! However, our sales manager also prepared Table 1.3, which compares warm and cold salesmen who did not have the special soft-sell training. Once again, we find those rated as warm do best, and we also note that those men with the special training were only slightly different from those rated warm but without the training. This might indicate that warm personalities tend to be better salesmen of the company's products than chillier personalities, but this could only be established as a "fact" when it could be shown that warmth and friendliness were the *only* characteristics distinguishing the better salesman. As for our sales manager's hypothesis, we can find no support for it from the data he collected.

The evidence can be summarized by the mean sales records of the groups. The means represent an estimate of the middle or central scores (sales) achieved by each group. We evaluate the effectiveness of the hypothesis by the differences among the mean scores of the various groups.

In our present example we have dealt with the *mean* (average), but there are other measures of central tendency. One can also use the most frequently obtained score in the group (the mode), or one can use that score which separates the upper from the lower half of the distribution (the *median*). The mode for salesmen in group A of Table 1.1 is 21. What is the number of sales which is the mode of the distribution of sales made by the men in group B?[1] The mean and the mode, both estimates of central tendency, differ in this example, i.e., the mean is not the same number as the mode. Furthermore, in each of the distributions the median does not equal either the mean or the mode.[2]

Which of these three common estimates of central tendency is the best to use depends upon the characteristics of the entire group of data, although where the number of cases is large, the mean score is often the most appropriate. When the number of cases in a group is small, the median is sometimes preferable. An important advantage of the mean, in general, is that it is an algebraic value, and hence it can be utilized in any further algebraic operations the investigator may wish to employ. The mode and the median do not have this advantage.

Knowledge of a measure of central tendency gives us some information about a group of numbers, whether they are sales

[1] Answer: 22 units.
[2] Since there is an even number of cases (ten) in each of the distributions of Table 1.1, there is no single number which has half of the numbers smaller than it and half the numbers larger than it. Therefore, the medians must be found by finding the number halfway between the fifth and sixth largest numbers. In the case of the salesman in group A it would be the number halfway between 19 an 20, i.e., 19.5. In the case of the salesman with the special training it would be the number halfway between 20 and 22, i.e., 21.

figures, scores from mental tests, or whatever. When, however, we add information about the *dispersion* of the numbers about their central tendency, we gain a great deal more information about the data.

MEASURES OF DISPERSION   At this point we can profit by introducing the concept of *distribution*. A distribution is nothing more than the arrangement of numbers under consideration. All the numbers representing the sales made by the two groups of salesmen arranged in sequential order from highest to lowest, as in Table 1.1, represent a distribution. Any time we have a set

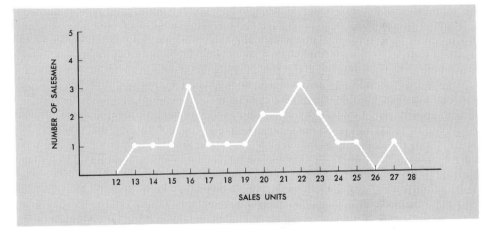

FIG. 1.1.   *The data of Table 1.1 redrawn as a frequency distribution. The two groups of salesmen have been combined.*

of scores and arrange them in such a manner we can call them a *distribution*. It is often helpful to rearrange our data in a *frequency distribution;* that is, according to the number of times, or frequency, each of the scores occurs. To do this we merely make an orderly progression of scores along the *x* (horizontal or *abscissa*) axis of a graph and plot the number of individuals who obtained each score on the *y* (vertical or ordinate) axis, connecting each point with a line. The sales of the two groups of salesmen given in Table 1.1 are combined and drawn as a single frequency distribution in Fig. 1.1. In frequency distributions the mode will always be the score on the *x* axis that is associated with the greatest (highest) point on the *y* axis. When two scores tie for the modal average, as occurs with the salesmen's scores, the distribution is called *bimodal*.

17

Statisticians have various rules which can be applied to describe the shape of distributions, but we shall not discuss them in this book.

Even with the unusual distribution in our example we can make some attempt to describe the dispersion (or variability) of the scores which constitute the distributions. We can give the *range* of the scores, e.g., from 13 to 27 for the salesmen of group A. The range is obtained simply by subtracting the lowest score from the highest score, i.e., 13 from 27. In this case the range is 14 sales units. We can also calculate statistical estimates of the amount of dispersion of the scores around the mean of each distribution. Some of these statistical measures are called the *average deviation,* the *standard deviation*, or the *sum of squared deviations*. Once again an extended discussion of these measures is beyond the range of our present intention. However, the student should be aware that these latter measures of dispersion are algebraic like the mean.

From the bimodal character of our frequency distribution we would be led to expect that two distinct types of individuals were represented. This is just what we found in our hypothetical example, namely, that the warm and friendly salesmen did better than the colder personalities, whether or not they received the special training.

NORMAL DISTRIBUTION Normal frequency distributions are those which are symmetrical around the mean and which fall

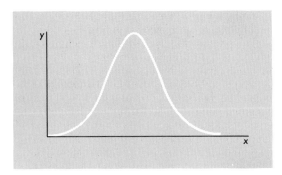

FIG. 1.2. *A normal distribution. Mathematically, this distribution describes a relationship between two variables. Often frequency distributions approximate this relationship. For frequency distributions, scores are plotted along the x axis and the number of individuals achieving each score are plotted on the y axis.*

off at a systematic rate from the mean. This phenomenon has highly desirable mathematical characteristics and, when plotted on a graph, takes on a bell-shaped curve, often called a *normal curve,* as illustrated in Figure 1.2.

When the frequency distributions of a large number of observations from many kinds of psychological experiments are studied they often tend to approximate a normal distribution. This allows the accurate description of the dispersion of the scores about the mean of the distribution through the use of the statistic called the *standard deviation*. When data approach a normal distribution and when the mean and standard deviations are known, the distribution is completely described. This is a great saving in description. By two numbers, the mean and the standard deviation, we provide as much information as by presenting all the individual scores which go into the distribution. In this sense statistics are highly valuable in their ability to summarize data.

INFERENTIAL STATISTICS Statistical description allows us to do more than summarize the data: it allows us to evaluate hypotheses about behavior. When we wish to know whether soft-sell methods are more effective than traditional methods of training, we naturally turn to statistics for summarization. We may use measures of central tendency and dispersion. However, we must be able to estimate the magnitude of the differences between groups of scores that is required for a hypothesis to be considered tenable. How large must these differences be?

For any particular experiment, we can postulate at least two possible outcomes; usually one outcome is based on a particular hypothesis or theory we hold, while the other is based on what is called the null hypothesis. From the former we might predict that, of two matched groups of subjects chosen from a larger population, the subjects in one will behave differently (or have different characteristics) from those in the other. The null hypothesis postulates that any difference between the two groups will be no greater than the chance variation normally expected to arise from the selection of our samples.

We know that in selecting any samples—particularly if they are small in proportion to the total population they represent —we are bound to obtain some differences owing to purely chance factors which may have nothing to do with the assumptions of our hypothesis. However, we can calculate the probable range of such misrepresentation that might have risen through selection of the samples; if the difference between the mean scores obtained for the two groups in our experiment (or the dispersion of individual scores) is large in relation to the *standard deviations* of the samples, the null hypothesis can be rejected. Thus, if the null hypothesis is to be disproven in favor of a test hypothesis, the differences between the two groups must be greater than those predicted by the null hypothesis. It is worth noting that all research aims at disproving the null hypothesis, rather than at proving the test hypothesis.

The following experiment demonstrates the effects of taking samples from a population. Take twenty small pieces of paper and write numbers on them according to the distribution of scores given in Fig. 1.3. On one piece of paper write the number 1; on another write the number 7. Continuing to work alternately with the scores at either end of the distribution, there will be two pieces of paper with the number 2 on them, and two pieces with the number 6 on them. Place numbers on the remaining pieces of paper according to the frequencies shown in

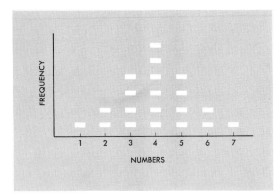

FIG. 1.3. *Example of distribution of a "population." Deviation of sample mean from population mean will decrease as the size of the sample increases.*

the figure. Place the twenty pieces of paper in a box or hat so that you cannot see the numbers and mix them thoroughly. Now draw out a sample consisting of three pieces of paper and note the average of the numbers on the three papers. Place the papers back in the box and mix them again. Now continue to take additional samples of these papers, and jot down the average in each case. Note the fact that the means of the samples of three papers differs from the mean of the entire population of the twenty slips of paper, often by a considerable margin. Now increase the size of your sample by drawing four slips of paper each time, and note the averages obtained in this part of the experiment. If you then continue to increase the size of the sample you take when reaching into the box, you will find that the means of the selected sample get closer to the true mean of the population as samples of drawings get larger.

The null hypothesis merely asserts that any difference between groups of scores comes from this kind of chance fluctuation, that is, the difference is due to the "luck of the draw" in obtaining the sample. In our original example we stated the null hypothesis; the difference between the two groups of salesmen was not significant.

When we wish to test whether two groups of scores differ, we usually test the obtained scores against those expected on the basis of the null hypothesis: We test whether the differences between groups might occur simply by chance. We usually do this kind of a test because it is simpler to test for the absence of a difference (a difference attributable to chance alone) than to test for the affirmative hypothesis. The student might do well to ponder this last statement. His understanding of why this is true will be valuable in gaining insight into the reasons why so much psychological experimentation requires this process.

We can make two kinds of mistakes in interpreting the results of experiments: we can accept the null hypothesis when we should reject it, and we can reject the null hypothesis when we should accept it. Each type of error is unfortunate, and we must avoid them both. Given the means and standard deviations of our two groups of subjects, it is possible to estimate the likelihood of significant differences (our hypothesis) or only chance differences (the null hypothesis). These estimates come only from information from the mathematics of probabilities and depend in part upon the extent to which the data obtained in the experiment approach well-known distributions such as the normal distribution.[3]

The results of a psychological experiment are often reported by use of a statistic that estimates the probability that the differences between experimental groups arose through chance-sampling fluctuations from the one underlying population. Some names of statistics for the evaluation of the differences between groups are the t test, the F ratio (or F) and Chi square (χ^2). For each of these, it is possible to find a related probability that

[3] Mention should be made of a recent development in statistical analysis. The procedures involved in evaluating the outcome of experiments for or against the hypothesis under test may change radically in the next few years with the application of Bayesian statistics to psychological research [4]. One of the major differences between Bayesian statistics and traditional statistics is that in the former the probability of acceptance of the hypothesis under test depends in part upon the experimenter's expectancies of finding support for the hypothesis before undertaking the experiment.

the null hypothesis should be rejected. In the future you will probably read a report of an experiment in a psychological journal which says that a difference between the scores of subjects in two groups in the experiment was significant beyond the .05 or .01 levels (meaning 5 and 1 percent, respectively) of confidence. Simply, this means that the difference in the scores of the two groups was large enough to justify the rejection of the null hypothesis because only 5 times in 100 attempts or 1 time in 100 attempts would drawing two samples from a single population give a difference as large as or larger than that found in the experiment. (Remember that this statement is justifiable only after making assumptions about the distribution of the underlying population from characteristics found in the data of our two groups.) Since the chances that our two groups represent one population are remote, that is, 5 in 100 or 1 in 100, we say the difference is *significant,* meaning the null hypothesis would be unlikely.[4]

CORRELATIONAL METHODS It is often desirable to express the results of an experiment in terms of the relationship between two measurements made upon a group of subjects. One way to do this is to express the relationship as a correlation coefficient, a statistic that expresses the degree of relationship between two sets of measurements.

The relations between two groups of measurements can be presented graphically as a *scatter plot.* Numbers representing measures of one characteristic of the subjects are given on the ordinate or *x* axis and numbers representing measures of the other characteristic of the subjects are plotted on the abscissa or *y* axis. A point on the plot is determined by the two respective scores representing each subject.

Once again an example is in order. Let us devise a hypothetical experiment in which we wish to relate the amount of "exploratory behavior" shown by animals with an amount of a hormone, let's call it hormone X, in their blood. First, we allow each animal to explore a box with a checkerboard floor for $\frac{1}{2}$ hour and count the number of squares it enters. Then, we take a blood sample from the animals and make a bio-

---

[4] The .05 and .01 levels of confidence are frequently, but not always, employed to satisfy the test of a significant difference. The specific level of confidence chosen or the criterion for significance depends on the degree of risk of being wrong in rejecting the null hypothesis which the experimenter wishes to employ in drawing a conclusion.

chemical analysis to find the level of hormone X in each subject. For each animal, we have two measures:

1. The amount of exploratory activity represented by squares entered in half an hour.
2. The amount of the hormone X present in 1 cubic centimeter of blood.

Table 1.4 presents the results of our hypothetical experiment. The first measure for each animal is given in one column and the second measure for each animal in the other column. The same results are plotted in a scatter plot in Fig. 1.4. By looking at

TABLE 1.4 HYPOTHETICAL DATA OBTAINED IN THE EXPERIMENT RELATING AMOUNT OF HORMONE X PRESENT IN THE BLOOD AND THE AMOUNT OF EXPLORATORY BEHAVIOR SHOWN BY THE ANIMALS

Animal	Amount of Hormone (in Arbitrary Units)	Number of Squares Entered in Exploratory Period
Q	7	6
R	6	4
S	10	7
T	4	3
U	7	4
V	4	5
W	9	7
X	12	8
Y	8	3
Z	8	6

this figure we can see that there appears to be some relationship between the two sets of measures. The relationship is not perfect, for if it were the data would fall in a straight line.

A statistical description of the data relationship is possible by calculating the statistic called a correlation coefficient for these data. The results of this computation is +.74, which indicates the degree of relationship present in our data.[5]

Because of their specific mathematical nature, correlations (short for correlation coefficients) range from −1.00 through zero to +1.00. A correlation cannot be lower than −1.00 nor

---

[5] In this case a rank-order correlation was used because it best fitted the characteristics of our hypothetical data. There are many types of correlation coefficients which may be used depending upon the nature of the variables being evaluated.

greater than +1.00. The minus and plus signs are arbitrary and only indicate the direction of the relationship. In our example large scores on one rating go with large scores on the other rating and *by definition* this is a positive correlation which is indicated by the +.74 value obtained. If we had measured the tendency for the animals to remain in one place, that is, the tendency not to explore, and compared this measure with the blood levels of the hormone, then we would have had a negative correlation. The significance of the results would be the same, however: animals high in the measured hormone move around more in our maze and this result could be described by a positive correlation with activity or a negative correlation with the animals' sedentary tendencies. It must be emphasized that the sign (positive or negative) of a correlation has nothing at all to do with the strength or degree of the relationship between the two measures.

The degree of relationship is conveyed by the extent to which the absolute value (disregarding the + or −) of the correla-

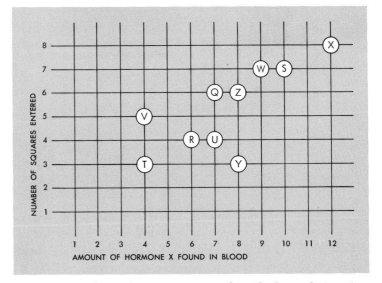

FIG. 1.4. *Table 1.4 drawn as a scatterplot. The letter designating each animal is encircled at the intersection of its hormone level and the number of squares it entered in the exploratory period.*

tion approaches 1.00. The closer the correlation is to 1.00, the greater the degree of association between the two sets of scores. A correlation of +1.00 or −1.00 represents a perfect correla-

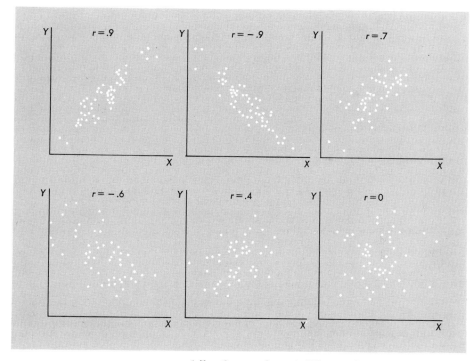

FIG. 1.5. *Scatterplots of different degrees of relationship expressed by the associated correlation coefficients.*

tion between two variables. A correlation of +.74 indicates the same degree of association as a correlation of −.74. Figure 1.5 shows scatter plots of various degrees of correlations. The reader should note that the closer the scores cluster along a straight line the greater is the size of the correlation coefficient.

Just as with differences between mean scores for groups of subjects, it is possible to determine correlation coefficients that represent a degree of relationship not likely to occur through fluctuations in the samples—that is, not due to chance factors. The technique for establishing significant correlations attempts to evaluate the probability that the two measures are completely unrelated and that they come from two populations of scores having no relationship with each other. The null hypothesis in the case of correlations would state that the obtained correlation was merely due to a peculiar stroke of chance in sampling from the two populations. From characteristics of the samples which are plotted on the *x* and *y* axes, it is possible to estimate probabilities that the null hypothesis is incorrect and that there *is* a relationship between the two sets of measures.

CORRELATION AND PREDICTION A perfect correlation allows perfect prediction of one measure or score from the other measure or score. If the correlation between exploratory activity hormone level had been +1.00 or −1.00 we could have predicted either of the ratings from the other. A high degree of correlation allows us to make predictions that are far better than chance.

Correlational predictions are usually made about groups of people and are often used in applied situations such as personnel selection or in the prediction of academic success. With relatively high correlation coefficients people high on one measure will tend to fall into predictable ranges on the other variable. Without a perfect correlation, however, some exceptions will occur. Thus, success in college achievement correlates approximately +.30 with scores obtained from the American College Entrance Examination [5]. This means that those who have low scores on the examination will tend not to do well in college and many of them will be asked to leave college. This is a statistical prediction that has been replicated many times. This information can be used in counseling prospective students and in selection by educational institutions of students who will best benefit from their programs.

This use of correlational data obtained from the performance of groups of individuals presents conceptual and ethical problems for science and society. If an organization can improve its efficiency, even by a moderate amount, by the selection of individuals who have personality characteristics correlated with success in their business, is it justified in giving personality tests to job applicants to screen out individuals who do not have the characteristics? Some of these individuals, perhaps quite a few, if the correlations are low, will not even be given the opportunity to try. Is the use of knowledge of statistical characteristics of a population justified when applied to individual cases? From the point of view of statistical conclusions the answer is "yes," since more correct judgments are made than wrong ones even though some errors also occur.

In one sense, less than perfect correlations reveal our lack of knowledge about a phenomenon. If we know that one personality characteristic correlates moderately, but far less than perfectly, with success in a business or profession, then knowing more about the characteristics of success would allow us to make the predictions approach 1.00. Then we would be able to apply the discovered method of prediction in both the group and the individual cases. But perfect knowledge may not lead to perfect predictions.

We know that many single nerve cells of the optic nerve are activated when the eye is flooded with light. Not all of them are activated, so our correlation is less than perfect. When we learn more about the codes used in the nervous system in the transmission of information from the eye to the brain, we may be able to improve our predictions about the activation of the nerve cells at the presentation of the light. However, and this point is essential, even if we know all about the functions of the nervous system, any single prediction may be only moderately accurate because of the imperfections of the measuring instruments. We may be able to know all possible responses of single cells in the visual system to light, but never be able to say with perfect certainty that our recording probe has reached any particular type of cell because of the minute size, physical similarities, and proximity of cells in the optic nerve. By the same token, we may never be able to measure, in a perfectly reliable way, those personality characteristics that we know to be related to success in business. This is most likely to be the case. Knowledge, even though it may reach perfection, may not allow the perfect prediction of the behavior of the single cell in the nervous system or of the individual in society.

STATISTICS AND DATA Almost always, the data used by psychologists are refined by the use of descriptive statistics. Measures of central tendency and dispersion must be used to reduce the quantity of the information resulting from even the most direct experiments. Inferential statistics are useful in estimating the likelihood that the differences resulting from the experimental manipulations are substantial enough to be accepted as greater than could be expected through chance fluctuations in the samples of subjects used.

There are many ways to describe and analyze experimental data, just as there are many ways to design an experiment that is well controlled. Not all are equally useful or appropriate to test the particular hypothesis under consideration. There is no one book to read, and there is no one academic course that will prepare a person to do good research or to be a scientist. As in most areas, experience and scholarship in the area of specialization will ultimately lead to a competent level of ability in experimentation. But the factors of ingenuity and creativity, and perhaps even genius if it is different from these two qualities, are necessary for significant research contributions.

Explanation

Psychologists want to explain human behavior. Earlier we talked about the role of theories and hypotheses in the prediction of behavior, and before moving on to Chapter 2 we shall consider more generally the relation between prediction and explanation.

Explanation and prediction have a great deal in common. In predicting behavior we take information already at hand and look toward the future. Given certain behavioral data we then expect (predict) certain other behaviors to follow. We expect these other behaviors because of theories that tell us what to expect. It is theory that makes observations of the present necessary precursors of the future.

The essential role of theory in predicting behavior can be illustrated as in Fig. 1.6. Here, a horizontal line represents the separation of a theory world of variables, concepts, and theoretical constructs, from the real world of observations and data. In the theory world there are rules whereby combinations of certain concepts lead to, or permit, certain other concepts to be inferred.

In a simple experiment using biological motives, we could have a theory that relates food-seeking to a state of hunger. If we want to predict how fast an animal will run down a long passageway for food, we might predict that the hungrier an animal is, the faster will be his running speed.

Hunger, the motive factor, is a theoretical concept. We can never see hunger directly. It is something inferred from observations made in the real world. We could infer the presence of this *motive construct* from the observation of the number of hours the subjects have been without food. (Note that our theory must include a statement that relates the intensity of the motive to the number of hours without food.)

To make a prediction of behavior, we must deduce from the theory. The theory might state that when biological motives are aroused, the organism will attempt to approach stimuli that satisfy this motive. It might go on to state that the greater the biological motive, the greater attraction food will have. We test

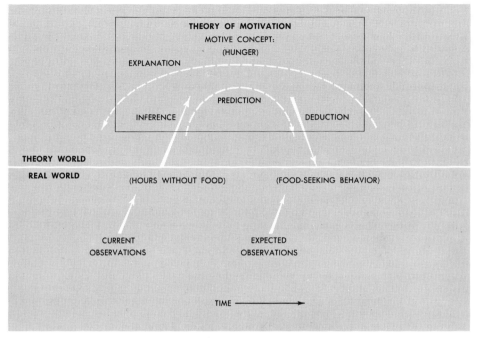

FIG. 1.6 *Schematic representation of the role of theory in the explanation and prediction of behavior.*

the deduction made from the theory by looking for data in the real world. We could measure how hard an animal works to obtain food, how much punishment it takes to deter his food-seeking behavior, whether or not it chooses food in preference to water or a sexual partner. These represent predictions generated by the general theory of motivation and by our current knowledge that the animal has, in fact, been deprived of food for a certain time.

On the other hand, explanation follows a similar pathway through the theoretical or the real world, but in an opposite direction. Suppose we notice an animal exhibiting persistent food-oriented acts. Why does it do this? We would accept the explanation that this behavior is attributable to hunger, provided that (1) we have a theory that relates hunger to food seeking and (2) we learn that the animal had been previously deprived of food.

The example is oversimplified, to be sure, but the general pattern holds even with more complicated examples. Given a theory relating academic performance to an individual's intellectual and emotional development, we can predict college success or failure from knowledge of measures of these factors made through objective tests. These allow inference to the theoretical variables and deductions from the theory are the predictions of how well individuals will do.

Given a student who is failing in college work, we feel his behavior can be explained when we have a theory that would predict such failure given certain earlier measures of personality and when the objective real-world measures of personality fit what the theory would anticipate. One can view the processes of prediction and explanation as being very similar in form, differing only in whether one is looking ahead to future events or looking back for causes.

In this first chapter, we have completed a full circle. We began by discussing the views of the layman about psychology and how the psychologist looks for firmer grounds and better observations before developing theories to explain them. The scientist wants well-controlled and highly reliable data and is not satisfied with a few observations made under uncertain circumstances. Once the real-world observations have been established, the psychologist looks for relationships between observations that are consistent and repeatable, and we have used the word *fact* to describe such firm relationships. But goaded on by a need to understand behavior, scientists develop theories or interlocking sets of hypotheses about behavior that, if useful will allow the prediction and explanation of behavior. Not all theories work well; only those theories that work best are retained in science.

Theories which are useful in predicting behavior are the goal of psychology. Theories are not necessarily true or false; they are more or less useful to explain and understand behavior. All scientific theories are evaluated against this pragmatic criterion.

Psychology comprises many kinds of theories. Some relate personality characteristics to complicated social behavior. Some relate early experiences to personality development, whereas others deal with foundations of behavior.

In this latter category we have theories concerned with the relationship between genetic influences and the development of the individual, theories relating neural structures and functions to behavior, theories describing the relation of our sensory mechanisms to perception, and theories of perception itself. We have theories of the basic mechanisms of all learning and remembering, and specialized theories of our verbal accomplishments. We have theories of motivation and emotion. But before we can have theories like these, we must have good, reliable data. This book is an attempt to provide a review of the data, facts, and theories that provide the foundations for the study of behavior.

References

1. Conant, J. B. *Science and Common Sense*. New Haven: Yale Univer. Press, 1951.
2. Boring, E. G. *A History of Experimental Psychology*. New York: Appleton-Century-Crofts, Inc., 1929.
3. Murphy, G. *An Historical Introduction to Modern Psychology*. New York: Harcourt, Brace & World, Inc., 1949.
4. Edwards, W., Lindman, H., & Savage, L. J. Bayesian statistical inference for psychological research. *Psychol. Rev.,* 1963, **70,** 193–242.
5. Fricke, B. G. *Opinion, Attitude and Interest Survey Handbook*. Ann Arbor: Evaluation and Examination Division, Univer. of Michigan, 1963.

TWO GENETICS AND PSYCHOLOGY: A RAPPROCHEMENT

A knowledge of the causes of the resemblances and differences among individuals is one key to understanding human behavior. Psychologists have sometimes overemphasized environmental influences to the exclusion of heredity. Other psychologists have naïvely assumed hereditary factors as causes even though they have not been established as facts. The result has been an artificial separation of genetics and psychology. There is no doubt that heredity and environment both contribute to the development of an individual and to the way he is like or different from other individuals.

A basic and fundamental understanding and knowledge of psychology demands a knowledge of genetics. Genetics and psychology must be considered as interrelated if we are to truly understand behavior. The influences of genetics on the individual's behavior in many respects can be considered as a preliminary to understanding the individual's behavior from a psychological point of view.

At chronological maturity an individual has had a considerable degree of cultural training. Twenty and more years of almost constant interaction between the individual and his surroundings have produced a person whose behavior is, in some major aspects, largely predictable from the social demands found in his culture. There is no doubt that the best predictors of some kinds of behavior are merely the social expectations of society. Think of your own behavior; what you wear, what and when you eat, what you say in practically every situation from the classroom to the intimate conversation of lovers are all predictable by our current social customs. Anyone who reaches maturity has had his behavior shaped and molded by the various environmental factors that go with being reared, educated, and group living.

Environmental factors act to determine behavior at all levels of development. The ways parents enforce desired behavior patterns in children, for example, in use of the toilet and by their punishment or praise, are techniques used for transmitting the prominent social values of the culture. But, there are other kinds of environmental influences that may affect the child even before his birth. For example, the amount of oxygen or other vital substances that are in the environment of the developing fetus will have a great deal to do with his ultimate adult characteristics.

At the meeting of the sperm and the egg, the genetic information from the father and mother are joined and the rest of the determination of the individual is up to the environment. At that point our ancestors have genetically done all they ever shall for us in terms of biological inheritance. How much of adult behavior is determined at the fertilization of the egg? How great is the effect of heredity on behavior? How do genetic influences manifest their controls of behavior? These are the questions that will concern us in this chapter.

33

Early Behaviorism and Genetics

The leading proponent of the behavioristic school of psychology, John B. Watson, threw out a challenge to those who believed that behavior was determined in any significant degree by heredity in this famous passage:

I should like to go one step further now and say, give me a dozen healthy infants, well-formed, and my own specified world to bring them up in and I'll guarantee to take any one at random and train him to be any type of specialist I might select—doctor, lawyer, artist, merchant-chief and, yes, even beggar-man and thief, regardless of his talents, penchants, tendencies, abilities, vocations, and the race of his ancestors. I am going beyond my facts and I admit it, but so have the advocates of the contrary and they have been doing it for many thousands of years [1, p. 104].

The reader must agree that this is a rather direct and unequivocal denial of the importance of genetic factors at the meeting of the sperm and the egg. If Watson was right, then any confluence of hereditary strains doesn't matter because through subsequent socialization and training any type of person could be produced. This statement, unusual in its strength as well as its argument, needs to be set against the background of psychology as it existed prior to 1930 and against the social and political atmosphere of the culture.

Watson was attacking both introspective psychology and instinct psychology. The first attempts to build theories of sensation and perception based upon an individual's analysis of his own mental experiences. The term *introspection* refers to an individual's attempt to see within himself, to become aware of his own conscious experiences. At the time of Watson's statement, psychology was just beginning to free itself from its bondage to "a study of mental experience" which had created endless series of controversy and debate without hope of adequate empirical resolution. In other words, Watson wanted less subjectivity and more objectivity.

Instinct psychology placed great emphasis on behavior which was instinctive. For example, McDougall considered much of human behavior to be influenced by innate psychological dispositions. Instincts according to McDougall were considered to be the fundamental source of all human activity and determined the ends of all behavior. Although conceded to be modifiable, the original behavior form was considered innate.

Watson with his desire to study human behavior more objectively became interested in the study of animal behavior. He was aware of the work of Pavlov, a Russian physiologist. This blossomed into Watson's firm committment to the Pavlovian view that the relation between stimulation and response, both objectively measured, was the proper study of those interested in behavior. Soon Watson was arguing that all learning was merely conditioning and was no different from a dog learning to salivate to the sound of a bell after the bell and the food had been paired many times.

Reviewing the history of modern psychology we find a steady progression away from introspective psychology as well as instinct psychology and toward the new view of behaviorism [2, pp. 292–299]. Consciousness was first attacked as inconsequential to psychology and later rejected as illusion. The influence of heredity upon behavior declined in Watson's writings until he reached the categorical denial expressed in the quotation given above.

On the positive side it must be said that behaviorism stressed the point of view that all we can know about another person is what we can observe of his behavior; we can never directly know another's perceptions or thoughts. If we accept this position, and if we recognize that psychology attempts to provide theories to explain observable behavior then we have come to the behavioristic position widely accepted by present day psychologists.

The denial of importance of the influence of heredity in controlling behavior was not without support from the social and political spirit of the times. Think of our heritage from American history for a moment. "All men are created equal," reads the Constitution. Does not Watson's view seem to fit in better with this philosophy than a view that holds that intellectual abilities are determined by heredity and therefore that men are not created equal? If some men are smarter than others, why shouldn't they rule the others? Is a view of behavior which stresses the importance of genetic inheritance undemocratic? Of course it is not, but it should be remembered that social and political factors have always influenced prevailing opinions on the extent of genetic influences. The challenge hurled by Watson was biased in part by his society.

To a considerable degree, the antigenetic attitude made explicit by Watson has prevailed in psychology. Only in recent years have psychologists begun to pay attention to the relation between behavior and heredity, and it is likely that there will be increasing intercommunication between the sciences of genetics and psychology. This reconciliation is one which promises to help in understanding behavior and to serve as a counterbalance to the excesses of early behaviorism.

The resistance among psychologists to crediting genetic influences with much effect in governing behavior also comes from another quarter. Clinical psychologists, psychiatrists, and psychoanalysts, the group attempting to evaluate and treat personality disorders, have tended to minimize the importance of hereditary influences in such disorders. An extreme reliance upon heredity as the cause of all such disturbances would negate the effectiveness of psychological methods of treatment. Clinical psychologists have found that most mental disturbances can be helped by treatment. But hereditary factors may still contribute to tendencies toward more-or-less disintegrated behavior. Other reasons for the resistance of clinical psychologists to the significance of genetic influences in behavior have been discussed in a provocative article by Meehl [3] which essentially states that schizophrenia, while its content is learned, is fundamentally a neurological disease of genetic origin.

Genetic Material

When the human sperm and egg unite, each provides twenty-three chromosomes—the hereditary background of the potential individual. Chromosomes are bodies of material in the nucleus of cells which are darker than the other cellular material. Because of their dark appearance after staining they are called chromosomes, or colored-bodies. Every cell in the body contains the same number of chromosomes. All human cells have forty-six chromosomes. Half have come from the mother and half from the father. Each species has its own special number of chromosomes.

Through its genetic inheritance each cell becomes a specialized unit of the body. Some cells become nerve cells, some blood cells, some muscle cells, and so on. Through determination of single-cell development, the information in the chromosomes

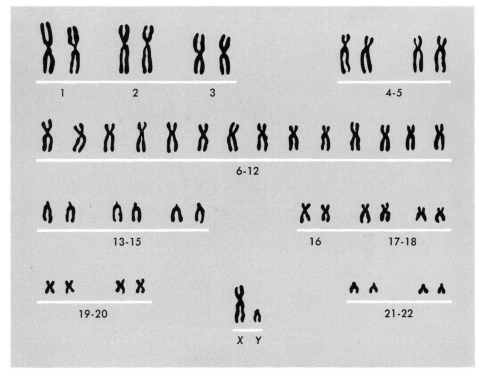

FIG. **2.1.** *Normal male chromosomes. Courtesy of M. Neil Macintyre, Western Reserve University, School of Medicine.*

determines gross bodily characteristics (e.g., hair color, eye color, and the number of muscle and nerve cells). In the horse and the dog, selective breeding has isolated pure strains with special characteristics especially suitable for hunting, running, and jumping.

Just how is information stored in the chromosome and how does this information exert such a powerful influence upon the development of the individual?

THE GENETIC CODE In 1962 the Nobel Prize for Medicine and Physiology was awarded to Francis Harry Compton Crick, James Dewey Watson, and Maurice Hugh Frederick Wilkins for their discoveries concerning the structure of the material of heredity. Their investigations have provided important insights into the composition of the chromosomes and, more important, how the genetic information is encoded in them.

Chromosomes are made up of long organic molecules whose substance, deoxyribonucleic acid (DNA), is found in the chromosomes as two long strands periodically connected by chemical bonds. These connecting bonds are four organic *bases* (in the chemical sense of the word). The two strands of DNA are curled in the form of a helix, a configuration similar to a spiral, but which does not come to a point (see Fig. 2.2).

In normal cell division the chromosomes form images of themselves just before the cell divides. Each chromosome forms a copy of itself so that the two cells resulting from the division have exactly the same genetic composition. Before cell division, the chromosomes form copies of themselves when the two strands of DNA separate at one end and peel away from each other, progressively from one end to the other. The four basic compounds connecting the two DNA strands determine what kind of molecules will be constructed to replace the DNA strand that pulled away. Given a type of connecting basic compound, only certain molecules can be attached to replace those which tore away. The missing strand of DNA is filled in from molecules in the immediate vicinity of the breaking DNA, and since each of the original strands fills in the missing structure, an exact replicate of the original DNA double strand is produced from each of the single, separated strands. This process is illustrated in Fig. 2.3.

The most constant feature of genetic material, after many cell divisions, is the order of the four basic compounds connecting the two strands of DNA. Genetic information *must* be constant in normal cell division, and therefore, all the genetic information an individual receives is encoded into the order of the four connecting compounds. Our hereditary information is not in the long strands of DNA, itself, nor in the four connecting compounds, per se. It is in their order of appearance between the two strands of the DNA helix.

We can think of this in another way. The four basic compounds can be thought of as representing symbols in a four-letter code. Their order of appearance will be used to indicate the messages. This would be like writing in a language that has only four letters in the alphabet instead of our twenty-six. We could send any message in this four-letter code. The organic molecules in the chromosomes are so long and the interconnections so numerous that there seems to be little doubt that all of the genetic information required to designate the special func-

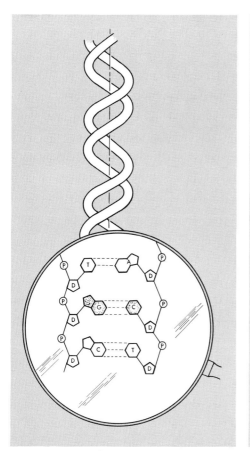

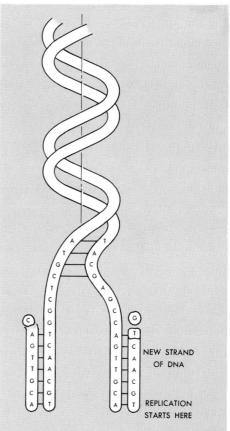

FIG. 2.2. *Highly schematic reconstruction of double helix formed by DNA molecule. Lower part of helix is enlarged to show bases adenine (A), thymine (T), guanine (G), and cytosine (C), and how these are linked with deoxyribose (D) and phosphoric acid (P).*

FIG. 2.3. *Replication of DNA during which the two strands of DNA are thought to separate, each serving as template on which new strand forms. Replication is beginning at lower ends of separated strands. Note that end result is two identical double strands.*

tions of cells in our bodies could be easily transmitted by this process—with plenty of room to spare.

Although all of the cells in the human body have forty-six chromosomes, this number is reduced by half when eggs and sperm are produced. At one stage of cell division, in the ovaries of the female and in the testes of the male, a special type of division takes place which reduces the normal chromosome number. This reduction in chromosomes prepares the way for the meeting of the egg and the sperm, each of which will have twenty-three. In this special type of cell division the regular tearing apart of the two strands of DNA is altered. In this case the basic compounds of DNA pull apart, but the other matching strand is not formed. Furthermore, the individual strands of DNA do not maintain their integrity. There is a mixing up of the DNA between the members of the chromosome pairs. It is this mixing at the stage of special cell division which prepares for the sperm and the egg which is responsible for the endless diversity found among people.

In normal cell division each new cell has an order of connecting bases identical to that of its former mate. If this condition prevailed in the formation of sperms and eggs, then every egg or sperm of a person would be endowed with the same order of bases. Therefore, all offspring of one set of parents would receive the same genetic information. We find a considerable degree of differences among the offspring of a given set of parents, and this diversity comes from a scrambling of the order of basic compounds in the DNA in one stage of cell division when the sex cells are made.

DETERMINATION OF SEX   The sex of the offspring initiated by the union of the sperm and the egg is determined by the presence or absence of a certain chromosome. One pair of chromosomes is concerned with the sex of the child. Girls have two similar chromosomes called X chromosomes. Men have an X and a larger Y chromosome (see Fig. 2-1). The special type of cell division which reduces the number of chromosomes preparatory to forming eggs and sperms can only result in eggs with X sexual chromosomes, because that's all there is to apportion to the new cells. The male, on the other hand, has both an X and a Y chromosome and when the sperm are produced, they may have either an X or a Y chromosome. If one of the X sperm unites with an egg, also carrying an X chromosome, then the child will be a girl. If a Y sperm meets an egg the offspring will become a boy.

Under rare circumstances chromosomal abnormalities occur. It may happen that more than two sex chromosomes result from the meeting of the sperm and egg. This condition produces a hermaphrodite, a person who has sexual organs and characteristics of both sexes. Such individuals have an extra chromosome in their genetic constitution, forty-seven chromosomes, three of which are concerned with sexual determination.

THE CONCEPT OF THE GENE   There is a considerable degree of confusion about the nature of a *gene*. The early anatomists thought the lumps which appear on the chromosomes in histological preparations were genes, but they are not. No one has ever seen a gene. Genes were inferred from an analysis of the lines of inheritance found in people and in animals. From the analysis of parents and offspring, rules of inheritance were discovered for certain bodily characteristics (e.g., eye color). When these traits are passed on from parent to progeny in what has come to be understood as a regular fashion, they are said to result from a certain gene in the chromosomes. A gene is *a hypothetical packet of genetic information determining a specific trait in the species.* Since all genetic information is in the chromosome material of the nucleus, the concept of genes in the chromosomes was invented, and it must represent a sequence of basic compounds existing between DNA strands. Recently we have learned that gene effects can be more or less localized in certain regions of chromosomes. The gene must represent the coding of information using the four organic basic compounds occurring over a limited extent of the long double-stranded DNA molecule.

Further, we know that genes controlling the same characteristics occur in matched positions on two paired chromosomes, i.e., in the same position along the extent of each pair of chromosomes. All chromosomes occur in matched pairs and the genes along one of them are related to the same bodily characteristics as the genes in similar positions on the other chromosome of the pair. We know very little as to the actual chemical composition of a gene, but we do know something of the mechanisms through which the information in the order of bases along the DNA effect the development of the body's cells.

HOW GENES WORK   The genetic information determines the development of each specific cell through the production of proteins. Protein synthesis is controlled by information encoded in the bases connecting the DNA strands. A messenger substance carries the protein-forming information in the DNA of the cell nucleus to the protein-manufacturing sites in the cytoplasm. This chemical messenger between the DNA of the cell nucleus and the extranuclear protein production sites, *ribosomes,* is a compound very similar to DNA. This substance is ribonucleic acid (RNA) and is different from DNA only in the

41

presence of an oxygen grouping in the molecule. The RNA picks up information contained in the configuration of nuclear DNA and transports this information to the ribosomes which are also made up of RNA (see Figure 2.4). The story is more complicated than this. Smaller molecules of RNA are soluble in the cytoplasm of the cell. This soluble RNA combines with specific amino acids (the stuff of which proteins are made) and with energy-packed phosphorous compounds. This package consisting of soluble RNA, a specific amino acid, and the phosphorous compounds which provide cellular energy, migrate to certain designated positions on the ribosome surface. There, the amino acid breaks free from the RNA bonds and joins with

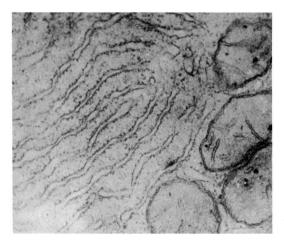

FIG. 2.4. *Ribosomes, the dark granules on the tube-like structures, are the sites of protein synthesis. The large, irregular spheres are mitochondria. The photograph was taken using an electron microscope at 50,000 diameters. From J. A. Moore.* Heredity and Development. *Cambridge: Oxford, 1963. By permission of L. D. Peachy, J. A. Moore, and The Oxford University Press.*

adjacent amino acids to form one kind of protein. The pattern of amino acid sequences, and consequently the type of protein formed, is thus determined at the surface of the ribosome and this in turn is controlled by the information brought by the messenger RNA from the nuclear DNA.

Genes are thought to be the fundamental units of biological inheritance and thus are the links of life between one generation and the next. By definition, all inherited traits are the results of genes. As we shall see, all of the genes which are inherited by the organism act together in determining characteristics. In some instances and in some species a few characteristics appear to be determined by only one or two genes. And it has been from the study of characteristics determined by a single gene that many of the rules of genetic inheritance have been discovered.

Dominant and recessive characteristics   Genes occurring in paired positions along the chromosomes carry contributions toward the same characteristics but can give information which would cause different kinds of development. One gene may act to cause the development of blue eyes, while the matched gene in the other chromosome may act to produce brown eyes. When both genes of the chromosomes act to foster the identical characteristic in the offspring, this is said to represent the *homozygous* condition. If the information concerning a given characteristic differs in the paired gene positions, the condition is called *heterozygous*. In many cases one of the tendencies of the pairs of genes found in the heterozygous condition will dominate. Thus, when a child inherits a gene for blue eyes from one parent and a gene for brown eyes from the other, the child will evidence brown eyes. Therefore, we call the gene for brown eyes *dominant*. However, the dominance of one gene over another is not absolute, and often the effects of the recessive gene can be seen in the offspring.

Mutations   Changes in genetic structure occur from time to time. There are several known ways in which these alterations can be produced. Some alterations are occurring all the time, but it has been shown that mutations occur faster than their "spontaneous" rate when the gonads of an organism are exposed to radiation. Often the effects of mutations are hidden because usually they are recessive and are obscured by the contribution of the dominant gene. However, some mutations are lethal and cause the death of the offspring. The mutant stock cannot, then, perpetuate itself. The effects of mutations are often masked by changes in the appearance of the offspring which stem from changes in the environment. Most geneticists and scientists in related fields are convinced that a low rate of mutation is preferable to a high one since few, if any, of the alterations caused by mutations help the organism to survive.

Genetic Influences

MENDELIAN INHERITANCE   In 1866 Gregor Mendel published the conclusions of his years of painstaking observations of cross-breeding strains of plants. Mendel discovered the rules of inheritance through the study of hybrid peas growing in the garden of an Austrian monastery. His principles of inheritance have been found to be applicable to both plants and animals when the particular characteristic under study is determined by a single gene. In several varieties of peas he found a number of differentiating characteristics. Once having found these characteristics that differentiated the plants, he studied the progeny that resulted from cross-breeding the different plants. Thus, he was able to study the inheritance of one characteristic at a time.

The Mendelian scheme can be summarized as follows: If a man who is homozygous for blue eyes marries a woman homozygous for brown eyes, the children of this couple will have only brown eyes. The genes determining this characteristic eye color can be called BB (brown) and bb (blue). The capital letters designate the dominant characteristic. The children of the homozygous couple will have one gene for brown eyes (B) and another for blue eyes (b). Now what happens if a heterozygous man marries a heterozygous woman? Figure 2.5 presents the outcome of this procedure. The distribution of children from this marriage will be such that one-fourth of them will be homozygous for brown eyes (BB), one-half of them will be heterozygous (Bb), and one-fourth of them will be homozygous for blue eyes (bb). Note that blue-eyed children will be born even though both parents were brown eyed. Judging only on external appearances, three-fourths of the offspring will exhibit the dominant gene trait of brown eyes.

Mendel's contribution reaches great significance because it points out that all genetic information comes to the individual in units rather than in a graduated series or continua. In other words, we receive from our ancestors genes controlling the development of specific unitary characteristics, not a mixture of various tendencies which has been blended together.

The view of Mendel that genetic inheritance came in gene packages was at odds with a long prevalent notion of biometricians (those who study the characteristics of various kinds of biological populations). Characteristics of men and animals tend to vary continuously along a dimension as is the case with intelligence. We do not find a cluster of bright people and a cluster of stupid people, but rather we find intelligence to be distributed in what appears to be a normal distribution (see Chapter 1). If our genetic inheritance comes in units, as Mendel suggests, then why do we have a continuously varying measurement of population characteristics like intelligence?

One answer to this issue was suggested by Mendel himself.

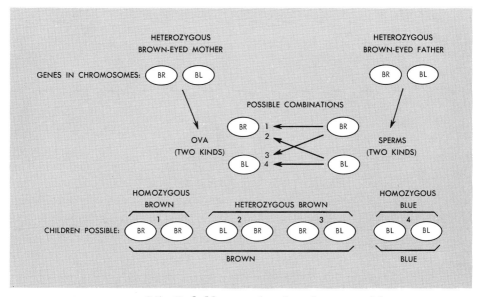

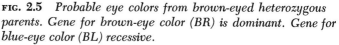

FIG. 2.5 *Probable eye colors from brown-eyed heterozygous parents. Gene for brown-eye color (BR) is dominant. Gene for blue-eye color (BL) recessive.*

He suggested that some characteristics might be determined by two or three elements (genes) acting together. In the early 1900s it was shown that if a characteristic was determined by several genes which had small but cumulative effects on the characteristic, the result would be a population which was continuous in that characteristic. Gradually the idea of continuous genetic inheritance in which hereditary influences from parents are blended was gradually discarded, and the rules offered by Mendel to explain genetic inheritance became the generally accepted rules for all inheritances.

POLYGENIC INHERITANCE The term *polygenic inheritance* refers only to the fact that some characteristics are determined by genes at more than one location in the chromosomes. Without doubt, most of the characteristics of the human that have been behaviorally studied are products of the action of many genes determining the functions of many kinds of organic systems.

SEX-LINKED INHERITANCE In some instances structural or functional characteristics of the body seem to be especially prominent in one sex rather than the other. This is due, it is believed, to the fact that the genes concerned with the development of the characteristic are part of the X or the Y chromosome. Color blindness of the red-green variety is a case in point. Men tend to be color-blind much more often than women. Perhaps as much as 5 percent of the male population suffers from a red-green defect in color perception, but only a fraction of 1 percent of the female population has a similar condition. The reason for this could be that the gene for color blindness is a recessive which is only found in X chromosomes. Since women have two X chromosomes, and the gene for normal color vision is dominant, a woman could only be color-blind if she is homozygous with the recessive gene. A man on the other hand would be much more likely to be color-blind in this way because lacking a color vision gene in his Y chromosome, one recessive color defect gene in his X chromosome would produce the imperfection in vision.

Other than red-green color blindness, few other sex-linked characteristics have been identified. Certain deficiencies in blood-cell conditions and a few other organic characteristics may be sex-linked, but as we come to identify more behavioral units effected by inheritance we must be alert to the possibility of sex-linked inheritance.

LIMITING CONSIDERATIONS The effects of genes upon behavior, as well as their effects upon the structure and function of the body, are difficult to understand fully for several reasons. One of these is the fact that the environment often acts to blur the differences among individuals which result from their various genetic backgrounds. Often environmental factors can mimic the effects of genes in the characteristics under study. Radical changes in the physiological environment can alter development of organic structures of the body. For example, a lack of oxygen in the environment of the very young fetus produces marked changes in the final structure of the organ systems undergoing the greatest degree of development at the time of oxygen privation. Less drastic alterations in the environment produce smaller changes in the developing organism, but these smaller changes tend to make the genetic inheritance less apparent.

Other confusions result from the possibility that one gene can mimic the effects of another. In lower animals it has been shown that genes located in quite different locations can produce the same behavioral effects.

Finally, it should be noted that there must be a complex interaction between genes at practically all of the gene locations. In principle this means that every gene influences the effects of all other genes in governing the developing cell. This is a most general principle and makes the study of the genetic influences upon behavior even more difficult to ascertain. At the same time this principle recognizes the fact that one gene affects bodily development or function only in concert with the many other genes inherited by the organism.

The Genetic Study of Animals

Experiments with selective breeding   The most commonly used technique for studying the effects of genetic inheritance on behavior has been the selective breeding of animals. This technique takes advantage of behavioral differences which occur in a population. Animals which exhibit a similar behavioral characteristic are mated together for many generations. Fast horses are inbred with other fast horses. If there is a genetic foundation to speed in running, after several generations of such inbreeding in which only the fastest are bred with the fastest, a strain of horses should emerge which is made up of very speedy animals. If, on the other hand, there is no genetic inheritance underlying the ability to run fast, this inbreeding technique should not work. Horses inbred for speed for many generations should be no better than randomly bred horses. The obvious fact is that horses and other animals can be successfully inbred for speed in running, as well as for other characteristics, and this provides a foundation for a belief in the genetic inheritance of these characteristics.

Bright and dull rats   By means of selective inbreeding, strains of rats have been isolated which have considerably greater maze-learning abilities than animals randomly mated [4]. By the seventh generation of the inbreeding procedure used by Tryon, there was little overlap between the bright and the dull maze learners. Inbreeding rats for maze-learning abilities has produced several strains of bright and dull rodent "students" [5, 6, 7].

Once two strains of animals which differed in their maze abilities had been isolated, the question remained of whether the genetic effects were due to a single gene or whether they were polygenic. If the behavior was due to a single gene, then cross-breeding the brights with the dulls should produce a type of animal represented by the dominant gene of the pair. If the strains were distinguished because of polygenic influences, the animals resulting from inbreeding the brights and the dulls should be intermediate between the two strains.

Tryon performed just this experiment. He found that the progeny of the bright animals and the dull animals fell into an intermediate position in ability and concluded that the maze skill was polygenic [4].

Research on bright and dull animals has indicated that the maze-learning abilities were but one manifestation of many differences between the strains. The bright animals were not merely smarter than the dull animals. The dull animals tended to respond to *visual* cues of the inside of the maze, whereas the bright animals responded more to *spatial* cues of the situation [8]. The dull animals were superior to the bright animals in a situation that required them to escape from water. The brights were more active in mazes but less active in the activity wheel, an apparatus which measures spontaneous running, than dull animals [9]. Some of the differences found between the bright and the dull animals may be incidental to the superior performance in the maze-learning situation. The question remains, however, which differences are incidental and which really account for the variations in maze learning of the animals.

More recently, extension of research on the characteristics of the maze-bright and maze-dull animals has developed along biochemical lines. While research has not reached a point of finality, it would appear that differences between the strains of animals may be accounted for by differences in the amounts of two chemicals in specific brain areas. As you will learn in the next chapter, one nerve cell (neuron) affects others by the release of transmitter substances. Chemical transmitters are being constantly produced and destroyed by chemical compounds at junctions between nerve cells in the brain. Efficient transmission of a nervous impulse from one neuron to the next depends upon the presence of just the right amount of transmitter substances. Rosenzweig, Krech, and Bennett [10] have argued that the balance between transmitter substances and the chemicals which act to break them down are determined through specific and separate genetic inheritance factors. It is possible that the balance between the transmitter substances and the breakdown chemicals determines the efficiency of the brain area. A favorable ratio in a visual area coupled with a less favorable ratio in nonvisual areas could act to produce animals which depend on visual cues of mazes.

Selection for other characteristics Inbreeding experiments have been used to separate strains of animals on many characteristics other than maze-learning ability. Strain differences in learning ability [11], vigor [12], wildness [13], agressive initiative [14], and the ability to win fights [15], have been reported in mice. Strain differences can be shown which are related to food hoarding and emotionality in the rat [16]. This relationship is of interest because of the work by Tedeschi [17], who found that rats hoarded food in adulthood to a greater extent if the animals had been handled early in development. It may be presumed that this early handling results in a decreased emotional reaction to fear-provoking stimuli which are present in the hoarding situations in which they are tested later in life. From the work of Tedeschi and in the light of other research it seems safe to regard food hoarding as an *innately* determined, response pattern which *can* be inhibited by excessive amounts of emotionality in later life.

Many other efforts have been directed toward the genetic separation of behavioral characteristics. But now let us turn our attention to a broad issue which has existed in the study of genetics and behavior since before the publication of Darwin's famous book which served as a foundation and stimulant to much of the later work in the area.

NATURAL SELECTION The theory of biological evolution had been advanced by the early 1800s. It had been accepted by some but rejected by others. The idea of a progressive change in the nature of animal life from lower to higher forms had a number of champions, even though the weight of many established religious and ethical organizations was thrown against the doctrine. Many famous scientists did not accept the evolutionary view of man's development on the grounds that there was just too little evidence for or against the theory. Erasmus Darwin, Charles Darwin's grandfather, had been one of the early proponents of evolutionary theory, and the famous zoologist, Lamarck, of whom we shall learn more shortly, had argued for a doctrine of transmutation of species in the course of evolutionary development. Today, however, it is the name of Charles

Darwin which is most closely associated with the establishment of evolution as a principle of biological life.

Charles Darwin's contribution stems from the fact that he recognized the need for more evidence on which to decide the acceptability of the evolutionary view. Accordingly, he sailed on the *Beagle* through the South Seas from 1831 to 1835. His detailed study of the forms of life existing in the regions visited led him to give considerable attention to the means by which nature "chose" which animals are to survive in their environments and which are not.

In the years following his trip through the South Seas, Darwin reviewed and studied his observations. He also read Malthus's *Essay on Population* during this period and this may have had an effect on his view of the determination of population sizes among the groups of animals studied. In 1859 his famous book, *The Origin of Species through Natural Selection,* was finally published. Keeping in mind that the evolutionary theory was not new, we must recognize that the importance of the work was due to its massive documentation of the theory with the result that the evolutionary view became a more reliable generalization among scientists.

The principle proposed to account for the survival of certain forms of animals and the death of others is the theory of natural selection. In this theory Darwin argues that the variations of animals which occur from time to time may be either a help or a hindrance to the preservation of that animal in its never-ending battle against the forces of nature. Today, we think of the variations found in animals of a species as reflecting mutations of the genetic material. If the mutation is of positive survival value then that animal will tend to survive and perpetuate the mutated characteristic. When the animal tends to survive, his progeny tend to survive. In natural settings the survival rate among offspring of a species is rather low. Mutations which hinder animals in their struggle for survival will result in decreased survival chances for the animal receiving the mutation; thus less progeny will occur, and the progeny will be less likely to survive. We can think of natural selection as a law of the animal world which describes the "survival of the fittest." Variations which make an animal better fit tend to be promulgated through later generations by the ever-increasing numbers of progeny arising from the mutations. Variations making an animal less fit tend to be extinguished.

Darwin also proposed a second principle of selection for survival which can be found in nature, the law of sexual selection. Darwin recognized that certain mutations occurred which were of no direct consequence for the immediate survival chances of the animal. Variation in the plumage of birds is a case in point. These nonfunctional variations of feathers could have indirect influences upon the question of survival, however. The mutation resulting in alteration of the bird's plumage could affect the sexual attractiveness of the birds. If more sexual attractiveness means more progeny then there is more likelihood that the variation would be perpetuated.

Nature selects animals which are best suited for survival through the principle of natural selection and selects others for increased chances of reproduction through secondary and indirect characteristics explained by the principle of sexual selection. But, what are the effects of the development of human societies and their cultural institutions regarding selection of the fittest humans?

When populations of animals leave natural settings of constant struggle against nature, selection for survival is based on different standards. In the laboratory situation animals are often maintained for countless generations. The principles which are important for their survival are quite different from those of the natural animals. Laboratory rats are favored for maintenance if they have a calm disposition, i.e., they do not bite their handler's fingers. The mildness of the laboratory animals would not serve the wild animals very well.

Strains of laboratory rats and wild rats have been compared. Several apparent differences were found between them which would be predictable on the basis of our current knowledge of physiology. Laboratory animals have smaller adrenal glands, for example. These glands serve the body's mechanisms for emergency reactions including aggression. Laboratory animals have sexual organs which mature more rapidly than the wild animals. In the laboratory a high fertility rate is desirable. This is an artificial selection criterion imposed by the laboratory caretakers which would favor the selection and breeding of animals with such characteristics [18]. Man's artificial environment imposes artificial rules of selection which effect the survival and perpetuation of people and their characteristics which are quite different from those favoring survival in the wilds.

In man's earliest stages of development the laws of natural

and sexual selection played a more important role than they do today. One of the effects of acculturization is to reduce the effectiveness of mutations on a person's chances to survive and contribute to new individuals. In its mercy, society acts to protect the weaker members from elimination through the harsh principle of natural selection. People with genetic backgrounds which produce rather drastic and unfavorable bodily problems can be cared for by social institutions, and the basic deficiency can often be compensated for by the use of medical know-how. Even Darwin's law of sexual selection is circumvented by the use of plastic surgery, cosmetics, and the effective use of clothes. From time to time certain objections have been raised against this role of society. People have pleaded that a continuation of genetic material which contains unfavorable mutations will ultimately result in a population of people too weak to survive despite all the remedial activities that can be undertaken. In general, people who argue for controlled breeding of humans, eugenicists, have not found a favorable reception among either laymen or scientists. There are too many unknown factors determining the structure of man to make the eugenic movement a forceful one. Even more important it is man's consideration and kindness for his fellow men that makes his perpetuation worthwhile.

LAMARCKIAN INHERITANCE The zoologist Lamarck (1744–1829) argued a theory of *transmutation* of genetic material. He believed that changes in behavior which came about through use or disuse and those demanded by changes in the environment could be passed on to subsequent generations through hereditary mechanisms. Even Darwin suggested this might be the case. *Lamarckian inheritance,* the doctrine of the inheritance of acquired (learned) characteristics, is still prominent in some circles, despite the fact that scientific data to support such a theory are lacking.

It is not quite clear why the theory of *Lamarckian inheritance* survives at all. With but a few doubtful exceptions, all of the evidence bearing on the Lamarckian hypothesis has been negative. For many generations animals have learned various kinds of discrimination and have been subsequently mated with other animals with similar learning without any evidence that the training of earlier generations had any effect upon later ones [e.g., 19]. The doctrine of the inheritance of acquired characteristics is not accepted by the vast majority of geneticists today with the exception of some Russian workers.

Genetic Effects in the Human

It has been noted that most of the significant characteristics which come to us through genetic inheritance are polygenic. Only a few characteristics can be shown to be determined by a single gene. Again as psychologists, we shall concentrate on investigations aimed at elaborating the contributions of inheritance along lines most related to our own domain of study, that is, to studies of the inheritance of behavioral characteristics.

Before going on, however, it should be pointed out that the direct study of the genetic make-up of human cells became possible only recently through advances in techniques and methods. It is likely that the study of human genetics will advance in the immediate future far more rapidly than before. Much of what will be said in the following paragraphs will undoubtedly be elaborated, and possibly changed in conception, in the next few years.

Only in the past few years, for example, has it been possible to show that mongolism, a condition of mental retardation with a specific kind of bodily development including slanted eyes and other unusual physical characteristics, results from the presence of an extra chromosome which is located somewhere among the smaller chromosomes. Today we also know that sex hermaphrodites have an extra sexual chromosome. Both the hermaphrodite and the mongoloid have forty-seven instead of the usual forty-six chromosomes.

EARLY STUDIES OF HUMAN INHERITANCES The modern study of the inheritance of human characteristics can be said to have originated with another grandson of Erasmus Darwin, Francis Galton (1822–1911). Galton was a man of many interests and has been described as an explorer, anthropologist, and statistician, as well as a psychologist. In his imaginative study of various topics in the area of psychology, Galton attempted many approaches to the study of man which are still being utilized today. At the moment, we are concerned with his study of the nature and extent of genetic inheritance in man.

From the observation that genius tends to run in families,

53

Galton argued for a strong genetic influence in behavior. He was not satisfied with merely pointing out the many instances in which this apparently seemed to be true (see Fig. 2.3) but went on to collect data to support his position. In this way he was much like his cousin, Charles Darwin, who became famous for his detailed support of the evolutionary point of view.

Galton suggested ways to discover men who could truly be called eminent, i.e., men whose talents were found only about once in every four thousand men. Galton discovered that many more than one in four thousand eminent men were found in families which had already at least one eminent member [20]. Furthermore, he found decreased instances of eminence as the degree of relationship to the eminent man decreased. These data, however, were not conclusive for his hypothesis and this fact was recognized by Galton, himself. The similarity among members of a family could result from common environmental conditions rather than from a common genetic inheritance.

Galton considered other kinds of evidence to substantiate his claim of the importance of genetics for creating the correlation of abilities in families. He pointed out that the proportion of eminent men was no greater in the United States than in England despite the greater range of educational opportunities in the United States. More directly, he compared the incidence of eminence in the adopted relatives of Roman Catholic Popes, who were granted many of the finest social and environmental advantages. But Galton found this background gave rise to fewer cases of eminence than were found among the sons of eminent men.

Another innovation of Galton was the study of genetic inheritance through the use of twins. Although he recognized the existence of similar and dissimilar twins, he did not distinguish between them in his analyses. Today we know that most of the similar twins are identical twins while the majority of the dissimilar twins would be fraternal. He reported that twins who were dissimilar at birth did not tend to become more similar even though their environments were almost identical. As we shall see later in the chapter, the use of twins for the study of human genetics is now an established procedure despite serious difficulties which underly this method.

THE INHERITANCE OF INTELLIGENCE Galton began the study of the genetic influence on the development of intelligence with his analyses of the families of eminent men. Many other studies have followed this general line of investigation. Some studies have reported correlations of intelligence between pairs of members of families as approximately $+.50$. Based upon these reported relationships, some people have argued that we cannot safely assume that this degree of similarity in intelligence is due to genetic factors. While the arguments take several forms, the most convincing is that bright people tend to provide better environmental conditions for their children. However, data like those provided by Galton which compared the adopted children of the Roman Catholic Popes with the sons of eminent men remain to be explained if the posture of the argument is to be sustained.

Studies of twins   There are two kinds of twins: identical and fraternal. Identical twins come from the same fertilized egg. Through a mischance in cell division two individuals arise from what was originally only one ovum. Identical twins have identical genetic inheritance. Fraternal twins come from nearly simultaneous fertilization of two eggs in the mother. They have no more necessary genetic correspondence than brothers and sister (siblings), since both the sperm and the egg in each fertilization have different assortments of genes just as do other siblings. In the past few years it has been possible to determine whether twins are identical or fraternal with greater precision. Identical twins must be of the same sex and must have the same characteristics of coloration and blood composition. Identical twins have been found to be very much alike in many characteristics, including the patterns of electrical activity of the brain which can be recorded from the scalp by means of the electroencephalogram (EEG). These findings are present even if the identical twins are brought up in differing environments from shortly after birth [21]. Identical twins have been reported to have very similar intelligence test scores even if they have been raised in separate environments, but dissimilarities in intelligence has also been reported [22]. The majority of investigations have indicated a close similarity in measured intelligence for identical twins, less similar intelligence between fraternal twins and least between brothers and sisters.

As has been pointed out, identical twins do not necessarily have identical environmental conditions. The findings of studies which compare fraternal and identical twins generally favor the genetic inheritance of some traits but are difficult to interpret, because the home environments of the identical twins *could* be more alike than that of fraternal twins. Furthermore, the development of identical twins before birth could be more uniformly effected by intra-uterine factors than the development of fraternal twins. But, positions in the uterus and other physiological occurrences could also act to make identical twins less alike and fraternal twins more alike than might be expected. Another difficulty is that studies of twins who have been reared apart often do not take sufficient account of the fact that the separated twins (separated by adoption, usually) are not randomly placed into new circumstances.

Studies of foster children   In general, the correlation in intelligence of foster children with their adoptive parents is much lower than the correlation between children and their natural parents. The intelligence of foster children tends to be fairly closely correlated with the measured intelligence of the foster parents, especially the mother [23], but the size of the correlation is much less than that of the correlation between the intelligence of mothers and their own children. Thus, the most striking resemblance is found between a child's intelligence and his true mother's intelligence even when the child has been raised with foster parents [24].

Generalizations about inherited intelligence   From the time of Galton to the present the available evidence appears to support the generalization that heredity does have an important influence on the development of the intelligence of the individual. One way to conceive of this hereditary effect is to imagine the genetic factors as setting limits, or ranges, for intelligence which can be attained by people under appropriate circumstances. Intelligence scores can be significantly influenced by differences in the environment, but the upper limit in intelligence which the person can reach through more favorable experience is set by genetic mechanisms.

What circumstances are more effective in stimulating the development of intelligence? It seems clear that the hereditary mechanism underlying intelligence is polygenic, that is, a great many combinations of genes act to produce a high score on intelligence tests. From data of other kinds of genetic experiments we know that environments which are beneficial to individuals with one set of genes may not be conducive to the proper development of individuals with other sets of genes, even though the polygenically determined characteristics produced by the two gene-types are very similar. Thus, there does not need to be any one kind of environment which guarantees to produce maximally beneficial development of intelligence. On the other hand it is clear that opportunity for development must be present in order for the "intelligence potential" to be fulfilled.

INHERITANCE OF OTHER PSYCHOLOGICAL CHARACTERISTICS

Attempts to assay the extent of genetic influence upon intelligence far surpass all other kinds of research on the genetic foundations of psychological traits. There are several reasons for this. First, and probably most important, is the fact that intelligence scores are relatively stable psychological measures. Intelligence test scores tend to remain rather constant over periods of time; and have shown themselves to be reliable and valid predictors of success in college and in certain occupations. Furthermore, they have standardized methods of administration and scoring. It is safe to say that no other kind of personality measurement technique provides as unequivocal data as come from intelligence testing. Stable test scores are absolutely necessary in order to determine the lines of inheritance which are used in tracing to establish genetic effects.

Scores on psychological tests of personality are far more variable and their interpretation is far less valid than are test scores of intelligence. In general, scores from different kinds of personality tests have low correlations with each other and there are many problems in obtaining valid predictions of behavior from such tests. Therefore, it is relatively difficult to assess traits of personality and this makes it far more difficult to assess the effects of genetic inheritance.

Personality patterns, like intelligence and other measures of performance, are most certainly the result of polygenic inheritance. A number of genes contribute to the characteristics exhibited in behavior. But, more important is the fact that several different kinds of genetic inheritance can contribute to the same behavioral effects. There is no reason to believe that one, and only one, assortment of genes underlies a given personality or behavioral characteristic. It is likely that, given the appropriate developmental environments, many different kinds of polygenic arrangements lead to the same psychological manifestation.

Studies which have used reliably measurable psychological

variables have tended to show the same pattern of findings as studies of intelligence. Correlations of motor skills, such as card sorting and manually following a moving target, tend to show higher correlations between identical twins than between fraternal twins [25]. Attempts at measuring inheritance patterns of temperament, mood, or other "personality variables" have, however, been indecisive. Some studies have reported positive results and others negative results. Here, the matter must rest for the present with an unsatisfying conclusion.

Mental disorders   The study of people with acute mental problems presents an indication of mental function that can be more or less readily agreed upon, at least when extreme. The fact that many kinds of personality disorders can be clinically recognized by many therapists makes them relatively easy to use in determination of genetic effects. The mental disorder that has been most carefully studied from the point of view of genetic inheritance is schizophrenia, a severe personality disorder characterized by a high degree of disorientation.

As a basic consideration, there can be no doubt that rates of incidence of schizophrenia are higher in families in which at least one member of the family has been previously diagnosed as suffering from the disease. For example, siblings of a schizophrenic parent have incidence rates of schizophrenia from 5 to 10 percent, whereas the incidence of schizophrenia in the general population is less than one in a thousand. The probability of schizophrenia rises rapidly when more than one sibling or one parent has been so diagnosed, and reaches probabilities of about nine in ten for identical twins of schizophrenic parents.

Those who do not favor a genetic inheritance hypothesis point out that as the genetic relationship between two individuals becomes closer, the similarity of their environments is also likely to increase.

Generally, the evidence seems to point toward a conclusion that some forms of schizophrenia are influenced by genetic factors, but such factors do not entirely account for their occurrence. In fact, Rosenthal [26] has analyzed data presented earlier (by Slater) which was obtained from the study of schizophrenia among twins, and found evidence supporting different hereditary patterns among the families of two types of twins. When both twins had been diagnosed as schizophrenic, histories of schizophrenia-like diseases were found in 60 percent of their families. When only one of the twins had been diagnosed as schizophrenic, schizophrenic case histories appeared in only 8 percent of their families.

Mental disorders indicated by psychopathic or neurotic behavior tend to have the same rates of incidence among identical twins as they do fraternal twins or siblings, [27]. While this result could imply that these two kinds of personality disorganizations have less of a genetic contribution, it could also mean that less reliable measurements or diagnoses of such disorders were made. This suggestion is given credence by the observation that scores of identical twins correlated .85 while scores of fraternal twins correlated only .22 on a "neuroticism factor" obtained from a special objective test of neuroticism [28].

Tendencies toward schizophrenia　It has been suggested that the genetic inheritance predisposing toward schizophrenia can be thought of as an inheritance of a defect in the "integrative ability" of the brain and the nervous system [3]. A precise definition of this "integrative deficit" is admitted to be beyond the present abilities of science, but Meehl argues that this concept can direct us to look for the nature of the genetic defect, namely a malfunction in the operation of single cells in the nervous system, while at the same time presenting us with the basic symptom of schizophrenia. This basic and biological deficit he labels "schizotaxia." On top of this genetic foundation the social environment adds learned reactions which tend to be common to all schizotaxic individuals. The schizotaxic individual uses characteristic type of reactions to the environment, but still may not become a schizophrenic as clinically diagnosed:

If the interpersonal regime is favorable, and the schizotaxic individual person also has the good fortune to inherit a low anxiety readiness, physical vigor, general resistance to stress and the like, he will remain a well-compensated "normal" schizotype, never manifesting symptoms of mental disease [3].

Schizotypes are people with schizotaxic tendencies but who do not come to the full degree of mental disorder resulting when individuals are not as "lucky" as those finding the favorable conditions mentioned in the above quotation. Thus Meehl suggests that the development of clinically diagnosed schizophrenia depends upon the inheritance of the schizotaxic tendency plus bad luck in having environmental conditions not hospitable to this tendency, and the inheritance of other indirectly related characteristics, such as the inability to resist stress.

One implication of such a view would be that the parents of the schizophrenic may not necessarily have the disease to the extent that it has become apparent through diagnosis, but could have less predominant symptoms which indicate the schizo-type. Meehl draws our attention to the report of McConaghy [29], who found that, among parents of ten schizophrenics not diagnosed as schizophrenics, at least one parent of each had symptoms of "thought disorders" which were not disabling but still apparent. This, Meehl suggests, is support for his position and would argue that the parents were schizotaxic but more fortunate in circumstances or in inheriting other personality characteristics which act to mitigate the schizotaxic tendencies.

The significance of Meehl's ideas for us is in his suggestion of the inheritance of personality dispositions which can be controlled or modified by other genetic or environmental circumstances.

Factors Influencing Development

In a now classical article about unlearned or instinctive behavior, Beach points to the importance of understanding the relationship between environmental and genetic factors [30]. In one experiment, two strains of mice were used; one strain was susceptible to audiogenic seizures (convulsive fits induced by loud, shrill sounds) while the other did not have the susceptibility. Crossing the two strains produced an animal intermediate between the two inbred strains which of course indicated a polygenic determination of the effects. One would expect that the susceptibility of audiogenic seizures came from genetic information which was the cause of the proneness to audiogenic seizures. But, further experiments showed *this need not be the case*. Fertilized eggs were obtained from the uterus or the fallopian tubes of one strain and implanted in the uterus of the other strain. Sometimes such implants will develop in this new environment and for those that "took" it was possible to determine the seizure-proneness of the "transplanted animals." In this study mice were always transplanted from the seizure prone animals to animals of the strain which was not seizure prone [31].

The transplanted, seizure-prone rats were intermediate, that is, less seizure prone than their parental strain and more susceptible than the strain into which they were introduced. One certain conclusion from this study is that prenatal environment can play an important role in the determination of behavior, and this, as Beach points out, should make us suspicious of attempts to attribute all of the characteristics found in an inbred strain of animals to specific genes for that characteristic. The genes may actually control other characteristics, such as uterine conditions, which may in turn affect the behavioral characteristics.

Hebb [32] suggests that six factors can be distinguished which effect the developing organism:

1. Genetic. This would be merely the gene structure of the egg after fertilization. It should be emphasized that this is the entire extent of the genetic information given to new organisms.

2. Chemical, prenatal. All of the nutritive and chemical factors in the uterus as the animal develops would be included in this class. In the study of transplanted eggs of mice discussed above, one is led to believe that the uterine environment of the new mother was different from that of the natural mother. Oxygen or other deficiencies in the prenatal environment as a rule tend to effect the organ system developing most rapidly during the shortage.

3. Chemical, postnatal. In this category would be the effects on development in the chemical or nutritive atmosphere of the neonate. Continued dietary deficiencies are the most likely cause of abnormalities although other factors could be included in this class.

4. Sensory, constant. Within any species of animal, certain kinds of sensory information will almost always be presented to the developing young. To some extent, the sensory environment of one species will be different from that of any other. When we evaluate the differences in behavior between species we must keep in mind that the sensory world of each of the species has been different and this could result in different learning and perceptions of the world. Thus, the reactions of one species to changes in the environment may be quite different from those of a second species and it is possible that the differences could result solely from differences in experiences during development.

5. Sensory, variable. While many kinds of sensory experiences must be the same for members of a given species, there

always will be differences between each and every member of the species. No two animals, even identical twins, develop in the identical environments. To understand behavior, we take into account the individual experiences during development which play a part in adult behavior.

6. Traumatic. A traumatic event is harmful to the individual, often culminating in the destruction of body cells. Traumatic events are brief and are often outside the normal sensory environment of the members of the species. These intense periods of unusual stimulation can result in changes in the organism which can be influential throughout its entire life. Such occurrences may range from the "trauma" of a harsh delivery, involving the use of forceps which clamp the head of the baby too securely, or they can be accidental events which befall a developing individual. In any case traumatic events are thought to provide a basis for many unusual modifications of behavior seen in adult behavior.

From this list of classes of factors which influence the development of behavior it is apparent that it would be all too easy to mistake the effects of factors 2 through 6 for genetic effects of factor 1.

The aim of research in the area of the genetic influences can not stop when behavior can be shown to be a result of a certain pattern of genes. Even though genes can determine behavior, we must know how they do so. Do the genes affect the secretion of biochemicals? Do they change the patterns of activity in the nervous system, the muscular system, or the hormones? Do the genes affect the development of certain clusters of nerve cells in the brain? Do they affect the structure or function of receptor systems?

To describe a pattern of behavior by calling it genetic is a beginning for research rather than an end. Once the genetic influence has been determined, then we are faced with the problem of finding the underlying mechanism of the characteristic.

In summary: In this chapter we have tried to present some of the information which is available today about the effects of genetic inheritance upon behavior. Presenting information about heredity was one goal, but in addition we tried to stress the possible contribution of genetics to psychology. Modern psychology has been too greatly divorced from the study of genetics because of its own course of development, and especially because of the downfall of instinct psychology and the rise of Behaviorism. The time for a convergence of the two sciences appears to be at hand and will in all likelihood result in stimulation of new developments in research and theory for both fields.

References

1. Watson, J. B. *Behaviorism.* New York: W. W. Norton & Company, Inc., 1924.

2. Pillsbury, W. B. *The History of Psychology.* New York: W. W. Norton & Company, Inc., 1929.

3. Meehl, P. E. Schizotaxia, schizotypy, schizophrenia. *Amer. Psychologist,* 1962, **17,** 827–838.

4. Tryon, R. C. Genetic differences in maze-learning ability in rats. *Thirtieth Yearb., Nat. Soc. Stud. Educ.,* 1940, Pt. 1, pp. 111–119.

5. Heron, W. T. The inheritance of maze learning ability in rats. *J. comp. Psychol.,* 1935, **19,** 77–89.

6. Heron, W. T. The inheritance of brightness and dullness in maze learning in the rat. *J. genet. Psychol.,* 1941, **59,** 41–49.

7. Thompson, W. T. The inheritance and development of intelligence. *J. nerv. ment. Dis.,* 1954, **33,** 209–231.

8. Krechevsky, I. Hereditary nature of "hypotheses." *J. comp. Psychol.,* 1933, **16,** 99–116.

9. Searle, L. V. The organization of hereditary maze-brightness and maze-dullness. *Genet. Psychol. Monogr.,* 1949, **39,** 179–325.

10. Rosenzweig, M. R., Krech, D., & Bennett, E. L. Brain enzymes and adaptive behaviors. In Ciba Foundation symposium, *The Neurological Bases of Behavior.* Boston: Little, Brown and Company, 1958.

11. Bagg, H. J. Individual differences and family resemblences in animal behavior. *Amer. Nat.,* 1916, **50,** 222–236.

12. Vicari, E. M. Mode of inheritance of reaction time and degrees of learning. *J. exp. Zool.,* 1929, **54,** 31–88.

13. Dawson, W. M. Inheritance of wildness and tameness in mice. *Genetics,* 1932, **17,** 296–326.

14. Scott, J. P. Genetic differences in the social behavior of inbred strains of mice. *J. Hered.,* 1942, **33,** 11–15.

15. Ginsburg, B., & Alee, W. C. Some effects of conditioning on social dominance and subordination in inbred strains of mice. *Physiol. Zool.,* 1942, **15,** 485–506.

16. Broadhurst, P. L. Determinants of emotionality in the rat.

III. Strain differences. *J. comp. physiol. Psychol.,* 1958, **51,** 55–59.

17. Tedeschi, J. Infantile stimulation in rats and the genesis of the disposition to emotionality. Unpublished doctoral dissertation, Univer. of Michigan, 1959.

18. Richter, C. P. Domestication of the Norway rat and its implication for the study of genetics in man. *Amer. J. Hum. Genet.,* 1952, **4,** 273–285.

19. Agar, W. E., Drummond, R. H., & Tiegs, O. W. Third report on a test of McDougall's Lamarckian experiment on the training of rats. *J. exp. Biol.,* 1948, **25,** 103–122.

20. Galton, F. *Hereditary Genius.* London: Macmillan & Co., Ltd., 1869.

21. Juel-Nielsen, N., & Harvald, B. The electroencephalogram in uniovular twins brought up apart. *Acta genet.,* 1958, **8,** 57–64.

22. Newman, H. H. Identical twins. *Eugen. Rev.,* 1930, **22,** 29–34.

23. Burks, B. S. The relative importance of nature and nurture upon mental development; a comparative study of foster parent–foster child resemblance and true parent–true child resemblance. *Yearb. Nat. Soc. Stud. Educ.,* 1928, **27(I),** 219–316.

24. Honzik, M. P. Developmental studies of parent-child resemblance in intelligence. *Child. Develop.,* 1957, **28,** 215–228.

25. McNemar, Q. Twin resemblances in motor skills, and the effect of practice thereon. *J. genet. Psychol.,* 1933, **42,** 70–97.

26. Rosenthal, D. Some factors associated with concordance and discordance with respect to schizophrenia in monozygotic twins. *J. nerv. ment. Dis.,* 1959, **129,** 1–10.

27. Slater, E. *Psychotic and neurotic illnesses in twins.* London: H. M. Stationery Office, 1953.

28. Eysenck, H. J., & Prell, D. B. The inheritance of neuroticism: an experimental study. *J. ment. Sci.,* 1951, **97,** 441–465.

29. McConaghy, N. The use of an object sorting test in elucidating the hereditary factor in schizophrenia. *J. Neurol. Neurosurg. Psychiat.,* 1959, **22,** 243–246.

30. Beach, F. A. The descent of instinct. *Psychol. Rev.,* 1955, **62,** 401–410.

31. Ginsberg, B. E., & Hovda, R. B. On the physiology of gene controlled audiogenic seizures in mice. *Anat. Rec.,* 1947, **99,** 65–66.

32. Hebb, D. O. *A Textbook of Psychology.* Philadelphia: W. B. Saunders Company, 1958.

THREE BIOLOGICAL FOUNDATIONS OF 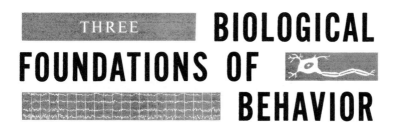 BEHAVIOR

Thousands of millions of years ago life began. In all likelihood our development stems from the first single-celled organism, although we must acknowledge the great mystery of creation. Evolutionary theory suggests that we are in continuity with this first creation of life and that we have evolved from whatever form the spark of life had at the beginning. Human life exists in a chain of development from this primeval life.

We presume to be the highest development from this beginning, and to understand our behavior it will be helpful to recognize our connection with all other forms of life. Doing so will offer a perspective essential to understanding ourselves. We believe that we are something special in the animal kingdom—"just a little bit lower than the angels." To understand just how we are different from the other animals, while learning ways in which we are similar, it is important to trace the development of man's structure and function through his lower relations in the phylogenetic scale. Success in understanding this development will provide us with greater ability to understand the mechanisms of our own bodies. Our ultimate goal in the present chapter is to understand the mature individual in biological perspective. If we want to understand man we must understand him biologically as well as behaviorally.

The single cell of original life had to perform all of the metabolic and behavioral acts requisite to keeping alive. As we shall see, these cells grouped together and later began to specialize according to structure and function. Groups of cells began to lose their general, nondifferentiated functions and to develop highly specialized ones. Of course, in man the life of the individual cell depends upon the functions performed by an incomprehensibly large number of cells elsewhere in the body. The life of every cell in the body is extinguished when the cells comprising the kidney, heart, lungs, or parts of the nervous system fail to do their jobs.

By bonding together into complex animals, the single cells lost the thread of eternal life in the sense that some fragment of one cell would exist in the progeny resulting from the almost infinite number of cell divisions that could occur without apparent end. On the other hand, the resulting complex organism developed a new step into eternal life through sexual reproduction and the passing on of genetic materials in the sperm and the egg.

But for whatever reason, cells did come together and specialization became the rule. As psychology students we are especially interested in the cells which developed to handle the problems of communication between the cells comprising the organism. The cells which became occupied with the transmission of information from the outside world, the environment, to the other cells of the organism were the early precursors of the nervous system. In the mature animal the nervous system is responsible for the detection of changes in the environment, the transmission of information from the receptor cells to a central station (the brain) for analysis, and the conduction of command messages originating in the brain to the muscles and glands.

The complexity of the nervous system in man is frankly overwhelming. We know only too little of its principles of operation. It has been likened to a cellular city of over twelve billion inhabitants. But even more, the number of interconnections between the cells probably exceeds 300,000,000,000,000. In addition, there is recent evidence to indicate that the connections between cells may not be fixed. Time-lapse photography of cells from the human brain grown in tissue cultures reveals the cells to be in continuous motion, constantly changing their connections with one another. While our comprehension of the nervous system is meager, it is vital to even a first understanding of behavior.

Our task will begin with an examination of the development of this marvelous machine, the human brain. We shall follow the course of development of the specialized neural cells phylogenetically. After discussing the differences existing between the invertebrate and vertebrate divisions of the nervous system we shall pause to look at the building block of the nervous system—the single nerve cell—the neuron. After attaining a degree of understanding of this specialized cell we shall then attempt to understand the organization of the mature nervous system of man.

These steps shall serve us as a basis for our comprehension of psychological knowledge to be presented in later chapters, but they are important in their own right. It may be that the breakthrough needed to understand man may come from the biological world before it comes from the behavioral world. Certainly, it is man's highly developed nervous system that accounts for his place of eminence in the animal realm. It is responsible for man's humanity and great accomplishments of all kinds, but it must also be the agent responsible for his miseries and problems.

Evolution of the Nervous System

Even before we consider the animal kingdom we can observe modifications of behavior in response to external stimulation in plant life. To be sure, trees do not respond to the chop of an axe as an animal would, but plants do have growth responses and rooted plants typically bend toward light falling on them. The relatively rapid reactions to tactile stimulation of plants such as Venus's-flytrap are known to many. In general seed plants exhibit many of the characteristics of all behaving organisms: sensitivity to certain stimuli, conduction of excitation from one part of the organism to another, and some variety in response patterns. However, the plants have followed different evolutionary paths than the animals, and our primary interest is in the evolution of animal behavior.

THE AMOEBA   The amoeba has been extensively studied and is of interest to us since many basic principles of behavior can be observed in this most simple animal. If we did not know

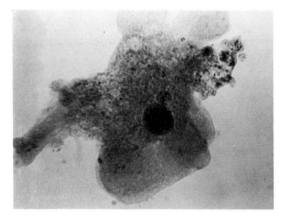

FIG. 3.1.   *Photomicrograph of an amoeba (enlarged about 130 times.) One of the simplest known forms of animal life, the amoeba nourishes itself by enveloping minute organisms and fragments of food. Courtesy of Chas. Pfizer & Co., Inc.*

that the animal was only one cell it would be easy to believe that its many responses had to depend upon the presence of many kinds of specialized cells. Consider the following facts about the amoeba:

1. *Its response is dependent upon the nature of stimulation.* When the side of an amoeba is stimulated there is an extension of protoplasm, the stuff of which it is made, toward the stimulation. If the stimulation becomes more intense the protoplasm flows away from the stimulated area and extends on the opposite side. Furthermore, the surface seems to have areas of greater or less sensitivity to stimulation.

2. *Continued stimulation alters the response to further stimulation of the same kind.* When the amoeba is brought in from the dark and placed under a microscope we observe several changes. Most pronounced among them is a general contraction. After a few minutes the animal adapts to its condition and

resumes its movements. Continued light stimulation does not produce any additional reactions.

3. *Internal states determine responsiveness to stimulation.* The amoeba will normally send a protoplasm probe toward particles near it. However, when it is well fed more stimulation than usual is needed before such a reaction will take place.

4. *The effects of several stimuli may summate to cause jointly a response neither one could elicit alone.* One level of stimulation of the surface of the amoeba may be insufficient to produce a response unless other stimulation is added. This additional stimulation may be in an adjacent area or could closely follow the other stimulation in time. The additional stimulation may be less than that normally required to elicit a response by itself. If the two stimuli, neither of which is capable of eliciting a response alone, determine a response when they are coupled in space or in time then we have a summation of their effects.

Parallels in behavior These four principles of behavior are readily apparent in the nervous system of man. First of all, man is quite apparently differentially responsive to external stimulation. Some men are even differentially responsive to blonds and brunettes. Also, man adapts to the constant stimuli of his environment. When a new worker begins his job in a boiler factory, the noise is very obvious to him. After a few weeks he may wonder what the fuss is all about when a more recent newcomer complains. A good number of our neural cells adapt more or less quickly to a steady state of stimulation. This illustrates adaptation at the cell level in a complex animal.

Internal need states of man influence his reactions. Your usual reaction to a hamburger will be considerably modified if you have just finished a T-bone steak. More generally, we shall find that our internal states, e.g., hunger and thirst, make us differentially receptive to stimuli related to these states. Advertisers bombard us with their ads partly in the hope that the effects of stimulation will last over some period of time and effect our future behavior. They hope that a number of ads may summate their effects and alter our behavior to their advantage and profit.

At a physiological level we find that single cells in the body respond like the amoeba. The effects of two weak stimuli occurring together on a cell may affect the cell whereas neither could alone. From these considerations we can see that many of the principles of behavior of total man and his constituent cells can be illustrated in an animal as low on the phylogenetic scale as the amoeba.

On a broader scale the behavior of the amoeba has another parallel with that of higher animals. We can interpret the responses of the amoeba as attempts to maintain some specific optimal conditions in its internal chemical make-up. Maier and Schneirla [1] define these optimal conditions as those which best promote the representative metabolic conditions for the organism, in short those internal conditions which favor the survival of the animal. This tendency toward the maintenance of suitable internal conditions foreshadows the theory of homeostasis made popular by Walter B. Cannon (discussed in Chapter 8 on motivation). In brief, the theory of homeostasis argues that all behavior is motivated toward the establishment of optimal conditions in the internal environment. It would be a mistake to infer that every animal, the amoeba included, has any "idea" of what these optimal internal conditions might be. However, animals which do not act to maintain optimal internal conditions will perish. The tendency toward optimal internal conditions should be interpreted as an evolutionary development through many successive mutations of genetic structure.

STEPS TOWARD A NERVOUS SYSTEM: THE INVERTEBRATES The amoeba has only one cell and therefore it can have no nervous system, muscle system, or receptor system. Ascending the phylogenetic scale we find animals which are aggregates of single cells and above them animals that are more than collections of cells—animals which have groups of cells with specialized functions.

The phylum Porifera represents a step toward the complex individual. This group of animals, commonly known as sponges, is characterized by a group of cells organized into two layers (See Fig. 3.2). Resembling a vase, the adult sponge is fixed to one location and water is drawn in and out of the animal by the beating of some specialized cells with flagella which take in fine organic materials from water which is forced in and out through the opening at the top of the sponge. This is a primitive way of obtaining food. Each of the cells in the area surrounding the opening at the top is individually irritable. These cells jointly control the size of the opening. Each of the cells surrounding the opening acts as a *receptor* in that it is responsive to the temperature and composition of the water; but in addition, each cell can be affected by the activities of its neighbors. Stimulation of one part of the border around the opening causes the cells in that area to contract. This contraction spreads slowly throughout the remainder of cells. Thus the whole opening closes. This contraction does not depend upon cells specialized for the transmission of excitation. The initial excitation spreads in wavelike fashion from one cell to another. While one may observe the beginnings of cells which are differentiated for special purposes, as a rule each cell functions autonomously.

In the phylum Coelenterata we come upon the first true nervous system, although it is quite unlike anything found in

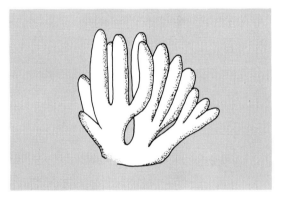

FIG. 3.2. *The sponge (phylum* Porifera) *represents a major step toward the complex individual.*

mammals. One of the representatives of this phylum is the hydra, which is probably familiar to all students of elementary biology (see Fig. 3.3). The tentacles wave about and the whole animal moves by elongation. When one of the tentacles is stimulated, the rest soon become active. The responsiveness of the tentacles to stimulation is determined by the state of the organism. The tentacles of well-fed hydra are less excitable than those of hydra deprived of food. The excitation at the point of contact in the tentacle is transmitted throughout the tentacle by specialized tissue. There are sensory cells in the outer layer (ectoderm) of the tentacle which have threadlike extensions that go to muscle cells beneath the surface. According to Parker [2], this is the second stage of development of cells in the nervous system. The first level is represented by cells which are both sensory and contractile such as those around the opening of the sponge. In the second stage there is a specialized sensory cell which has an extension to a muscle system. The third stage is also found in the phylum Coelenterata and is called the *nerve net*. The nerve net is a complex mesh of cells between the receptor cells and muscles. This nerve net is diffusely organized and acts to stimulate cells of the tentacles in a widespread fashion. When one tentacle is excited, the other tentacles become excited because

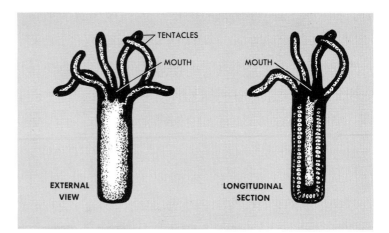

FIG. 3.3. *The hydra (phylum* Coelenterata). *Left: external views; right: internal view of longitudinal section.*

of activity of the neural net, although this excitation lacks direction.

Although some improvement in the coordination of behavior of a "nerve ring" is found in the echinoderms (starfish), we come upon our next most interesting improvements in the nervous system of the worms. One of the simple flatworms, the planarian, has been extensively studied. It is a bilaterally symmetrical animal, and has both a physiological and sensitivity *gradient* from head to tail. The head region is more active, metabolically, and is more sensitive to stimulation than the posterior regions. A drawing of a planarian is presented in Fig. 3.4. The animal has receptor cells and neural nets in the periphery. These connect with neural strands running into the head ganglia. These ganglia are merely enlargements of the nerve strands, and are thought to be responsible for the coordination of movement. However, when these ganglia are removed, the animal still moves appropriately, although more slowly and less smoothly. Excitation of the ganglia can produce swimming movement. Superficially, the head ganglia would seem to be nature's first tentative step toward a brain.

Phenomena which resemble conditioning in some ways have been found in planarians. A group of investigators, led by McConnell [3, 4], has demonstrated that planarians can "learn" and, even more exciting, can pass along something of this learning to its offspring. Through a procedure called *classical conditioning* they have shown that these flatworms will contract to a light which was previously ineffective in producing the contractile response. The first step in such a classical conditioning experiment is to ascertain that the stimulus used as the conditioned stimulus does not produce the response. Therefore, in the studies under consideration the worms were exposed to light until the experimenters were convinced no contractile responses were being made. Then the conditioned stimulus (*CS*), light, was associated with a stimulus which is effective in producing the desired response. In the present case electrical shock to the worm was the unconditioned stimulus (*US*) which was used to produce the contraction response. The response produced by the *US* is called the unconditioned response or reflex (*UR*). After a number of pairings of the *US* and the *CS,* the light and the shock, the animals will come to make a response similar to the *UR* (con-

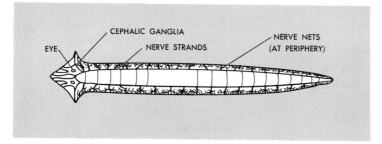

FIG. 3.4. *Drawing of a planarian.*

traction to shock) to the *CS* (light). This contraction made to the previously ineffective *CS* is called the conditioned response or reflex (*CR*). Generally speaking the *CR* is very much like the *UR,* but it is more than a matter of simple substitution of stimuli. The *CS* does not elicit a response exactly like the one elicited by the *US*. This classical conditioning model will be of importance to us throughout this book, and it may be helpful to master the simple steps in this conditioning *paradigm* early (see Fig. 6.2, p. 216).

It has been found that the planarians are capable of acquiring what very much appears to be a conditioned response, but the fascinating part of the story is yet to come. This kind of worm can reproduce by a regeneration of its separated parts. If one of these worms is cut across the middle creating a head-half and a tail-half animal, both ends will regenerate into complete animals. Interestingly, both parts show retention of the learned response acquired by the previous whole animal. The head ganglia are included in only one of the two parts of the animal. Yet the results clearly show that both the new animals learn the avoidance problem faster than animals re-generating from cut but untrained animals. If anything, the animal from the tail portion seems to relearn the contraction response faster. This means that the effects of the training, learning the avoidance response in our example, are not dependent upon changes in the head ganglia in the planarians. These studies suggest that alterations in the animal's chemical make-up could be responsible for this transmission of infor-mation from separated parents to regenerated offspring: Today we believe a great amount of learning of higher animals to be the result of changes in the pattern of interrelated activity of groups of neurons acting on one another. The fact that the tail-region animal inherits some knowledge of the avoidance problem suggests that there may be more than one bodily mechanism underlying the learning and memory processes.

In the cephalopod popularly known as the octopus we note several improvements in the nervous system and in its range of behavior. The nervous system of the animals con-tains several head ganglia not dissimilar to those found in the worms, but in addition a specialized receptor for visual stimuli has developed. The octopus has an eye with a movable lens which can focus light on sensory cells behind it. The effects of changes in illumination are transmitted by nerve fibers to the ganglionic lobes at some distance from the eye. This primitive visual system is efficient enough so that the octopus can use visual cues to direct attacks on its main foodstuff, crabs. The nervous system of the octopus is still rudimentary, and the behavior of the animal is limited in range. For example, it does not seem to be able to respond to barriers placed between it and the food. If it is "aware" of the barrier, it does not seem to be able to coordinate its movements to circumvent the barrier. However, the octopus can learn to inhibit its usual response of catching and eating a crab when one is placed in front of him. By appropriate administration of an electric shock as a punishment when the crab is placed on a given colored card, the octopus learns not to move about and enclose the food [5]. The octopus will continue to attack the crab when it is on a card of a different color. Surgical interference with one portion of the octopus' brain (the vertical lobe) can produce an astounding change in the animal's reactions. When the animals are tested after surgery, they can still remember not to attack a crab on the "wrong" card if the experimental trials are within five minutes of each other. When the intertrial interval is lengthened to two hours, the animal does not restrain his attack and is punished. In the cephalopod's neural lobes there must be different systems for long-term memories which are distinct from those involved with short-term memories. This represents our first contact with two kinds of memory, but it will not be our last. We will come to find that higher forms of life, including man, seem to have several kinds of memory processes.

The octopus seems to be the result of an evolutionary growth that is an offshoot from the main course of development leading to the vertebrates. The direct path of phylogenetic development is believed to run via the nonsegmented animals, the segmented worms, and insects. Herrick describes the neural organization of the segmented worms and the insects in a way difficult to improve:

The body of a worm may be compared with a loose federation of separate states, each with autonomous self government and responsible to a central power only in its foreign relations. In the insect, to carry out the analogy, the central governing power (head dominance) is stronger, the states (segments) are united in three subsidiary federations (head, thorax, and abdomen), and yet each state retains a measure of autonomy. The machinery of government is almost entirely inflexible, as if it were merely the execution of immutable laws [6, p. 143].

Both the worm and the insect can exist admirably well without their heads and even show definite signs of learning. However, some activities which occur in normal animals will not occur if they are decapitated, but changes in the external environment can compensate for this loss. For instance, decapitated moths will not lay eggs spontaneously, but will with certain special kinds of sensory stimulation. This illustrates the fact that the loose neural confederacy of the segments is not entirely dependent on the central power, the head ganglion. The organization of the nervous system of the vertebrates is entirely dependent on the centralization of the brain.

With the insect (phylum Arthropoda) we reach a peak of complex behavior for the invertebrates. The bees even have what can be described as a language of their own. The ants have a complex social order. But as Herrick has pointed out their behavior seems to be governed by certain inflexible laws. While their behavior is complex it is inflexible. It is important not to confuse these two concepts. We can obtain some insight into some characteristics of the laws which seem to govern the behavior of such animals by inspecting the spider spinning his web. Different species of spiders tend to spin their own distinctive webs. The number of webs they spin is proportional to their food intake. Again, as we have seen as far down the phylogenic scale as the amoeba, the internal environment of the animal, especially as determined by recent food intake, is important for controlling even unlearned reactions.

As with much of the behavior of insects, the spider's behavior appears to be and is indeed complex. Yet it consists largely of many fixed responses to various stimulus patterns.

To some extent the spider's motion seems dictated by the growing web, which may be considered as a gradually developing field of force. The varying tensions of long and short segments, the distances between intersections, the lengths of filaments and the angles between them—each furnish stimuli to which the instinctively driven spider is compulsorily obedient [7, p. 118].

This quotation by Savory illustrates the complex control which the environment, as interpreted by the animal's sensory system, exerts upon behavior of the lower animals.

Of a seemingly more complex nature is the communication of bees. Karl Von Frisch, an Austrian zoologist, has spent years studying how bees learn the location of food from other bees. Watching a bee's return to the hive, Von Frisch found that it communicated its find to the other bees in the hive by a dance [8]. The vigor of the dance indicates the amount of nectar left at the source. When the nectar supply is running out the bees returning to the hive dance slowly or not at all. When the supply is plentiful, the dance is more vigorous. The direction to the food source is given by the angle of inclination from horizontal. This angle is related to the position of the sun in the heavens. The intricacies of the sensory determinants of this complicated bee behavior are enormous and not fully investigated. For instance, Von Frisch has found that the bees are capable of relating direction of the food source to the sun's position even though the sun is itself obscured. (Whether this involves a capacity to respond to infrared light or to polarization of the light is unknown.)

Here at this level of insect life we find an elaborate communication system. It is a type of symbolic communication. In many ways it can be considered as similar to our use of language for symbolic communication. Equally fascinating is the capacity of these animals to use the position of the sun in the sky as a reference point in their communication of the position of the food source. Since they can use the sun's position as such a reference point, they must make use of stimuli that we do not normally use (i.e., the polarization of light or the infrared rays). Thus the sensory world of the bee must be one which is quite different from ours.

We have seen that the insects communicate symbolically. They also show what might be called social behavior.

When groups of army ants are placed on a flat surface, free of obstacles, they begin a death march. They march in eccentric circles, controlled by stimuli arising from their own group and a counteracting centrifugal force. In the jungle the army ants run into many obstacles which more or less randomly alter the group's path. Where there are no obstruc-. tions the geometry of the forces is unaltered and results in an almost certain formation of suicide mills [9]. The behavior of an individual army ant is completely determined by the group. The behavior of groups of humans is much more flexible, less determined by specific sensory patterns, than the behavior of ants.

In both the bee and the ant we can find prototypes of caste systems. For example, some bees are workers, some drones, and generally there is a queen. Each bee or ant has a certain role to fulfill in its community and generally follows a certain behavioral pattern commensurate with this role. Animals adopt such roles, however, because of their biological make-up, whereas the caste systems of human society are determined by a social not a biological heritage. Our position in any caste system is one which is subject to modification by the individual and by changes in the social structure.

Throughout the study of the invertebrates we have learned of many instances of complex behavior and even of group or social organization typified by the army ant. Yet invertebrate behavior is rigid to a great extent. It lacks the flexibility of human behavior, or even the behavior typical of vertebrates generally. Furthermore, the behavior of the insects consists largely of innate responses to stimulation. The spider builds a type of web whose structure is predictable if we know the species of spider. A particular spider's response to a strand or filament of the web is determined by genetic information acquired from his ancestors. The spider is equipped for survival by nature with innate responses. We are equipped for survival by the great flexibility of our nervous systems and our capacity to change our activities to meet the present conditions of the world. Both types of systems work effectively.

Because we are a part of the animal world, we might assume that we are born with certain kinds of responses to stimulation which are determined to some extent by our genetic inheritance. To understand the nature of any of our genetic dispositions, we should study the nature of genetically determined behaviors in other members of the animal kingdom. The general adjective used to describe responses which are exhibited by animals without any chance of their having been learned is *instinctive*.

Instinctive Behavior

Instinctive behavior occurs without being learned. We think of such behavior as species-predictable and passed on from generation to generation through hereditary mechanisms. For example, spiders build webs that are predictable if we know their particular species. The belief that this information is passed on through the DNA of the genes (see Chapter 2) is a presumption. But to classify a response as instinctive, we must be able to show that it exists even when we have deprived the animal of all chances of learning it. Since it does occur in the absence of learning and is exhibited by all members of a species, we assume that the genetic material common to the species contains the information requisite to building the physiological mechanism underlying the response.

Psychologists tend to think of instinctive responses as *elicited responses.* By this we mean that the responses are triggered by a stimulus in the environment. The notion of a stimulus-response model has been inherent in much of our discussion, but when we use the word *elicited,* we make the proposed relationship more concrete. Thus we come to a conceptualization of instinctive responses as unlearned reactions of the organism which are triggered or released by particular kinds of environmental stimulation. That the stimuli eliciting the innate behavior pattern may be complex has already been suggested by our study of the spider.

However, studies of the instinctive behavior of fish and birds suggest that the stimuli which act to release instinctive behavior can be quite restricted. The zoologist N. Tinbergen has studied the behavior of the three-spined boney stickleback. This fish displays a number of instinctive responses, some connected with the mating cycle. The male stickleback assumes control over a portion of the sandy bottom of his tank or pond. Once in possession of such a territory he will defend it from male intruders. The male stickleback will also show courtship behavior when a female comes into his area. The courting behavior leads to actions which help to squeeze the eggs from the female and which result in the fertilization of the eggs. The courting behavior, known as the zig-zag dance, is determined by heredity. Timbergen has investigated the stimulus characteristics which are sufficient to release this courting behavior [10].

One technique Tinbergen has used is to introduce various shapes into the water near the male stickleback. By altering the character of the stimulus it is possible to determine specific attributes of the entire pattern which act to release the innate behavior of the zig-zag dance. He finds only a few characteristics of the female form are responsible for the elicitation of the response. The specific attribute which calls out a particular kind of instinctive behavior is called the *sign stimulus.* The sign stimulus for the zig-zag dance is a protruding underportion of a figure that needs be only vaguely fishlike. The characteristic of a bulging underside of a figure is the important feature of the environmental situation. The bulge is the sign stimulus. In Fig. 3.5 the various stimuli used to test for the sign stimulus of the courting behavior are presented. The sign stimulus responsible for eliciting the aggressive behavior appropriate to a male intruder seems to be the size and color of the underbelly of a fishlike form.

Tinbergen can manufacture better sign stimuli than those provided in nature. He can emphasize and enlarge the sign

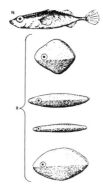

FIG. 3.5. *Models of stimuli used by N. Tinbergen in his studies of instinctive behavior in the stickleback. From N. Tinbergen.* A Study of Instinct. *Oxford: Clarendon Press, 1951. By permisson of the author and the Clarendon Press.*

stimulus characteristics in his models. When these special stimuli are presented, they exert more effect upon the animal than any stimulus naturally found in the environment. These artificial and exaggerated sign stimuli are called *supranormal sign stimuli.*

If the male fish has been stimulated time and time again to make a courting response, the presentation of yet another protruding female form will not usually elicit another zig-zag dance. In short we find adaptation of the response through repeated occurrences. However, if we present one of the supranormal sign stimuli this may be potent enough to release the behavior. On the other hand Tinbergen has observed that if the response has not occurred for some time in the past, instinctive responses often occur even when no sign stimulus is present. It is almost as if energy for a particular response builds up to a certain point and then the response will occur with a minimal amount of stimulation. The *energy* of a particular innate response is specific for a specific stimulus. The effect is not one of general fatigue. The number of recent occurrences of the aggressive responses to other males does not affect the amount of sign stimulation required to release a courting response to a female.

From this work it would seem that animals are instinctively

responsive to certain attributes of environmental stimulation. Only a part of the whole stimulus pattern is important.

From the preceding chapter we have become aware of the maturation and development of man. In the world of lower animals we find a type of instinctive activity for which genetically determined preparations have been made but whose fulfillment depends on (1) a critical period of postnatal development and (2) the occurrence of special stimulating conditions.

The sight of a group of goslings following a mother goose is a common enough sight in rural areas. But in Fig. 3.6 we find a group of goslings following Dr. Konrad Lorenz just as naturally as they would their mother. Through the work of Lorenz [11] and others we know that most fowl will follow *any stimulus* presented to them at a critical time

FIG. 3.6. *Goslings following Dr. Konrad Lorenz, having been imprinted on Lorenz at an early stage in their development.* Courtesy LIFE Magazine © 1955 Time Inc.

after hatching. They do not *learn* to follow the object in the usual sense, rather they *immediately* follow the object presented to them. The object, whatever it may be, is *imprinted* into a following-response behavior system. When the imprinted object is presented, the birds follow it. In fact it appears now that ducks will imprint sounds and tactile sensations as well as visual objects.

Studies of the imprinting process by Hess [12] suggest that the manner of presentation of the stimulus to be imprinted is of crucial importance. Hess keeps his newly hatched ducks in the dark for about 15 or 16 hours after hatching, then they are placed in a circular runway while an object moves around it. The duck follows the object for four turns around the runway. These conditions prove to be very effective in eliciting durable imprinting. Generally, Hess finds that conditions in which the animal is aroused and required to do some work are desirable for imprinting responses. If the young animals are tranquilized with drugs, the following response is poorly imprinted.

Of greatest interest to us now is the extraordinary nature of this instinctive reaction. No innate reaction to a specific stimulus is prepared; rather the nervous system is prepared to incorporate any stimulus-object into ready-built motor sequences providing that the conditions of stimulation and of the organism are right. The work of Tinbergen, Hess, and Lorenz just discussed illustrates some of the exciting frontiers of research on the instincts found in animals. We have avoided the word *instinct* because it readily lends itself to the suggestion that a behavior is easily explained. When we use the word *instinct* we should mean no more than an unlearned response of the organism. We should not then abandon further attempts to understand the mechanisms of behavior responsible for it. The mechanisms of the instinctive responses could be the fundamental units of all behavior; in the higher, more tractable animals learned characteristics may overlie and modify the structure and functions already provided by heredity.

Development of the Human Nervous System

As Herrick pointed out, the nervous systems of the vertebrates are as different as they can be from those of invertebrates. The segmental, body-state federation character of the invertebrate plan is lost, and a central control agency of the whole organism is established in the vertebrates. The parts lose their autonomy and accept commands issued by the central nervous system and its chief unit, the brain. Messages from the senses pour into the central command station of the brain and there they are sorted, catalogued, and evaluated before being transformed into new messages for the individual muscles. All that man is, or can be, depends on the functions carried out by the central nervous system. It will be our next task to try to gain some understanding of its development, structure, and function.

Embryologically, the nervous system of all vertebrates develops from a neutral tube of nerve fibers. The longitudinally organized tracts of the neural tube (in man the forerunner of the spinal cord) allow the greater central control of all activities. Possessing the centralized nervous system typical of

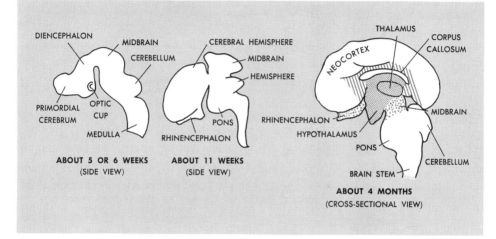

FIG. 3.7. *Stages of brain development of human embryo. Stripes show phylogenetically "old" cortex; shaded area represents the diencephalon (thalamus and hypothalamus), and the dots indicate the midbrain.*

the vertebrates, man has a vast number of elaborate reflexes and, more important, the possibility of considerable modification of behavior through experience.

Neither the brain nor spinal cord ever loses this tubelike organization. As maturation progresses, the cells of the tube in the region which will become the brain show the greatest number of divisions and alterations, and as a result certain early prominences appear which are the precursors of later adult brain structures.

Figure 3.7 shows the structure of the anterior portion of the nervous system of the human embryo at five or six weeks, eleven weeks, and four months after conception. In the four-week embryo the region that will become the medulla and the region which will become the midbrain area of the adult have begun to separate. The beginnings of the visual system are seen in the rapidly developing optic vesicles. The endbrain and the betweenbrain can be distinguished to some extent.

In the three-month embryo a great amount of further differentiation is observed. Now the endbrain has become clearly separated from the betweenbrain, and similarly the betweenbrain is distinct from the midbrain. The primitive cells from which the cerebellum will develop have begun to appear. Also the region of the medulla is more distinct from the rest of the brain or spinal cord.

The region of the medulla will contain cells which are concerned with the regulation of many internal organs and the facial muscles. The cerebellum will become a neural center controlling posture and act as one of the coordinating centers of sensory information from many of the senses. The midbrain is a region containing relay nuclei for some of the senses and contains regions concerned with modulating the information coming in from all of the senses and the outgoing information on the way to muscle cells. The betweenbrain will include in addition to certain other structural parts two regions of particular interest, the thalamus and hypothalamus. The thalamus is primarily a relay station for information from all of the sensory systems but in addition has groups of cells which act in more general fashion to regulate activity of other areas of the brain. The endbrain will differentiate into many different clusters of cells in many different kinds of arrangements. Certain of these will be cells spread over the upper regions of the brain in layers. These cells arranged in layers and overlying the upper end of the brain we call the *cortex*. We shall soon see that there are several kinds of cortices. Each kind develops at different phylogenetic stages of development and presumably each is related to different kinds of behavior in the human. We shall soon learn that the cortex is not homogeneous in structure or in function. Specialization of function is a very prominent feature of the central nervous system.

Although our discussion and illustrations may have given the impression that the brain is a discrete series of segmental structures, this is not the case. All brain regions are intimately related. The brain is continuous and interconnected, one part with the other. Some of the developing brain regions will be concerned with rather specialized functions, but each part operates in cooperation with many other parts and each cell is influenced, directly or indirectly, by almost every other cell in the brain.

THE SINGLE CELL OF THE NERVOUS SYSTEM   The units from which the nervous system is built are single cells called *neurons*. The nervous system is a massive collection of thousands of millions of neurons. To understand how the nervous system operates we must understand the construction and workings of the units of which it is composed.

There is of course a functional resemblance between the single neural cell found in the adult human and the single cell with which we started the chapter, the amoeba. Each

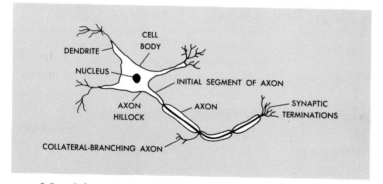

FIG. 3.8.   *Schematic drawing of a neuron.*

must have nourishment and ways to handle the elimination of waste products. Both the amoeba and the neuron have cell membranes, nuclei, other protoplasmic structures, and patterns of reactions to appropriate stimulation. Neurons differ from other cells in the body in that they are specially constructed to transmit excitation swiftly from one end to another, even though the distances between the point of excitation to the end of the neuron may be considerable.

Our brains are essential to our existence, and the brain is nothing more than interconnected masses of cells. Our perceptions, experiences, behavior all depend on the brain. Our hopes, dreams, and aspirations must be explicable in terms of the activities of the single cells of the brain. Investigations

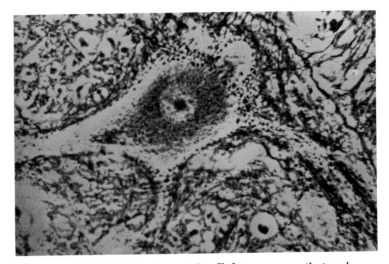

FIG. 3.9. *Cell body of a neuron. Small dots are synaptic termi-nations of axons from other cells. Photomicrograph from a slide prepared by Grant L. Rasmussen, in A. Brodal.* The Reticular Formation of the Brain Stem: Anatomical Aspects and Functional Correlations. *Springfield, Ill.: Charles C Thomas, 1956. Used by permission of the author and the Trustees of the William Hender-son Trust.*

into the brain which have attempted to reveal more than mere brain cells in action have failed. In the single cell and their organization we must find our understanding of ourselves.

In Fig. 3.8 we have diagramed the structure of a single nerve cell in a schematic representation, and in Fig. 3.9 we have presented a photomicrograph of a single nerve cell. In Fig. 3.10 a photomicrograph is presented to illustrate the com-plexity of connections of any given cell with others. Because of the myriad of interconnections between neurons it is mis-leading to think of a neuron in any other context than as closely and intimately connected with thousands of others.

Formally, the nerve cell is thought to be divisible into three functionally discrete parts. One part, the *dendrite,* re-ceives excitation from preceding cells. If this excitation is sufficient to cause a reaction in the dendrite, this reaction spreads to the *cell body,* the second part, and then along to the end of the *axon* portion, the third part. When this spread-ing reaction reaches the end of the axon, its effects may cause the next neurons to react in a similar way. Each cell is a unit, structurally distinct from other cells. The connection between

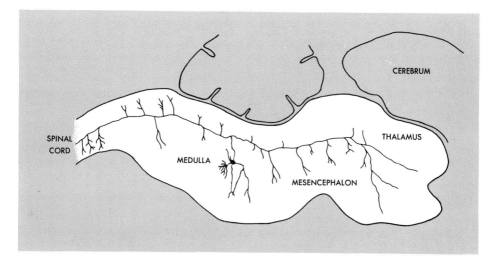

FIG. 3.10.   *Sagittal section of the brain of a 2-day-old rat, showing a large reticular cell projecting forward and backward for considerable distances. Adapted from Madge E. Scheibel & A. B. Scheibel.* Reticular Formation of the Brain. *Boston: Little, Brown and Company, 1958. By permission of the authors, the Henry Ford Hospital, and Little, Brown and Company.*

the axons of one cell and the dendrite of the next is the *synapse.*

Today, we are aware of other types of junctions between cells which may be different from the axon-dendrite arrangement just described. According to Eccles [13] some axons connect directly with cell bodies of subsequent cells. This kind of synaptic arrangement can be called an axon-cell body junction. Eccles found that in some spinal-cord cells which are linked by axon-cell body connections, stimulation of the dendrites could not be great enough to cause the reaction to spread to the cell body or axon. Only the activities of cells with processes ending directly on the cell body could cause the resultant reaction, or excitation, to spread to the cell body and axon.

What is meant by excitation of a neuron? Upon examining the membrane of a neuron at rest, we find a preponderance of sodium (Na^+) and chlorine (Cl^-) ions on the outside of the membrane. (Ions are electrically charged particles of various chemical elements.) On the inside of the cell we find a preponderance of potassium ions (K^+). We are not at all sure of the chemical mechanisms that maintain the separation of the ions across the membrane; but this separation does exist and

87

is called the *polarization* of the membrane, as it exists when the cell is in a resting state. Neural excitation refers to a change in this resting condition. During this change, the positive ions of sodium (Na^+) flow inward, and the polarization of the membrane breaks down. This process is called the depolarization of the cell membrane. Almost as soon as this depolarization has occurred, certain chemical processes begin which act to reestablish the former polarized state. The Na^+ ions are forced outward again to the exterior of the membrane. The original polarized state is reestablished. The time required for all these activities is extremely brief. The depolarization and restoration processes sufficient to allow another depolarization are accomplished in about one-thousandth of one second. Some nerve cells can fire about one thousand times a second for indefinite periods of time.

One fascinating problem of neurophysiology is how the excitation crosses the synapse. The answer now seems to be that the conduction of excitation across the synapse is accomplished by chemicals, released by one neuron, which cause the second neuron to be depolarized. When the excitation reaches the end of the axon, little pockets release certain chemicals (transmitter substances) which flow to the cell body or dendrite of the next cell. These pockets of chemicals in the terminations of the axons are illustrated in photograph made by the electron microscope in Fig. 3.11. When these chemicals reach the membrane of the next cell, a depolarization of the membrane is begun. Most likely there are several kinds of transmitter substances, or chemicals, which are released at synapses. There is evidence that some transmitter substances do not cause a depolarization of the next cell's membrane, but rather act to increase its polarization (even more Na^+ and K^+ ions on the outside of the membrane; more Cl^- on the inside). The increase in polarization results in inhibition of the activity of the neuron. There may be several kinds of chemicals acting to either increase or decrease the polarization of cell membranes.

When a depolarizing substance reaches a cell membrane, it always has some depolarizing effect. However, this effect may not spread to the rest of the cell body and in turn down the axon. There is a segment of the cell body which chemically "decides" whether the net depolarization effects of all of the transmitter substances acting on it are large enough to precipitate a complete reaction of the cell body and axon. This portion of the cell body acts to integrate all of the chemical influences acting on the cell at every moment. If the net depolarizing effect is sufficient, the cell reacts. If the totality of the influences is insufficient, no total reaction of the neuron will occur. When sufficient depolarizing influences impinge on a cell to trigger a reaction, the depolarization of cell body and axon is complete. It does not matter whether the depolarizing influences were just barely enough or much more than required.

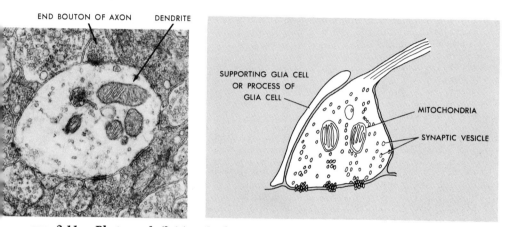

FIG. 3.11. *Photograph (left) and schematic drawing (right) of a synaptic ending based on electron microscopy. Photograph courtesy of Dean E. Hillman, Kenneth A. Siegesmund, and Clement A. Fox; drawing adapted by permission of The Rockefeller Institute Press from E. De Robertis. Submicroscopic changes of Synapse after nerve section in the acoustic ganglion of the guinea pig. The* Journal of Biophysical and Biochemical Cytology, *1956, 25 (September 25), 503–512.*

If the cell responds, it responds completely. This phenomenon is the classic all-or-none law. If a cell fires, it fires all the way.

The depolarization of the cell body and axon is referred to as the *spike* potential because of the sharp spikelike waveform observed in oscilloscopic recordings of the neuron reaction. In Fig. 3.12 the reaction of an entire nerve, a collection of axons, is presented and in Fig. 3.13 a record from the axon of a single cell is shown. After the quick, sudden change the cell returns to its resting state. This recording of a spike discharge illustrates in dramatic fashion the basic electrochemical activity of the brain—the excitation of the individual nerve cells. We can record other electrochemical activities of the brain and nervous system. Records are often made of the activity of a nerve, which is composed of a group of axons.

Another technique records the gross electrical activities occurring in an area of brain tissue. Somewhat similar techniques are used in each case. Small wires or other electrically conducting substances are placed near or in the material from which recordings will be made. The electrical changes in the area under study are picked up by these conductors (electrodes) and then are sent through several stages of amplification before they become large enough to be seen on an oscilloscope or to deflect a pen in an ink-writing device. The recent advances in our knowledge of the electrical activities of the brain have depended upon the development of recording techniques and equipment. Thus our knowledge of the neurophysiological bases of behavior could only be gained when the technology of other fields, notably electronics, developed appropriate techniques and equipment.

This pattern of interdependence between technology and basic research has been prominent throughout the history of science. Investigations of the activity of the single cell and the

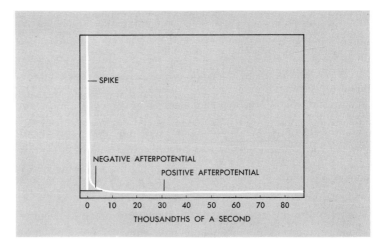

FIG. 3.12. *Scale diagram of complete action potential of a large, myelinated nerve in the cat. Adapted from H. S. Gasser. Electrical signs of biological activity.* J. appl. Phys., *1938,* 9, *88–96.*

related electrical phenomena of the brain are searches for basic knowledge. They are attempts to learn just how the nervous system works. Applications are sure to follow the accumulation of basic knowledge, but at this point the student should seek to gain understanding of the principles of neural function.

We have spoken of neurons, synapses, and the principles of their excitation and conduction in a way that the student could easily conclude that each cell is a passive unit only activated when stimulating situations are appropriate. However, the nervous system is continuously active. Cells are firing spontaneously all

FIG. 3.13. *Action potential of a nerve fiber. Adapted from H. S. Gasser. The classification of nerve fibers.* Ohio J. Sci., *1941, 41, 145–159.*

the time. Stimulation of a cell results in an increase or decrease of the rate of activity, depending on whether the transmitter substances act to depolarize or hyperpolarize the membrane.

Even though the neurons of the brain and central nervous system are electrically active, and possibly physically active, at all times, studies of the nervous system have revealed *units of organization.* By this we mean that a given animal, e.g., man, has groups of cells whose functions are somewhat well defined and known. Understanding of the brain depends on knowledge of these organizational principles.

Anatomy of the Nervous System

To be effective a football team must work together to gain common objectives. The results of the team depend on every player doing his assigned task. In the nervous system various units act to perform different specialized functions, and again the result of their work is dependent upon the appropriate functioning by all of the parts. Just as we might analyze the functions of one player on a football team, we can try to isolate the functions of one or another anatomical parts of the nervous system. In both cases we should keep before us the fact that we have isolated but one part from an ongoing process. The activity of the part under study is normally determined by activity in all of the other units and the constant flux of external events.

This section will take the nervous system apart in order to present some of the known anatomical units for study. First, we shall look at the peripheral aspects of the nervous system concerned with (1) providing us with the information about the outside world and (2) controlling muscular activities. Then we shall move inward to the central nervous system and upward toward the brain. We shall move from specific systems to more general ones which exist in the nervous system and, at the end of this section, present some of the brain structures which modulate all incoming and outgoing messages.

THE SENSES AND THE AFFERENT SYSTEMS   One of the essential functions of the nervous system is to detect changes in the physical stimuli surrounding us. We can think back to the amoeba and recall that stimuli tended to arouse the whole animal, but it is generally true that as we go higher and higher in the scale we find that more and more cells are specialized for the detection of a limited range of stimulus changes.

Cells which are sensitive to changes in specific kinds of stimulation are called receptor cells. Some are found in collections of cells with a similar function called *receptor organs* or *receptors,* others are scattered about in the skin and muscles. Receptor cells come in a wide variety of sizes, shapes, and functions. We shall discuss the general features of receptors and discuss more elaborately the nature of those in the visual and auditory systems in the next chapter.

The over-all picture of our peripheral sensory systems is presented in schematic display in Fig. 3.14. From the receptor organs, groups of axons of cells (located in or near the receptor organs) run into the central portion of the nervous system: the spinal cord and the brain. These constitute the nerves connecting the receptors to the central nervous system. In the spinal cord, the impulses originating in the receptors course toward the higher centers. Usually, the ascending fibers end on cells in restricted portions of the thalamus, and these thalamic cells in turn send axons to restricted areas of the neocortex.

The nerves which carry information from the receptors to

the thalamic areas and brain are called *afferent nerves* (afferent fibers if we are talking of single axons). The neocortical areas which receive the information from a specific thalamic area, and consequently from a specific kind of receptor, are called *projection areas.*

Receptor cells are different from other neural cells in that they can become excited by physical energy changes which do not affect other cells. In the chain of cells which carry impulses toward the brain in the afferent systems only the first cells, the receptor cells, have this function. The other cells in the chain are excited by normal processes, namely the transmitter substances of the synaptic junction.

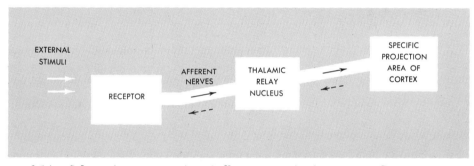

FIG. 3.14. *Schematic representation of all sensory-projection systems. Sensory fibers run from receptors toward cortex by way of the thalamic relay nuclei. The broken arrows indicate anatomical pathways running from the cortex to the thalamic nuclei, and from the thalamus to area of the receptor, presumably allowing central control of the peripheral receptor mechanisms.*

In the receptor cell, physical energy is transformed into changes in the spontaneous activity of the receptor cells. This has great implications for us. It means that the brain does not receive *redness, loudness, burning sensations,* or *smells,* per se. But it does receive changes in the activity of millions of single neurons, and the brain in turn transforms these changes of activity in such a way that redness, loudness, burning, and smells are created. These qualities are products of the brain.

One of the most fascinating areas of research is that concerned with understanding the relationship between the physical energy changes and the changes in the activities of single neural cells. This task could be described as an attempt to crack the neural code used to transmit information about the states of the receptors to the brain.

93

MUSCLES AND THE EFFERENT SYSTEMS   Some nerve cells have axons that end not in a synapse with another nerve cell but rather in muscle. Chemicals released at the termination of the axons produce a contraction of the muscle. The contractions of all kinds of muscles are governed by nerve fibers: both the somatic muscle system that moves the body and the muscles of the internal organs are controlled neurally by the central nervous system. The nerves that run to somatic muscles are called, collectively, the *somatic motor system.* The nerves which end in the muscles of the internal organs and glands are called the *autonomic nervous system.*

The autonomic system can be further subdivided into two categories: the *sympathetic division* and the *parasympathetic division.* Anatomically, the sympathetic division is localized by two long nerve trunks *outside of the spinal cord,* extending from the base of the skull to the "tail bone." One is on each side of the spinal column. The nerve fibers of these trunks, their fibers extending to visceral organs and their connections to the rest of the nervous system, are known collectively as the sympathetic division of the autonomic system. Generally, the sympathetic division readies us internally for stress and emergency reactions.

The parasympathetic division includes the cranial nerves supplying visceral and facial organs and a component which leaves the spinal cord near its base and supplies internal organs in the pelvic area. Generally, the parasympathetic division acts to maintain processes such as digestion, food metabolism, and excretion, and its effect on other internal organs is to maintain the normal vegetative functions of the body.

The organization of the peripheral somatic motor system is less complex than the peripheral organization of the autonomic nervous system. Cells in the motor areas of the neocortex initiate impulses which arrive at cells in the spinal cord. These cells in turn send impulses to the appropriate muscles. If anything happens to damage the nerves from the spinal cord to the muscles, the muscles become limp and cannot be contracted by normal means. In other words, a complete flaccid paralysis is produced when the motor nerve supply to the muscles is interrupted. Interestingly enough, muscle activity also depends upon the nerves which run *from* the muscle to the cord and higher centers (the *afferent* nerves). If these afferent nerves are severed the muscles are paralyzed just as though the motor nerve was interrupted. Our muscle movements depend upon a complex interplay in the cord of afferent (sensory) and efferent (motor) impulses.

Certain simple behavioral acts are organized within the cord. For instance, when the patellar tendon is struck, the muscles of the leg contract, sending your foot forward in the knee-jerk reflex often demonstrated in the physician's office. This reflex *can* occur without assistance of the higher areas of the nervous system but normally is modulated by higher nervous centers. We should recognize the extent of this modulating effect even in simple reflexes. Even though the physician taps your crossed knee with his rubber hammer, you *can* consciously inhibit the reflex. Excitement or arousal increases the size of the reflex. The basic mechanism is built into the spinal cord, but it is under the direct influence of the brain.

THE AUTONOMIC SYSTEM It is much more difficult to provide an overview of the autonomic system. Fibers associated with the sympathetic system seem to act in some cases as if they should be classified with the parasympathetic system. Some experts believe it would be better to divide the autonomic system into two branches on the basis of the transmitter substances involved in a chain of neurons or the effects of certain drugs on the synapses in the systems. It is sometimes difficult to separate the two systems anatomically. For example, the heart receives fibers from both divisions of the autonomic system. It is extremely difficult to separate the fibers from the cranial nerve of the parasympathetic division and those coming from the sympathetic trunks. However, for the present we shall continue with the traditional separation of the two components based on anatomic structure. Figure 3.15 shows some of the internal organs and their relation to the autonomic systems.

There are many mysteries still to be solved regarding the autonomic nervous system. One of the most pressing problems is the relation of the autonomic system to the brain areas. While we know the specific neocortical areas of origin of the somatic motor system, we know very little about the origin of the fibers going into the divisions of the autonomic system. At the moment, however, we know that portions of the limbic system and the hypothalamus exercise various amounts of control over the autonomic system.

The internal conditions of the body are partly regulated by the nervous system, as we have learned. There is another

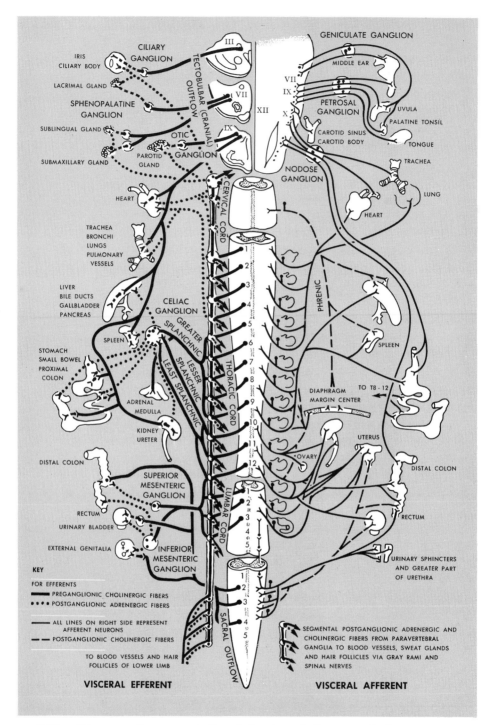

FIG. 3.15. *Diagrammatic representation of the visceral efferents and afferents.*
From T. C. Ruch & J. Fulton. Medical Physiology and Biophysics (18th ed.).
Philadelphia: W. B. Saunders Company, 1960.

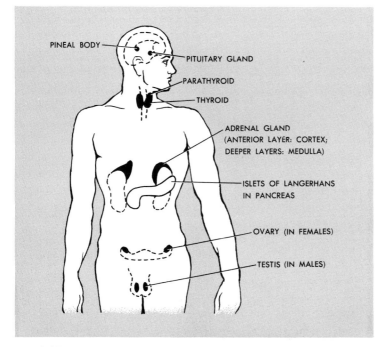

PINEAL BODY

PITUITARY GLAND

PARATHYROID

THYROID

ADRENAL GLAND
(ANTERIOR LAYER: CORTEX;
DEEPER LAYERS: MEDULLA)

ISLETS OF LANGERHANS
IN PANCREAS

OVARY (IN FEMALES)

TESTIS (IN MALES)

FIG. 3.16. *Diagrammatic representation of the endocrine glands.*

controlling and regulating system that merits our attention: the endocrine system.

THE ENDOCRINE GLANDS The body's glands can be categorized on the basis of whether they secrete their contents through a duct or not. If they do not secrete through ducts they are called *endocrine* glands. Substances secreted by the endocrine glands, called *hormones,* are sent into the blood stream and, therefore, may cause effects of a more widespread nature. Many hormones are of extreme importance in the individual's behavior and development. Although the endocrine glands are so important to behavior that they cannot be omitted from our discussion, their relation to behavior is so complex that much of what will be said represents a vast oversimplification. Figure 3.16 illustrates the position of the major endocrine glands.

There are many hormones secreted by the *pituitary* gland, which lies below the anterior margin of the hypothalamus. This gland is often called the master gland of the body, for its hormones influence the secretions of many other endocrine and duct glands. One of the pituitary hormones is the adreno-corticotropic hormone (commonly abbreviated ACTH), which influences the activity of the adrenal gland. Other hormones from the pituitary assist in the regulation of the output of the thyroid (thyroxine) and the pancreas (insulin). Still other hormones from this body are concerned with the development of sexual organs, the secretion of milk from the mammary glands, and the conversion of fats and proteins to carbohydrates. Hormones secreted by another portion of the pituitary control the body's loss of water through the kidney. The pituitary also helps to regulate blood pressure.

The thyroid gland secretes a number of hormones which help control the basal metabolic rate of the body and its growth. The parathyroid glands work to maintain the calcium and the phosphorous balance of the blood.

Insulin is a hormone secreted by the pancreas which acts upon individual cells to allow blood sugars to enter them as nourishment. People unfortunate enough to produce too little of this hormone are commonly called *diabetics*. When there is an insufficient amount of insulin, the individual cells cannot absorb and use the available blood sugars and the blood sugar level climbs. With the injection of insulin the cells can absorb the sugar, and the blood sugar level drops toward normal. The actual mechanism whereby insulin controls the cell's membrane to allow sugar to enter is still unknown.

The adrenal glands secrete hormones from their surface layer (cortex) and their centers (medulla). The hormones produced in the adrenal cortices control the carbohydrate and sodium balances of the body, while the adrenal medulla produces adrenalin (epinephrine) and noradrenalin (norepinephrine). Adrenalin stimulates secretion of sugar by the liver, increases the heart rate, and raises the blood pressure by increasing the heart rate. Noradrenalin raises the blood pressure through constriction of the peripheral blood vessels.

Our secondary sexual characteristics, such as beard and body hair, are controlled by hormones secreted by the sexual glands. In the male these are secreted from the testes, but the female hormone system is much more complicated. There are hormones secreted from different kinds of cells in the ovary as well as from the placenta during pregnancy.

These and many other hormones act in a coordinated fashion with the sympathetic and parasympathetic systems in maintaining the body during periods of normal activities and in times of emergencies. Adrenalin produces many of the same effects as does increased activity in the sympathetic system. Thus, the adrenal medulla and the sympathetic system often are jointly referred to as the sympathetic-adrenal system. Since insulin is so necessary for body maintenance the term parasympathetic-insulin is sometimes used to describe the functional convergence of the two systems, one neural, the other hormonal.

THE BRAIN At the top of the spinal cord, we reach the pinnacle of man's neural development, the brain. We may think

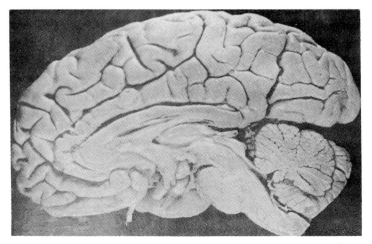

FIG. 3.17.   *Brain sectioned in the median plane. From E. Gardner.* Fundamentals of Neurology *(4th ed.). Philadelphia: W. B. Saunders Company, 1963.*

of it as beginning at the medulla oblongata and continuing upwards through pons and cerebellum, midbrain, hypothalamus and thalamus, before reaching the cortex (see Figs. 3.17 and 3.18). In man the neocortex covers the surface of the brain and is extremely convoluted, as can be seen in Fig. 3.19. The major neocortical areas are labeled in the sketch provided in Fig. 3.20. The significance of these convolutions can be appreciated when one recognizes that about one-half of all of man's neocortex lies hidden from sight in the valleys (sulci) between the convolutions (gyri). Neocortex ranges in depth from about 1.5 to 4.0 millimeters in different cortical areas.

At the top of the spinal cord is an enlarged region, called the medulla, or medulla oblongata, and pons. All of the fiber

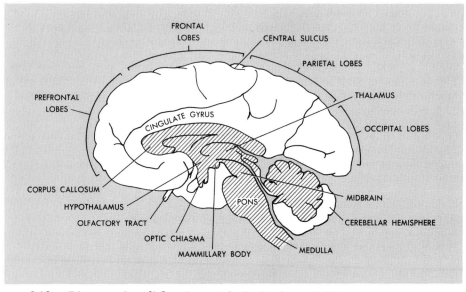

FIG. 3.18. *Diagram of medial surface of the brain shown in Fig.* *3.17.* *Adapted from E. Gardner.* Fundamentals of Neurology (*4th* *ed.*). Philadelphia: W. B. Saunders Company, 1963.

tracts carrying information from the body ascend through this region, as do the nerve fibers descending from higher regions of the brain which control bodily movements. In the pons and medulla, however, there are groups of nerve cells which send axons downstream into some of the most important internal organs. These clusters of cells (nuclei) act as centers for the activities of the heart and lungs and their integrity is essential to life. Throughout the center of the midbrain and pons there is a network of cells which are believed to exert general and diffuse influences upon the activity of the higher regions of the brain and motor movements of the body. The central core of this region is called the brain-stem reticular system (see pp. 104–107). Finally, in this same region of the brain there are important interconnections with the cerebellum, usually thought to be important for maintaining balance and posture, and clusters of cells (nuclei) which help in the refinement and coordination of bodily movements.

Above the pons is the midbrain. The ascending and descending fiber tracts also pass through this region, and in it the reticular formation occupies a central position. At the top of the midbrain there are reflex centers for movements related to vision and audition. At the bottom there are nuclear groups which participate in coordinating motor movements.

Immediately above the midbrain is the small but important area called the hypothalamus. The border between the midbrain and hypothalamus is marked by the mammillary bodies which are part of the hypothalamus. This region contains many groups of nerve cells which function as centers for many kinds of behavior related to maintaining the individual and perpetuating the species (see pp. 328–329).

The hypothalamus is above and extends both ahead and behind the optic chiasm. This is the point at which the optic nerves, one from each eye, come together; and it is at this point that some fibers are exchanged between the two optic nerves before the fibers continue back to reach a relay station in

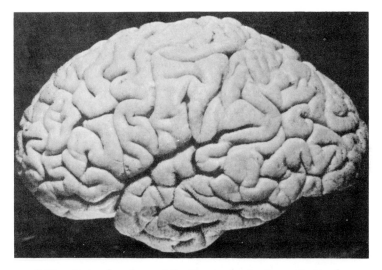

FIG. 3.19. *Lateral surface of the human brain. From E. Gardner.* Fundamentals of Neurology *(4th ed.). Philadelphia: W. B. Saunders Company, 1963.*

the thalamus. From the thalamus (see Fig. 3.18) visual information will be transmitted by neural impulses to area 17 of the occipital lobe and then to surrounding areas 18 and 19.

The corpus callosum, a most prominent feature of Fig. 3.17, is a collection of a large number of fibers which connect areas of one hemisphere with corresponding areas of the other hemisphere.

The thalamus, located above the hypothalamus, has several

kinds of cell groups (or nuclei). One type contains cells which receive axons from one of the sensory systems and relay this information to the brain's neocortex. Another type contains cells which project to wide regions of neocortex and other higher brain regions. Since cells in these nuclei diffusely bombard brain regions, their role in behavior will be discussed in the following section on diffuse systems. We already have learned that certain thalamic areas contain cells which project to restricted neo-cortical areas.

The fibers leaving the thalamus from the relay nuclei for vision all go into the visual projection areas in the occipital lobes. The fibers from cells in the thalamic relay-nuclei for hearing reach cells in special areas of the temporal lobes, and neocortical cells just behind the central sulcus receive impulses originally arising from receptors in the muscles, joints, and skin (the somatosensory system). Note areas 1, 2, and 3 of Fig.

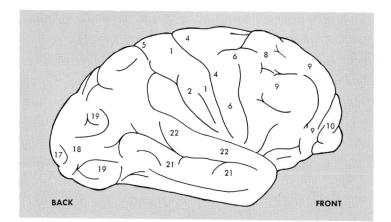

FIG. 3.20. *Lateral surface of the human brain showing the numerical designations of cortical areas developed by Brodmann.*

3.20. These projection areas are again presented pictorially in Fig. 3.21, but in this figure we may compare the relative amounts of brain surface occupied with the reception of sensory information. As one goes higher and higher in the phylogenetic scale the amount of brain committed to a given sensory (or motor) responsibility becomes less and less. Areas of neocortex that have not been identified with specific sensory or motor tasks are caller *association areas.* In passing we should note that it is often assumed, implicitly at least, that the greater the amount of uncommitted association area the greater will be the behavioral flexibility of the animal.

The thalamic relay cells of the somatosensory system project to cells behind the central fissure in a rough approximation to the location of the receptors in the body. Today, we know there are many cells, other than those located in the primary somatosensory areas, which receive the fibers coming in from specific body receptors. For example, the primary motor areas in front of the fissure receive a number of afferent fibers [Woolsey, 14]. Thus, while there is anatomical and functional evidence for describing certain areas as motor and others as sensory, we must recognize a considerable overlap in function throughout the cortex.

The primary motor areas just mentioned lie just anterior to the central sulcus (areas 4, 6, and 8 of Fig. 3.20). The term *motor cortex* or *motor strips* refers to areas of cortex in which

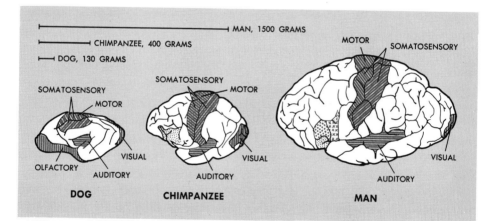

FIG. 3.21. *Lateral views of three mammalian brains drawn to scale to show the relative sizes of primary sensory and motor areas of (a) the dog, (b) the chimpanzee, and (c) man. Adapted from G. W. Bartelmez, Man from the point of view of his development and structure, in* The Nature of the World and of Man *by H. H. Newman by permission of the University of Chicago Press. © 1926 by the University of Chicago. All rights reserved.*

the majority of cells have axons which extend down to the cell bodies of motor neurons in the cord. These motor neurons send projections out to the somatic musculature. The motor cortex is not arranged haphazardly. There is a systematic organization in which adjacent cortical cells influence neighboring muscle cells. One interesting facet of the organization of the motor cortex is the ratio of the number of neural cells to the number of muscle cells in a given body area. In general we observe that those areas of the body which are concerned with fine discriminations and delicate movements have the greatest number of controlling cells in the cortex.

However, the axons which run to the motor neurons in the cord originate in many other places in the cortex than the "classical areas" just in front of the central fissure. There are secondary and tertiary motor areas for most muscle groups. Lilly [15] has demonstrated that stimulation of any area of the neocortex can produce bodily movements when the animal is unanesthetized and free from physical restraints. There may be a great number of highly organized motor areas of the brain of which we know little, and *all areas* of the cortex may be involved in the production of our normal behavioral acts. There is probably no area of the brain that is entirely motor or entirely sensory in function.

The mechanisms responsible for coordinating the contractions of many muscles into a complex movement of the hands or face are poorly understood, but we know that some areas in the medulla are essential to this coordination. In addition, some neocortical areas just outside of the classical motor areas of the cortex seem to have similar functions. These cortical areas lying immediately anterior to the classical motor area are essential to the complex tactual movements, but their removal does not seem to cause any disturbance of gross movements.

THE DIFFUSE SYSTEMS   A more complex type of regulation of the motor systems is effected by the *diffuse system* of the reticular formation of the brain stem and spinal cord.

Up to this point we have assumed a simple model of neural activity: sensory pathways going toward the neocortex and motor tracts running down from the neocortex to muscles. While our presentation has been oversimplified, the underlying model represents the classic view of the afferent and efferent systems. Usually it is assumed that the *integration* of signals arising from the different senses takes place in the neocortical association areas.

Within the past ten to fifteen years a body of research findings has developed which makes it necessary for us to add some new features to our views of neural organization. These findings relate to the discovery of new functions for parts of the brain and spinal cord and may be briefly summarized as follows: Most generally, certain areas of the upper brain stem and thalamus can act so as to regulate the activity in the following:

1. The sensory afferent fibers and possibly the activity of receptor cells themselves
2. The neurons controlling muscle movements
3. The neocortex and other higher centers

Because the effects of these thalamic and brain-stem areas are generally widespread and because cells in these areas project to wide areas of cortex, these thalamic and brain-stem regions are considered to be parts of a diffuse system of brain

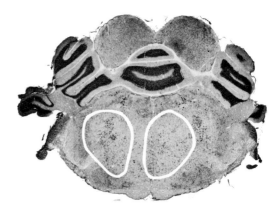

FIG. 3.22. *Photomicrograph of the brainstem of a rat. Enclosed areas represent portions of the brain stem reticular formation. Photograph by R. L. Isaacson.*

function. Most of the research on the diffuse systems has been in the brain-stem areas. Therefore, we shall discuss this portion of the diffuse systems in greatest detail.

Throughout the spinal cord and running to the forward margin of the midbrain, there is a region of nerve cells that appear netlike when stained and viewed under the microscope. In the upper regions it is referred to as the brain-stem reticular formation. Figure 3.22 shows a cross section of the upper spinal cord with this area outlined. At first it seemed to be capable of almost magical things. It was described as the neurological basis for learning, motives, and general alertness of the body and brain. As research progressed claims about its functions have become more cautious. However, there is little doubt that this region is very important in regulating many of our sensory and motor activities. We shall have occasion to speak of brain-stem reticular formation several times later in the book, and at this time we shall discuss only some of its most widely known properties.

Cells in the brain-stem reticular formation act upon cells located in upper regions of the brain with a diffuse rain of nervous impulses. Whether or not the bombardment is completely diffuse is unsettled. It may be that not all areas of the reticular formation bombard all areas of the upper levels of the brain. Brodal [16] has pointed out the likelihood of a considerable specificity in the activities of this system. In other words, certain portions of the brain-stem reticular formation may send impulses to restricted cortical areas. However, some theories in psychology have assumed a complete generality of diffuseness of reticular formation activity. Assuming a general diffuse bombardment, these theories then relate this bombardment to an activation or arousal of the brain. Evidence supporting this view can be obtained from studies of the electrical activity that can be recorded from the neocortical surface of the brain.

By electronic amplification, one can record the changing patterns of electrical potentials from the brain surface or even from the overlying scalp. These patterns originate in the neocortex and are thought to be related to the arousal or alertness of the person or animal from whom the records were obtained. French *et al.* [17] stimulated the brain-stem reticular formation electrically and found that this stimulation could alter both the waking and drowsy EEG patterns to ones that are indicative of greater arousal. Some of their EEG recordings obtained before, during, and after brain-stem reticular formation stimulation are presented in Fig. 3.23.

The brain-stem reticular formation also can produce facilitation or inhibition of reflex movements of the extremities. The response of a leg to a tap of the patellar tendon reflex (the knee jerk) is easier to obtain and of greater amplitude when certain areas of the brain-stem reticular formation are stimulated. Today we conceive of the brain-stem reticular formation as a system (or systems) of neurons which modifies the activity of the higher regions of the brain as well as the motoneurons in the spinal cord. Presumably, it does this by controlling the excitability of the individual neurons. Today we also recognize that the brain-stem reticular formation is regulated in turn by sensory stimulation from all receptors and by output from the cortex and higher subcortical areas.

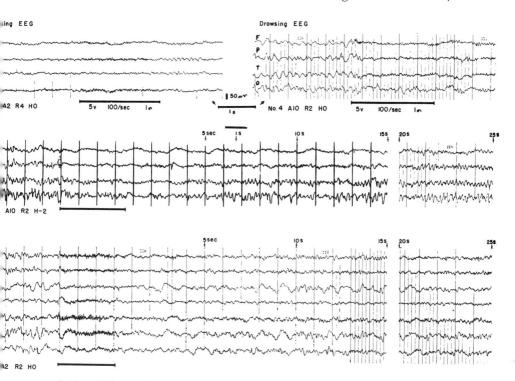

FIG 3.23.   *Effects of stimulation of the reticular formation upon the waking (upper left) and drowsing (upper right) electroencephalograms. Two lower tracings illustrate long lasting effects of such stimulation on the activity of the brain in a drowsy state. From J. D. French, F. K. von Amerongen, & H. W. Magoun. An activating system in the brain stem of monkey. AMA Arch. Neurol. Psychiat., 1952, 68, 577–590.*

Later in the book we shall discuss the theoretical significance of the brain-stem reticular formation under several topic headings. For instance, in discussing sensation we will find that the brain-stem reticular formation can influence the activity of receptor organs themselves.

THE LIMBIC SYSTEM   Between the great grey mantle of neocortical cells and those of the thalamus there are several varieties of cell masses which are distinct from neocortex. Some of these cell groups are related to the modification and coordination of movements (the basal ganglia). Other cell groups are collectively called the *limbic system,* and this group of structures seems to be especially important for many psychological phenomena.

The term was first used by Broca in 1878 to designate the phylogenetically old cortex which surrounds the upper portions of the brain stem. It presents a common denominator [18] of brain tissue for all of the mammals. Figure 3.24 shows the area of the brain which is called the limbic system in the rabbit, cat, and monkey. As one ascends the phylogenetic scale, the *relative* amount of brain tissue in the limbic system decreases as the amount of neocortex increases. (The neocortex is anatomically differentiated from older cortex in that it either has, or went through, a developmental stage that has six layers of cell bodies. Phylogenetically older cortex does not have, and never had, this many layers of cells.)

In general the limbic system develops from portions of the brain devoted to olfaction (smell). The limbic system is

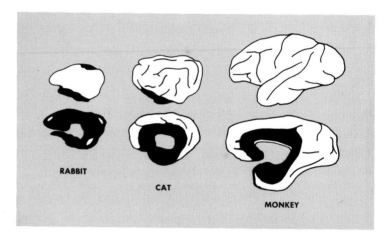

FIG. 3.24. *Lateral and medial surfaces of the brains of a rabbit, a cat, and a monkey. The limbic lobe (shaded area) forms a common denominator in brains of all mammals and seems physiologically to be a common base for a variety of behaviors involved in self-preservation and preservation of the species. Note how limbic lobe surrounds the thalamus.* (Limbic means "forming a border around.") *Redrawn from P. D. MacLean, Studies on the limbic system ("visceral brain") and their bearing on psychosomatic problems, in E. Wittkower & R. A. Cleghorn (Eds.). Recent Developments in Psychosomatic Medicine. London: Pitman Medical Publishing Co. Ltd., 1954.*

especially large in animals that depend for their adjustment to the environment upon smell. However, in the higher animals the limbic structures do not have any important connection with the sense of smell and seem to have taken over new functions far removed from olfaction. For our purposes, the major divisions of the limbic systems are as follows:

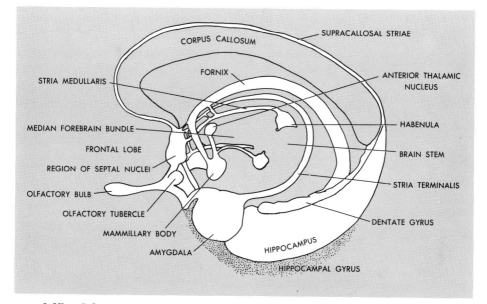

FIG. 3.25. *Schematic representation of the relationships among various subcortical structures of rhinencephalon, as if seen through lateral surface of the brain. Adapted from P. D. MacLean. Psychosomatic disease and the "visceral brain:" recent developments bearing on the Papez theory of emotion. Psychosom. Med., 1949, 11, 338–353.*

1. The hypothalamus
2. Nuclear masses of the amygdala, septal area, anterior nucleus of the thalamus
3. Older cortical areas: hippocampus, cingulate cortex, orbito-frontal cortex, temporal pole, etc.
4. Fiber tracts connecting various regions of the limbic system, e.g., the fornix, medial forebrain bundle

(These areas and nerve tracts are illustrated in Fig. 3.24.)

The hypothalamus is an area at the base of the brain just anterior to the upper end of the brain stem proper. About the size of a large marble in adult man, it is an extremely complex structure. In Fig. 3.25 one can see the medial forebrain bundle running through the hypothalamic areas and along the base of the brain. The fornix can be seen descending from the septal area and terminating in the posterior hypothalamus near the two prominences at the rear, the mammillary bodies. The hypothalamus itself is made up of several subgroups or nuclei.

Most of the limbic system is involved in the regulation of the internal organs, the viscera. Some refer to the limbic system as the visceral brain because of this control. Kaada [19] has shown that electrical stimulation of practically all of the various parts of the limbic system alters the activities of the internal organs. Since we believe the functioning of our internal organs to be intimately related to our mental states, emotion, motivation, and behavior generally, we can infer the importance of the limbic system, itself.

Since the limbic system is concerned with the internal organs, it must be closely involved with the autonomic branches of the nervous system. Such an intimate relationship has been found in the hypothalamus where an anterior-posterior division of function has been found.

Electrical stimulation of the anterior hypothalamus, through implanted electrodes, produces effects which are typical of those mediated by the parasympathetic division of the autonomic nervous system. Stimulation of the posterior portions of the hypothalamus results in activities of the emergency type served by the sympathetic division, such as increased heart rate, blood pressure, and respiration. These anterior and posterior divisions of the hypothalamus easily lead to a view that control centers for the respective portions of the peripheral nervous system exist in the hypothalamus.

The concept of centers in the hypothalamus which tend to control or regulate behavior has been very fruitful in our understanding of the central organization of the brain. Today, we know that there are regions in the hypothalamic area which seem to regulate the sleep-wakefulness patterns of the animal [20]. In addition, centers regulating the initiation and cessation of eating behavior, water intake, and aggressive behaviors have been reported as localized in the hypothalamus. (For an introductory review of these functions see [21].)

These represent only some of the important controlling and regulating functions believed to be localized in the hypothalamus. Considering even the ones we have listed, one cannot but be impressed by the significance of this relatively small amount of neural tissue.

Recent work suggests that electrical stimulation of parts of the limbic system may produce effects on behavior that may be most easily explained on the assumption that it elicits pleasurable sensations in the animal.

In his original experiments Olds was attempting to stimulate a specific subcortical area of the brain. He wanted to obtain an increase in the general arousal of the animal. In planning this experiment he thought that it would be desirable to have some means of controlling for possible painful or unpleasant sensations that might be produced by the stimulation. Therefore, he placed the experimental animals with electrodes embedded in parts of their brains into a large box and stimulated the brain regions with minute amounts of electrical currents when the animals wandered into one part of the box. He reasoned that if the stimulation of the brain was unpleasant the animals would not return to the region where they had had their brains stimulated. To his surprise the animals kept coming back for the electrical stimulation. Olds then set up a situation where the animals could press a bar which would close an electrical circuit and send the small electrical current into their own brains. This particular response, the bar press, is a very common type of testing situation for animals. Most often, however, the animal is rewarded by food for each depression of the bar. In Olds' experiment the reward was an electrical stimulation of a particular region of the brain. Olds found that electrical stimulation appeared to be as good a reward as food was for the hungry animal, as measured by the rate at which the animals pushed the bar [22].

Since the original bar-press experiments, Olds has found that animals will cross an electrically charged grid which gives them a painful shock to obtain this stimulation of the brain. In fact they seem to be willing to withstand a more painful shock to reach a place of electrical stimulation of the brain than they will to reach food when hungry. Generally speaking, stimulation of certain brain regions produces effects which are stronger than the effects of most, if not all, natural reinforcements [23].

In Fig. 3.26 we can see an X-ray of one of Olds' experimental animals. Under careful anesthetic and surgical techniques, a pedestal is screwed into the skull which has insulated silver wires extending beneath it. The silver wires are very small and extend into the brain region that Olds wishes to stimulate later. Only the very tips of the wires are uninsulated. When current is passed through the wires, it passes only between the tips of the electrodes in the brain and only stimulates neurons in this area. With the small amounts of current used by Olds, only cells in the immediate vicinity of the electrode tips are excited by the electricity.

With self-stimulation techniques the rat brain has now been

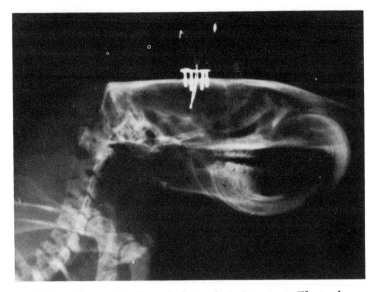

FIG. 3.26. *X-ray of implanted electrode in intact rat. Electrode pedestal is held to skull by four screws while two insulated wires, which reach deep into brain, have insulation broken only at tips, stimulating the brain only at this point. From J. Olds, & P. M. Milner, Positive reinforcement produced by electrical stimulation of septal area and other regions of rat brain.* J. comp. physiol. Psychol., *1954,* **47,** *420.*

explored for regions that seem to act like rewards for the animals [24]. At this time it appears that positive reward behavior can be produced by stimulation of any portion of the medial forebrain bundle which courses along the base of the brain. Other areas tend to give less rewarding effects or what seem to be mixtures of rewarding and punishing effects.

From these kinds of results one can conclude that the electrical stimulation of the medial forebrain bundle produces pleasurable sensations in the animal. Indeed this might be the simplest explanation. However, psychologists are trying to explain the results obtained by Olds without recourse to inferences regarding the mental states of the animals. To date none have been entirely successful.

The hypothalamus has a plethora of neuronal connections to the rest of the central nervous system, but is more directly connected with other limbic system structures. Because of its considerable connections with the other limbic structures, the limbic system is thought to be the most direct source of regulation for the hypothalamic centers. Unfortunately, very little is known about the functions of the structures comprising the limbic system. However, some findings are so important and substantial that they should be discussed.

Evidence indicates that surgical damage in certain areas of the limbic system can alter the emotional responses of animals. If the septal area is damaged (see Fig. 3.23) the animal becomes more ferocious than he was prior to the surgical intervention [25]. On the other hand, if the damage is restricted to an area called the amygdala, a nuclear mass in the temporal lobes, the animal tends to show evidence of being more placid than before [26]. Evidence from observations and tests of human patients who have had to have surgery involving the limbic structures of the temporal lobe suggests that these people suffer deficits in recent memory [27]. These patients have difficulty recalling events happening as recently as ten minutes before testing although their memory for older, more established facts seems relatively unimpaired. However, similar results are not found when temporal lobe limbic structures are damaged in animals.

It would be exciting to be able to tie together the many present and future research findings on the limbic system at this point, but this is not possible. We have only tried to suggest some of the kinds of research that lead to the belief that the limbic system is important for many psychological functions, including the emotions, learning, and memory.

OTHER SUBCORTICAL STRUCTURES As mentioned there is more than the limbic system underlying the great neocortical layers of the brain. In the thalamus we already know of two kinds of groups of cells. There are the direct relay nuclei for vision, audition, kinesthesia, etc. Impulses arriving at these nuclei are sent by cells located there to specific segments of the neocortex. Thalamic nuclei of the other variety have more diffuse effects on the neocortex, similar to the effects of the brain-stem reticular formation. Cells in these nuclei send impulses to *segments* of the brain and regulate the excitability of cells in these segments.

There are many other masses of subcortical cells and tracts of nerve fibers. The functions of many of these are just now becoming apparent. Some have to do with the coordination of the messages arising in the motor system of the brain, others have to do with the sensory systems, and there are others whose functions are practically unknown. A thorough understanding of the actions of this enormously complicated structure, the brain, will not be attained until these other areas are better understood.

The most striking and obvious neurological feature of animals highest in the phylogenetic scale is the great grey mantle which covers the brain in man, the neocortex.

One widely held general view is that the cortex assumes the functions of many of the lower centers as the amount of cortex increases. Marquis [28] has provided evidence for this principle in the visual system. The first visual representations in the brain are subcortical nuclei found in the upper brain stem. These are used by the lower animals for every visual function, but in the higher animals these visual functions depend on the neocortex. While the subcortical centers still may subserve some rudimentary visual reflexes in higher animals, vision, as we know it, is not dependent on them. Our perception is a fortunate result of the development of neocortical development in our species.

Finally, we must remember once again that the fractionation of the living brain into centers, nuclei, areas, and tracts tends to make us forget the continuous activity and interaction between the many parts. Further, we should remember that man's great development of neocortex has provided him with the most adaptable and tractable brain yet developed. The most important and valuable characteristics of mankind are those which he *acquires* from his environment rather than those he inherits genetically.

The maturation of the human brain underlying the acquisition of speech and language and all related symbolic and intellectual performance does not proceed *in utero*. Instead, these capacities only begin to be acquired about a year after birth and go on to develop through much of our lives. While the capacity for these characteristically human developments is transmitted genetically, each individual must cultivate them for himself after birth, by education [18, p. 108].

References

1. Maier, N. R. F., & Schneirla, T. C. *Principles of Animal Psychology*. New York: McGraw-Hill Book Company, Inc., 1935.
2. Parker, G. H. *The Elementary Nervous System*. Philadelphia: J. B. Lippincott Company, 1919.

3. McConnell, J. V., Jacobson, A. L., & Kimble, D. P. The effects of regeneration upon retention of a conditioned response in the planarian. *J. comp. physiol. Psychol.,* 1959, **52,** 1–5.

4. Jacobson, A. L. Learning in flatworms and annelids. *Psychol. Bull.,* 1963, **60,** 74–94.

5. Boycott, B. B., & Young, J. Z. A memory system in octopus vulgaris Lamarck. *Proc. Roy. Soc. (London),* 1955(B), **143,** 449–480.

6. Herrick, C. J. *Neurological Foundations of Animal Behavior.* New York: Holt, Rinehart and Winston, Inc., 1924.

7. Savory, T. H. Spider webs. *Sci. Amer.,* April, 1960, 115–124.

8. Frisch, V. K. *Bees: Their Vision, Chemical Senses and Language.* Ithaca: Cornell Univer. Press, 1950.

9. Schneirla, T. C., & Piel, G. The army ant. In *The First Book of Animals, Sci. Amer.* (Eds.), New York: Simon Schuster, Inc., 1955.

10. Tinbergen, N. *The Study of Instinct.* Fairlawn, N.J.: Oxford Univer. Press, 1951.

11. Lorenz, K. Z. The evolution of behavior. *Sci. Amer.,* 1958, **199,** 67–78.

12. Hess, E. H. Imprinting. *Science,* 1959, **130,** 133–141.

13. Eccles, J. C. *The Physiology of Nerve Cells.* Baltimore: Johns Hopkins Univer. Press, 1957.

14. Woolsey, C. N. Organization of somatic sensory and motor areas of the cerebral cortex. In H. F. Harlow and C. N. Woolsey (Eds.), *Biological and Biochemical Bases of Behavior.* Madison: Univer. of Wisconsin Press, 1958.

15. Lilly, J. C. Correlations between neurophysiological activity in the cortex and short-term behavior in the monkey. In *ibid.*

16. Brodal, A. *The reticular formation of the brain stem. Anatomical Aspects and Functional Correlations.* Springfield, Ill.: Charles C Thomas, Publishers, 1956.

17. French, J. D., Amerongen, F. K. von, & Magoun, H. W. *Arch. Neurol. Psychiat. (Chicago),* 1952, **68,** 577–590.

18. MacLean, P. D. The limbic system with respect to two basic life principles. In Mary A. B. Brazier (Ed.), *The Central Nervous System and Behavior,* Trans. Second Conf., Josiah Macy, Jr., Foundation, New York, 1959.

19. Kaada, B. R. Somato-motor, autonomic and electrocorticographic responses to electrical stimulation of "rhinencephalic" and other structures in primates, cat, and dog. *Acta physiol. Scand.,* 1951, **24,** Suppl. 83.

20. Gellhorn, E. *Autonomic Imbalance and the Hypothalamus.* Minneapolis: Univer. Minnesota Press, 1957.

21. Stellar, E. The physiology of motivation. *Psychol. Rev.,* 1954, **61,** 5–22.

22. Olds, J., & Milner, P. Positive reinforcement produced by electrical stimulation of septal area and other regions of rat brain. *J. comp. physiol. Psychol.,* 1954, **47,** 419–427.

23. Olds, J. Positive emotional systems studied by techniques of self-stimulation. *Psychiat. Res. Repts.,* 1960, **12,** 238–258.

24. Olds, M. E., & Olds, J. Approach-avoidance analysis of rat diencephalon. *J. comp. Neurol.,* 1963, **120,** 259–295.

25. Brady, J. V., & Nauta, W. J. H. Subcortical mechanisms in emotional behavior: affective changes following septal forebrain lesions in the albino rat. *J. comp. physiol. Psychol.,* 1953, **46,** 339–346.

26. Schreiner, L., & Kling, A. Behavioral changes following rhinencephalic injury in cat. *J. Neurophysiol.,* 1953, **16,** 643–659.

27. Penfield, W., & Milner, B. Memory of deficit produced by bilateral lesions in the hippocampal zone. *Arch. Neurol. Psychiat. (Chicago),* 1958, **79,** 475–497.

28. Marquis, D. G. Phylogenetic interpretation of the functions of the visual cortex. *Arch. Neurol. Psychiat. (Chicago),* 1935, **33,** 807–815.

FOUR MECHANISMS OF PERCEPTION

We live in a world of people and things—books, trees, sunshine, snow, friends, loved ones, strangers. We take our perceptions of them for granted, just as we take for granted that they really are the way they seem to us. But is this book, for example, *actually,* really, and permanently the thing that we believe it to be? We sometimes have a suspicion that some things seem different to us than they do to others. Do you see your girl friend as the rest of your friends do? Is there some doubt about whether she is quite as pretty to them as she is to you? Even the relatively stable world of objects causes us some doubts at times. If this book is placed in a position at which the light strikes it from an acute angle oftentimes the color seems different. Has the color of the book changed? No, you will say, it is an *illusion* caused by the angle of incidence of the light. Yes, but how can we decide which appearance is the illusion? Plato proposed that all of our *real* objects are but illusions.

The philosophical question of the ultimate truth or falsity (the veridicality) of perceptions lies outside the domain of scientific psychology. Such questions may lead to interesting hours of discussion, but as behavioral scientists we want to understand the mechanisms whereby we perceive the world. Assuming that we live surrounded by a world of objects that we can come to know through our senses, what are the mechanisms whereby we feel, hear, see, and smell? Perceptions of the world of objects begin with the reception of changes in the physical energies impinging upon specialized organs. In the case of visual perception these energies take the form of light waves or quanta of light. In hearing, the energy is in the form of waves of increasing and decreasing compressions of the atmosphere. For touch, the skin must be compressed. Before any kind of perception can occur, there must be some interchange of energy between the environment and the individual.

In the body there are many kinds of specialized organs, collections of cells which act to achieve a common result and which are only sensitive to certain kinds of changes in physical energies. We might think of these organs, or receptors, as similar to television cameras on the outer edges of the body which tune in on events taking place in the environment. This is an especially appealing analogy in the case of the visual mechanism. However, with a little imagination one could extend the analogy to all the senses. In fact there seems to be some kind of a myth perpetuated by magazine articles and some "scientific" books intended for the layman that the actual mechanisms do work in such a fashion. Let us for the moment examine the analogy. The eye is the television camera. The receiver is back, somewhere in the brain. Electrical energies (pictures) are relayed to the receiver in the brain. But what do we have to assume then? What good would such a picture be if there was no one back in the brain looking at the picture screen? Our problem is not solved by the television analogy, for we must investigate the "someone" back in the brain who is watching the pictures transmitted to this region from the eyes.

We would have to start all over again investigating this new being watching the TV set. Our problem is much more difficult than understanding a biological TV transmission scheme. We must try to understand how the changes in energy at the receptors are utilized into a form such that the nervous system, as a whole, can alter the body's activities to reach new adjustments to the external situation.

This problem raises some important yet difficult conceptual issues. Information concerning the state of the external world is encoded into a neural code at the receptors. Changes in the physical world outside effect changes at the receptor level. Then these receptor changes are transmitted to the brain in the form of a code which uses the changes in the rate of activity of single neurons. These changes in neural firings represent the basis of the neural code. But it is not a code which is broken down into the original message once again in the brain as a TV set would do. Rather, this encoded sensory message from the receptors is integrated into the ongoing activities of the 12,000 million cells of the brain and can somehow result in changes in the neural code going out to somatic and autonomic muscles.

The assumption of a little man in the head is the easy way out. It is too bad we cannot take this way. Rather, we must learn the brain's various codes and rules of integration. We are not yet very close to this goal. However, in the first sections of this chapter we shall present some of the available information about sensory systems generally and the visual system in particular. We shall soon find that the immediate sensory environment cannot explain all perceptual phenomena. In the next chapter, therefore, we shall look at the studies which explore the effects of internal and individual factors such as sets, motives, and attitudes on perceptual phenomena.

Toward a Definition of Perception

Let us examine the problems that bear on a definition of perception. First, let us bear in mind that all we can *know* about anyone else is that which comes to us via our own receptor systems. Let us set aside, for a few moments, the problem of our own perceptual processes and concentrate on the fact that other people *behave,* and usually seem to be using information about their environment in appropriate ways. We can know only about behavior. This means that while you may assume that your neighbor *sees* a red light at an intersection, it is still only an *assumption*. You might base your assumption on the fact that he stops his car at the traffic signal you call "red." Here you are basing your assumption on his behavior, which results in his stopping his car. Still, this tells us only that he can discriminate between certain stimulus conditions. It does not tell us that his perception of the traffic light is just like yours. But, you may say, "He says it is a red light." Here you are basing your assumption on his use of a verbal labeling response. You only know that he can discriminate different colored

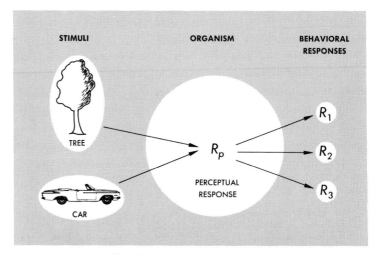

FIG. 4.1. *A possible theoretical interpretation of perception.*

stimuli and can label them with appropriate terms. Still, you do not *know* whether the perception he labels *red* is similar to your perception of a stimulus labeled *red*. In fact you know nothing more than that given specifiable stimulus conditions he can make specific kinds of responses. We can never know about the mental processes of others except by inferences from their behavior.

Let us consider the diagram of a general perceptual situation given in Fig. 4.1. We present a stimulus to a person. Let the large circle represent the person. Then the individual emits certain verbal or other behavioral responses. Psychology's job is to build theories which accurately predict responses. As we shall see in our subsequent chapters on learning, there are psychologists who do not believe we need to say anything about perception to account for behavior, and who assume other factors to be at work (see pp. 213–232). Other theorists say we must have theories which assume that certain perceptual responses occur within the organism. (These perceptual responses are labeled *Rp* in Fig. 4.1.)

What should determine whether or not a psychologist assumes perception to occur in others? What should be the basis of a decision on whether or not to include *Rp*'s in the theoretical schema used to understand behavior? As of the moment there are many competing theoretical approaches to explaining behavior. They have not as yet merged into one stable framework. Throughout the book, the reader should be alert to the values and liabilities of each of the several types of theoretical approaches which will be presented.

In this chapter we shall be making the assumption that perceptual responses do occur in the individual and that they are susceptible to study by the use of specified *indicator responses*. Furthermore, we shall assume that it is necessary to know about the sensory apparatus of the human in order to understand perceptual phenomena properly. We would justify this assumption by our belief that the simplest explanation of a phenomenon is the best. In the present instance this means we would prefer to explain perception—insofar as it is possible—on the basis of structure and function of the sensory systems. Those phenomena not susceptible to sensory system explanations must then be handled by higher-order theories. In order to be able to know which phenomena are explicable at the sensory level we must study them in some detail.

General Properties of Sensory Systems

Conceptually, we may think of ourselves as involved in two worlds: the external physical world around us and the inner world beneath the skin. The physical world is composed of things and people and (the theorists of physics and chemistry tell us) atoms, molecules, and energy. The inner world beneath the skin is a world of atoms and molecules too, but patterned so as to constitute the person. People are made of many systems usually working harmoniously to maintain the larger system of the individual. At this point the systems of primary importance to us are the sensory systems. These systems generally are localized close to the skin, which is the membrane separating the inner and outer worlds. The skin is not simply a separating wall but also permits interchange of information between the two worlds. This interchange takes place at the receptor organs. We perceive changes in the outer world because of corresponding changes in our receptors and their associated sensory systems.

In man, we become aware of changes in electromagnetic waves through the visual sensory system, of changes in air pressure through our auditory system, of changes in the chemical composition of our environment through the olfactory and taste sensory systems. In addition we are aware of alterations of the skin itself and of the underlying musculature through other sensory systems.

SPECIALIZATION OF RECEPTOR FUNCTIONS It is a readily apparent fact that our receptor organs have become highly specialized. For example, our eyes do not respond to smells or sounds. Rather, each of our receptor organs has developed so it only responds to certain kinds of stimulation. In addition it is only sensitive to a narrow portion of the total energies which could effect it. We do not hear all possible sounds or see all possible lights. The ear is responsive to sound waves of frequencies between 20 and 20,000 cycles per second. Changes in air pressure of greater or smaller frequencies are not detected by normal auditory apparatus. We should bear in mind that other species need not have these same limitations. Dogs can detect frequencies much greater than 20,000 cycles per second, and as a result dog whistles which we do not hear can be used to call them. Some insects seem to be able to detect the plane of polarization of light waves which we cannot. Many animals can detect changes in electromagnetic waves at wavelengths beyond the spectral wavelengths visible to ourselves. The anatomical structure of the various central nervous systems of the animals leads to certain hypotheses about their perceptual world. The dog, for example, may live in a wonderful world of smells whereas we live in a wonderful world of visual impressions. This idea stems from the greater development of neural structures related to smell in the dog.

All sensory systems share various aspects in common. First

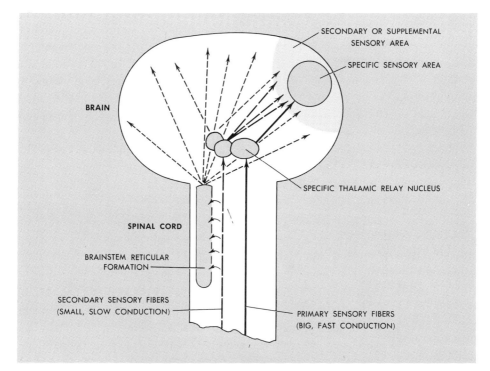

FIG. 4.2. *Primary (unbroken lines) and secondary (broken lines) afferent fibers in somatosensory system.*

of all there are specialized receptor cells grouped into a receptor. These cells act to translate activity in the physical outer world into changes in the inner world beneath the skin. Essentially, these changes are alterations in the firing of afferent neurons going to the central nervous system and the brain. *The receptor cell must therefore be sensitive to specific physical and chemical changes in its immediate environment and in turn effect changes in neurons to which it is connected.*

PROJECTIONS TO NEOCORTEX   The phylogenetically most recent acquisition in the brain is the neocortex, the great grey mantle. Although the assumption is open to some discussion, we generally assume that most of the higher perceptual and intellectual functions involve neocortex. Therefore, special efforts have been made to trace the neural pathways between the receptor organs and the neocortex. In many instances it has been possible to localize these pathways and also to specify the regions of neocortex which receive information from a particular sensory modality.

The neurons connected with the receptor cells proceed to higher levels of the central nervous system. Usually, cells in the sensory systems projecting toward the neocortex go first to the thalamus, where they end on cell bodies in specialized nuclei. The thalamic cells then send axons to cells in the sensory areas of neocortex as well as to other higher brain regions. The general organization of these specific sensory systems is schematized in Fig. 4.2.

Diffuse Systems

In addition to the direct projection systems there are other routes of transmission of information arising in the receptor cells to the brain. These consist of smaller nerve fibers which reach other thalamic nuclei and project to wider regions of neocortex. These supplementary sensory systems include the diffusely projecting systems of the brain, notably the brain-stem reticular formation and certain thalamic nuclei which have cells which relay this activity to wide areas of neocortex. These other sensory systems are diagramed in Fig. 4.2. In the primary or specialized sensory systems information proceeds rapidly to highly specialized neocortical areas. Receptor activity initiating changes in the diffuse systems help to regulate the allover activity of the neocortex.

Central control of receptor activity Sensory systems are not one-way systems proceeding always upward to neocortex. It is now clear that most, if not all, sensory systems also involve efferent pathways, probably beginning in the primary sensory receiving areas in neocortex and going down to act on receptor cells or on cells near them in the chain of transmission to the brain [e.g., 1, 2]. These efferent tracts can suppress or alter the information sent toward the brain. Thus, the central nervous system itself can turn on or off the information coming to it from the peripheral receptors.

From the Physical World to Neural Changes

In order for the individual to be aware of receptor activity caused by the correlated changes in the physical world, changes in the physical world must be rewritten into a neural code. The receptor cells must alter in some way the activity of neurons. This means that the single neuron's state of membrane polarization must be broken down, and the resulting depolarization of the neuron must be sufficient to trigger the total cell body and axon depolarization so that it spreads as the *spike potential* or firing of the nerve cell.

RECEPTOR POTENTIALS The means by which changes in the external environment are translated into changes in neural activity are highly individualized for each receptor system. While all of the cells in each sensory organ operate according to the same principles, each of the sensory organs has a different mechanism to affect the neurons which will carry their information to the brain. In the visual system cells at the back of the eye initiate impulses in neurons by means of a breakdown in light-sensitive chemicals (photopigments) within them. In the auditory system cells located deep in the inner ear are physically compressed by waves of fluids induced by "sound waves" through a complex chain of bones and membranes. Other types of sense organs use still different mechanisms. In every case environmental changes become reflected in changes of activity of single neurons that reach toward higher regions of the nervous system and the brain. Electrical recordings from every kind of sensory organ reveal that there are special kinds of activities aroused in them when activated by a stimulus. These responses, found when recording from sensory organs, are called the receptor potentials.

Each specific receptor organ initiates its own particular pattern of electrical activity when it is stimulated. The receptor potential is a product of single cells. When a receptor organ is activated many single cells work together and it is possible to record the sum of the resulting electrical changes. The combined receptor potentials are referred to as the *generator potential* of the sensory receptor organ. When one floods the eye with light a characteristic change in potential is recorded in the eye which does *not* result from the activity of afferent axons going brainward. This is the generator potential of vision called the electroretinogram [3]. In Fig. 4.3 one can observe an electroretinogram (ERG) recorded from man. It is a complex electrical pattern. Various components of the ERG can be sorted out experimentally, and there are several of these components which seem associated with different kinds

125

of receptor cells in the eye. Generally speaking, we must recognize the fact that receptor organs are *not* simply collections of cells all of which are exactly alike. To be sure, all the cells of a receptor are sensitive to the same kind of physical energy (e.g., sound), but some may be sensitive to only a smaller portion of the energy received by the whole receptor.

In the eye, for example, there are two major divisions of receptor cells, the rods and the cones. While both are sensitive to light they are differentially sensitive to conditions of illumination and lights in various regions of the spectrum. The rods are best activated after the eye has been without light for some time and operate best at night. The cones, on the other hand, are

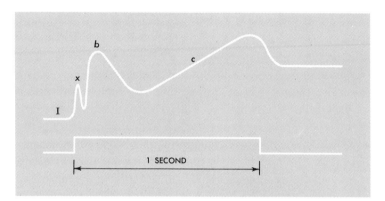

FIG. 4.3. *Approximate representation of human electroretinogram.*

most responsive in normal daylight conditions. There are probably several varieties of rods and cones. Later in this chapter, we shall discuss the mechanisms of action in these receptor cells in greater detail.

RECEPTOR FIELDS Up to this point we have discussed some of the general notions concerning sensory-receptor systems. Another general problem needs to be elaborated which is the concept of receptive fields. Essentially, *receptive field* refers to a characteristic of all receptor organs, namely that the functional unit of analysis of the receptor is larger than that of the individual receptor cell. For example, each axon running in the optic nerves from the eye to the thalamic relay nucleus for vision responds to stimulation of a considerable number of actual receptor cells. One inference drawn about the nature of sensory systems is simple: many receptors feed into other cells before the sensory information goes toward the brain. This intermediate cell collects information coming from many different individual receptor cells. The information reaching the brain has already been "packaged" to reflect changes of stimulation over given areas of the receptor organ. It does not receive, directly, information as to the state of any one particular receptor cell.

Research in the visual system has yielded some of the best analyses of receptor fields. It is possible to record from single axons in the optic nerve. By moving a light across the retinal portion of the eye in which the receptor cells are located, the areas which affect changes in the electrical activity of particular optic nerve axons can be determined [4]. It is the changes in rate of firing of these axons which carry visual information to the brain. There are several kinds of fields of receptor cells. Some of these clusters act to increase the activity in an optic nerve axon when the latter is stimulated by light. Others, when stimulated lightly, act to inhibit activity in the same axon.

Convergence and divergence of sensory information in the visual system As yet, we have neglected a detailed consideration of the microstructure of the receptors. But, following our discussion of receptor fields, it is appropriate to discuss the minute structure of receptors. As with sensory systems generally, we find that several different receptor cells feed into collector cells. These collector cells sometimes feed into larger collecting cells in, or close to, the receptor organ itself. In the retinal portion of the eye the rods and cones are the primary sensory cells. These feed into bipolar cells and the bipolar cells in turn feed into what are called *ganglion cells*. The long axons of these ganglion cells leave the eye and proceed to the thalamic relay nucleus. *The axons of the ganglion cell constitute the optic nerves.* (The optic nerve also contains efferent fibers going to the retina. The locus of termination of these efferent sensory fibers in the retina is as yet unknown.) Thus, the recordings made from optic nerve fibers which indicate that these fibers are responsive to stimulation over a large area is explained by the fact that many receptors converge on bipolar cells and probably many of these in turn converge on the ganglion cells. It is likely that similar convergence takes place in all sensory systems.

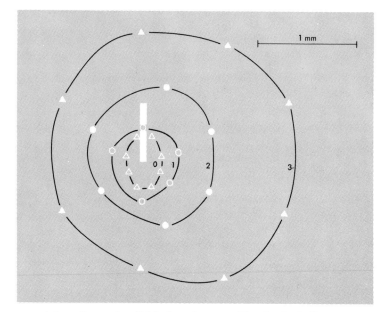

FIG. 4.4.   *Receptive field of optic nerve fiber in the bullfrog.*
Four intensities of illumination of the eye were used, represented
by the numbers (logarithms). Note that as these are increased,
area on retina, which produces responses in the fiber, increases.
From H. C. Wagner & M. L. Wolbarsht. Receptive field of
bullfrog. Amer. J. Ophthal., 1958, 46, 46–59.

Receptor fields can also be measured by recording the
responses of single cells in the visual neocortex. This type of
research uses the same method of moving a light across the
retina and recording from single cells in areas of the neocortex which receive, predominantly, input from the visual
system. Single cells in visual neocortex tend to have smaller
receptor fields than the visual fields defined on the basis of
recording effects on ganglion cell axons in the optic nerves [5].

There is a great amount of divergence in the sensory systems. Many more cells in the neocortex receive input from the
visual system than there are ganglion cells in the retina or
cells in the visual relay nucleus (lateral geniculate). Information from many receptor cells converge upon single
cells in the neocortex and, at the same time, every receptor
unit projects to a large number of cells in the neocortex.

Inhibition and excitation   The story is more complex than
that which we have presented thus far. A receptor field, defined as the retinal area which affects a cell in the visual

system, is composed of two portions. One portion is excitatory, and the other inhibitory. If the central portion of the receptive field is excitatory, that is, if visual stimulation of the retina *increases* activity in the ganglion cell axon, then there usually will be an annulus, or ring, surrounding this center which is inhibitory in nature. If the center is inhibitory, that is if visual stimulation decreases activity in the ganglion cell axon, then there often will be an excitatory annulus around it. Not all fields have a center and surrounding annulus, but receptive fields can be found which are of many different shapes with surrounding areas of antagonistic functions. A representative receptive field is shown in Fig. 4.4.

The knowledge of inhibitory and excitatory processes at the receptor level has explained some puzzling findings from studies recording from single cells in the neocortex. Many investigators have noted the remarkable observation that there are many cells in the visual neocortex which do not seem responsive to illumination of the retinal elements. But recently some of these cells have been found to be responsive to a light

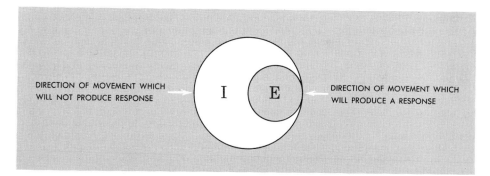

FIG. 4.5. *Schematic distribution of excitatory and inhibitory fields of the retina which allow cells of sensory system to respond only when light is moved across it from left to right. Movement of light in opposite direction would stimulate inhibitory field first, inhibiting reaction when light reached excitatory field. Simultaneous stimulation of both fields would elicit no response.*

source that *moves* across the retina. Some cells become excited when the light source moves in one direction but not the other [5]. We can explain this on the basis of the distribution of peripheral fields of excitation and inhibition. For example, consider a hypothetic neocortical cell which has the field illustrated in Fig. 4.5.

129

Under the assumptions made about the distribution of excitatory and inhibitory areas of the visual field, the illumination of both *E* and *I* would not affect the cortical cell because the *I* area would act to inhibit *E*. A stimulus moving from right to left, stimulating *I* then *E,* would not be effective either, for the inhibitory effects would prevent *E*'s affecting the cortical cell. On the other hand a stimulus moving left to right would excite the cortical cell because it would strike the excitatory position of the retinal field before striking the inhibitory portions. This would be one explanation of the fact that many cells observed in the visual neocortex do not respond when the entire retina is flooded with light [6].

We are a long way from knowing all of the different arrangements of receptive fields in sensory systems. Evidently, combinations of the inhibitory and excitatory receptive fields are many and varied. Recently, it has been demonstrated that the frog has cortical visual cells that are responsive to different shapes and curvatures entering into the animal's visual fields [7]. Probably all species of animals have somewhat different patterns of excitatory and inhibitory regions in their receptive fields. Yet, as investigators use more and more complicated stimuli, more and more cells in the visual cortex become understood.

OVERVIEW OF RECEPTOR ACTIVITY   While the idea of receptor fields is not a new one, we have only begun to scratch the surface of knowledge about them. Our knowledge, or lack of it, must make us aware of the enormous organizational complexity of the sensory apparatus. We find that every receptor generates a steady potential when activated; this in turn produces the depolarization typical of excitation in any neuron. Thus, subsequent cells in transmission chains carry information to the specialized neocortical areas by way of the thalamic relay nuclei. Throughout this chain we find increasing degrees of convergence and divergence.

Not all cells in the specialized areas of the cortex are responsive to changes in the related sensory system. Some "silent cells" have been found that will be effected by highly specialized activity in the sensory system, e.g., movement in one direction. While many of our examples were obtained from research upon the visual system, we believe the general principles of organization to be similar in all sensory systems.

The Visual System

Earlier we noted that the different specialized receptor cells acted in different ways to translate physical energies into neural activities. The actual techniques of these changes are fascinating but we shall have space only to discuss in detail the change of electromagnetic energy into neural signals responsible for vision.

Man can discriminate only a small portion of the spectrum of electromagnetic radiation. While the nature of electromagnetic waves is incompletely understood, it can be easily measured (in terms of wavelengths). The common techniques for measuring electromagnetic radiation provide us with a spectrum running from the small peak-to-peak wavelengths of gamma rays to the long peak-to-peak wavelengths of waves used to transmit radio signals. The electromagnetic spectrum is illustrated in Fig. 4.6. The small portion of this spectrum to which man can respond lies between the wavelengths of 450 to 750 millimicrons. As mentioned before, other animals have somewhat different capacities of wavelength discrimination.

We have been careful to talk of *electromagnetic waves,* not *light waves,* a term which refers only to the wavelengths to which man is sensitive. The same problem of terminology exists with color. Within the visual spectrum we can discriminate different wavelengths. We show our wavelength discriminations in words (*red, green*) or by behavioral responses which indicate the discrimination has been modern, e.g., stopping at a red traffic light. Our discrimination between wavelengths is the basic operation, and the appearance of color is due to the organization and structure of our visual sensory system.

STRUCTURE OF THE EYE A study of the eye reveals a finely constructed device which acts to focus the images of objects from the outer world upon the rods and cones in the retina. The electromagnetic waves come in through the cornea, the aqueous humor, the lens, and vitreous humor. The lens and cornea focus them to provide a clear image. In this process the image is inverted so that an upward pointing arrow actually is pointing downward on the retina. A simplified

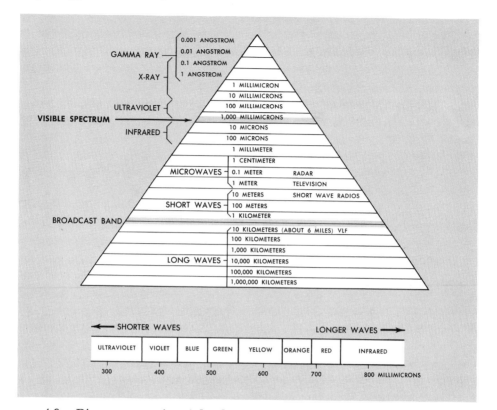

FIG. 4.6. *Diagram suggestive of the electromagnetic spectrum, with closeup of segment of visible light (below). The entire spectrum encompasses so wide a span of wavelengths that they cannot be expressed in a single unit of measurement.*
Adapted from John L. Chapman, The expanding spectrum, Harper's Magazine, July, 1964, pp. 70–78. © 1964, by Harper & Row, Publishers, Incorporated. Reprinted from Harper's Magazine by the artist's permission.

picture of the eye is presented in Fig. 4.7. The image upon the retina excites, in various ways, the receptor fields. The complex changes in neural activities of the ganglion cells in the eye are transmitted to the specific relay nucleus for vision, the lateral geniculate body; then fibers from geniculate nucleus cells go to the visual cortex. Cells also project fibers to the older neural centers for vision in the midbrain (the superior colliculi) and to the diffuse systems of the brain (brain-stem reticular formation and diffuse thalamic nuclei).

The two basic receptor cells in the human eye are rods and cones. These are different in anatomical structure, although the difference is not very pronounced. A photograph of rods and cones is shown in Fig. 4.8, and the layers of the retina can be seen in Fig. 4.9. In our previous discussion of the general receptor systems we noted the fact that the rods and cones converged into bipolar and thence into ganglion cells. The actual diversity of cells in the retina is apparent in Fig. 4.10. We are not completely sure of the functions of all of the retinal elements pictured here.

Distribution of rods and cones As we know, the rods and cones make up the sensory elements of the retina. They are distributed over the back of the eyeball and, with the ganglion and bipolar cells and the clusters of supporting cells, make up the retina. In the central portion of the retina there is a great preponderance of cones compared with the number of rods. At the approximate center of the retina there is a depression called the *fovea* or *fovea centralis* which is believed to contain only cones. In and around the fovea there is the greatest density of cones, but the ratio of cones to rods becomes less and less toward the periphery of the retina until the only receptor cells are rods.

The depression of the fovea results from the fact that in this one area of the retina the ganglion and bipolar cells are

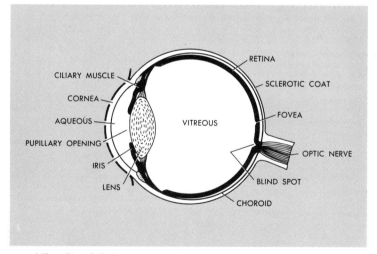

FIG. 4.7. *Simplified representation of the human eye.*

not piled on top of the receptors. Elsewhere in the retina the incoming light must go through the other cells stacked between the receptors and the light sources. This would seem to be an inefficient design, but the cell bodies and their processes lying between the retina receptors and the lens are almost

133

FIG. **4.8.** *Low-power photomicrograph of portion of retina, choroid, and some of the sclera of the human eye. Numbers correspond to layers of the retina shown in Fig.* **4.9.** *Adapted from* A. W. Ham & T. S. Leeson. Histology *(4th ed.).* Philadelphia: J. B. Lippincott Company, *1961.*

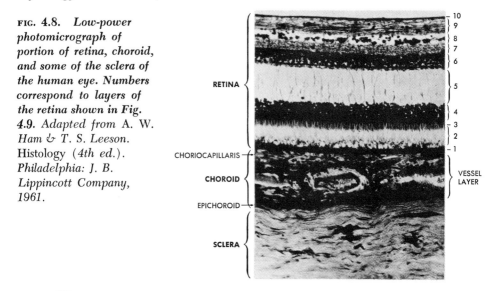

RETINA
CHORIOCAPILLARIS
CHOROID
EPICHOROID
SCLERA
VESSEL LAYER

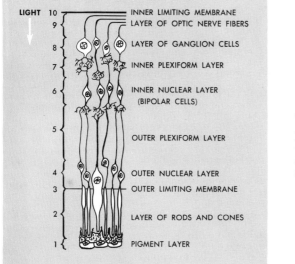

LIGHT

10 — INNER LIMITING MEMBRANE
9 — LAYER OF OPTIC NERVE FIBERS
8 — LAYER OF GANGLION CELLS
7 — INNER PLEXIFORM LAYER
6 — INNER NUCLEAR LAYER (BIPOLAR CELLS)
5 — OUTER PLEXIFORM LAYER
4 — OUTER NUCLEAR LAYER
3 — OUTER LIMITING MEMBRANE
2 — LAYER OF RODS AND CONES
1 — PIGMENT LAYER

FIG. **4.9.** *Diagram of layers of the retina. Adapted from* A. W. Ham & T. S. Leeson. Histology *(4th ed.).* Philadelphia: J. B. Lippincott Company, *1961.*

transparent. We cannot complain of the results of this system for calculations made on the basis of optical properties of the eye indicate that as little as one quantum of light per receptor element may be sufficient to cause perceptible activity [8].

One other structural feature of the eye is of some importance in understanding perception. At the place where the axons of the ganglion cells leave the eye at the optic nerve there are no receptor cells at all. This region is called the optic disc.

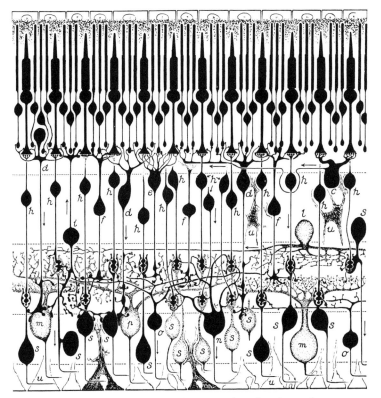

FIG. 4.10.   *Reconstruction of primate retina showing primary neuron types and their synaptic relations.* c: *horizontal cells;* d, e, f: *diffuse or polysynaptic bipolar cells;* h: *individual cone* (*midget*) *bipolar cell;* i, l: *amacrine cells;* m, n, o, p, r, s: *ganglion cells. Reprinted from* The Retina *by S. L. Polyak by permission of The University of Chicago Press.* © *1941 by the University of Chicago. All rights reserved.*

Ordinarily, however, we do not notice any gap in our visual experience unless conditions are specially arranged for us to do so. Somehow we fill in this deficit in sensory information. In our discussion of Hebb's theory of perception (see Chapter 5) this optic disc will become of theoretical importance.

Other visual structures   The optic nerve leaves the eye at the optic disc and travels back toward the brain. A short distance from the eye the optic nerves from the two eyes cross. This junction is called the optic chiasm, and there is actually an interchange of some fibers from each optic nerve. Beyond the chiasm, fibers from the left side of the retina of the left eye and fibers from the left side of the right eye travel along together to the left lateral geniculate nucleus of the thalamus.

From the optic chiasm the fibers from the right sides of both retinas travel together to the right lateral geniculate nucleus in the thalamus. This exchange of fibers is represented in Fig. 4.11. Traditionally, the nerves which carry the visual information from the optic chiasm to the lateral geniculate bodies are called the optic tracts, and the fibers from lateral geniculate nucleus to the visual neocortex are called the optic radiations.

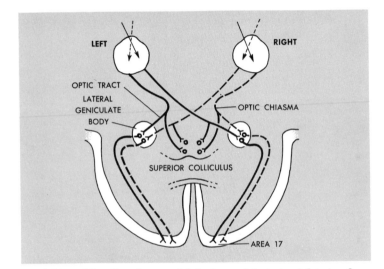

FIG. 4.11.   *Visual pathways. Light from objects in right visual field reaches left half of retina; Light from left visual field reaches right half. Note that information from right or left half of retina is transmitted to same right or left hemisphere. Collaterals from optic tracts reach visual reflex centers in the midbrain. Determine visual effects of damage to visual pathways made before and after optic chiasma.*

In higher animals, notably man and the monkeys, the lateral geniculate body is composed of six layers of cell bodies. Each layer contains cells receiving special kinds of information. Some layers receive visual information originating in one eye while others receive information originating in the other eye. Cells in certain layers of the lateral geniculate nucleus have been identified as being selectively responsible to certain wavelengths of light. This could be very important information for understanding color perception (see pp. 148–151).

In man, the visual neocortex is localized in the occipital lobes. In lower animals the cells of the lateral geniculate body project to wider areas of neocortex. Using a numbering system developed by Brodmann, we designate the area receiving neural projections directly from the lateral geniculate nuclei area 17. From this area cell axons go to other cells located in neighboring neocortex (Brodmann areas 18 and 19) and to cells in visual neocortex on the other side of the brain. Although areas 17, 18, and 19 are all referred to as visual cortical areas, area 17 is the only neocortical area to receive direct projections from the lateral geniculate nucleus. While the visual system projects directly only to area 17, messages originating in the retina reach the entire brain from axons projected from cells located in area 17.

Visual displays at the neocortex As mentioned in the first pages of this chapter, we should not think of a televisionlike arrangement whereby there is a faithful display of the retinal image on a neocortical screen formed by area 17. It would not help us to explain perceptual phenomena.

We already know that some of the cortical cells in the visual areas respond to excitation in receptor fields; we know that the different effects of excitation and inhibition at the retina "select" special groups of cortical cells to be aroused. What we need to know is more about the code used to transmit information about the changes in the outer world and how these neurally coded messages act on the ongoing activities of the brain. The sensory information must be integrated into ongoing activities and be able to change the direction of an individual's motor activities. The adjustment of the individual to his environment is the end product of all sensory discriminations and detection.

To better understand the nature of the neural codes used by organisms, we must once again return to the retina and begin with the translation of physical energies into neural information.

PHOTOPIGMENTS In every rod and cone there are outer segments filled with chemicals called, collectively, the *photopigments*. Coresponding to the rod-cone division there are two classes of photopigments: rhodopsin and iodopsin. Rhodopsin is only found in the rods, and iodopsin only in the cones.

When light strikes these photochemicals, a bleaching process begins which alters the energy state of the photopigment. This alteration is the process which acts to change the polarization of the cell membrane. This change in cell membrane polariza-

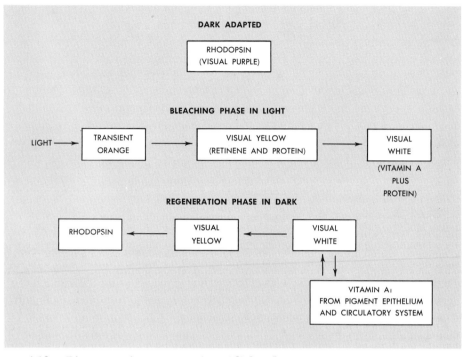

FIG. 4.12.   *Diagrammatic representation of light effects on photopigment rhodopsin, and its subsequent regeneration in the dark.*

tion initiates the neural impulse used to signal a change in the electromagnetic input to the receptor cell.

The study of visual pigments has a long history and a promising future [9]. Today we know a great deal about the synthesis of rhodopsin and are rapidly learning about iodopsin. A summary of the rhodopsin cycle is presented in Fig. 4.12.

RHODOPSIN AND NIGHT VISION. Rods contain the photopigment, rhodopsin. This chemical is bleached by the incoming light and this releases energy which triggers the cell's response. After a rod's rhodopsin has been bleached, a considerable amount of time is required (in the dark) for the resynthesis of rhodopsin. This must take place before the cell can be excited again. During normal daytime vision the rods remain bleached and therefore relatively unresponsive. But after we have been in the dark for some while, rhodopsin regenerates and the rods recover their sensitivity. This process is called *dark adaptation.*

There is a period of time after entering a dark motion picture theater during which we can see only very poorly. *The recovery of our visual perception in the dark follows just about the same time course as the regeneration of rhodopsin.* The cones which contain iodopsin are less sensitive to the bleaching effects of light than are the rods of the retina, which are the cells most sensitive to even small amounts of light when they have been able to regenerate their supply of rhodopsin in the dark. Our best night vision then is accomplished by actions of our rod system. Figure 4.13 shows that the longer an animal stays in the dark, the more sensitive his eye becomes to test flashes of light. Curve (a) shows the quick drop in threshold that can be attributed to the dark adaptation of the daytime (or photopic) receptor system. Curve (b) reflects the slower but more extensive adaptation due to regeneration of rhodopsin in the night or scoptic system. Since the rods are found in greatest concentration at the periphery of the eye, night vision is best at the edges of the retina. Our chances of detecting small sources of light at night are much better if we do not look directly at the spot where we expect the light to be. By looking to the side of the light source, the light will fall on the periphery of the retina,

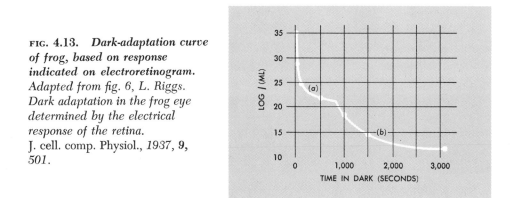

FIG. 4.13. *Dark-adaptation curve of frog, based on response indicated on electroretinogram. Adapted from fig. 6, L. Riggs. Dark adaptation in the frog eye determined by the electrical response of the retina.* J. cell. comp. Physiol., *1937, 9, 501.*

the area of greatest rod population. Lookouts scanning the horizon for lights of ships are therefore directed not to look directly at the suspected target.

CONES AND IODOPSIN. Much less is known about the cone system of the retina. Only recently have we been able to chemically identify iodopsin, although its presence had been predicted long before its discovery. The regenerative cycle of iodopsin is similar to that of rhodopsin, and the principle by which the iodopsin acts to initiate the activity of a single neural element is essentially the same; but there are some important differences.

The iodopsin reaction is faster than that of rhodopsin. Time spent in the dark will increase the sensitivity of cones to light, Fig. 4.13(a), but the cones do not achieve the same degree of sensitivity to light as do the rods following dark adaptation. While the cone system is less sensitive to light than the rod system, it provides us with the highest visual acuity in the fovea and with color vision.

THE PERCEPTION OF COLOR   Color perception refers to discriminations the human and some animals can make within the realm of the visible spectrum. In order to be described as color discriminations, these discriminations must not be based on brightness or other features of the stimulation but must be based on a special sensitivity to specific wavelengths of the electromagnetic spectrum.

It is not likely that the rods are capable of providing a neural basis for discriminations of wavelengths. There may be more than one kind of rod in the eyes of higher animals, but the general belief is that they could only provide a limited discrimination between portions of the short wavelengths (blues) and the remainder of the spectrum. There is little doubt that the cone system is responsible for most color discrimination.

Let us accept the proposition that the cone system does mediate color discriminations. Does this mean that there must be more than one kind of iodopsin? In order for us to live in the world of multiple colors, which we do, we must have receptors built to discriminate among many different wavelengths. This in turn means that we must have cones containing pigments which will be bleached more effectively by one wavelength than another. This differential bleaching due to wavelength of illumination must be the peripheral basis of color discrimination.

Like all sensory experiences color exists as a response within the individual. Color is not to be found in the nervous system. All neurons are the same color, and their electrical responses are not colored either. Differential sensitivity to certain wavelengths provides us with the neural basis of discriminations in the visual spectrum.

Traditional color theories Probably the importance of vision and the beauty of the perceived world of color account for the early and continued attempts to explain color generally. Theories of color vision were among the very first theories proposed to explain behavior. Modifications of old theories and the creation of new theories proceeds to the present. No one theory is perfectly satisfactory and each contains something of special merit.

THE YOUNG-HELMHOLTZ THEORY. In 1801, Thomas Young suggested that there were three types of nerve fibers running from eye to brain. He thought these corresponded to the three primary colors. Some fifty years later, Helmholtz extended Young's theory which had not received a great deal of attention. Through Helmholtz's successful efforts to relate this theory to the facts of color mixture, the modified theory became widely accepted. It is probably the most well known of all theories of color perception.

The Young-Helmholtz theory assumes three varieties of cones which have different photopigments. Each photopigment is presumably most sensitive to one portion of the visual spectrum. One type is specially sensitive to short wavelengths (blue cones), another specially sensitive in the middle range (green cones), and the last type specially sensitive in the long wavelength area (red cones). While each type of cone has a region of greatest sensitivity, all have *some* sensitivity to other wave lengths. Color is determined by the brain on the basis of the relative amounts of excitation coming from the three different cone systems.

When we perceive a colored object we can make a discrimination of the wavelength. This reaction is referred to as hue discrimination. We say "that is aqua," "that is chartreuse," "that is magenta," and so on. We have learned to make color discriminations, and, also, we have learned to label and discriminate in accordance with the rules accepted by the majority of people in our culture.

Two stimuli can be of the same hue but differ in other visual qualities. A color can be more or less saturated. The saturation of a particular hue refers to the amount of white mixed with it. The less white mixed with a stimulus of a given hue the more saturated it is. Brightness is yet another quality which is different from both hue and saturation, and it correlates with the intensity of the light reaching the eye.

The Young-Helmholtz theory suggests that it is possible to explain saturation and brightness in terms of the responses observed in the three cone systems. The perceived hue is determined by the *relative* amounts of activity in the three cone systems. Brightness is determined by the absolute level of activity in all three systems. How can the Young-Helmholtz theory explain the quality of saturation, or the degree to which the hue is diluted with white? White light, e.g., sunlight, had been known for a long time to be a mixture of many hues. When a prism is held appropriately a ray of white light can be changed into a full spectrum of all the visible wavelengths. The Young-Helmholtz theory proposed that we see all of the spectral hues through three basic color receptors, red, green, and blue cones. White was believed to be a combination of activity in all three cone types. Thus, saturation as a quality of color perception, was explained by the balance existing between the red-green-blue cone activities aroused by the light.

HERING'S THEORY. A second major color-vision theory was developed by Hering and stemmed from the introspective analyses of color sensations. Many people who have tried to analyze impressions into primary sensory components have felt that the experience of yellow is somehow a "primary experience," not susceptible to further analysis. Today, this sort of introspective evidence is less impressive than it was historically. But introspective analysis did lead to a theory of color vision designed to accomodate *four* basic colors instead of the three of the Young-Helmholtz theory. It is based on the assumption of specialized photopigments in the cones, but it postulates rather different characteristics of photopigment reactions. Hering assumed cones contained three kinds of photopigments: (1) a white-black pigment, (2) a yellow-blue pigment, and (3) a red-green pigment.

This theory assumes a breakdown of the photopigments to produce white, yellow, and red, whereas the reconstitution of the pigments was assumed to elicit the black, blue, and green in the appropriate cones. The basic objection to the Hering theory came from the necessary assumption that a given neural fiber had to carry two kinds of sensory information, e.g., black *and* white, blue *and* yellow. This went against one of the basic notions of nerve physiology, the *doctrine of specific nerve energies*. According to this doctrine a nerve fiber could carry only one quality of sensation, and certainly the doctrine of specific nerve energies seems widely applicable in the nervous system. However, recent evidence to be presented later makes us seriously question this doctrine for all levels of the visual system. We shall also find evidence that some neural cells in the visual thalamus respond in accordance with the Young-Helmholtz theory while others act like those presumed by Hering's theory.

Today, the most widely held theory of color vision is a modification of the Young-Helmholtz theory. Its greatest strength comes from data from experiments of color mixture, and yet these very experiments present problems which suggest the incompleteness of the theory.

Color mixing Artists mix paints, psychologists mix lights. Different laws describe the results of mixtures of paints and lights, for when an artist uses a pigment that appears yellow, he is using material that reflects only electromagnetic energy of wavelengths in the region of the spectrum called "yellow." If he mixes this yellow pigment with a blue pigment he will obtain a greenish mixture. This occurs because his pigments reflect only the wavelengths common to both pigments and each pigment reflects some "green" wavelengths.

On the other hand mixing yellow and blue lights produces a whitish achromatic result. In mixing lights the wavelengths combine to form a new appearance. With colored lights the effects of one wavelength add to the effects of other wavelengths. For this reason the laws describing the addition of colored lights are called *additive laws.* Since the mixing of pigments reduces the number of wavelengths *that reach the eye,* the laws of the mixing of pigments are called *subtractive laws.*

COMPLEMENTARY COLORS. When mixing colored lights, we find that certain hues combine with other hues at appropriate intensities in such a way that their joint effect on us can best be described as neutral in hue—achromatic, or colorless. The pairs of colors that will add together to form a neutral experience are complementary colors. Mixtures of hues that are not complementaries produce a hue somewhere in between them. In theory every color has a complementary, although in fact some complementaries are practically unobtainable. The mixing and matching of colors have been studied in great detail, and we shall find it necessary to limit our discussion to some aspects most important for the development of theories of perception.

PRIMARY COLORS. If we presented a test patch of color from

any portion of the spectrum to a normal observer, we would find that he would produce a hue which matches the test-patch hue by adjusting the proportions of two of the three color primaries, taken one each from the red, green, and blue regions of the spectrum. The exact wavelengths used for the primaries have tended to vary somewhat from one experimenter to another; but the important fact is that observers are able to match the hue of test patches with combinations of two of the three primary colors.

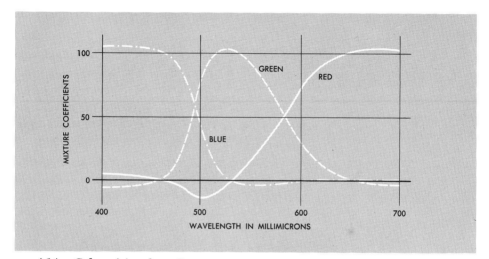

FIG. 4.14. *Color-mixing data. Curves represent proportions of each of the three primaries required to match each region of the spectrum. Adapted from S. Hecht. The development of Thomas Young's theory of color vision. J. Opt. Soc. Amer., 1930, 20, 23.*

However, even though the match made by the two primaries will be perfect for hue, the combination of our two primary colors would not always be sufficiently saturated. In order to have a perfect match for hue *and* saturation sometimes we must add some of our third primary color to the test patch. This reduces the saturation of the test patch. There is no other way to obtain a perfect match for saturation and hue for all test colors. Figure 4.14 shows the proportions of three primaries used to obtain perfect matches of test patches from each spectral region. Where a color primary curve dips below the horizontal line marked "0," that color must be added to the *test patch* to allow a perfect match.

The strength of the Young-Helmholtz theory was that it

assumed three primary color processes: red, green, and blue. The fact that all hues of the spectrum could be matched by manipulating primary colors is indirect but supportive evidence for the theory. It appeared to be more powerful than in fact it was because not everyone recognized that the third primary had to be added to the test patch to obtain a perfect test-patch-primary color-mixture match. This was partially obscured by transformations of the curves such that the curves all appear above the 0 line.

Data from color-mixture experiments provide only indirect inference for a theory of the physiological basis of color vision. Recently, with the development of equipment and techniques that allow recording from single neural cells in the visual system it is possible to take a more direct approach to the study of the neural basis of color vision.

Neurophysiological bases of color For a number of years, it has been possible to record the electrical activities of a sensory nerve (a collection of axons); but the recording of the activity in a single cell or its axon is a much more difficult undertaking. One of the first techniques for recording from a single sensory fiber was that of dissecting out a single nerve fiber from the collection of fibers that make up a nerve. This dissection technique was extended to the visual system of the frog, and recordings were made by Hartline [4] of the excitation of single fibers in the frog optic nerve. Hartline's study of the responses of neural elements in the frog optic nerve revealed that about 20 percent of the fibers began firing and maintained an increased discharge rate while the receptors were stimulated with light; 50 percent of the fibers responded at both the onset and the termination of the visual stimulus; and 30 percent fired *only* at the termination of stimulation. These three kinds of fiber activities were labeled the "on," "on-off," and "off" responses, respectively. Not all neurons in the visual system act strictly in accordance with these three types of response patterns. In addition we should be alert to possible variations in the response characteristics of cells in the visual systems of animals in different species.

Granit [10] has studied the activities of neural elements in the retinas of many kinds of animal eyes. Unfortunately, it is not possible to say definitely which link in the neural chain from receptor cell to ganglion cell was studied, although the ganglion cell itself is the most likely candidate. Granit has

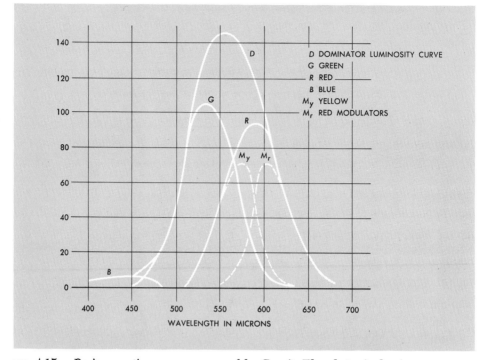

FIG. 4.15. *Basic sensation curves proposed by Granit. The photopic dominator curve (D) is a synthesis of modulator functions. Adapted from R. Granit.* Sensory Mechanisms of the Retina. *New York: Oxford University Press, 1947, p. 332. By permission of the author and Oxford University Press.*

found two general types of responding units: *dominators* and *modulators*. Dominators and modulators must be defined in terms of Granit's techniques. Essentially, after a stable location for recording from a cell in the retina is obtained through a microelectrode, the intensity of light sufficient to cause a noticeable difference in the recorded neural activity is determined for hues in all regions of the spectrum. Then for every neural unit in the retina a "sensitivity curve" can be obtained. In such a curve, wavelength is plotted horizontally and a measure of the intensity of light (of a given wavelength) required to alter the neural response of the cell is plotted vertically. Figure 4.15 shows the dominator and modulator curves found by Granit.

Modulators are defined by narrow, peaked response patterns. Retinal elements which give modulator effects are found less frequently than cells which give dominator effects. The modulator curves shown in Fig. 4.15 are found only under light-adapted conditions and are presumably initiated by activities in the cone system. Narrow response curves (modulator cells) are found with peaks at many wavelengths but they tend to cluster in certain regions. Granit believes his work supports the general position advocated by the early theory of Thomas Young, but others have interpreted Granit's findings as support for theories postulating more than three types of receptor cells. It should be pointed out that the average values of modulator curves do not resemble the three curves postulated by the Young-Helmholtz theory since rare yellow modulators have been found. If Granit's recording techniques reflect activity in single receptor elements, the yellow modulator presents another difficulty to the traditional theory of three cone types, which assumes yellow to result from the synthesis of red, green, and blue primaries.

RETINAL CONVERGENCE. There must be a considerable convergence taking place in the retina and optic nerve. In man there are 4 million to 7 million cones and about 125 million rods in the retina. In the optic nerve there are between 800 thousand to 1 million fibers. Therefore, many individual receptor cells must converge upon and feed into the ganglion cells and few (if any) receptors have "private lines" to the brain. What is the scheme of this retinal convergence?

Figure 4.16 diagrams the convergence pattern proposed by Rushton [11]. It contains some novel and important ideas about the structure and function of the visual system. Note that rods and cones feed into "excitation pools," and in turn these feed into ganglion cells. The anatomical correlate of the excitation pool is uncertain but the evidence of Rushton and others makes the assumption of some such structure necessary.

Now, let us look closely at the diagram. The existence of several types of rods seems likely, and two varieties are indicated by the filled and open rectangles. Note that *both rods and cones feed into the same excitation pools*. Also, one receptor cell sends impulses to more than one excitation pool. Several excitation pools send impulses to the same ganglion cell. All of these arrangements are necessary to account for the data assembled through the use of a technique of *silent substitution*, developed by Rushton. In one experiment, microelectrodes were inserted into the retina of the frog and the activities of neural units, presumed to be ganglion cells, were monitored. The retina was illuminated with a given intensity and wavelength of light. Then a sudden transition was made to a new wavelength

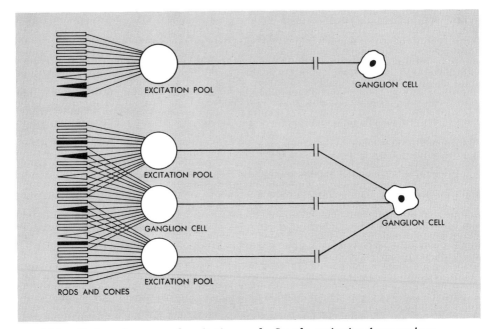

FIG. 4.16. *Rods and cones and excitation pools. Steady excitation from various receptors is transmitted to the pool, and any changes in the pool's level are transmitted to the ganglion. The simplest model is shown above, but more recent data requires the more complicated model shown below. Adapted from W. A. H. Rushton, Excitation pools in the frog's retina. J. Physiol.* (*London*), *1959,* **149,** *327–345.*

and intensity of light. If an intensity could be found for the new wavelength which makes the transition silent, i.e., no change in the ganglion cell's activity is recorded, then this would imply that the level of activity reaching the ganglion cell under the two conditions was the same. This theory assumes the ganglion cells to be responsive to the *total amount of activity* reaching it. Silent substitution can be achieved from many modifications of the basic design too detailed for presentation here. Since silent substitution can not always be made, it is necessary to assume that the retina must be organized as in the lower portion of Fig. 4.16 rather than as in the simplified version shown first.

THALAMIC ACTIVITY. Another approach to gaining understanding of the sensory systems is to "listen in" at the relay nuclei in the thalamus.

The thalamic relay nucleus for vision is called the lateral geniculate body. The lateral geniculate nucleus (LGN) is organized into six layers of cell bodies representing three *pairs* of layers. One member of each pair receives input from the right eye while the other member receives input from the left eye. In other words there seem to be three functional subdivisions in the LGN each consisting of two layers and each receiving impulses from separate eyes. Figure 4.17 presents a cross-section of the LGN stained to show the six layers of cell bodies. To record from cells in this structure, exceedingly small microelectrodes must be lowered deep into the brain.

Once the microelectrode reaches the LGN and a cell body is isolated, its responses to various illuminating conditions of the retina may be studied.

The two dorsal layers contain cells which increase their rates of activity when the retina is illuminated. Most of these cells continue this increased discharge rate for a period of time

FIG. 4.17.   *The lateral geniculate nucleus of a monkey. The dark regions are densely packed cells which are organized into six layers.*

before returning to their normal rates even though the light remains on. When the light is turned off, these same cells show a decrease in discharge rate which is below the level of their "spontaneous" activity [12].

Cells in the bottom two layers respond to changes in illumination by decreasing their activity rates until the light is extinguished. Then they exhibit a burst of activity. We can think of these cells being inhibited by light and then becoming active when the light is turned off.

However, it is the activity of the cells in the middle two layers that demands our attention for their exciting implications for theories of color reception. Cells in these layers react strongly when the retina is illuminated by one wavelength but not by another, and in general their reactions are similar in form to the "modulators" discussed by Granit. However, these "color cells" show a most peculiar phenomenon: *a lateral geniculate cell may be excited (increase its rate of firing) to one color and be inhibited (decrease its rate of firing) by the complementary color.* As an example, suppose the cell increases its rate of firing when the eye is illuminated by green light, then this cell will be inhibited by red light. If it is excited by yellow light it can be inhibited by blue light.

We might recall that Hering's original proposal was discounted because of the basic physiological dictum called the *doctrine of specific nerve energies* according to which a given nerve cell could only mediate one quality of experience. In the studies of the lateral geniculate nucleus, a cell has been shown to signal the experience of one color by an increase in rate of activity and signal another color by a decrease in rate. Thus, the doctrine of specific nerve energies must be modified, and the Hering theory of color vision must be reconsidered. All theories proposed to explain color in neurophysiological terms must be able to incorporate the results obtained from the middle layers of the LGN.

The results from the LGN do not represent a clear victory of the original Hering theory. In the first place, the cells in the LGN are considerably removed from the receptor units. The excitation or inhibition of the LGN cells may come from complicated neural interaction in excitation pools or ganglion cells in the microstructure of the retina, or be the result of the summation of effects from retinal ganglion cells feeding into a lateral geniculate cell. We cannot decide upon the types of receptor cells from research on the thalamic nucleus. In addition, cells in the upper two layers of the LGN respond as modulators but without being inhibited by a complementary color. Thus, the findings obtained from microelectrode studies of the LGN suggest that our color vision must be a result of processes like those postulated by Young and Helmholtz as well as like those postulated by Hering.

But we are a long way from being able to understand color phenomenon. The theories of color vision we have studied refer to theories of the construction of the receptor organ, and neurophysiological studies are just beginning to offer hope of learning the ways in which peripheral visual information is translated into the code used by the brain. We know, on the other hand, that the quality of perceived color, the color we observe in natural objects, depends on the context in which the object occurs and the object itself. We are unable to integrate relatively simple perceptual phenomena like these into our theories as yet. Further, we still are puzzled by many of the types of color vision defects which can be found in the clinical literature.

VISUAL ACUITY The studies of the peripheral mechanisms are essential to understanding sensory phenomena, for if we know how the peripheral system is organized and responds, we will know the nature of the changes imposed upon the information coming in from the periphery to create *perception,* as we commonly use the term. We are just learning about some of the complexities that can be found in the peripheral sensory organs. A case in point can be illustrated by recent studies of visual acuity.

When we think of visual activity most of us think of the Snellen eye chart. This is the chart we read in the physician's office. Usually it hangs about 20 feet from the line on which we stand. The chart has rows of letters which diminish in size from top to bottom. This is a crude measure of visual acuity, and there are many other types of tests for acuity which reduce the unwanted effects of language attainment and letter-design cues on a person's performance. Some of these improved tests use circles with gaps in them (Landolt rings). A series of these circles with the direction of the gap varied is presented, and the subject must report this direction. In another test the subject is required to decide whether two parallel lines are actually separate or not. Most of us have had some experience with tests of visual acuity.

Visual acuity depends upon several factors. A sharp image must be focused on the retina. If the image is blurred through defects of the lens or cornea, our acuity will be decreased. On the other hand the eyeball may be too long or too short for the lens to focus a distinct image when the stimulus is far away or close up and the result is clinically either far- or nearsightedness. The ultimate limits of our visual acuity depend upon the retinal mosaic of receptor fields and their modes of action. It turns out that our visual acuity is exceptionally fine. We are able to detect lines whose thickness is *less than the diameter of one cone.* Calculations of the energy required for the perception of a visual stimulus reveal that the reception of one quantum of light by one receptor cell is sufficient to be detectable. Our vision is excellent, then, almost too good, for it poses the question of how we can detect lines which are smaller than the width of a receptor unit.

EYE MOVEMENTS. The perception of stimuli smaller than a receptor cell can be accounted for on the basis of eye movements. The eye continuously exhibits several kinds of movements. Small and very rapid oscillations of the eye are sufficient to throw the image on the retina over several receptor cells and thus create patterns, or distributions, of excitation over a larger area. Resolution of this larger pattern caused by the eye movements must be accomplished by neural interaction at the level of the bipolar or ganglion cells or higher up the neural chain to the brain.

When discussing visual fields we noted that there is good evidence that one retinal area can influence an adjoining area. This interaction, in which one retinal area inhibits or excites neighboring areas, may also serve to *sharpen* the neural activity caused by the retinal figure. Thus, the images we perceive represent great accomplishments in both the anatomical system of the eyes and the neural mechanisms of the entire system beginning at the retina itself.

Other Sensory Systems

How many other senses do we have? Certainly we hear, we smell, we taste, we feel tactile sensations of the skin, we are aware of the orientation of our body in space and relative to gravitational forces, we know when our stomach "growls." On top of this, we are sensitive to changes in temperature and we can feel several varieties of pain.

As we have already mentioned, our preference is to concentrate our attention upon some of the functional characteristics of the visual system. Many of the functional characteristics found in the visual system are common to all sensory systems. For example, each kind of sensory system has some kind of a receptor field. Receptors in the skin respond to deformations over a rather well-defined spatial area. Receptor fields for these skin receptors can be mapped by recording from single neurons in sensory nerves, or by recording from the neocortical areas receiving this kind of information. Principles of transmission of sensory information from receptor to thalamus to cortex have many points of similarity in all sensory systems. The greatest *difference* among the several sensory systems is to be found in mechanisms used to change physical energies into neural activity at the receptor organs (generator potentials).

THE AUDITORY SYSTEM The external, shell-like structure of the ear (the pinna) probably is useful in funneling changes in sound pressure into the auditory receptors of the lower animals, but in man these external features serve little function. Just inside the pinna, through a short passage (the external meatus), is the ear drum which moves in and out in response to changes in air pressure. This vibration of the ear drum is

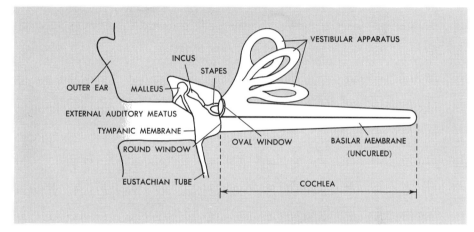

FIG. 4.18. *Diagram of the peripheral mechanisms of audition. The cochlea, straightened here, is naturally twisted about three and a half times—rather like a sea shell.*

transmitted by a mechanical linkage of the three bones (malleus, incus, and stapes) of the middle ear to the inner ear. Inside the inner ear are the receptor cells which change physical vibrations into neural events for final translation into changes in neural activity. Figure 4.18 presents a schematic diagram of the human ear. The inner ear is filled with fluids. The mechanical vibrations of the bones of the middle ear are translated into moving waves in these fluids through the in and out movements of the oval window. The motion of the inner-ear fluids is translated into neural changes by receptor cells located on the basilar membrane.

In Fig. 4.18 the basilar membrane has been drawn as a straight, flat surface. Actually, it is curled up inside a boney structure resembling a snail's shell. The name of this boney housing of the basilar membrane comes from its appearance: it is called the *cochlea*. The basilar membrane extends throughout the length of the cochlea. Waves in the fluid medium produce oscillations of the membrane. The place of greatest oscillation of the basilar membrane is determined by the frequency of the vibration of the oval window. The actual receptor cells, *hair cells,* are located on the basilar membrane. As the basilar membrane oscillates, the hair cells are distorted and this causes them to produce neural changes just as light causes neural reactions in the rods and cones of the retina. These changes in neural activity originating in the hair cells is transmitted through a series of neurons to the auditory areas of the neocortex found in the temporal lobes, via the thalamic relay nucleus for audition (the medial geniculate nucleus). The frequency of the fluid vibrations of the inner ear is signaled to the brain by the pattern of distortion of the basilar membrane. Different patterns of distortion result in different groups of hair cells being activated.

The ears function to apprise us of changes in the air pressure around us. However, our auditory mechanism is only sensitive to changes in air pressure occurring within a certain range of frequencies. Generally speaking, the human can hear frequencies between 20 and 20,000 cycles per second. Changes in air pressure of slower or faster frequencies do not effect us. Remember that in the case of vision we found that we were sensitive to only part of the electromagnetic spectrum. In hearing we are sensitive only to a portion of the frequency spectrum. Other species are sensitive to different ranges of frequencies.

Air pressure changes of appropriate frequencies are translated into mechanical changes by the middle-ear mechanisms. These mechanical vibrations are changed into hydraulic vibrations in the inner ear. The receptor cells are affected by these changes in the movement of fluids in the cochlea. In the ear we find an interesting series of translations of air pressure changes to mechanical changes to hydraulic changes to neural changes. The signals arriving at higher centers of the brain from the auditory system are encoded as alterations in the activities of single neurons just as are signals arriving from all sensory systems.

SMELL AND TASTE Smell and taste are two of the chemical senses we have. In the nose the particles in the air combine with the fluids over the receptors to form a chemical solution to which sensory cells in the olfactory epithelium respond. The patterns of excitation set up in the receptors by these solutions are carried to the brain over the olfactory nerves, and then are projected to certain portions of phyletically old brain. The taste receptors are located on the tongue. Because of their shape they are called *taste buds*. While most of these are located on the top, tip, and side of the tongue, there are some on the top of the mouth, in the glottis, and in the pharynx and larynx.

Impulses initiated by the chemical solutions on the tongue are relayed to the brain over several nerves. Once they reach the central nervous system they become connected with impulses arising from the somatic musculature of the body, and their projection to neocortex probably is through relay nuclei which carry the somatic information. This mixing, however, does not mean that taste-initiated neural activity becomes integrated with the neural activity initiated by the muscles. The taste activity and the somatic activity are projected by thalamic relay nuclei to quite different areas of the neocortex.

Psychologically there seems to be four distinct kinds of tastes: sweet, sour, bitter, and salt. Other tastes are believed to be compounded of these four basic tastes. However, records of the activity of single taste buds reveal that none of them seems to represent a single kind of basic taste receptor. Single taste buds may respond to combinations of several of the basic tastes. A given taste bud may respond to both salt and sweet solutions, for example. Because it is possible through the use of certain drugs to eliminate the response of this kind of taste bud to sweetness but maintain its response to salty solutions, it is now believed that taste buds may have specific locations, or sites, which are sensitive to certain kinds of solutions but not others.

The fact that single receptor units do not respond in the four ways suggested by the four psychologically basic tastes implies that the latter are compounded or created by the central nervous system. (For reviews of modern information about smell see [13] and for taste see [14].)

SOMATIC SENSATION The information about the position and the actions of our body comes from fibers embedded in muscles, from receptors in tendons, and from receptors located in the skin. For many years efforts were directed toward locating specific receptor units which corresponded to each of the types of somatic sensation. For example, investigators tried to associate a specific type of receptor cell for the sensations of heat loss (cold) and another specific kind of receptor cell for the sensation of touch. However, the work of Weddell suggests that this search for basic receptor types may be fruitless. Information concerning warmth, cold, touch, tickle, and pain can all be transmitted by free nerve endings which do not appear to have any specialized receptor units at their extremities [15]. As with the sense of taste, the organization of peripheral information into psychologically elementary sensations seems to be accomplished in the central nervous system. Different kinds of stimulation arising from the periphery of the body produce different patterns of excitation in free nerve endings, muscles, joints, etc. From the patterns of stimulation arising in the periphery of the body the central neural apparatus imposes organization.

Somatic sensations travel to the brain in the spinal cord. In general we can recognize two kinds of pathways from the spinal cord to the relay nuclei of the thalamus (spinothalamic tracts). The first system is a group of large, heavily myelinated fibers which are located toward the back (dorsum) of the body and are called the dorsal columns. These reach a thalamic nucleus and then are projected in to neocortical areas just in back of the central fissure (see p. 102). An outline of the muscles of the body can be found in the neocortical projection area and in the thalamic relay nucleus. No pain sensations are carried over this big-fiber system, and there is reason to believe this system is recent in the phylogenetic development of animals [16]. This system would represent the primary sensory stem illustrated in Fig. 4.2 (p. 123).

Somatic sensations also reach the brain from the spinal cord over other ascending columns or tracts. These are located more toward the side of the cord (lateral spinothalamic tracts) and toward the stomach (ventral and anterior spinothalomic tracts). The fibers in these somatic systems are much smaller than in the dorsal columns and reach the thalamus after many synapses with other cells. These smaller fiber systems give off collaterals to the diffuse systems of the brain including the reticular formation of the brain stem. Upon reaching the thalamus they go into different thalamic areas from those entered by the bigger fibers of the dorsal columns. Then they project to areas of the neocortex adjacent to the somatosensory areas innervated by the dorsal-column fibers.

The smaller fiber columns of the spinal cord carry different kinds of somatic messages from those in the dorsal columns. Activity in their fibers can be initiated by wider regions of the body and their thalamic nuclei receive input from more than one type of receptor. For example, a thalamic neuron in the area receiving somatic input from the lateral spinothalamic system may respond to muscle changes, tendon changes, and possibly auditory stimulation [17].

The behavioral significance of the two types of somatic sensation has not been completely specified. Yet we do know some of the functional characteristics of each kind of system. We know, for example, that neural impulses giving rise to pain are carried over the lateral spinothalamic system. This knowledge allows neurosurgeons to help people who have continuing unbearable pain in some portions of their bodies by selectively severing these tracts. This operation reduces or eliminates the sensation of pain without loss of sensation or muscular coordination of the affected region.

In summary: Although there are specialized aspects of each sensory system, in broad detail certain similarities can be found among them. Each sensory system seems to be organized at the periphery in terms of receptive fields, that is, in terms of relatively broad areas of a receptor surface. Stimulation in these areas will produce a change in the response of one of the neurons in the chain from receptor to brain. Receptive fields may be arranged in different shapes of excitatory and inhibitory areas and can be measured by recording from cells close to the receptors or at the neocortical areas receiving the specific sensory information. As a general rule receptive fields are smaller when measured at the neocortical level than nearer the receptor. This suggests, along with related evidence from many sensory systems, that the qualities of sensation result from the central organization of the brain and nervous system.

Information from the sensory systems reaches the neocortex through afferent nerve tracts and through a synaptic relay nucleus of the thalamus. There are two categories of afferent nerve fibers: the fast, myelinated nerve tracts which go to the main sensory receiving areas of neocortex and the slower, smaller fiber nerve tracts which reach the supplemental sensory areas and which give off collaterals to the diffuse systems.

Finally, we must recognize that the central nervous system is actively concerned with modifying the peripheral input close to, if not at, the level of the receptor units. This is accomplished through systems of sensory efferent fibers. The entire sensory process must be conceived of as a constantly active relationship between input from the receptors and modifying outflow to the receptors.

References

1. Kuffler, S. W., Hunt, C. C., & Quilliam, J. P. Function of medullated small-nerve fibers in mammalian ventral roots: efferent muscle spindle innervation. *J. Neurophysiol.,* 1951, **14**, 29–54.
2. Hagbarth, K. E., & Kerr, D. I. B. Central influences on spinal afferent conduction. *J. Neurophysiol.,* 1954, **17**, 195–307.
3. Granit, R. *Receptors and Sensory Perception.* New Haven: Yale Univer. Press, 1955.
4. Hartline, H. K. Impulses in single optic nerve fibers of the vertebrate eye to illumination of the retina. *Amer. J. Physiol.,* 1938, **121**, 400–415.
5. Hubel, D. H., and Wiesel, T. N. Receptive fields of single neurons in the cats striate cortex. *J. physiol.,* 1959, **148**, 574–591.
6. Jung, R., & Baumgartner, G. Hemmungsmechanismen und bremsende Stabilisierung an einzelnen Neuronen des optishen Cortex. *Pflüg. Arch. ges. Physiol.,* 1955, **261**, 434–456.
7. Lettvin, J. Y., Matwiana, H. R., McCulloch, W. S., & Pitts, W. H. What the frog's eye tells the frog's brain. *IRE Proc.,* 1959, **47**, 1940–1951.
8. Hecht, S., Shlaer, S., & Pirenne, M. H. Energy, quanta, and vision. *J. gen. Physiol.,* 1942, **25**, 819–840.
9. Wald, G. The photoreceptor process in vision. In J. Field (Ed.), *Handbook of Physiology. Section 1: Neurophysiology.* Washington, D.C.: Amer. Physiol. Soc., 1959.
10. Granit, R. *Sensory Mechanisms of the Retina.* London: Oxford Univer. Press, 1947.
11. Rushton, W. A. H. Excitation pools in the frog's retina. *J. Physiol.,* 1959, **149**, 327–345.
12. DeValois, R. L., Smith, C. J., Kitai, S. T., & Karoly, A. J. Response of single cells in monkey lateral geniculate nucleus to monochromatic light. *Science,* 1957, **127**, 238–239.
13. Adey, W. R. The sense of smell. In J. Field (Ed.), *op. cit.*

14. Pfaffman, C. The sense of taste. In J. Field (Ed.), *op. cit.*

15. Weddell, G. Receptors for somatic sensation. In Mary A. B. Brazier (Ed.), *Brain and Behavior*. Washington, D.C.: Amer. Inst. Biol. Sci., 1961.

16. Bishop, G. H. The relation between nerve fiber size and sensory modality: phylogenetic implications of the afferent innervation of cortex. *J. nerv. ment. Dis.,* 1959, **128,** 89–114.

17. Mountcastle, V. B. Duality of function in the somatic afferent system. In Mary A. B. Brazier (Ed.), *op. cit.*

FIVE PERCEPTUAL BEHAVIOR: EXPERIMENTS AND THEORIES

How many ways can we perceive the moon? Does the moon appear the same on an autumn hayride with your favorite partner as it does in an evening astronomy class? Do we *see* the moon differently after learning about its craters and landmarks in the astronomy class? Why does the large moon seen at the horizon change in size if we bend over and look at it through our legs? In asking these questions we are asking if our actual perception of the moon is different under the several conditions we have mentioned, not whether our emotion or behavior is different. If our perceptions are different then these differences must be caused by influences quite apart from the sensory determinants of perception discussed in Chapter 4. In this chapter we shall discuss experiments and theories which concern perceptual behavior of the entire individual. We have already suggested that perception is more than reactions of the sensory systems. "Man, not his eyes, sees."

In the first section of this chapter we shall discuss some modern aspects of an area of psychology called *psychophysics*. This branch of research has roots extending back to the beginnings of scientific psychology. Early research in psychophysics attempted to determine the relation between physical stimulation impinging on an individual and his mental experiences. Today, we would say that psychophysics attempts to describe the relationship between changes in physical stimulation and changes in those responses which indicate recognition or detection of the physical changes. Like all branches of psychology the aim is to understand man; in this case man as an observer. We shall discuss both early and modern techniques in this attempt to coordinate the physical world about us with our internal reactions.

Next we shall examine the reasons why some psychologists began to assert that we must study the total "form" rather than "elements" of perception. At the same time we shall consider some explanations which have been offered for the perception of forms and the relevance of psychological research using perceptual illusions. This will lead us to a theory of perception developed by D. O. Hebb which has important implications for behavior theory generally.

In the later sections of the chapter we shall discuss the influence of bodily activity, values, motives, and personality variables on perception. The fact that psychologists discuss the possibility that variables like these can affect perception reflects a relatively recent change in emphasis in psychological research. In fact research with these variables has been called the *New Look* in perceptual studies.

Psychophysics

As the name implies, psychophysics suggests a marriage of psychology and physics. If we think of the setting in which the marriage took place in the middle of the nineteenth century in

Germany, this is a reasonable union. In those days physics and psychology were very different from what they are today. Physics was fairly well established in its Newtonian tradition with a strong emphasis on measurement. In fact many philosophers of science held that it was because of this emphasis on measurement that physics advanced so rapidly. Psychology was primarily the study of mental experience. Furthermore, many scientists were active in several areas of research. What would be more natural for a scientist with biological, physical, and psychological interests to want to study and measure *sensation?* Psychophysics refers to research which aims to do just this: to study the changes in perception which occur when changes in the physical stimuli are made. While many psychologists still believe the methods of psychophysics do measure mental experiences, the behavioristic influence suggests that we confine ourselves to speaking of the relation between physical stimuli and response. It will be most useful to consider perception as a "theoretical variable" which is inferred from certain kinds of responses. We cannot know by inference the mental states of any other person but we can know and study his behavior.

One of the founders of psychophysics, Gustav Fechner, began his studies because of an interest in attacking the current materialistic philosophies existing in Germany in the middle 1800s. Fechner believed he could prove his own philosophic view through psychophysics. This view illustrates the early attempts to use psychophysical methods as a means to measure mental experiences by finding laws relating the two worlds.

WEBER'S RATIO AND FECHNER'S LAW One of the earliest psychophysical observations made was the general rule that the amount of change in sensory stimulation required to allow the observer to report that he perceives a perceptual change is proportional to the amount of the sensory stimulation. This is Weber's law. Another way of stating this, using symbols, is

$$\frac{\Delta I}{I} = K$$

where ΔI = increase or decrease in stimulation

  I = amount of original stimulation

  K = a constant which depends on the particular sensory modality and other variables

A simple example of Weber's ratio which is often found on examinations is the following:

Q. If a theater sign had a dense grouping of 1000 bulbs, and if the Weber ratio for the particular situation was 0.10, how many bulbs would have to burn out before they were noticed?

A. $\dfrac{\Delta I}{I} = K$ If $K = .1$ $\dfrac{X}{1000} = .1,\ X = 100$ bulbs

$I = 1000$

$\Delta I = X$

Therefore, we can predict that if less than 100 bulbs were burned out (randomly), observers would not report any change in stimulation. However, this problem is greatly oversimplified. In a real situation the Weber ratio could not be applied to a situation like a theater sign where the grouping of the stimulus elements is important. In our illustration a cluster of burned-out bulbs would be noticed more rapidly than if the burned-out bulbs were evenly dispersed.

Fechner applied mathematically the basic Weber equation to obtain a general statement about the relation between physical stimulation and mental sensations.

$$\frac{\Delta I}{I} = K \quad \text{(Weber's Law)}$$

$$\int \frac{\Delta I}{I} = k \log I$$

This result is often interpreted to read

Sensation $= k$ log stimulation

This equation asserts that sensation varies in a logarithmic relation to stimulation. In effect this means that small changes in the lower ranges of the physical-stimulus scale will produce greater changes in sensation than the same amounts of physical-stimulus changes superimposed upon stimuli of greater magnitude. We have displayed the "sensation $= k$ log stimulation" relationship graphically in Fig. 5.1. From it we observe that a small change in skin pressure (*a* to *a'*) will produce a greater change in sensation when it is imposed on a slight previous pressure than on a great previous pressure (*b* to *b'*). If the initial pressure is high enough, an increment of 2 ounces per square inch may not be reported as any change at all. This would be the case if the ratio of a 2-ounce increment to the original pressure is less than the particular Weber's constant for this type of stimulation.

JUST NOTICEABLE DIFFERENCES AND THRESHOLDS   Weber's fraction ($\Delta I/I$) is based on the concept of a *just noticeable difference* (JND). It assumes that changes in existing stimulus conditions are either large enough to cause a perceptual difference or they are not. If they are not large enough then the observer will perceive no change whatever in the stimulus. A JND refers to the smallest change in a stimulus which can be

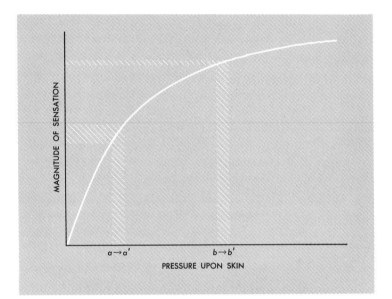

FIG. 5.1.   *Logarithmic relation between stimulation and sensation. Vertical axis presumably reflects the magnitude of observer's perception of skin pressure. The same increase in physical pressure on the skin (the distance between a-a' and to b-b') creates a greater difference in perception at lower end of stumulus scale than at higher end.*

detected by the observer. This concept rests in turn upon the concept of a threshold. The threshold is a theoretical concept which indicates a boundary condition. If one applies increasing amounts of pressure on a balloon, say by squeezing it, at some point the balloon will burst. The amount of pressure needed to break the balloon can be thought of as a threshold condition. Any pressure less than the boundary pressure will not break the balloon; any pressure greater than the boundary pressure will. Changes in any sensory stimulation which fall below a threshold will not cause any perceptual change in the observer.

Changes in sensory stimulation above this threshold amount of stimulation will produce changes in the observer's perceptions.

We can talk about two kinds of thresholds: a *difference threshold* and an *absolute threshold*. In fact they are very similar concepts, both based on change from prior conditions. An absolute threshold refers to the smallest amount of stimulation which can be *detected* by an observer. In measuring an absolute threshold we begin with no stimulation at all and add energy until the observer reports a perceptual experience. If we want to measure the absolute threshold for a spot of white light, we could present this spot to subjects looking at a dark target area in a blackened room (after sufficient time for dark adaptation to occur). We would present the spot at different intensities and instruct the subjects to respond in a certain way when they saw the white spot. If we wanted to measure difference thresholds, we must present an increment or decrement of illumination in the spot and ask when this difference is noticed. When measuring absolute thresholds the experimenter wants the subjects to report the presence of a stimulus; in measuring difference thresholds the experimenter wants the subjects to report a change in stimulating conditions.

Measurement of thresholds Psychophysical methods are techniques used to measure absolute and difference thresholds.

Measurements of thresholds can be done in several ways. The primary methods were reported by Fechner in 1860. Three methods are still widely used today.

1. The first method is often called the *method of constant stimuli,* despite the fact the stimuli presented to the observer are not constant. When using this technique, stimuli are presented to the observer one at a time in a varying order. If the method is being used to determine an absolute visual threshold the observer is asked to report when he sees the stimulus. After each stimulus has been presented many times and the observer has reported his perceptual changes, it is possible to relate the intensity of the stimulus to the number of times that the observer reported seeing it. A hypothetical curve, representing the frequency of detection for five stimuli, is presented in Fig. 5.2. As the stimuli increase in intensity, the greater is the frequency defined as that stimulus intensity which is reported as perceived Furthermore, as is typical in psychophysical experiments, the frequency of reports of perceptual changes increases most rapidly in the middle range of the stimulus intensity scale. This

is reflected in the shape of the curve which resembles a slanted *S*. Using the method of constant stimuli, a threshold is usually defined as that stimulus intensity which is reported as perceived half the number of times it was presented. This definition is

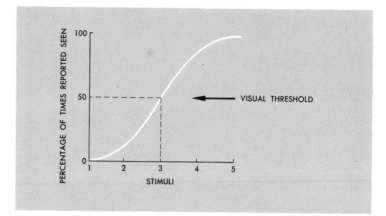

FIG. 5.2. *Hypothetical relationship between the proportion of times a stimulus is presented and reported seen and the intensity of the stimulus. Stimulus 1 is the least intense, 5 the most intense.*

arbitrary and other definitions could serve as well. For example, would not a stimulus whose intensity was such that it was perceived 75 percent of the time be an equally good threshold?

2. When an experimenter uses the *method of limits,* he presents the subject with a graduated series of stimulus intensities either from the smallest intensities to the greatest intensities or from the greatest to the smallest. The experimenter begins by presenting the subject with one of the stimuli from either end of the continuum. Then, he asks the subject if he sees the stimulus. Usually, the extreme intensities are selected so that there is no doubt that the subject will report that he sees it if the greatest intensity stimulus is presented and will not report seeing it if the minimal stimulus is presented. Each stimulus in the series is presented and the subject again reports whether or not it is perceived. The series of stimuli is presented in order through the entire range of stimuli or until the subject changes his report from "seeing" to "not seeing" or the other way around, depending on whether an ascending or descending series is being presented.

3. In the third method, *the method of average error,* the subject adjusts a stimulus until it matches some given standard.

The subject has control of a knob or dial by which he can increase or decrease the stimulus intensity. The basic operation of matching is repeated many times. The difference between this method and others is that the subject is required to make a judgment of equality between the stimulus under his control and the standard. Thresholds are determined by the mean (average) stimulus intensity set by the subject. This presumably is the point at which the sensation reaches a region of intensity indistinguishable from the standard. The conditions of the experiment influence the calculated thresholds, and the thresholds obtained by this method often fail to correspond to those obtained by the method of constant stimuli or the method of limits.

Should we assume a threshold? Each of the three methods described above produces a number, expressed in physical units of measurement, which is called a threshold. These numbers are often considered as more or less reliable estimates of some "real threshold" in the person which cannot be measured directly. This real threshold would be a boundary between sensation and no sensation or between a change in sensation and no change in sensation, depending on whether we were speaking of absolute or difference thresholds. The threshold

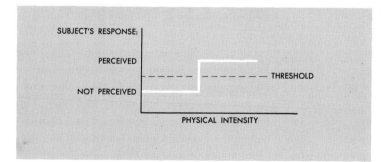

FIG. 5.3. *Graphic presentation of the threshold assumption. As the physical stimulus increases, some point is reached when the excitation is sufficient to cause a perceptual response to it. Crossing the threshold is an all-or-none event on any presentation of stimulus.*

concept can be illustrated by the steplike graph of Fig. 5.3. Along the abscissa, we have represented a physical-energy scale. It could be a scale of light intensity, for example. On the ordinate we have represented essentially two conditions: stimulus perceived and not perceived. As the intensity of the stimulus is increased, some point is reached at which perception takes place. As we already know, this point is often called the threshold. Yet, curves like this are never found when data from psychophysical experiments are analyzed.

Usually, a slowly rising curve is obtained as represented earlier in Fig. 5.2. This, plus the fact that different psycho-physical methods often yield different estimates of the threshold point, raises doubts as to the usefulness of the concept of sensory thresholds. But there are still other problems for the concept of thresholds.

REWARDS AND EXPECTANCIES If one considers the task of the subject in a psychophysical experiment, it becomes apparent that both his expectancies about the experimental situation and the reward system set up by the experimenter must have a profound influence on behavior. Even though the subject tries to report his experiences honestly, the *sequence* of stimuli presented by the experimenter and the pay-offs to the subject affect the observer's reports.

For an illustration, let us think of a radar operator watching the face of his scope. The radar operator may be part of an early warning system and he knows that any blip appearing on his scope face could be an enemy missile on the way toward the United States. Detection of the missile is important for the initiation of countermeasures.

Radar screens tend to have some degree of background activity, or noise. The blip is really an intense point of light superimposed on a background of less intense and constantly varying light. If the radar operator has been observing the screen for months without a signal or blip occurring, and nothing has been said to make him think there is any change in the world situation, he probably believes that it is unlikely that a blip will occur. However, the payoffs for his possible responses are interesting too.

The radar operator, at any moment, can report the activity on his scope as "missile" or "no missile." At any moment a missile could be present or not. Two kinds of mistakes can be made. If a missile is on its way toward the United States, a mistake in not reporting it might have terrible consequences. The other type of mistake, reporting a missile when there is none, would waste some interceptor missiles which may be expensive; but not nearly as much damage would be inflicted by an enemy missile. Therefore, it is likely that the radar operator would tend to make the second kind of error in preference to the first. Thus both the observer's past history as it influences his expectations of the occurrence of a blip and the pay-offs for the various kinds of correct and incorrect responses influence perceptual *reports*. These factors have been incorporated into a theoretical model of how the human observer detects stimulus change.

THE DECISION ANALYSIS MODEL   Tanner and Swets [1] have proposed that our detection of sensory signals can be compared to the performance of an electronic device designed to detect signals against a background of noise which is an unpredictable pattern of activity. This comparison allows us a fresh look at the basic perceptual mechanisms. In the example of the hypothetical radar observer, the detection task faced by the human can be one where signals must be detected against more or less intense backgrounds of noise. One suggestion made by Tanner and Swets is that all sensory detection can be thought of in the same way. We all must sort out signals of interest from noisy backgrounds. Noise can be external, as in a radar screen or a poor radio, or internal, caused perhaps by the spontaneous activity of the nervous system. In any case the problem posed for signal detection is how do we reach a decision regarding whether we are observing signal and noise or noise alone. Because the theory proposed by Tanner and Swets explicitly provides a model for how this decision is reached, it is called the *decision analysis model*.

Noise and signals   In the decision analysis model every problem of sensory detection is viewed as one in which a signal is added to a noise background. Noise is postulated as a basic feature of the model and the organism. There may be more or less noise at any moment. Noise can occur in every sensory modality. While it is possible to think of various sources of noise both in the external world and in the person, *for our purposes let us merely assume that there always is some noise as part of the background for all sensory observations.*

By definition, noise refers to a pattern of activity which is unpredictable. Auditory noise usually refers to an unsystematic sampling of auditory frequencies which change rapidly. Noise in the visual system could refer to an unsystematic pattern of visual wavelengths which also change moment to moment. The intensity of the noisy background can also change moment to moment. While the precise characteristics of the noise at any instant would be impossible to predict, it is possible to make assumptions about the average values of the noise when observed over a period of time. For example, if your radio is tuned so that you get only static, you can not know how loud that static will be at any one instant. But by turning the gain (volume or loudness) of the radio you can arrange to have the average value of the static greater or less. When the radio is loud, the average value of the static has been increased. Turning the radio down would decrease the average value of the static. So it is possible to talk about average values of noise and, even more, to talk about the distribution of noise patterns. By distribution we mean the way in which the unsystematic noise occurrences of noise range about an average value. In the Tanner-Swets theory distributions are similar at all intensities.

The important parts of the decision analysis model are (1) a background noise is postulated to always exist and (2) the average value and distribution of the noise can be specified to some degree. If this is accepted, then the next assumption is that *the effect of a signal is to displace the average value of the noise distribution.*

Let us assume in a case of auditory detection that there is a background noise level with an average intensity of X. Subjects attempt to detect a signal presented against this noise background. The signal is assumed to have a *constant intensity* (not varying moment to moment like the noise) of Y. The decision analysis model asserts that the mean value of the signal *and* noise is $X + Y$. Mathematically, it can be shown that the distribution of the signal-plus-noise distribution will be the same as the distribution of the noise alone, although it is displaced along the intensity scale. Figure 5.4 shows a hypothetical noise distribution and the effect of adding a signal to this background distribution.

Moment to moment the noise distribution fluctuates about the average value of X, and the signal-plus-noise distribution fluctuates about the average value of $X + Y$.

In the normal course of events an observer in real life or in the reduced laboratory situation never can observe the entire range of either distribution. We must make decisions with less than complete information. If we must decide whether a signal is being presented we decide on the basis of a sample which can come from either of the two distributions.

Sampling from the distributions   In the decision analysis model the observer is thought to be given a sample from one or the other of the distributions. This observer's job is to decide whether the sample comes from the noise or the signal-plus-noise distributions.

In effect we can interpret this to mean that the observer is given one value from the intensity scale of Fig. 5.4. This is a

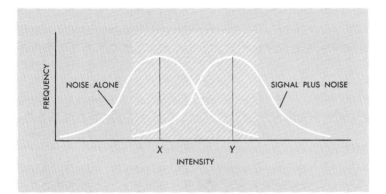

FIG. 5.4.   *Effect of adding a sensory signal to a noise distribution as proposed in the Tanner-Swets theory. Ordinate represents frequency with which a given intensity is obtained; abscissa represents a hypothetical intensity scale. Mean of noise distribution is located at* X; *mean of signal + noise is located at* X + Y. *Generally, effect of adding stimulus is to intensify noise distribution. Distributions of noise and signal + noise are assumed to be identical.*

restricted sample, of course, but can serve as the prototype for samples of larger size. Suppose we were to give our observer this sample: an intensity value below the shaded area in Fig. 5.4. Clearly, this sample must be from the noise alone. The signal-plus-noise distribution can never produce such a small intensity. By the same reasoning, intensity samples greater than the shaded area can occur only when the signal is added to the noise. But, values in the shaded area can be from either the noise or the signal-plus-noise distribution. To make decisions in this area of uncertainty, the observer must set up a *criterion,* a value on the intensity scale somewhere in the shaded area, and report any value greater than this criterion as most likely to have come from the signal-plus-noise distribution and any value below the criterion point as most likely to have arisen from noise distribution alone. What determines the point where this criterion is placed by the observer?

The setting of the criterion Tanner and Swets propose that the location of the criterion point is determined by (1) the pay-off to the subject of the possible outcomes of his responses and (2) the observer's estimates that the signal-plus-noise or the noise alone was presented.

TABLE 5.1. PAY-OFFS FOR OUTCOMES IN MISSILE EXAMPLE

| | Outcome of Observer's Responses | |
Actual Event	"Signal" (Missile)	"No Signal" (No Missile)
Missile coming	Save area from destruction	Destruction of area
No missile	Waste of expensive interceptor	Continued tranquility

The pay-offs to an observer can vary for each possible outcome of his response. If the subject can say only, "Yes the signal was presented," or, "No the signal was not presented, noise alone was there," then a pay-off table can be constructed. Table 5.1 presents a possible pay-off table for our radar operator in the earlier example, and Table 5.2 presents a possible pay-off table for an observer in an experiment. Tables like these represent both the rewards and penalties for correct

TABLE 5.2. PAY-OFFS FOR OUTCOMES IN EXPERIMENT

| | Outcome of Observer's Responses | |
Actual Event	Signal	No Signal
Signal + noise	$+10\not{c}$	$-10\not{c}$
Noise alone	$-10\not{c}$	$+10\not{c}$

and incorrect responses. Too often, in many real-life situations it is impossible to calculate the pay-off for certain entries in the table. In the laboratory, however, a pay-off system can be exactly specified and explained to the observers. Table 5.2 represents a balanced pay-off in which both kinds of correct and both kinds of incorrect responses are rewarded and penalized equally. It is easy to create pay-off tables which are not balanced. The pay-off for correct identification of the signal as a signal can be heavily rewarded and the penalty for saying "signal" when noise alone is presented can be made minimal. Such a pay-off table would bias the observer toward reporting signals at the expense of his "noise" responses. In the formulation the effect of this biased table would be to set the criterion lower, more toward the bottom of the shaded area than the top of Fig. 5.4.

The observer's estimates of the likelihood of the two events, a signal plus noise or the noise alone, will also alter the

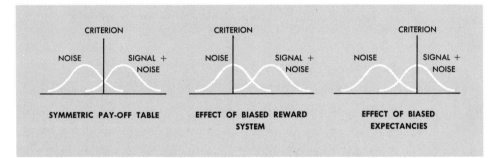

FIG. 5.5. *Effects of pay-off and observer's expectancies of outcomes on criterion placement according to the decision-analysis model. Left, placement of observer's criterion for discrimination when reward for correct identification (S + N) is balanced by some degree of penalty for incorrect identification, and observer's expectancies have not been biased; middle, observer shifts criterion when reward for correct identification is greater than penalty for error; right, criterion is shifted to accommodate observer's expectancies when he has been led to expect noise more than the signal, although reward and penalty are balanced.*

position of the criterion. The effect of increasing the probability of one or the other of these is to move the criterion away from the favored distribution. If the observer expects that noise alone is more likely to be presented to him, the criterion will be placed near the top of the shaded area. If he believes the signal plus noise is more likely to occur, then the criterion is moved lower. Figure 5.5 shows the effect of rewards and penalties and the effects of the observer's expectancies on the location of the criterion. If the pay-offs are biased and the noise-alone and signal-plus-noise presentations are not subjectively equal, then the effects of each manipulation combine to produce a joint effect. The location of the criterion can be calculated by use of a maximum likelihood ratio which takes into consideration both rewards and penalties and the probabilities of occurrence of the two possible stimulus conditions.

Significance of the decision analysis model   First, we might ask what has happened to the familiar concept of the threshold in the decision analysis model? We began by assuming a noise distribution which provides a background for all signals. Then, we assume certain effects of signals on this background noise. Next, we learned that a criterion was established to decide whether the sample should be assigned to the signal-plus-noise or the noise-alone categories. The word *threshold* did not once occur. One of the most interesting features of considering sensory detection in light of the decision analysis model is that the threshold concept need not be used. Perhaps this concept is not needed to understand perceptual phenomena.

We know of course that intense signals are easier to detect against a noise background than are weak signals. The decision analysis model explains this by assuming that weak signals add a smaller constant to the noise distribution than do intense signals. Very strong signals could displace the average value of the signal-plus-noise distribution so far along the intensity scale that there could be little or no overlap of the two distributions and thus little or no range where decisions would be uncertain. Weak signals might only displace the signal-plus-noise distribution a short distance on the intensity scale and result in making practically the entire distribution a zone of uncertainty.

One advantage of viewing sensory detection as Tanner and Swets do is that rewards and expectancies can be incorporated into the perceptual decision. Thresholds, on the other hand, are usually felt to be some inherent property of the individual and insensitive to changes in expectancies or rewards. When we think of a threshold for the detection of light, for example, we think that there is some intensity of light which is just sufficient to produce a perceptual response. But, how do we then incorporate the fact that rewards and expectancies can alter this inherent property, the visual threshold?

Perception of Complex Patterns

Hermann von Helmholtz, the great physicist and physiologist concerned with understanding the sensory systems, held that a belief in a mechanism of "unconscious inference" was needed to explain normal perception of figures. He held that we perceive those figures or objects which are most likely to have produced the sensory information reported to the nervous system from the receptors. This inference of the most likely object is based on our past experiences with objects and the stimuli arising from them. The inference was supposedly made on the basis of things we had learned about the world about us.

The concept of unconscious inference in perception has been attacked, especially by Gestalt psychologists. *Gestalt* is a German word meaning *configuration* or *form*. The basic arguments against unconscious inference have been that inference is a conscious phenomena and that it does not occur instantly, though perception itself does seem to occur at once. Yet people do not report "feeling" that they make inferences, nor do they seem to require time to make them when perceiving objects.

However, despite the fact that the battle between unconscious inference and Gestalt psychologists began before the turn of the century, no clear-cut victory has ever been won by either side. There is no doubt, however, that the work of Gestalt psychologists has resulted in the gathering of many important and interesting observations of perceptual phenomena.

THE GESTALT MOVEMENT   In the later part of the nineteenth century a controversy existed between two groups of people concerned with perceptual phenomena and their origins. This controversy divided interested parties into two groups:

1. Those who believed perceptual phenomena were innately given as parts of our physiological apparatus
2. Those who believed that past experiences were crucial in determining how we see the world around us

Helmholtz belonged to this latter group, for his unconscious inferences depended upon the person's past experiences with objects. Gestalt psychologists tend to identify with the former group. The philosopher Immanuel Kant sided with those who believed in the innately given characteristics of perception, whereas the British Associationists stressed the acquired characteristics of perception (see pp. 212–213). It was in this medium of controversy that Gestalt psychology arose as a movement in psychological theory. In essence, Gestalt psychologists believe that perception is determined jointly by the nature of the stimuli falling upon the receptors and the innate organization of the nervous system. They hold that the proper study of perception involves strong dependence upon phenomenology, by which they mean the study of a person's own sensations. Because of their interests, they were drawn to consideration of erroneous perceptions, or illusions.

What is an illusion? Probably no experience exactly copies reality. All our perceptions are illusory to some extent. Because

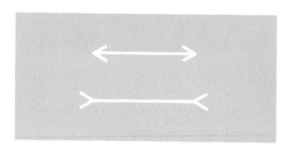

FIG. 5.6. *The Müller-Lyer illusion.*

of this we cannot usefully employ the term, *veridical perception: No perception is an entirely faithful representation of objects or qualities found in our environment.* Philosophers have struggled with many different approaches to the nature of truth and what a true perception might be. Despite the lack of a philosophic solution to the general problems of truth and falsity, we must recognize the fact that there exist a number of prominent examples of stimulus patterns which initiate perceptual activities which deviate from what we accept as appropriate perceptions.

Visual illusions The well-known Müller-Lyer illusion is reproduced in Fig. 5.6. The two horizontal lines are the same length, although the one on the right in the figure clearly seems to be longer. What is it about the two forms which causes the difference in the perception of length? Gestalt psychologists have pointed out, most forcefully, that our perceptions are a great deal more than any retinal figure could be. For example, we can perceive three dimensional figures even though the retinal image cannot be more than two dimensional.

One of the illusions presented in Fig. 5.7 is more aptly described as an ambiguous figure. This is the famous vase-profile form, and it is possible to see either two faces opposing one another or a vase. What determines which figure will be seen? The perception divides itself into two categories: figure and ground. The drawing will appear as a vase when the white portion acts as figure and as two faces when the black is figural. Generally speaking, ground serves as the backdrop for figures.

The figure in a figure-ground relationship always seems to have the quality of a unitary perception. This ability to separate the sensory world into figure and ground does not seem to depend upon past experience. Such figure and ground perception is found both in rats reared in darkness and in human patients following the removal of cataracts. In other words it seems to be primitive and independent of early experiences both in man [2] and the rat [3]. *In general, Gestalt psychologists believe that the illusory experiences occurring when the geometrical designs of Figs. 5.7 and 5.8 are observed are the result of the innate structure of the nervous system.* It is on this point that controversy exists. Other psychologists believe that most perceptions depend upon early sensory experiences and learning.

It is perhaps too easy to identify the Gestalt movement with the study of optical illusions. Gestalt psychologists are active experimentalists and, as is often profitable in research, have moved the study of illusions into the laboratory. Through

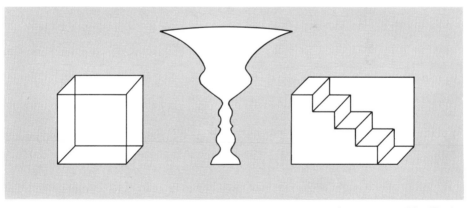

FIG. 5.7. *Examples of reversible illusion.*

laboratory experiments the scientist is often able to isolate relationships between the variables under study. Some Gestalt psychologists use geometric patterns to isolate more easily the characteristics of stimulus patterns which affect our perceptions. It must be remembered that Gestalt psychologists are interested in explaining normal adult perception and use the study of illusory or abnormal perceptions as one approach to that end.

Two products emerged from the Gestalt studies of perception: a set of laws which described the perceptual experiences occurring as a result of specified stimulus conditions and an explanation of the ways in which perception occurred.

Laws of perception As many as 114 laws have been reported to have been formulated by Gestalt psychologists from their studies of perception [4], although this list has been abbreviated by some authors, and there are many interpretations of them. Probably the most comprehensive is the law of Prägnanz. This principle is simply that perceptual figures tend toward the "best figure" possible. This is a law of "good form."

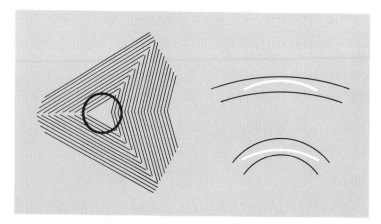

FIG. **5.8.** *Examples of apparent distortion of figures by their surroundings.*

According to one of the leading exponents of Gestalt psychology, Kurt Koffka, the law of Prägnanz "can briefly be formulated like this: psychological organization will always be as 'good' as the prevailing conditions allow. In this definition the term 'good' is undefined. It embraces such properties as regularity, symmetry, simplicity and others" [5, p. 110].

Of course this law hinges upon the definition of good form. Koffka leads us to believe that the more regular, symmetrical, and simple the form is, the better it is. If this is understandable, we can now subsume a number of other Gestalt laws under it. For example, the principle of closure, one of the more widely accepted Gestalt laws, says that if a figure is presented which has an open area or gap in its boundary the observer will tend to perceive the figure with a closed boundary, *other forces permitting*. In other words, if we present a triangle with a portion of one side missing, and if the exposure is brief enough so that the forces aroused by the missing portion are not too great, then the observer will tend to see a completed triangle. By presenting the stimulus only briefly we do not allow the observer to make the gap figural—or in Koffka's terms to arouse *other forces*. Another way to exhibit the closure of the boundary of the triangle would be to present the stimulus so that the open portion of the triangle falls on the blind spot of the eye. As we have learned in the preceding chapter, no receptor cells exist in the blind spot of the eye, and so information reaching the brain would provide information about all of the triangle *except the area of the gap*. No information at all would be sent to the brain about the area of the gap. Under these conditions—perception should be in accord with the closure principle and the perception should be of a closed triangular figure.

As with many of the Gestalt laws, the principle of closure is often used in contexts somewhat removed from direct sensory or perceptual realms. For example, some might say that the reason a mystery story holds our attention is because we have been given parts of a *verbal figure* but the parts have not been assembled into a *good figure* until the end. Thus, forces are instituted toward closure (or good form), and these remain active until the author closes the figure for us.

Gestalt theory was appealing because it could be applied to many diverse phenomena. Such terms as *closure* and *Gestalt* are useful descriptive terms, but they are also vague and general. There is no doubt that the phenomena described by the Gestalt psychologists are observable and that the perceptual behaviors they describe do happen. However, the existence of the perceptions and related behaviors does not mean that the Gestalt explanations of them must be accepted. The laws developed by Gestalt psychologists may best be considered as labels for descriptions of these perceptual and response tendencies in man. They do not explain *why* these tendencies are exhibited. In this sense these laws are similar to the word *instinct,* which is a label for certain kinds of unlearned reactions (see pp. 78–82). Having stressed the more general view of Gestalt psychology— that our perceptions are unlearned reactions which depend upon the innate organization of the sensory and nervous systems and the sensory patterns presented to the observer—we shall discuss the innate properties of the nervous system which are assumed by Gestalt psychologists to account for our perceptions.

The principle of isomorphism Gestalt psychologists seek explanations of perceptual experience in terms of physiological activities in the central nervous system. Their basic principle is that for every perception there is a corresponding physiological activity in the brain which is *isomorphic* to the mental experience. (The mathematical relation of isomorphism is that two figures are isomorphic if the points of which they are comprised are connected in the same way. If we were to draw a figure of a triangle on a piece of elastic material, like rubber, then no matter how we distort the rubber surface, the connections between the adjacent portions of the figure are always the same. Each new figure created by distorting the rubber surface is isomorphic to the original triangle and to other figures produced by distortion of the figure.) This principle asserts that when we perceive a triangle, there exists in the brain a physiological representation of a triangle which maintains certain aspects of triangularity. What kind of triangularity could exist in the brain, where the neocortex is a highly convoluted mass of cells? Almost every single portion of its surface area is curved. A perception of a flat triangle could not depend on the existence of a flat triangular form on the surface of the brain. Nonetheless, the Gestalt principle of isomorphism asserts that in the brain there must be a form of physiological excitation which maintains "triangularity" in order for the related perception to occur.

In effect, the Gestalt view holds that when a pattern of excitation on the retina is transmitted to the brain, a form is produced in the visual projection area of the brain which is isomorphic to the retinal image. Our visual perception of any geometric form is based upon the presence of a form of physiological activities in the visual projection areas of the brain.

In the Gestalt theory the form existing in the brain is in part determined by the form of activity transmitted to the brain from the receptors, but it is also determined by the structure of the brain itself. The "form" existing in the brain is a pattern of excitation in the electrical fields provided by the brain tissue. This brain form is influenced by electrical forces existing in adjacent brain areas. For example, in the Müller-Lyer illusion (Fig. 5.6) the fact that one horizontal line appears longer than the other is explained on the basis that the forms of excitation in the visual area of the brain corresponding to the horizontal lines in the stimulus are in fact different lengths. The form corresponding to the perceived longer line is longer than the form corresponding to the perceived shorter line. The field effects produced by the different types of lines at the end of the two longer lines influence the electrical brain fields of the two forms in different ways. The arrowlike endings act to shorten the figure in the brain fields, whereas the inverted arrow endings act to stretch out the electrical fields. Thus, the ends of the stimulus patterns have actually altered the *physiological forms.* The explanation is based upon electrical phenomena which would occur in any similarly constituted electrical field. Thus, the Gestalt movement explains perception on the basis of the physical characteristics of forms found in electrical fields in the brain. Our perceptions correspond to the final electrical form in the brain, according to the Gestalt view.

CRITICISM OF ISOMORPHISM. If we were to accept the principle of isomorphism and the corresponding belief that perception is some way related to the electrical form existing in the visual areas of the brain, would this be enough to explain perception? One thing we must avoid is a theory which only provides us with a display in the visual area which then must be observed by a "little man in the head." Thus far Gestalt psychology would have us assume that figures in the world are transmitted to the visual areas, and sometimes the transmitted figure is distorted because of the nature of the material in the brain and activity in other areas. But, what then? We must have some theory to explain how these physiological forms are capable of instigating behavior, and some theory by which these brain forms are translated into awareness to account for the mental experiences of perception. One of the serious problems which exist for the Gestalt theories of psychology is that these next links in the theoretical chain leading to behavior have not been forged. Whatever else, we must have a theory which gets us further than the existence of a television-like projection of images to the brain's visual cortex.

There are other bases for doubt about the usefulness of the principle of isomorphism. These center on the results of studies of the nervous system. First, the size of the visual projection area which receives fibers from the foveal area of the retina greatly exceeds the size of the visual projection area receiving fibers from the rest of the retina. Shouldn't this produce a considerable amount of perceptual distortion? Yet, our visual experiences do not seem distorted in this way. We do not see portions of figures in the center of our visual fields larger than other portions falling more on the periphery of the retina.

A second type of observation which casts doubt upon the isomorphism principle is represented by studies which create electrical or physiological disturbances of the brain tissue in the visual projection areas. It has been pointed out that tumors and accidents of brain pathology in the visual areas do not produce the expected disturbances of perception. In one study gold foil, an excellent electrical conductor, placed across the visual projection areas of a chimpanzee trained in a visual discrimination problem did not interfere with the animal's behavior in a visual task. The gold foil was placed so as to disturb any *forms* which might exist in the electrical fields of the visual brain areas [6]. Gold pins inserted in the visual projection area of another animal did not interfere with the animal's responses in the same task. These examples make it difficult to assume that the integrity of a form of electrical activity in a sensory projection area is essential to perception.

HEBB'S THEORY OF PERCEPTION In 1949, a book by D. O. Hebb of McGill University [7] was published which has had a great influence upon certain areas of psychology. For some time previously Hebb had studied the development of perception, and his findings led him to formulate a general theory of behavior based in large part on perceptual phenomena. In Hebb's theory sensory information becomes perception. Hebb's theory is not the kind of associationistic theory against which Gestalt psychology reacted. Gestalt psychology objected to psychologies which accounted for behavior through the then current principles of association. Gestalt psychologists argued that the form of the electrical activity in the brain was responsible for perception. In their view past associations did not affect perception directly, although they could influence our interpretation of a perception. Perception, *per se,* was not influenced by experience.

From the start it should be recognized that Hebb's proposals are tentative. However, even in this form they represent one of the most thought provoking contributions yet made to behavioral theory: explanations for phenomena in the areas of learning, perception, emotion, motivation, and even abnormal psychology. The most essential of all the assumptions made by Hebb is one concerning growth processes occurring at the synapse between two neurons. This assumption, in turn, is intimately related to certain postulates about the anatomical organization of the nervous system.

Reverberatory loops   The nervous system can be considered to be a collection of individual nerve cells whose basic physiological properties we have discussed before (Chapter 3). Their arrangement is such that one can find loops of several cells through which excitation may travel around and around. It can be likened to a parking lot with so few spaces that the cars may travel around it several times before they obtain a space. Within the neural loop the firing of cell A would excite cell B and it in turn would excite cell C. Cell C then would activate cell A once again. A highly schematic loop arrangement of neurons is presented in Fig. 5.9. These loops of cells could hold recurrent

FIG. 5.9. *Hypothetical arrangement of neurons which would underlie prolonged reverberatory activity. Neurons would fire in numerical sequence; i.e., neuron (1,4) fires first and again in fourth position. This multiple-path arrangement would "hold" activity for longer periods than simple closed loops of neurons. Adapted from D. O. Hebb.* The Organization of Behavior. *New York: John Wiley & Sons, Inc., 1949.*

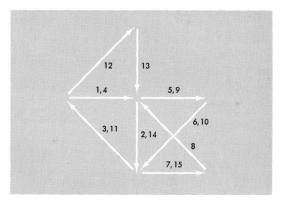

activities, although they would not continue their firing forever. These circular arrangements which would permit impulses to go around in them for some time after the stimulation originating the activity has ceased are *reverberatory circuits* or *holding mechanisms* [8].

The reverberatory circuits *could* provide the physiological basis of memories. If a loop arrangement like this were activated by a specific type of sensory input, then the reverberatory activity in the loop could represent a kind of memory for the input that originally started the activity. However, it is likely that activity in such closed loops would be disrupted after a short time. Therefore, it would provide a neural basis only for relatively recent memories and not what we might call permanent memories. The actual reverberations of the holding mechanisms might only last for a matter of minutes even under the most ideal conditions. *Yet, one might use these reverberating systems as the basis for developing other changes representing the physiological underpinings of more permanent memories.*

The growth principle   Given the assumption of the holding mechanisms, we now state the major assumption of the theory: "When an axon of cell A is near enough to excite cell B and repeatedly or persistently takes part in firing it, some growth process or metabolic change takes place in one or both cells such that A's efficiency, as one of the cells firing B, is increased" [7, p. 62].

There are many ways in which a growth process like this could take place. For instance, the axon of A might grow closer, physically, to the cell body of B. The end feet on the axon of cell A could enlarge and cover more of B's surface; and there is the possibility that the release of the chemical transmitter substances from the end feet of A might become more efficient. Despite the fact there is very little evidence for any one of these assumptions today, they are not unreasonable; and most people are willing to concede there must be some permanent changes in the nervous system which correspond to long term, or permanent, memories. Remember that Hebb does not say that these must be the mechanisms involved. He only says that as a function of reverberation cell A has greater control of the firing of cell B.

Cell assembly   With these assumptions we are able to progress to the functional organization of the brain proposed by Hebb. Most of our discussion will center about the visual system, but we hope that the conclusions based on analyses of the visual system will be general and apply to other sensory systems as well.

All neocortical areas of the brain have been numbered. These numbers are labels given to the areas on the basis of their structure, function, and origins in development. There are four important numbered visual areas: 17, 18, 19, and 20 (see Chapter 3, p. 102). In man all of the visual fibers which reach the neocortex come into area 17. From area 17 impulses are relayed to areas 18, 19, and 20.

As we have learned, neurons of the brain and central nervous system have a remarkable number of interconnections with other cells. Each neuron is probably connected with hundreds, if not thousands, of cells. Any input which fires a given cell in area 17 must effect the firing of many other cells in the other visual areas and, indirectly, cells in many other brain regions. Probably, the preponderant effect is a fanning-out from the original and rather restricted region of excitation in area 17 to other regions of brain; and for any *pattern* of cells activated in area 17 specific neurons in many areas of the brain would be activated. Any group of cells indirectly excited by any particular pattern of excitation arising in area 17 could form a loop capable of maintaining reverberatory activity over a period of time. The types of cells in the loops would vary. Some would be cells which receive information from other sensory systems, some neurons which interconnect with other cortical or subcortical cells, other cells whose axons descend to motor cells in the spinal cord. The inclusion of motor cells in these reverberatory loops is important because it provides a basis for the incorporation of motor activities in perceptual learning.

As a loop of cells is activated repeatedly by identical patterns of activity in area 17, the neurons comprising the loop will become bonded together. This follows from application of our growth principle. After repeated arousal of the same pattern in area 17, the whole group of loop neurons may be so completely tied together that it functions as a unit. If any portion of the loop is activated, activity in every cell of the loop will follow. These reverberatory loops are the units of perception. They take time to form. Each loop must be activated many many times before the growth occurring between the neurons bonds them together permanently. When the connections between neurons of a reverberatory loop have become established to the extent that activity in one portion of the loop is sure to trigger reactions throughout the loop, we can consider that the loop of neurons constitutes what Hebb calls a *cell assembly,* the basic building block of all perception.

PERCEPTUAL DEVELOPMENT A collection of reports dealing with patients who were born blind [2] is quite relevant to Hebb's theory. These patients were born with congenital cataracts, a clouding of the lens of the eye. Through surgical removal of the lens the eye can function adequately when appropriate glasses are used. Thus vision is restored. When tested postoperatively these patients could distinguish between certain forms, i.e., between a square and a circle. They seemed to do this by searching for corners, which seemed to be focal points for them. They could also distinguish between figure and ground and were able to distinguish colors. However, while the patients responded quickly and directly to different forms, the patterns did not seem to have a consistent *identity*. They could name a given form (triangle, square, etc.) only after a great deal of experience with it.

It is difficult for us to imagine the difference in the perceptual abilities required to distinguish a triangle from a square and the ability to recognize a triangle *as a triangle*. Yet the patients born with congenital cataracts could not identify a triangle *as a triangle* when it was presented differently or from different angles. This ability to recognize the identity of an object took a considerable period of time to develop even though they did have the ability to distinguish between the forms.

One other observation reported by Senden needs to be emphasized, namely the role of eye movements in learning the figure identity. When presented with a visual form some patients learned to respond "triangle" only when they could count the corners and reach a total of three. After practice, eye movements followed the corners in the same way as a finger had been used earlier to pick out the corners. The counting of corners still occurred, but in a less observable way. After months of practice, some patients reached a stage where they could identify the figure at a glance.

These data suggest that adult perception, as we usually think of it, is based upon a vast amount of experience. The recognition of patterns does not seem to be the immediate and innate reaction which is postulated by the Gestalt psychologists.

Early and later perceptual learning In Hebb's theory the development of perception can be categorized into early and later stages. Normal infants and patients like those born with congenital cataracts are in the early learning stages. They have adequate visual mechanisms but the neural impulses arising from the visual receptors must be integrated into meaningful units before perception, as we know it, can occur.

In the early perceptual stage the individuals are developing cell assemblies for vision. What sort of stimulus patterns would be first incorporated into these cell assemblies? Hebb assumes that most of our early perceptual learning involves the development of cell assemblies which represent "lines and corners." There must be a special cell assembly developed for each of many types of corners and lines. The number of perceptual units, or cell assemblies, needed to build the adult perceptual world must be staggering. Just how many types of different cell assemblies must be formed is beyond estimate, but however many there are, they represent the building blocks for all perception. For our purpose cell assemblies can be considered as groups of cells which have been cemented into a functional unit by the growth principle. The various cells of each group may be widely scattered throughout the brain.

The phase sequence   According to Hebb's position, forms like a triangle *would be a complex perceptual entity,* which becomes recognizable only after cell assemblies for the respective

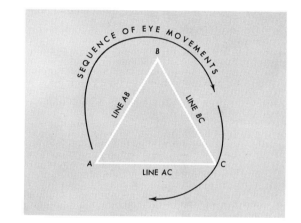

FIG. 5.10   *Triangle (ABC) and the sequence of eye movements which might be produced by observer viewing it. Eyes first fixate angle at A; then progress along the line AB to angle C; etc.*

angles and lines, as well as the relations between them, have been formed.

Phase sequences are defined as particular orders of cell assemblies and eye movements. Consider the triangle *ABC* in Fig. 5.10. When a person centers his visual attention at *A,* a cell assembly *a* is presumed to be activated in the brain. Then, this point of fixation of the eyes is altered and the eyes move to the line *AB,* and a corresponding cell assembly *ab* is activated. The points of fixation progress from corner to line; line to corner, etc., around the triangle. Each point of fixation elicits the cell assembly which has developed from past experiences with similar corners and lines. The eye movements which bring about a change in visual fixations are important, too, for the sensory feedback from them, may act as neural units themselves, in the development of the neural counterpart of the perceived triangle.

The figures of our perceptual world are built from the cell assemblies, and are represented in Hebb's theory by their order and interconnecting eye movements. Thus, the triangle in Fig. 5.10 would be encoded as an order of cell assemblies and eye movements which might be: corner *a,* eye movement$_1$, line *ab,* movement$_2$, corner *b,* movement$_3$, line *bc,* movement$_4$, corner *c,* movement$_5$, line *ca.* This sequence would represent the *phase sequence* or perception of the figure triangle. Perception of a triangle would differ from perception of a square in both the types of cell assemblies and interconnecting eye movements. Triangles of all sorts would be similar in some types of corner cell assemblies and in some types of eye movements. Categories of perception, e.g., "triangle," "square," are created by the occurrence of similar perceptual elements.

Once again, it is through repeated experiences that cell assemblies and eye movements become connected into other and more elaborate perceptual units. With experience, synaptic growth occurs between the neurons of the units involved in the cell assemblies and eye movements. After repeated exposure to a triangle, a certain facilitation develops between the cell assemblies initiated by the sensory activities. It becomes easier for cell assembly *a* to instigate the subsequent eye movement, and for the eye movement, to instigate arousal of cell assembly *ab,* and so on. The occurrence of cell assembly *a* readies, prepares, or *sets* us to make the next movement and perceive the next cell assembly in the phase sequence. Ultimately, sufficient growth occurs among the clusters of neurons to allow a *short circuiting* of the cell assembly chain. When this happens a triangle can be identified before all cell assemblies and eye movements of the figure have been triggered by sensory input.

In summary: A phase sequence is the collection of cell assemblies and related eye movements which, through experience, have developed a mutual interfacilitation. Sensory information which initiates activity in any part of a phase sequence results in the facilitation of the subsequent arousal of all parts. The perception of a figure as an entity first depends upon the firing of all the elements of the phase sequence by the appropriate sensory stimulation. After further perceptual learning, however, it may be possible for a part of the phase sequence to exert strong enough facilitating effects to trigger the other units. This represents a functional short circuiting of the phase sequence. Even beyond this, however, it is possible to postulate a neural counterpart to what we think of as *perceptual classes* of stimuli.

The superordinate phase sequence   After we learn to perceive objects through phase sequences, we can develop a neural shorthand for the figure. In Hebb's theory this is a *superordinate phase sequence* and results from the development of a new cell assembly which stands for the whole complex figure. This is represented in a schematic order of cell assemblies as t.

Going back to our triangle example, we can diagram the perception of the triangle

$$a - ab - b - bc - c - ca -$$
$$\begin{array}{ccc} \backslash \;/ & \backslash \;/ & \backslash \;/ \\ m_1 & m_2 & m_3 \end{array}$$

When the whole triangle is identified as an entity, without demonstration of all the eye movements and all the fixations of eye movements at the corners of the figure, Hebb assumes that the phase sequence itself has built a new cell assembly, t.

$$a - ab - b - t - bc - t - c \qquad \text{and so on}$$
$$\begin{array}{cc} \backslash \;/ & \backslash \;|\;/ \\ m_1 & m_2 \end{array}$$

According to the theory, we would recognize specific figures when a cell assembly t has been formed which acts as a label for the whole complex. When t is activated, we experience the triangle *as a figure* which can be identified, labeled, and manipulated as an entity in itself. Due to the growth assumption it becomes easier and easier for any of the cell assemblies of the complex to elicit t, and unless there is competing sensory input we would expect the occurrence of any constituent cell assembly to lead to t. Thus if an incomplete triangle was being viewed, and the incomplete portion fell on the blind spot, we would expect to see a whole triangle. No sensory input at all comes from the blind spot. If the incomplete triangle falls on the retina so that the gap is on a normal portion of the retina, then this gap would be perceived because receptors are activated which send conflicting information to the brain. In general, we would expect a facilitation for those perceptual complexes, or configurations, that have occurred most frequently in the past. This facilitation is due to the growth processes between the cell assemblies involved in each pattern in theory. This is in contrast to the Gestalt position which postulates that closure, or the tendency for figures to be seen as completed forms, results from the structure of the nervous system. Hebb's theory explains closure on the basis of inter-neuronal growth, taking place at the synapse and depending upon the prior sensory experiences of the organism.

Acting like one of the cell assemblies in the phase sequence, the superordinate phase sequence unit, *t,* can facilitate the occurrence of the other members. Thus, no matter how *t* is initiated, the cell assemblies and movements comprising the entire phase sequence would be easy to instigate through this facilitation. Therefore, we might expect that a subject might give evidence of the eye movements normally involved in look-ing at a triangle when merely told "to think of a triangle."

Motor movements and phase sequences The cells involved in the loops of which cell assemblies are composed contain some cells which control motor movements primarily. When cell assemblies and phase sequences are acquired, these moto-neurons are incorporated; perhaps even large packages of motoneurons become parts of phase sequences. From the be-ginning, movements are an integral part of perceptual develop-ment. In Hebb's theory movements develop along with per-ception and in accordance with the neuronal growth principle which underlies the entire theory. As a consequence, no little man in the head is needed to explain our responses to stimulus patterns, and no isomorphic figure of electrical activity in the visual cortex is required. The motor and cognitive aspects of perception are both natural consequences of Hebb's assump-tions about neural activities and may be thought of as a pos-sible neural basis for the phenomenon of *set.*

Perceptual Readiness, or Set

One of the most common observations made about perceptual experiences is that we tend to perceive what we expect to see. This phenomena is often ascribed to the effect of *set.* The word *set* can be used almost interchangeably with words like *expectancy* or *readiness* and refers to a disposition to perceive a certain type of stimulus in a given situation at a particular time. Outside of a perceptual framework the word *set* can be used to describe a disposition to respond in a particular way.

For example, when a sprinter on a track team is given a ready signal ahead of the starting gun, he is able to leave his position faster than if he were not given this preparatory signal. Often it is possible to observe the physical and physiological aspects of motor sets, but it is more difficult to observe preparatory sets for perceptual events. Nonetheless, there is little doubt that preparatory perceptual sets do exist and are influential in determining our perceptual experiences.

Perceptual sets may be established by the context or past experiences in a situation, by the instructions to the perceptual task, and by the general strategies we use to deal with perceptual tasks.

SITUATIONAL EFFECTS   As an example of how the situation, itself, can operate to affect perception, consider the not improbable situation of being alone in a house at night. You pick a book to read, a ghost story. You get along into the book and become absorbed in the narrative. All of a sudden you see a figure on a wall or in the next room. A ghost! Whatever the stimulus might be in reality, for instance, the light from a passing car, you are *set* by the story and the circumstances to perceive a ghost. Walking at night through a cemetery while taking a shortcut home is another very good way to establish a preparatory perceptual set.

Yet the environment can prepare us for certain types of sensory experiences in a more subtle fashion. In one experiment students were engaged in what they thought was merely an attempt to determine their thresholds for a tone of 1000 cycles per second [9]. The method of constant stimuli was used in which the tone was presented at different intensities in intervals marked off by flashing lights. Some of the tone intensities were so low that none of the subjects reported hearing them, while others were so high that all subjects indicated their presence perfectly. Most of the tone intensities presented fell between these limits. The subjects were told to report *any sound at all,* and were warned that tones which are just barely audible often seem to be of different frequencies. During the course of the experiment, the experimenters occasionally substituted tones of different frequencies for the 1000 cycles per second tone. Very few subjects reported the latter tones although they were presented at usually audible intensities. Even after the experiment, the subjects had a difficult time hearing the other relatively loud tones. For example, at the conclusion of the experiment, the experimenters would turn on one of the loud tones of a different frequency which had been intruded into the 1000 cycles per second tone series and ask the subjects if they heard anything. About half the subjects heard it immediately, but the other half would not hear it until the experimenter explicitly called their attention to the tone by humming at a frequency near the 1000 cps and then "sliding" the hum to one near the different tone. When the subjects finally heard it, it appeared suddenly. Some often would claim the experimenters had just then turned it on, because it sounded so loud that they could not understand why they had not heard it before.

This experiment can be interpreted in terms of a set which was established by the sequence of 1000 cycles per second tones. When tones which were divergent from this target frequency were presented, the subjects could detect them only poorly. At times the cue tones were higher than the subsequent tones; at times they were lower. Thus the effect of the cue tone was due to the informational value of the tone.

The establishment of preparatory sets for stimuli in different frequency ranges by signals (cue tones) which indicated whether the next stimulus to be presented would be high or low has been studied [10]. The cue tones enable subjects to recognize subsequent tones better than when they are not presented.

We can look at the phenomena of perceptual set as a preparation for certain categories of stimulation: With our ghost story example we might say that the reader was prepared for the appearance of ghostlike stimuli, weird and bizarre figures. When a set was established on the basis of a sequence of 1000 cps tones or by a cue tone, we might say that the subjects were prepared for auditory stimuli in a narrow frequency range.

Many methods can be used to make one or another perceptual event most likely in any situation. Information which limits the perceptual possibilities which are likely to occur aids us in perception. The important question is, however, just how sets or information about likely perceptions act to make perception easier. In Hebb's theory we could explain this by assuming preparatory sets facilitate certain phase sequences. This partial facilitation means that less sensory input is required to initiate the activation of the entire phase sequence and, in the theory, the associated perception.

PERCEPTION AND CLASSIFICATION Some psychologists most actively concerned with understanding perceptual processes propose that we consider the process of perception as the organization of stimuli into *classes*. To these psychologists the sensory information provides us with a basis for discrimination, but this basic process of discrimination must be elaborated in the central nervous system to place these activities into classes or categories.

What do we mean when we say we perceive an apple? We usually mean that we have assigned certain sensory signals transmitting information about forms, colors, sizes, textures, and so on, to a class of objects labeled *apples*. The establishment of such classes is usually accomplished relatively early in life, but not without difficulties. Confusion among such classes as oranges, balls, and wax apples, probably takes a considerable number of years to resolve.

The basis for the establishment of perceptual classes is the effect of this classification upon the internal and external environment. We learn the perceptual classes used by our parents, friends, and playmates, because of rewards, social approval, and the ability to respond adaptively to our environment. If the effects of our perceptual classifications are not satisfactory, then reclassifications can be made, and our perceptual categories are shaped by their effects. The most fruitful ones in terms of their practical benefits and their ability to anticipate the results of dealing with objects in the class (reducing surprises) are retained.

Every perception is assigned to a large number of classes. Stimuli are assigned to *object* classes, e.g., apples, chairs, John Jones. This assignment we can call identification and labeling. However, stimuli are also categorized as good-bad, light-heavy, hard-soft and so forth. Perception depends upon a classification of the stimulus input and the related judgments of the attributes of the object class: goodness, heaviness, uses, etc.

Psychologists who hold to the view that perception can be represented by a process of categorization of stimuli, are saying that perception is the result of decisions about the categories to which a stimulus should be assigned. For them, perception is an act of judgment, and they follow in the footsteps of Helmholtz's principle of unconscious inference. The original statement of this principle was attacked on the grounds that perception was instantaneous and did not require an interval of time for inference to occur. However, with the development of Hebb's theory of perception we have a hypothetical mechanism whereby the classification (inference) could be almost instantaneous. The sensory input is classified by the nature of the phase sequences which were elicited by the particular pattern of excitation coming in from the receptors. These phase sequences in turn facilitate other, related phase sequences which could represent further classes of evaluation, i.e., goodness, heaviness, etc. The neural basis of classification could be found in something like the mechanisms proposed by Hebb. One advantage of using Hebb's concepts of cell assemblies and phase sequences as the neural basis for perceptual classification is that we tend to avoid the assumption of a little man in the head who classifies and makes inferences from these classifications.

CLASSIFICATION AND RESPONSE   Considering our earlier discussion of the effects of set upon perception, we can now rephrase the matter by use of the general concepts of perceptual classification. We could speak of set as a bias on the part of the person to expect certain classes of input. In a grocery store we are prepared to use our perceptual category for *apple.* The grocery store environment facilitates the phase sequences of all grocery store products. When we enter a toy store, we are prepared for classifications like that of *ball,* as a result of corresponding facilitation of phase sequences related to toys. After reading a ghost story, we are prepared for classification of stimuli into categories of a more terrifying nature.

This way of talking about set allows us to say that the individual and situational variables which determine perceptual sets do so by preselecting categories of classification. If the stimuli which are presented actually do fit into the preselected perceptual categories then perceptual recognition will be more rapid than if preselection were not made. On the other hand the preselection of categories will hinder proper recognition of an external stimulus if it does *not* appropriately belong to the preset categories. That is, in a grocery store a small red object will be perceived easily and quickly as an apple. However, if a boy's red ball becomes mixed up with the apples in the store we may not recognize the discrepancy between apple and ball until discrepancies in weight or texture make the distinction imperative. Generally speaking, the selection of prior categories as ones likely to be useful in a given situation will be reflected in greater facility in making responses suitable to the preselected categories.

PERCEPTION UNDER UNCERTAIN STIMULUS CONDITIONS   In a normal adult with sufficient time and opportunity a ball and an apple are correctly placed into different perceptual categories. Confusion between balls and apples will only occur when we are disposed toward the perception of one or the other and when the sensory information is less than complete, for example when we only glance at the object for a moment. Greater attention to the stimulus input resolves the confusion. Yet, some of the most fruitful techniques found in the study

FIG. 5.11.   *An ambiguous figure which can be seen as a pretty woman or an ugly one. The observer's "set" helps determine which profile will be seen. From E. G. Boring. A new ambiguous figure.* Amer. J. Psychol., *1930, 40, 444.*

of perception use stimulating conditions in which it is *impossible* to determine the exact nature of the physical stimulus. Several techniques are used by psychologists in situations purposely designed to introduce uncertainty in perception, i.e., to prevent absolute identification (classification) of the stimulus.

Ambiguous figures   In our earlier discussion of illusions we discussed the famous figure which can be interpreted as two faces or a vase (Fig. 5.7). This is typical of ambiguous figures: there is no single response which occurs when the figure is observed. In another example the figure can be seen as either a pretty or a horrible-looking woman, depending on the prior instructions given to the observer (Fig. 5.11). If a set for beautiful women is established, the more attractive profile is more often seen. Whereas if a set to perceive "your mother-in-law" is established, the alternative form is readily observed. Many kinds of ambiguous stimuli exist. They range from pictures which are interpreted by observers in many different ways to the ink blots used in personality tests.

Impoverished stimuli It is possible to reduce the clarity or details of a stimulus to the extent that responses to it become variable. Stimulus objects can be placed behind cloudy glass to give the object a hazy and indefinite appearance, they can be poorly illuminated, or they can be placed at a great distance from the subject. Probably the most common technique presents the stimulus to the observer for only a very brief time. Instruments which present stimuli for short durations at specified degrees of illumination are called *tachistoscopes*. With a tachistoscope the duration of exposure can be systematically varied so that a threshold (expressed in the length of time the stimulus is presented for viewing) can be determined by use of traditional psychophysical methods.

The effect of uncertain stimuli upon the perceiver is that the stimuli lose properties which usually allow the perceiver precise categorization of them. Therefore, these techniques can be used to force a subject to make judgments which reflect his preselected categories of perception. These preselected categories may reveal interesting qualities of the person making the observations. They could reveal information about the frequencies with which such categories are used by the person and information about his interests, attitudes, values, and motives. Looking at the problem another way, we might say that values and motives affect the perceptual categories used by the observer. Whether or not values and motives directly affect perception is still a hotly debated issue in psychology. No one questions that attitudes, values, and motives may affect the responses made to stimuli or the interpretations given perceptual phenomena. The central issue is whether we should assume that the *mental experience of the perception* can be influenced by nonperceptual variables like attitudes and motives.

THE CORE–CONTEXT ARGUMENT Many psychologists believe that the mental experiences of perception are determined solely by the sensory information. It has been argued that we should distinguish between a *visual field* and a *visual world*.

The visual field would be the composite of sensory impressions occurring at any moment, whereas the visual world would be the world of objects and things. The visual world would be created with the help of the experiences of the person, whereas the visual field would be independent of these influences. Others who support a similar distinction have argued that we should distinguish between pure stimulus processes initiated by receptor activity and the result of these pure stimulus processes interacting with memory traces of earlier perceptions, which would create something like a visual world.

Pure sensory processes, or visual fields, represent the sensory core upon which all perception is built. This core is determined only by receptor activities and the structure of the nervous system. The context, or visual world, surrounding the sensory core refers to the meaning we have attached to the components of the core. The accretions to the sensory bases of perception which we call meaning are the learned reactions deriving from our individual experiences. But in the core–context theories these only influence the outer context of perception. The central sensory core of perception remains fundamental.

In contrast, psychologists who suggest that our perceptions are really the product of almost instantaneous classifications reject the primitive and unassailable sensory core. For them our perceptions are entirely formed by the classifications which we make. This issue is lively and not likely to be resolved for some period of time. The question is which one will be the most fruitful approach? Will we be better able to understand perceptual activities if we consider them to be elaborations of a central and innate sensory core, an edifice built by experience around a base provided innately by our receptor systems? Or will it be more profitable to conceive of perception as the product of learned classification of stimulus inputs? Sooner or later, after more data and knowledge are acquired, the view which will lead us further toward understanding perception in all of its many aspects will prevail. But for now we have to be patient and explore.

General Factors Influencing Perception

Psychologists often tend to talk of visual perception, auditory perception, tactual perceptions, and so forth, as if they exist independently of one another. This fractionation of the study of perception is founded on the belief that it is possible to advance our understanding of the complex of perception fastest by the isolated study of various components of perception in the laboratory. Yet in everyday life our visual perceptions occur against an active background of auditory, tactual, and other perceptual activities. Furthermore, since perception can be influenced by the perceptual set or readiness of the individual, we must consider these effects when moving from the isolated study of one kind of perception to understanding the perception of the active individual in his busy life. If attitudes, values, motives, or even language can influence our perceptions, then these too must be studied. In this section we shall discuss information which has been gained about such general influences upon perception.

INTERMODALITY PERCEPTION   It sometimes happens that when a person receives certain auditory stimulation he has a perception which is best described as "visual." This is known as a form of synesthesia. For example, when a musical note is sounded, a person may "see" a color. It has been reported that one subject had relatively consistent color responses when tested over the period of several years [13]. This subject reported that the note C generally produced a red color, whereas F sharp tended to produce blue-green. Only a few people demonstrate a great amount of this "color hearing." However, most of us tend to think of certain kinds of visual images when auditory stimuli are presented and often associate certain colors with sounds. A soft brown color is more likely to be associated with soft auditory stimuli. Our language reflects an intermodality association of perceptual qualities by allowing us to use adjectives like *soft,* to describe visual, auditory and tactual sensations. Many words in our language produce perceptual responses which are similar in some way to the thing or object labeled. Many words in our language probably stem from phonetic similarity to the object portrayed: for example, *babbling* brook, *chirping* bird. Nonetheless, we should distinguish cases where certain verbal responses can be made to stimuli of different sensory systems through social convention from true synesthesia which is probably quite rare.

MOTOR EFFECTS   The effects of background sensory information can be rather subtle. The problem of just why the moon looks larger at the horizon than when above us in the sky has troubled many competent philosophers and scientists. According to one researcher it depends upon the eye muscles, which are used differently depending on the moon's position [14]. If a person rests on an inclined board to watch the zenith moon and does not have to rotate his eyes upward, then this moon appears as large as do moons on the horizon. This then is an example of how motor activities (and quite likely the sensory reports of tensions in the various eye muscles) alter visual perception without producing noticeable effects appropriate to their own sensory modality. The illusion of the moon being larger at the horizon than when directly above has been shown to be caused also by cues related to distance and size, e.g., trees and buildings, being present as the moon is viewed near the horizon [15, 16]. The importance of such cues can be easily observed. On a clear night make a fist so that you can see through a small hole and look at the moon when it is near the horizon. You will observe the moon's apparent size shrink. Looking through your legs at the moon will reduce its size, but not so much as will looking through the small hole of your fist which acts to eliminate other stimuli from around the moon.

In many studies the effects of other muscles and sensory systems upon visual perception have been demonstrated. For instance, a person's perception of a vertical line can be displaced by applying an electric shock to one side of the subject's neck or by inclining the subject to one side [17]. These results could be due to activities aroused in motor systems of the central nervous systems controlling the muscles or due to the sensory feedback to the central nervous system from the muscles and tendons. Evidence can be sighted for either view, although it is most frequently assumed that the sensory feedback aspect is of major importance. Since the effects of the muscle tonus can play such a significant role in perception, we must keep in mind that all normal perception occurs against a background of specific muscular positions and activity. Study of the motor contributions to our perceptual activities has been somewhat neglected in the last half century. Certainly it is true that the end product of successful perception is measured in the practical usefulness of action, behavior, and effective motor responses.

EFFECTS OF VALUES AND ATTITUDES We already have discussed some effects of sets on behavior and perception. Social context, one's own past experiences, and other factors can prepare us for one type of perceptual event or another. This readiness for certain perceptions, or set, prepares us for stimuli of certain categories. Now we shall find that sets may be established by still other factors.

In one experiment, in which men who had been placed under conditions designed to provide impoverished stimuli were asked to write stories, hungry men mentioned more food-related objects than did men who were not hungry [18]. Even though the stimuli were supposed to be the basis for the stories, this experiment only provides evidence of what the subjects *wrote* in their imaginative stories. The occurrence of food-related objects could be explained by the fact that the subjects were thinking about food and incorporated these thoughts into their stories. While the hungry subjects wrote about more food-related objects than nonhungry subjects, the stories of the hungry men did not include more direct references to food than did the stories of the nonhungry men. This could have occurred because the subjects were in a situation in which going without food could have been interpreted as a patriotic duty. This might have tended to suppress any direct conscious expression of food objects.

A better example of an effect of motivation upon perception was provided by an experiment (see Chapter 8) in which subjects who were evaluated high in the motive to achieve were able to recognize achievement-related words at faster speeds of presentation in a tachistoscope than subjects low in this motive [19]. This experiment would seem to suggest that perceptual changes can be determined by the motivational states of the observers. Yet one could argue that people who were evaluated high in the achievement motive would tend to respond with more achievement-related words when they could not be sure what the word was. However, this response-likelihood explanation loses some of its strength because there was no difference between subjects high and low in the achievement motive in the number of achievement-related guess responses made before recognition of the word occurred.

Earlier, Postman, Bruner, and McGinnies [20] had studied the relation between a person's values and his tachistoscopic recognition threshold for words related to these values. Subjects were given a written test which measured the relative interest a subject had in six value areas. The experimenters predicted that people with considerable interest in one value area would have a lower threshold for words related to that area than subjects with different values. In general the predictions were upheld. A person who obtained a rather high score in the area of economic values tended to have a low threshold for words like *income*.

One basic criticism of studies dealing with the relation between motives and perception is simply that people who are high in a particular motive or value area are merely more familiar with words related to these motives or values than other people. Familiarity with words, by itself, can produce lower thresholds in tachistoscopic experiments [21]. This criticism was answered in an unusual way in one experiment. The subjects in this study were selected on the basis of the amount of motivation toward affiliation. The subjects were instructed to indicate the clearest and most apparent picture out of a group of four which were presented briefly in a tachistoscope. In every group of four pictures one contained people and three contained only inanimate objects. Subjects who were high in the motive toward affiliation selected the picture containing people as clearest more than subjects low in the affiliation motive [22]. It is difficult to explain these results on the basis of a greater familiarity with faces by the group high in the affiliation motive. The problem of how an affiliation motive could enable the subjects to see a picture of a person more clearly has yet to be solved. Perhaps subjects high in the affiliation motive have some lasting readiness to classify stimuli into categories associated with people.

EFFECTS OF REWARD AND PUNISHMENT ON PERCEPTION

Motives may operate to establish sets, that is, a perceptual readiness for certain kinds of stimuli. These then affect our perceptions of the world about us. Can we establish changes in perception through application of rewards or punishment?

In one study [23] pairs of figures were presented to subjects after a training period in which one of each pair of training figures was arbitrarly chosen to elicit a reward when named by the subject and the other to elicit a punishment by the awarding or taking away of pennies. After this training, the test figures were presented and subjects were asked which figure they saw. They could respond by naming the figure for which they were either previously rewarded or previously punished. No rewards

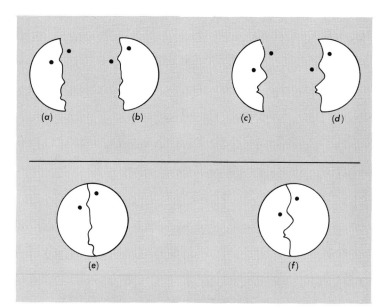

FIG. 5.12. *The figures used in the Schafer and Murphy experiment. Perception of each pair above the line was rewarded or punished; test figures appear below the line. Adapted from R. Schafer & G. Murphy. The role of autism in a visual figure-ground relationship. J. exp. Psychol., 1943, 32, 335–343.*

or punishments were given when the compound figure, which contained both the reward and punishment figures, was presented. The experimenters believed that the effects of the rewards and punishments would be to make the reward figure clearer and more readily perceived than the punishment figure in this compound figure. The reward figures tended to be perceptually selected by the subjects.

Before interpreting this experiment as a demonstration of the effects of rewards and punishments upon perception we must recognize that the subjects' verbal responses were rewarded, and that we have no information concerning whether their perceptions were altered. The results could be explained simply on the basis that one name could have become more frequently reported than another. Thus, the experiment could be interpreted solely in terms of reinforcement and punishment of a verbal response and not a change in perception. Supreme care must be exercised to determine the effects of other types of variables upon performance when attempting to measure perceptual changes. However, other experiments have demonstrated that stimuli associated with rewards tend to be seen more frequently and more clearly than those not associated with rewards [e.g., 24].

The effect of associating a figure with punishment is less clear-cut. Small amounts of punishment tend to have little if any effect upon figure selection. Where the punishment is stronger, say an electric shock of moderate unpleasantness, the figure associated with the shock is seen less well than figures which does not result in punishment. However, when a figure has been associated with a very unpleasant shock, there is some evidence to suggest that the figure becomes *better selected* by subjects [25], at least under conditions which allow the subjects to "get away from" the unpleasant stimulation. The names *perceptual defense* and *perceptual vigilance* are used to refer to behavior which indicates poorer recognition of some figures and better recognition of others due to degrees of pleasantness or unpleasantness. Often the pleasantness or unpleasantness is inferred from information about the subject's personality. In a moment we shall return to this topic which is a much-debated issue in perception today.

VALUE OF OBJECTS AND PERCEIVED SIZE People who believe in a central sensory core in perception find it difficult to imagine that rewards or punishment can directly affect the perception of figures, although the evidence continues to mount in this direction. Can such an obvious and straightforward perceptual quality as size be affected by the value of the stimulus to the observer?

One of the first experiments relating the object's value to perception was that of Bruner and Goodman in 1947 [26], and it has assumed the stature of a classical experiment in psychology. Two groups of children were asked to estimate the size of coins both when the coins were present and when they were not physically present. Two experimental groups were established on the basis of their social backgrounds. One group came from relatively poor and the other from relatively wealthy families. The subjects turned a knob to regulate the size of a circular patch of light projected on a screen in front of them. It was expected that the children from the poorer backgrounds would value the coins more than the wealthier children. If value affects perception, in this case perception of the size of coins, then the group of children from the poorer family conditions should overestimate the size of the coins. The experimental results confirm this prediction when size judgments were made with the coins present. In addition the amount of overestimation increased with the monetary value of the coin up to the half dollar. When the size of the coins was estimated only on the basis of memory (actual coins not present), the degree of overestimation of size by children from less wealthy families was less. The children from wealthier backgrounds only overestimated the quarter and half dollar.

Earlier, we discussed the necessity of controlling for the effects of familiarity in studies relating motivational variables to perception. The experiment in which individuals high in the achievement motive recognized achievement-related words more readily than individuals low in this motive could be criticized because the results could be due to the greater familiarity with achievement-related words in the group with high achievement motive. Can the results of the Bruner and Goodman experiment be explained on the basis of familiarity with coins? To do so, we would have to assume that the wealthier children had more experience with coins and their greater familiarity led them to be more accurate than the children of poorer circumstances.

While this is a possible explanation, it does not appear to account for the results of more recent experiments. In one instance subjects under hypnosis were given false biographical information to accept as their own [27]. A subject was instructed to believe he was from a poor home at one time and from a wealthy home at another time. When provided with poor backgrounds, subjects overestimated coin sizes; with rich backgrounds they underestimated the sizes. Since every person was both rich at one time and poor at another, the experiment controls for degree of experience or general familiarity with coins. Other experiments have shown that poker chips can be overestimated after a history of association with other valued objects [28].

We must conclude that the evidence points to acceptance of a view that motives, rewards, punishments, and values can and do affect our perceptions. At the same time we must hold some reservations. Some experiments aimed at replication of earlier findings have not been successful. Furthermore, there is the possibility that motivational effects are especially effective in altering memory traces of stimuli. Probably it is safest, although least satisfying, to reserve final decision regarding whether the perceptions of figures or the memory of them can be altered. The issue can be resolved only by further experiments. Perhaps you will be one of those who help decide the issue.

PERCEPTION WITHOUT AWARENESS The concept of threshold is a pervasive one in perception. *If* we assume a threshold to exist as a boundary between awareness and a lack of awareness, then it becomes meaningful to ask questions such as "Is it possible to have perceptual discrimination below the threshold for awareness?" Certain evidence suggests that this question should be answered in the affirmative. In one experiment nonsense words made from uncommon combinations of letters were associated with electrical shock to the skin during training sessions [29]. Other nonsense words were not paired with this electric shock. Electric shocks produce a change in the electrical resistance of the skin which reflects activation of the autonomic nervous system. This change is called the galvanic skin response, or GSR. After a number of pairings of the nonsense words and the shock, the nonsense words came to elicit a GSR which they had not done originally. Then both the nonsense words associated with shock and those not associated with shock were flashed to subjects in a tachistoscope at an intensity and for a duration such that they could not be identified. Even though they were not identified, a GSR tended to occur following the words which had been paired with the electrical shock. This result means that sufficient information must have reached the subject to alter the response of his autonomic nervous system but not enough to allow verbal identification of the words.

This finding, and others like it, present a difficult problem for psychological theories. If a GSR response occurs, and yet the subject reports he does not recognize it, how is it possible to have an autonomic alerting reaction to it? Is there a perceptual mechanism which acts to filter or censor the information arriving from the senses and which allows only certain kinds of information to reach awareness? Can stimuli influence unconscious mechanisms in the individual without influencing conscious mechanisms?

PERCEPTUAL VIGILANCE AND DEFENSE In discussing the effects of punishment on the perception of figures, we point out that subjects defended against seeing figures associated with moderate punishment and showed vigilance for figures associated with intense punishment. It is time now to return to these concepts and dig somewhat deeper into this problem.

Both vigilance and defense can be discussed in terms of changes in thresholds. When thresholds for words are lowered we speak of perceptual vigilance and when they are raised we refer to it as perceptual defense. The mechanisms underlying both vigilance and defense *could* be operating at a "lower perceptual level," gathering and regulating the sensory data before they reach awareness. We have suggested that these perceptual mechanisms could be controlled or regulated by degrees of punishment alone, but some psychologists believe that the controlling factors are more likely to be more permanent constellations of personality characteristics in the person.

Repression is a name which describes the tendency not to remember certain information. Most personality theorists believe that the material below awareness can affect our lives in many different ways. Repression is one defense mechanism used by people to guard awareness from intrusions of painful memories. Perceptual defense could be the result of a mechanism like repression which operates to scan incoming sensory messages. The potentially threatening or painful perceptions would be prevented from reaching consciousness.

Both perceptual vigilance and defense depend upon the assumption of several levels of mental and perceptual life. This assumption is a common one for personality theorists but remains rather foreign to other psychologists. The data from future experiments will decide whether or not it is necessary to assume several levels of mental processes.

LANGUAGE AND PERCEPTION Three separate aspects of the relation between language and perception need to be stressed. First, we can never directly be aware of the mental experiences of another person. All we can know are verbal reports, written or spoken, or indicator responses of some kind. These reports constitute the basic materials of perceptual study. We talk to each other about the view from our windows, our perceptions of others, about the colors in a painting, but the only thing available to us which can be used to understand perception in others is verbal behavior. Verbal behavior is a subject unto itself and we must be careful to recognize that it can introduce error into our experiments and into discussions of perceptual phenomena. We might fall into the conceptual mistake of assuming that every descriptive word must refer to some perceptual activity. Or we might make the opposite error of assuming the absence of a perceptual event because it is not labeled with a word. The problem exists even though we restrict the subject to "yes" or "no" responses used to signal the occurrence of perceptual events.

Second, we must recognize the dramatic yet utterly common fact that verbal messages from others are the most common means used for the establishment of sets. If a ghost story prepares us for special classes of stimuli it must do so by means of the information encoded in verbal materials. When we perceive an ambiguous figure as an old shrew rather than a beautiful woman, the set is established by words. Once again, we must admit to practically no knowledge of just how words act to perform these perceptual miracles, although Hebb's concepts of cell assemblies and phase sequences may help if we are willing to assume that the verbal labels of an object can activate at least part of the phase sequences associated with the object itself.

Third, we must recognize the possibility that language itself can act to shape our perceptions. Whorf has suggested that language influences (or alters) the nature of the perceptual processes themselves rather than merely the verbal responses and the reporting of perception [30]. One of the most common illustrations in support of Whorf's theory is that people who speak *Iakuti* do not have separate words for the green and the blue portions of the visual spectrum and that they may actually see green and blue more alike than speakers of languages which make verbal distinctions between them. The question of the effects of language is open, but it represents a fascinating although difficult area of research. It may turn out that the rules and content of a language may affect the encoding and memory aspects of perception but not the basic perceptual discriminations.

The perceptual activities of man are one exciting facet of his life, but they are far from being the only aspects of behavior which we must consider. Our next step in understanding the fundamentals of behavior takes us into studies of how we learn. Although the study of learning developed from philosophical interpretations of perception, the two area have developed rather independently.

References

1. Tanner, W. P., Jr., & Swets, J. A. A decision-making theory of visual detection. *Psychol. Rev.,* 1954, **61,** 401–409.

2. Senden, M. V. *Raum—und Gestaltauffassung bei operierten Blindgeborenen vor und mach der Operation.* Munich: Johann Ambrosius Barth, 1932.

3. Hebb, D. O. The innate organization of visual activity: I. Perception of figures by rats reared in total darkness. *J. genet. Psychol.,* 1937, **51,** 101–126.

4. Helson, H. The fundamental propositions of gestalt psychology. *Psychol. Rev.,* 1933, **40,** 13–32.

5. Koffka, K. *Principles of Gestalt Psychology.* New York: Harcourt, Brace & World, Inc., 1935.

6. Lashley, K. S., Chow, K. L., & Semmes, J. An examination of the electrical field theory of cerebral integration. *Psychol. Rev.,* 1951, **58,** 123–136.

7. Hebb, D. O. *The Organization of Behavior.* New York: John Wiley & Sons, Inc., 1949.

8. Hebb, D. O. *A Textbook of Psychology.* Philadelphia: W. B. Saunders Company, 1958.

9. Karoly, A. J., & Isaacson, R. L. Scanning mechanisms in audition. Paper read at Michigan Acad. Sci., 1956.

10. Venier, Florence A. Signal detection as a function of frequency ensemble. *J. Acoust. Soc. Am.,* 1958, **30,** I: 1020–1024, II: 1075–1078.

11. Boring, E. G. A new ambiguous figure. *Amer. J. Psychol.,* 1930, **42,** 444–445.

12. Allport, F. H. *Theories of Perception and the Concept of Structure.* New York: John Wiley & Sons, Inc., 1955.

13. Langfeld, H. S. Note on a case of synesthesia. *Psychol. Bull.,* 1914, **11,** 113–114.

14. Holway, A. H., & Boring, E. G. The moon illusion and the angle of regard. *Amer. J. Psychol.,* 1940, **53,** 109–116.

15. Kaufman, L., & Rock, I. The moon illusion, I. *Science* 1962, **136,** 953–961.

16. Rock, I., & Kaufman, L. The moon illusion, II. *Science,* 1962, **136,** 1023–1031.

17. Wapner, S., & Werner, H. Experiments on sensory-tonic field theory of perception: V. Effect of body status on kinesthetic perception of verticality. *J. exp. Psychol.,* 1952, **44,** 126–131.

18. McClelland, D. C., & Atkinson, J. W. The projective expression of needs: I. The effect of different intensities of

the hunger drive on perception. *J. Psychol.*, 1948, **25,** 205–222.

19. McClelland, D. C., & Liberman, A. M. The effect of need for achievement on recognition of need-related words. *J. Pers.,* 1949, **18,** 236–251.

20. Postman, L., Bruner, J. S., & McGinnies, E. Personal values as selective factors in perception. *J. abnorm. soc. Psychol.,* 1948, **43,** 142–154.

21. Howes, D. H. & Solomon, R. L. Visual duration threshold as a function of word-probability. *J. exp. Psychol.,* 1951, **41,** 401–410.

22. Atkinson, J. W., & Walker, E. L. The affiliation motive and perceptual sensitivity to faces. *J. abnorm. soc. Psychol.,* 1956, **53,** 38–41.

23. Schafer, R., & Murphy, G. The role of autism in a visual figure ground relationship. *J. exp. Psychol.,* 1943, **32,** 335–343.

24. Sommer, R. The effects of rewards and punishments during perceptual organization. *J. Pers.,* 1957, **25,** 550–558.

25. Reece, M. M. The effect of shock on recognition thresholds. *J. abnorm. soc. Psychol.,* 1954, **49,** 165–172.

26. Bruner, J. S., & Postman, L. Tension and tension-release as organizing factors in perception. *J. Pers.,* 1947, **15,** 300–308.

27. Ashley, W., Harper, R., & Runyon, D. The perceived size of coins in normal and hypnotically induced economic states. *Amer. J. Psychol.,* 1951, **64,** 564–572.

28. Lambert, W. W., Solomon, R. L., & Watson, P. D. Reinforcement and extinction as factors in size estimation. *J. exp. Psychol.,* 1949, **39,** 637–641.

29. Lazarus, R. S., & McCleary, R. A. Autonomic discrimination without awareness: a study of subception. *Psychol. Rev.,* 1951, **58,** 113–122.

30. Whorf, B. L. *Language, Thought, and Reality.* New York: John Wiley & Sons, Inc., 1956.

SIX BASIC THEORIES OF LEARNING

It is difficult to imagine anything we do which has not been influenced by training in social customs. Even if you select activities used to satisfy your bodily needs, such as eating and drinking, it is readily apparent that the ways in which these needs are satisfied stem largely from your early training and general culture. People living in other cultures satisfy their needs in ways which often seem strange to us. The Chinese cannot understand how we could ever eat spoiled milk (cheese) whereas we would be revulsed by the thought of eating rotten eggs. A Moslem would rather die of thirst than drink wine or beer which are prohibited by his religious creeds. We consider some foods and drinks as pleasant or unpleasant, some actions as good or bad, some goals and motives as acceptable or not, all due to *learning*. As we grow older, we keep learning more and more of the rules and standards laid down by our social environment. Psychologists want to understand the empirical relationship between our environment and what we learn, and more generally the rules which govern changes in our behavior which have resulted from changes in our experiences.

In this chapter we shall present the basic theories which try to explain changes in behavior through learning. Learning is inferred from changes in performance. However, all changes in performance are not necessarily a result of learning. Often our behavioral patterns change because we are tired or because we are under medication. These are changes in *performance* and, while they are interesting objects of study for a science of behavior, they do not represent changes in *learning* as psychologists use the term. Learning refers to changes in performance of a rather special kind.

A definition of learning is by no means easy. Underwood has mentioned several considerations which should be kept in mind when *learning* is inferred from behavior. The following considerations have been adapted [1, pp. 340, 341] with the omission of a reference to a "strict" operational definition of learning, and interested readers are recommended to Underwood's text for a more thorough consideration of a definition of learning.

1. The performance change (from which learning is inferred) must result from practice.
2. The response measured must show an increment or an improvement with practice.
3. At least two observations of performance must be made since learning is inferred from a *change* in behavior.
4. Learning is the acquisition of new responses or the enhanced execution of old ones.

The important distinction between the concepts of learning and performance will become clearer as the chapter progresses and we attempt to see how different psychologists treat them. As you will soon realize, there are many different types of theories of learning. All share a common heritage of associationism, which refers to the idea that elements of behavior become more closely tied together through learning. Most learning theories have developed rules, more or less complex, which are supposed to govern the strength of association of these elements of behavior, usually stimuli and responses.

In this chapter we shall examine (1) the background of association theory, (2) some modern examples of associational learning theories, (3) various criticisms of learning theory, and finally (4) we shall review some representative data from experiments initiated by men who try to remain independent of formal theories.

Background of Association Theory

It is impossible to understand the current status of learning theory without some idea of how it evolved to its present forms. One of the main influences upon American learning theorists stems from philosophy. The British Associationists are the men to whom psychology owes its debt for its current *rules* of learning [2, 3]. Other influences on learning theory can be found in the pragmatic and functional philosophies. The American view of learning resulted from the need for dealing only with observable behavior, from the widespread effects of the work of Ivan Pavlov, from the orientation to behavior problems provided by the evolutionary views of Darwin and from the advances made in the physiological study of the body.

THE BRITISH ASSOCIATIONISTS In the eighteenth and nineteenth centuries, philosophers were especially interested in the origin of knowledge. Where does our individual knowledge come from? Do we inherit some knowledge? Are we born with any innate knowledge? Socrates long ago had argued that knowledge of the natural laws was within each of us, and by questioning an uneducated slave about the Pythagorean theorem he showed that he had managed to elicit from the slave information that he had not directly given to him. Kant also argued for the acceptance of knowledge which seemed to come through other than direct experience. On the other hand, some philosophers maintained that people are born with no inherited information and that the mind of man at birth may be compared to a blank slate on which experiences are written. This group of philosophers denied that any knowledge was innate and believed all knowledge must come to us through sensory information provided by the receptors. The problem for this group was how we combine the mental experiences we have into a meaningful, regular, and consistent world. Their solution to the problem may be summed up as *mental chemistry;* they said we construct a perceptual world out of basic sensory elements. According to the views of the British Associationists, objects may or may not exist; we only *know* about sensory *impressions.* In fact the Bishop of Cloyne, George Berkely, concluded that there was no objective world, but that which we call *object* is merely an idea in the mind of God.

Our debt to the British Associationists does not stem from their concern with philosophical problems but from their efforts in working out rules of association by which elementary sense data forms ideas (objects in the perceptual world). The rules developed by the philosophers of the British Associationist movement represented something like a mental chemistry. These rules varied somewhat from one philosopher to another, but they were in general agreement in regard to the effectiveness of two factors in forming associations: *contiguity* and *frequency.* In the philosophers' terms, sensations which occur close together in time or in a perceptual field tend to become associated (contiguity). The more often sense data occur together the stronger the association between them (frequency). Modern learning theories have accepted the importance of these two rules of learning, but they have rejected portions of the British Associationist theories.

INFLUENCE OF AMERICAN BEHAVIORISM Physics and chemistry seemed to be making tremendous advances because they were able to make precise measurement of their objects of study. And so learning theories developed with the view that they could only have the same success as physics and chemistry when all things which were not objectively definable and measurable were rejected. Thus the trend in American psychology was away from the mentalistic concepts used by the British Associationists and toward the concepts of measurable *stimuli* and *responses.* These were definable in strict physical terms. The stimulus could be defined in mass and acceleration for mechanical stimuli or in other physical units for visual and auditory stimuli. Responses could be measured in terms of muscle movements or in countable acts. For example, the number of times a rat presses a lever can be objectively measured. The trend was to take the subjectivity out of psychology and to make experimental manipulations open for examination and replication.

American psychologists who emphasize the importance of being able to objectively measure the *stimuli* and the *responses* of an organism in a learning situation are known as *behaviorists*. A psychologist who explains behavior by using rules associating stimuli with responses is called an *associationist*. Because behaviorists were most often associationists too, the term *behaviorist* usually implies a belief in some variety of an association learning theory.

Behaviorism has dominated the thinking of practically all of the psychology of learning. In fact the only areas of psychology not greatly affected by association theory are Gestalt psychology (treated in the previous chapter) and the personality theories based on the work of Sigmund Freud. However, it should be pointed out that there is no one universally accepted behavioristic theory today. There are many types of learning theories which are both associational and behavioristic.

CONDITIONED REFLEX   Ivan Pavlov contributed indirectly to the behavioristic movement in the United States through his studies of conditioned reflexes. The basic functional unit of the nervous system is the reflex. Pavlov summarized the reflex as follows:

> An external or internal stimulus falls on some one or other nervous receptor and gives rise to a nervous impulse; this nervous impulse is transmitted along nerve fibers to the central nervous system, and here, on account of existing nervous connections, it gives rise to a fresh impulse which passes along outgoing nerve fibers of the active organ, where it excites a special activity of the cellular structures [4, p. 7].

This account of the reflex shows the mechanical, telephonelike concept that Pavlov held of the nervous system. Two kinds of reflexes could be distinguished. First, there were permanent connections built into the organism. We could think of these as unlearned and innate reflexes. Second, there were the temporary connections which came about through the association of a neutral stimulus with the first kind of unlearned reflex. This new connection was the conditioned reflex.

While there are many different kinds of reflexes available to the organism, most of Pavlov's work was with the acquisition of alimentary reflexes, which involve the autonomic nervous system, and the defensive reactions (escape or withdrawal) of the body to painful or destructive stimuli. His work with the reflex in which saliva is reflexively secreted to food is most widely known today. A picture of a dog in the experimental situation used for the conditioning of the salivation response is shown in Fig. 6.1.

In Pavlov's work we find one of the earliest examples of a laboratory learning situation. The dog stands moderately restrained in the apparatus. The equipment allows meat powder to be introduced into the animal's mouth. By earlier surgery a

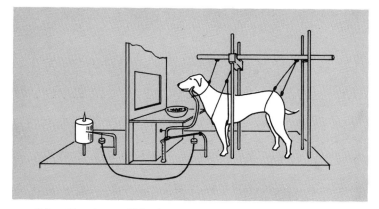

FIG. 6.1. *Dog in conditioning apparatus used by Pavlov.*

tube has been implanted in the dog that allows saliva excreted from one of the glands in the mouth to be observed and measured. Through the physiological mechanism of the innate reflex, a flow of saliva is always produced by the meat powder. Pavlov discovered that if he repeatedly presented a sound (bell, buzzer, or metronome) just before the introduction of the meat powder, the sound alone would come to elicit a flow of saliva. This kind of learning is called *classical conditioning* in which an otherwise ineffectual stimulus becomes one which can elicit a response. In the saliva experiment the learned response of salivation is very similar to (but not identical with) the natural salivation occurring to the meat powder. Because of the great similarity of the learned response to the natural response, classical conditioning is sometimes thought of as simple stimulus substitution of the new sound for the meat powder. However,

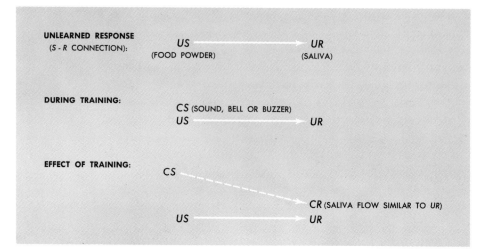

FIG. 6.2. *Symbolic model for Pavlovian, or classical, conditioning.*

since the salivation in the two cases *is* different, it is unlikely that the learning can be understood this easily; the unconditioned reflex involves salivation with chewing, while the conditioned reflex involves salivation without chewing.

From the model of learning created by Pavlov certain terms have come to be accepted as part of the language of psychology. The meat powder used to elicit the reflexive flow of saliva is the *unconditioned stimulus* (*US*) because it always leads to the salivation response presumably without prior learning. The salivation itself is the *unconditioned reflex* (*UR*). Today it is more often called an *unconditioned response*. The stimulus which does not produce a response like the *UR* (salivation) before training but which does so after training is the *conditioned stimulus* (*CS*). The response which is acquired through training is the *conditioned response* (*CR*). Figure 6.2 presents the model for classical conditioning using these symbols. The terms can be used to describe any learning situation in which a response similar to the unconditioned response (*UR*) is conditioned to another stimulus (*CS*) previously ineffective in producing the *UR*.

We should note that the classical model of learning is a switchboard, association model. The *CS* and *CR* come to be associated so that the *CS* is more and more likely to produce the *CR*. This associative tendency is one of the vital features of all learning theories. In all of them, things become bonded together, or associated. In some theories stimuli become associated with other stimuli; in other theories stimuli and responses become associated; and in still others the association is between responses. In any case learning theories all involve some kind of association principle whereby one activity becomes connected with another activity in a more or less permanent manner.

INFLUENCES FROM BIOLOGY At the time formal theories of learning came into prominence, scientists were very much aware of man's place in, not apart from, the animal kingdom. Darwin's work made popular the argument that man represented one point of evolutionary development. Early psychologists were aware of man's continuity with the other animals and justified the experimental study of animal behavior as one way of gaining new insights into the behavior of man. Darwin's doctrine of natural selection focused the scientific world's attention on the importance of behavioral and physiological competence in dealing with an uncertain environment. At the same time the American physiologist, Cannon, and the French physiologist, Bernard, had made popular the concept of homeostasis. Homeostasis refers to the tendency of the body to maintain a constant and generally favorable internal environment (see pp. 330–332). The effect of these ideas can be seen in the prominence of *biological usefulness* as the most important measure of the correctness or success of behavior.

In summary: Learning theories were molded into an associative pattern by the philosophic traditions of the British Associationists and the physiology of Pavlov. From Pavlov, was obtained an inheritance of a model for learning (classical conditioning) and a specific symbolism for this model.

From the evolutionary movement prominent at the turn of the century came both a stress on the biological utility of behavior and a justification for the use of animals in studying the learning of new responses. At this point we are ready to examine some of the types of theories of learning which developed largely in this century.

Modern Theories of Learning

In this section we shall first present Edwin Guthrie's views of the association process, the reinforcement theories proposed by

Thorndike and more elaborately by Hull, and then the position of Edward C. Tolman where behavior is explained on the basis of *expectancies.*

GUTHRIE'S POSITION: SIMPLE CONTIGUITY There could be no better introduction to the behavioristic learning theories than the position of Edwin Guthrie. Like many psychologists, he defines stimuli as follows: "Stimuli are changes in the world order to which sense organs or receptors respond by exciting impulses in sensory nerves" [5]. This means that physical changes must be effective in altering the state of the nervous system to serve as a stimulus for learning. Not all physical changes become registered as changes in the activity of the nervous system, and Guthrie recognizes this by his definition. His emphasis, however, is on the stimulus as a change in the physical environment which is observable and of such a nature that a number of observers would agree upon it. This is about the same thing as requiring the physical changes of stimuli to be measurable. Guthrie defines a response as specific movements whether of somatic or autonomic muscles, and he points out a distinction which we would do well to remember. This is a distinction between *movements* and *acts.* Movements are merely the contractions of somatic and autonomic muscles, whereas acts are movements which are considered in relation to the goals attained by the movements. Walking into a classroom, reaching for a pen, and opening a notebook, for example, are acts rather than movements. When we are concerned with the outcome of a series of movements, and consequently we talk of the movements in terms of their results, than we are talking about acts. Guthrie believes that it is confusing for understanding the problems of learning if we try to create laws of learning for *acts.* He prefers to think of learning as the association of stimuli with movements.

All learning theories are attempts to connect observable stimuli with measurable responses through certain rules of association. For Guthrie there is only one rule and it is taken directly from British Associationism: *contiguity.* When a stimulus occurs at the same time as a response, a maximal association is at once made between the two. On this basis, all we must do for learning to occur is to arrange for a stimulus to occur when a given response is going to take place. When the S is presented again, the R should follow. Obviously this simple rule doesn't seem to work most of the time. There are many times when movements occur in the presence of a given stimulus and yet do not occur at the next presentation of the stimulus. Most of our adult learning seems to require many training trials, i.e., a lot of practice. Certainly Guthrie is aware of this apparent contradiction between his theory and the actual conditions of learning in real life. How is this contradiction resolved? Consider yourself at any instant in time. There are millions of different stimuli impinging upon your receptors. Not only do these stimuli come from the object world around you but also from the inner world of organs and glands. Hunger, thirst, muscle tension, and internal emotional reactions all contribute to the total stimulus pattern which is constantly changing. If a stimulus is presented to us twice in succession, it will not occur in the same total stimulus context on each occasion. In fact no stimulus can appear in the same total stimulus pattern twice. Any new stimulus situation can only be *similar to,* not identical with ones of the past. Normal learning requires a large number of trials because of the complexity of the stimulus pattern. The appropriate stimulus *figure* must be isolated from the *ground* of other irrelevant stimuli through repetition.

Another reason that adult human learning requires practice and cannot be acquired at once is that most responses that we want to learn involve a sequence of movements. Remember, Guthrie believes that movements, not acts, are learned.

The learning of a sequence of muscle movements depends upon maintaining a complete sequence. There are stimulus effects for each movement we make. These effects include the new position of the body, the tension in muscles, and perhaps the effects of glandular secretions. All of these contribute to the total stimulus context to which individual movements are associated. It is important for the sequences of complex behavior to remain in a constant order.

In practical advice to parents Guthrie suggests that if you want your children to learn to hang up their coats when coming inside, you should *not* have them go back to the chair in which they flung their coats to pick them up and hang them in the closet. Rather, you should make them put on their coats, go outside, come in again, go to the closet, hang them up, and then close the closet door. By doing this, each movement produces stimuli for the next movement in the sequence to be learned.

Whether we acquire a given response pattern gradually by learning the constituent responses of the whole pattern one at a time, or whether we learn each of these small responses all at once as Guthrie suggests, is still a controversial matter. For example, some experimenters have reported evidence that word associations are not the result of a slow growth of a connection between the words [6]. However, because of the necessarily complex nature of verbal learning studies, the matter has not been finally resolved.

Thus, Guthrie's learning theory requires the immediate association of movements with the stimuli which elicited them. The stimuli must be regarded as compounds of many different types of sensory stimulation, including the sensory feedback from previous movements. Therefore, if a sequence of movements is to be learned the entire sequence should be kept intact. The basic rule of learning is *contiguity*. Nothing else is needed. We shall see that this view of learning by contiguity alone is quite distinct from the group of theories which postulate that a reward or reinforcement is essential for learning.

REINFORCEMENT THEORIES   Psychologists' use of the word *reinforcement* may at first seem somewhat different from the way it is used by the man on the street. Reinforcing a crumbling wall means to shore it up, to strengthen it. When we speak of reinforcing a response we think of strengthening the hypothetical (learned) association between a response and its stimulus. This strengthening through reinforcement is a basic feature of several theories of learning. A reinforcement is always a stimulus that is presented to the subject following his response. On certain occasions the reinforcing stimulus acts as a reward.

Thorndike and the law of effect   First, let us consider the contributions to modern learning theory of Edward L. Thorndike, a famous learning theorist and educator. Thorndike felt that *repetition* was an important factor in the acquisition of responses. Previously, Watson had held that repetition was necessary for learning, and as we have seen, it was one of the two principles which stemmed from British Associationism. However, Thorndike believed that more than repeated occurrences of stimuli and responses was necessary for an association to be built up between them, and that *motivation and reward* played important roles in learning. For efficient learning motivation must be present at least to the extent that rewards will be satisfying to the organism. Thorndike proposed three laws of learning:

1. the law of exercise
2. the law of effect
3. the law of readiness

As a function of all three laws, *connections* or *associations* are formed between observable stimuli and observable responses. The first law states that the more times the stimuli and responses are paired, the stronger is the association between the two. When psychologists use the terms *association* and *connection* they refer to the phenomenon that links a particular stimulus with a particular behavioral response which an organism makes as a result of exposure to that stimulus. The more likely a given response is to occur after presentation of the stimulus, the stronger is the association between them considered to be. An increase in the probability that a given response will follow a particular stimulus is what is meant by a strengthening in the association between the two.

The laws of effect and of readiness are closely related. The readiness law merely states that for rewards to be effective the animal must be physiologically prepared for them. Food will only be useful as a reward when the animal is hungry. A lollipop serves as a reward to a small child, but it will not be very effective if the child has just finished a box of chocolate cream candies. If the organism is ready for a certain kind of reward and that reward is given after every response that is paired with a certain stimulus, then, according to Thorndike, the connection or association between the stimulus and response will be made faster than if the reward is not given.

Reward for Thorndike means a stimulus which produces a "satisfying state of affairs" in the organism. By this he did not mean that we need to resort to an evaluation of the subjective mental experiences of the rat to determine what would constitute a reward. Thorndike said that a "satisfying state of affairs" could be inferred from the behavior exhibited by an animal. Those things which an animal approached and with which he maintained contact could be presumed to be rewards. However, with this basis of determining which objects would serve as rewards, one would have to test each and every object to determine whether or not it could serve as a rewarding stimulus. In the next section we shall see that a very much refined reinforcement theory, developed by Clark Hull, approached this problem in a different way.

The law of effect was an important milestone in the development of modern theories of learning. It represented a departure from Guthrie's theory in that the *effects* of the response determined the extent to which it was learned. If the effect of the response was to produce a "satisfying state of affairs" for the organism then the strength of association between the preceding stimuli and the response was increased. If we can

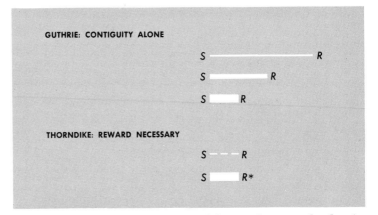

FIG. 6.3. *Schematic illustration of difference between the theories of Guthrie and Thorndike. Degree of association is represented by width of bars connecting S and R; reward is indicated by asterisk. According to Guthrie's views, only closeness determines amount of association or learning; Thorndike believes rewards are necessary to learning.*

think of those stimuli which produce a "satisfying state of affairs" as rewards, then Thorndike's law tells us that rewards act as the agents which strengthen the associations between stimuli and responses.

The theories of Guthrie and Thorndike are contrasted in Fig. 6.3. The separation of the *S*s and the *R*s indicates the amount of closeness in time or space (contiguity). In Guthrie's theory only the proximity of the *S* and *R* is important for learning. Therefore, the bottom pair of the three *S-R* pairs in the upper portion would have the strongest association. For Thorndike the closeness of association has no effect by itself. A response must be followed by a reward, indicated by the asterisk. If reward does follow, the connection between the stimulus is strengthened. If no reward follows the response, the connection is not strengthened.

We should note that the effects of a reward work *backward* in time. The reward strengthens an association between a stimulus event occurring earlier and a response which also has preceded the reward. Just what the mechanism is which allows this backward effect of rewards on prior events is not certain, although many psychologists postulate the existence of *traces* of stimuli in the nervous system as a basis of memory. The physiological effect of reward could be to act on the neural traces of preceding events. Yet, the problem is one which is very much alive in psychological research because the physiological mechanisms of learning are still obscure.

The formal theory of Hull You will be able to see many similarities between Thorndike's ideas and those proposed by Clark L. Hull. Hull was Sterling Professor of Psychology at Yale University until his death in 1951. His formulations of the laws of learning remain the closest approximation to a formal deductive theory in psychology. Yet Hull did not think his theory was in a final or complete form. He was constantly changing it through publication of articles in psychological journals and notes from his seminars. In the form of his theory which we present [7] we find typified many similarities to learning theories described earlier: (1) it is an association theory; (2) it is based on a *survival model* of life, which means it was influenced by Darwin's principle of natural selection and the popular notion of survival of the fittest; (3) it is based on biological needs and their fulfillment; and (4) many of the laws Hull derived about the nature of learning originated with Pavlov.

UNLEARNED BEHAVIOR. In Hull's system there is a recognition of the importance of unlearned stimulus-response associations. Few learning theories attempt to provide a place for such unlearned (instinctive) responses, and this is due to some extent to the rejection of any kind of inherited characteristics by the early Behaviorists. Unlearned *S-R* connections are found more frequently on the lower phylogenetic levels than on the higher, and it may be wise to view learning as a superstructure built upon these inherited connections. The nature of inherited response patterns was formulated on the basis of association doctrine. They were thought to be unlearned *S-R* connections. We shall see that Hull developed an elaborate symbolism for his theory, and in it the symbol $_sU_R$ stands for the unlearned stimulus-response connection. U was an abbreviation of *unlearned*. The $_s$ and $_R$ represent the stimulus and response components of learning respectively.

THE STIMULUS. While behaviorists measure the objective physical stimulus, their *theories* usually relate the internal neural activities (initiated at receptors) to a response. For Hull responses are conditioned to the neural aftereffects of stimuli rather than to the stimuli themselves. The effective stimulus in learning is the trace in the nervous system caused by the environmental object. The effects of a stimulus trace were postulated to be greatest about a half-second after the external stimulation begins. This figure was determined on the basis of behavioral experiments not physiological measures of neural activities. Hull did not change his behavioristic perspective, but he did remove the variables used in his theory one step beyond direct observation. Thus for Hull the stimuli in the object world give rise to stimulus traces in the organism. The first we might designate S and the second $_s$. Learning involves the $_s$ not the S.

THE RESPONSE. At the same time, we may distinguish between a tendency within the person to make a response and the actual response itself. If we designate the muscular overt response $R,$ we can refer to the preexisting neural activities which initiate the response as $_R$. These internal response tendencies are not observable, and are inferred from behavior. However, Hull postulated that learning involved an association of the stimulus trace with an "effector activity," presumably meaning the overt, observable response. At this point the authors would suggest that the more appropriate association would be with the internal motor tendency rather than the overt response. This is due in part to an experiment which indicated that a leg-lift response could be conditioned to a tone in cats who were prevented from making the response during learning [8]. These cats were trained either under a drug which blocked transmission of nerve impulses to the muscle or after the nerve which energized the muscle had been crushed, which temporarily blocked all neural impulses from reaching the leg. This experiment seems to argue convincingly for a view that the associations of learning must be between internal stimulus traces and internal response tendencies. Therefore, we have taken the liberty of modifying Hull's theory on this matter.

Symbolically the learned association of $_s$ and $_R$ is represented $_sH_R$. In unlearned reactions the connecting link U referred to an unlearned association, but in those reactions acquired through the experiences of a single organism the connecting link H should be thought of as an abbreviation for *habit* or *habit strength*. Changes *in* $_sH_R$ constitute learning in Hull's system. In Fig. 6.4 the distinctions between the various internal and external stimuli and responses are illustrated.

LEARNING AND BIOLOGICAL NEEDS. Hull, like Guthrie, makes a distinction between learning and performance. Many factors can affect performance, but learning itself ($_sH_R$) is influenced only by one factor in Hull's theory: the number of times the

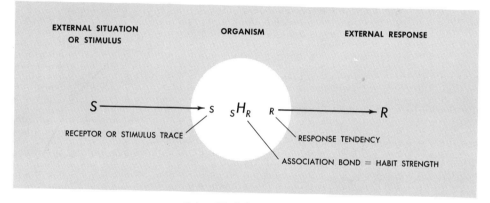

FIG. 6.4. *Modified representation of stimulus and response variables in Hull's theory.*

particular stimulus and the particular response occurring together (contiguity) *have been followed by a reinforcement.* You will find that the word *reinforcement* is often used by psychologists like the word *reward* although Hull's *reinforcement* is quite different from Thorndike's *reward.* A reinforcement is defined in a particular way by Hull and we must be careful to understand what this definition means. To do this properly we shall approach the definition through a brief historical comment.

DEFINITION OF REINFORCEMENT. Hull believed that all behavior has its origin in the biological needs, which are most demanding early in human life and in the lower animals. Yet very few of the many patterns of action we exhibit as adults seem directly related to the fulfillment of these bodily needs. To be sure, we eat and drink and sleep; but the ways, times, and places in which we fulfill our needs are not dictated by the biological conditions themselves. The means to biological fulfill-ment are social accruements which differ from one person to the next and from one culture to the next. Still, Hull believed all complex adult behavior to be indirectly based on our biological needs.

One insight into how adult behavior may be based on bio-logical needs occurs when we look· at Hull's principle of re-inforcement. Reinforcement is like Thorndike's reward in one way; it is a *stimulus* which has the ability to alter the proba-bilities of certain *Rs* following certain *Ss*. When a response is reinforced this means that it has been followed by one of a certain class of stimuli. What defines this special class of rein-forcing stimuli? We would like to be able to have an inde-pendent method of identifying "reinforcements" and not be con-fined to the observation that its presentation alters response probability because *it would then be possible to predict what stimuli would have reinforcing properties ahead of time.* Thorn-dike said that rewarding stimuli produced a "satisfying state of affairs in the organism." These are hard to observe. On the other hand, Hull postulated *that reinforcing stimuli were those which reduced stimuli uniquely associated with the biological drives.*

A biological deficiency in the organism produces a state of *need*. This can be defined in an experiment by depriving an ani-mal or person of food or water over a period of time. One es-sential characteristic of the need is the pattern of internal stimuli which is always associated with this kind of deprivation con-dition. The stimuli uniquely associated with a specific need are called *drive stimuli*, S_D. It is only when these drive stimuli are diminished that the animal is reinforced. Whether or not the animal experiences a "satisfying state of affairs" is immaterial.

Drive stimuli may result from a dry throat due to thirst or stomach contractions due to hunger. In fact, they could be signals in the nervous system from hypothalamic centers or other centrally located neural systems. Reduction of S_D, reinforce-ment, is usually accomplished by the common method of feeding the hungry animal or watering the thirsty one. The definition of reinforcement is flexible, however, and does include the oc-casions when S_D are reduced by unnatural means. One could reduce the stomach contraction component of hunger S_Ds by filling the stomach of an animal with nonnutritive substances. To the extent that the stomach contractions (S_D) are reduced by the inert bulk inserted into the stomach, reinforcement would be produced.

REINFORCEMENT AND LEARNING. For Hull, learning depends on reinforcement. Neither contiguity nor frequency of S and R are sufficient in and of themselves. Hull's basic rule of learning is that a response is associated with a stimulus trace to the extent that the response has been followed by a reduction of the drive stimuli. While the definition may seem a little elaborate, it is nonetheless clear.

The learning rules for Hull can be written as follows: *A stimulus in the environment (S) is presented to the organism; this causes a neural trace of (S) in the organism ($_s$). This trace then becomes conditioned to a response tendency ($_R$) occurring simultaneously with the trace if followed by a stimulus with reinforcing properties.*

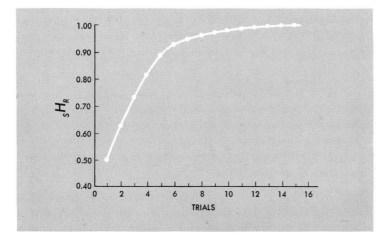

FIG. 6.5. *Representational curve of $_sH_R$ as number of trials increases.*

The growth of habit strength is a function of the number of reinforced pairings of S and R (N). *No other factors influence the growth of learning.* Hull wrote this in equation form:

$$_sH_R = 1 - 10^{-.0305N}$$

This equation implies that as N gets larger the successive increments to $_sH_R$ get smaller. It indicates that when we learn a response to some stimulus, the first few trials build up habit strength faster than do later ones.

Figure 6.5 presents the typical growth curve of $_sH_R$ as determined by the number of reinforced pairings of S and R and Hull's theoretical equation.

According to this theory, we now know all the rules necessary to describe the learning process but not all the rules which go into determination of final behavior. We must be aware of the *distinction between learning* and *performance*. Which factors operate on what an organism has learned so that this learning is evident or not evident in performance?

DRIVE AND PERFORMANCE. First of all, we must look at the role of motivation in performance. Thorndike argued that unless an animal is motivated, it will not learn. In his laws of readiness and effect we note the explicit common-sense notion that an organism must be physiologically ready for a reward for it

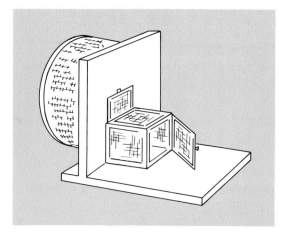

FIG. **6.6.** *Activity wheel. Animals live in small cage at right.*

to be effective in producing learning. Hull indirectly asserts the same thing when he stipulates that drive stimuli must be reduced for reinforcement to occur. But, in addition to the effects of drive stimuli on learning, Hull maintained that a general concept of drive was necessary in order that the animal alter his behavior and demonstrate what it has learned. As we have seen, Hull assumed that each different biological need produces a unique pattern of S_D. He also assumed that every need contributes *in the same way* to D (drive). Drive then is a general concept. To illustrate the general nature of D, we can consider data recorded on animals housed in activity wheels (see Fig. 6.6). The animals are kept in the housing units connected to their particular wheels. When the animals are well fed and watered, they will occasionally exhibit spontaneous running in the connecting wheels. But when deprived of food or water, all animals show an increase in the amount of time they spend running in the wheels. Generally, they will keep up this increased amount of activity until they weaken from lack of food or water. In this environment, increased running in the activity wheels is truly purposeless. No biological goals are fulfilled by running; in fact, their physiologic reserves are reduced. This increase in activity is believed to correspond to an increase in drive of the organism. Note that the increase is not dependent upon a specific deficit. Lack of food, water, or hormonal changes (in the case of the female rat) can produce an increase of drive measured in this way. (For a more detailed analysis of the role of motivational concepts in learning theories see pp. 342–348.)

While D is a common result of all bodily needs, there are differences between hunger and thirst as well as between all the other biological deficits. Hull argued that our discrimination between needs was based entirely upon the different patterns of drive stimuli associated with them.

Drive serves to energize behavior. Habit strengths formed in reaction to the many stimuli around us guide behavior. Presumably no behavior at all will occur unless there is a sufficient level of D to produce behavior. Drive does not direct behavior, it acts to arouse and intensify it, like an amplifier of our habits. It does not selectively energize the person toward one or another response. The direction of behavior depends on the relative strengths of the stimulus-response associations formed in the past and aroused by the external situation and the drive stimuli present at the moment. Drive operates in conjunction with habit strengths to produce the observable behavior.

Let us take an example of how drive, habit strength, and drive stimuli effect behavior. Class has just been dismissed. You have a free hour and *hurry* from the classroom. The fact that you are doing something and doing it with some intensity reflects a significant amount of drive. Sometimes it is possible to feel restless and move without knowing just what it is you want. This active but nondirected behavior may be a counterpart to the aimless running activity of rats in the activity wheels under food or water deprivation (high drive condition) and your behavior would only reflect the general drive level. If on the other hand you know you are hungry or thirsty, this discrimination between the biological origins of drive would occur on the basis of the S_D present. If you turn promptly and go to the coffee shop for liquid refreshment or to the cafeteria for food, these responses would be initiated because of the development of stimulus-response associations activated by the S_D present and your past experiences in the situation.

The energizing effects of drive are made explicit in the formal context of Hull's theory by the relation:

$$_sH_R \times D$$

All habits active at any moment are multiplied by drive. As we shall see in the next section, other variables also stand in this multiplicative relation to learning ($_sH_R$) in the final determination of behavior.

OTHER VARIABLES INFLUENCING PERFORMANCE. Drive is not the only multiplier of $_sH_R$. The value or desirability of the goal stimulus (K), the intensity of the external stimulus paired with the response (V), and drive (D), multiply the quantity $_sH_R$ to obtain a new number called the *reaction potential* ($_sE_R$).

$$_sE_R = H \times D \times V \times K$$

All of these other factors have an energizing effect upon reaction potential but none as strong as D. Hull has made explicit the differential qualities and specifications of each of these variables, but they are not vital to our presentation of the basic model. However, it is important to remember that the two most important contributors to $_sE_R$ are $_sH_R$ and D.

Hull was a behaviorist and as such demanded that his theoretical variables be closely tied to measurable experimental conditions. As we have seen, $_sH_R$ is defined in terms of the number of times the response has occurred followed by a reinforcement. The other variables have similar defined conditions. In the animal experiments from which the data were obtained which both lead to formulation of the theory and at least partial confirmation of it, the following were the definitions used to obtain numerical values of the theoretical concepts.

Concept	Definition Used in Experiments
D	Hours deprivation of food or water
K	Weight of food or quantity of other incentive
V	Intensity of external stimulus

The theory was recognized as only a beginning of a general theory for adult human behavior, and as such Hull did not believe it necessary to formulate definitions suitable for all learning situations. In one sense he left it up to others to extend and broaden it.

What is this $_sE_R$? First it is a numerical quantity like $_sH_R$, D, K, and V. This number represents the tendency to make the response *in the theory*. It is strictly a theoretical, or conceptual, variable, useful only in so far as the theory is concerned. It is only the product of the various numbers multiplied together. It represents an intermediate step toward the prediction of the response. It is only an intermediate step because other variables of learning must now be considered before the response prediction can be formulated.

RESPONSE INHIBITION. We must expend energy to make any response. It costs us something in fatigue to do anything at all, and at times it seems as though the muscle fatigue is concentrated in some region of the body. One example would be the localized fatigue of the hand after continuously taking notes for an hour. After any task we have been working on for some time, there is a tendency to do something else. However, only part of the explanation of this tendency to change our behavior can be attributed to muscle fatigue per se. For example, if a person has been drawing lines on sheets of papers until he feels it is no longer possible to continue because of hand fatigue or actual cramps, it is easy for him to shift to a slightly different writing task *which uses the same muscles* without fatigue or pain [9]. Thus, there must be a considerable psychological component in the tendency to alternate performances.

Hull would explain the muscle-fatigue effects and the psychological-fatigue effect by two different inhibitory mechanisms. First, there is reactive inhibition (I_R) which is the theoretical counterpart of muscle fatigue caused by the response. The second is conditioned inhibition $(_sI_R)$ which is a *learned* tendency not to respond in the same way. The two combine to form a combined inhibitory potential $(\dot{I}_R)$. After a series of responses, there is this aggregate tendency not to repeat the R again. The conditioned inhibition $(_sI_R)$ is akin to habit strength $(_sH_R)$ in that it is learned and does not dissipate with mere passage of time. The fatigue component does become reduced with time. The aggregate of inhibition detracts from the $_sE_R$ generated by the earlier formula: $_sE_R = {_sH_R} \times D \times K \times V$. After the inhibition effects have been subtracted from $_sE_R$ the new quantity is the effective reaction potential, $_s\bar{E}_R$.

$$_s\bar{E}_R = {_sE_R} - \dot{I}_R$$

Both the inhibition variables are experimentally defined by the amount of work required in making the response. But we are not yet in a position to predict behavior. We must first consider the phenomenon in which a person's responses tend to show fluctuations from one situation to the next and from one time to the next.

BEHAVIOR PREDICTIONS The effective reaction potential is not considered to be constant but rather to fluctuate in an unsystematic fashion. The momentary value of $_s\bar{E}_R$ fluctuates and the effects of these fluctuations must be considered in predicting behavior. By mathematical manipulation it is possible to always subtract the oscillation effect ($_sO_R$) from $_s\bar{E}_R$. By this subtraction a new term is defined, momentary reaction potential ($_s\dot{E}_R$).

$$_s\dot{E}_R = {_s\bar{E}_R} - {_sO_R}$$

Behavioral oscillation does not have any important ties to experimental observation. It is a concept which lives entirely in the theory world of Hull; but it can be thought of as a device which adds in theory the spontaneous fluctuations repeatedly found in neural and muscular systems of the body.

The momentary reaction potential, $_s\dot{E}_R$, is the end product of the formulas of Hull used in the prediction of behavior. If it is greater than some necessary threshold ($_sL_R$), then the specific behavior will occur. If the $_s\dot{E}_R$ is less than threshold, the response will not occur. If several $_sH_{RS}$ are activated in the same situation, that which is associated with the greatest $_s\dot{E}_R$ will take place. A diagrammatic summary of the Hull variables is presented in Fig. 6.7.

The quantity of the $_s\dot{E}_R$ is used to predict:

1. The probability that the response will occur (the probability that $_s\dot{E}_R$ is greater than $_sL_R$).
2. The response amplitude.
3. The response latency (the time it takes the response to occur).
4. The number of trials for which the response will continue to occur after the reinforcement is no longer given following the response.

All these are measures used by psychologists to measure performance. For Hull, these are a function of the $_s\dot{E}_R$ as derived

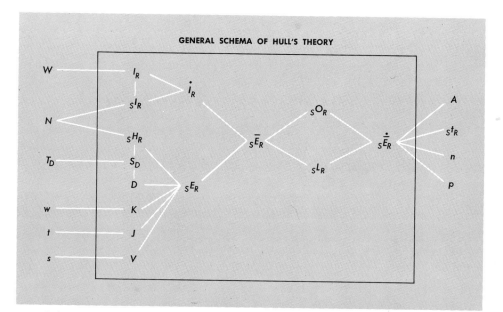

FIG. 6.7. *Schematic representation of Hull's theoretical variables. Left: antecedent measurements from which properties of first-order variables of theory are inferred (center box). Right: variables measured on response side. Second- and third-order variables resulting in momentary reaction potential are illustrated in box. Adapted from Edward L. Walker with permission.*

from his theory. Let us take a simple learning situation and try to use Hull's theory (1) to describe the problem and (2) as an aid to designing an effective situation for learning and performance.

EXAMPLE 1. Suppose we want to train an animal to solve a simple maze problem. Perhaps we would use a simple **T** maze of the kind illustrated in Fig. 6.8. The animal begins a training trial at the bottom of the **T** and proceeds to the point where the horizontal arms join the vertical section. Here the animal can choose to (*a*) turn right or (*b*) turn left. We will assume there are no significant special stimuli in the maze which would distract the animal from the task and that both horizontal arms of the maze are equally illuminated. By a flip of a coin or some other means of random selection we choose one side to terminate in a goal box containing food. Our task is to train the animal to run down the starting arm and into that arm which leads to food. To use food as an incentive we must make the animal hungry by a schedule of food deprivation.

This amount of deprivation contributes to two variables in

Hull's system: the S_D and the D. D arouses the animal to behavior while S_D reduction will constitute reinforcement. We place the animal repeatedly in the bottom of the T. It runs to the choice point and enters one or the other of the arms. When it reaches the end of an arm, it is lifted out of the maze and replaced in the starting box for another trial. If the animal chooses the correct arm (containing the food) it is allowed to eat for a few seconds before being removed. This reduces the S_D caused by the deprivation of food and acts as a reinforcement. As the number of times that it turns to the correct side, proceeds to

FIG. 6.8. T *maze often used in animal learning studies. Animals run down starting arm to choice point where they may turn left or right. Striped background is to control background around maze. Courtesy of R. J. Douglas.*

the end of the arm, and obtains food increases (N), the habit strength for this behavior also increases. In this case habit strength refers to the building up of a connection between the stimuli of the maze *and* food deprivation and the response of turning toward and running to the end of the correct arm. Only the number of reinforced responses is important in the determination of the amount of learning the animal will have in the T maze.

However, all of the variables, D, K, V, and J, help determine the behavior of the animal once it is placed in the maze. We should obtain better performance when the animal is well motivated by hunger (D), when there is a goodly amount of food

(K), and when the stimuli of the maze are readily discernable (V).

In discussing the learning of the rat in the T maze, we have so far not mentioned either the inhibitory factors or the oscillation function which Hull postulated. The amount of inhibition which will become attached to the response and result in a diminution of the $_s\dot{\bar{E}}_R$ would be a function of the work involved in making the response. If we make the arms at the top of the T slant upwards at 30 degrees, then this would require more work of the animal to reach the ends of the arms. Inhibition would be greater in this case and thus would diminish $_s\bar{E}_R$ to a greater extent. This would result in a lower performance rate, greater latency, and fewer correct responses if the food was omitted from the goal box. We could dissipate the temporary inhibition by allowing greater intervals between trials. This is important for all responses where a significant amount of work is required in making the response. Time should be allowed the subject to dissipate the temporary inhibition of fatigue. Where little work is required, the trials can occur closer together. Hull's use of the oscillation function would be apparent if we observed an animal that had a great deal of training, was well motivated, and had all of the other performance variables arranged so as to be at a maximum value. The animal would not always turn and run down the correct arm as we might expect. Occasionally the animal would still run to the wrong arm and be disappointed (along with the experimenter).

EXAMPLE 2. Let us take some liberties with Hull's strict formulations and use his terminology in the analysis of a common behavioral situation—the examination period. Let us imagine a student in college takes a multiple choice test in his introductory psychology course. A week later he receives his paper back with an F for failure written across the top. After looking at the exam once more, even the student recognizes the poor performance. What happened?

Had the student learned the material covered in the test? Hull would say that from the test itself, it would be impossible to determine the answer to this question. Why? Because any or all of the factors which contribute to $_s\dot{\bar{E}}_R$ could have been low and caused the poor performance. As we already know, the two greatest factors are learning $(_sH_R)$ and motivation (D). If the student had learned the material, then was there anything wrong about his motivation which caused his poor performance? Many poor examination performances are brought about by insufficient motivation. Occasionally, we may find a detrimental effect on performance if the level of drive becomes too great. In such cases the high drive level activates responses incompatible with the ones required in the exam. As a teacher, we would want to examine the situation to see if the incentives offered for correct responses are sufficiently attractive. Are the stimuli to which the student is asked to respond clear and emphatic? Lastly, what about the student's responses? Is there any chance that inhibitions had built up through previous study or work to reduce the performance? If all else seems in order, we might then feel safe in concluding that the student had not learned the content of his course in psychology.

ANIMALS IN LEARNING EXPERIMENTS   This may be as good a time as any to point out that nearly all learning theories have made great use of the laboratory rat as it solves its various tasks. Some have argued that it is useless to study the behavior of animals in any learning situation if we are really interested in principles of learning *for the human*. Naturally, psychologists *are* interested in human behavior; yet there are many impelling reasons behind the use of laboratory animals in research on learning and performance.

There is no doubt that animals are different from man. Even the inbred albino rat, who suffers from many of our own diseases, cannot be said to be similar to man in all important psychological characteristics. But probably millions of valuable hours have been spent in observing its behavior in laboratory learning tasks. Most psychologists who spend time observing this behavior believe that it is only with laboratory animals that we can control enough of the important variables (such as the amount of previous learning, capacity, motivation, rewards, etc.) to make any firm conclusions about basic learning processes. From the observations of the rat or monkey or cat or dog we hope to make better informed predictions regarding the conditions which would be relevant for the human. We do not assume that man and animals learn in identical ways, but we hope that what we find out from the lower animals will lead to *testable ideas* and *theories* which can be later tried with people. After all, from Darwin's work we can assume some form of continuity.

SECONDARY REINFORCEMENT AND MOTIVATION In Western society little of man's behavior is directed toward direct fulfillment of biological needs. To be sure we work for money, which we exchange for the physiological necessities of life. Yet money itself does not reduce drive stimuli. It is not a reinforcement, as we have learned in Hull's theory. In addition only a small percentage of the money we earn goes toward the fulfillment of physiological needs. Millionaires who are assured of enough money to provide handsomely for themselves seem motivated to acquire more. The fruits of our labor are many beyond money itself. Words of praise or esteem and self-realization of success are but a few of the other sorts of goals toward which behavior seems to be directed. These certainly seem to be far removed from the drive stimuli of hunger or thirst.

The learning theorist recognizes that but a few of the actions of modern Western man are guided by food or drink incentives. However, a behavioristic learning theorist believes that the goals of human behavior can be understood through the same basic theory developed on the basis of direct reduction of biological needs through the concepts of *secondary motivation* and *secondary reinforcement*. These concepts allow us to extend the relatively bare theory of Hull to situations where the reduction of primary drive stimuli (biological needs) is not suitable as a condition of reinforcement and consequently to situations more relevant to human behavior.

At the outset we should like to point out that much of the literature of psychology contains references to the concepts of secondary reinforcement and motivation. Not all definitions of these terms are made using Hull's terminology. Yet, if one once understands the basic definitions used by Hull, all other modifications can be more easily understood. As with primary reinforcing stimuli, secondary reinforcements and motivations are certain *classes of stimuli*. The defining characteristics of the classes of stimuli are described below as well as their presumed theoretical effects upon the organism:

Secondary reinforcements are stimuli that have been paired with *reduction* of drive stimuli (S_D) and have the property of *reducing* drive stimuli in the organism when they are presented in the future.

Secondarily motivating stimuli are stimuli that have been paired with an *increase* in drive stimuli (and their subsequent reduction). They have the property of increasing the amount of drive stimuli in the organism when presented in the future.

Both of these concepts are intimately connected with the concept of drive stimuli. Their effect on one's behavior are mediated through acquired capacity to alter the drive stimuli existing at any moment. Secondarily motivating stimuli produce drive stimuli in the person and secondary reinforcements have the acquired capacity to reduce certain drive stimuli.

An example from animal behavior In order to develop secondary reinforcements according to Hull's rules, we can train animals to value stimuli they have associated with reductions of biological needs almost as highly as the natural stimuli which reduce the needs. Chimpanzees will work to accumulate poker chips which are paired with food [10]. The animals are trained with a Chimp-o-mat, into which poker chips are inserted and food subsequently is obtained. They will seek these poker chips, work for them, hoard them—in other words act toward them as most people act toward money.

New responses can be learned to new stimuli by using secondary reinforcements with the stimulus-response pair. Even painful stimuli can lose at least some of their sting when they have been paired with drive-reducing stimuli and take on secondarily reinforcing properties [4].

The nature of secondary reinforcements and motives can be illustrated with further observations about the chimpanzees trained to value poker chips. When a chimpanzee sees a poker chip lying outside of its cage, the animal becomes agitated and tries to find sticks and tools to get the chip inside the cage. The poker chip outside the grasp of the animal does not appear reinforcing, but rather has motivational effects. The unpossessed chip acts like a secondarily motivating stimulus. The two conditions, poker chip possessed and not possessed, alter the chimp's reactions differently. The poker chip in the possession of the animal serves as a secondary reinforcement. The same poker chip not in the animal's possession acts as a secondarily motivating stimulus.

Human behavior Some learning theorists view early childhood experience in the light of reinforcement and motivation. Think how consistently a mother is associated with primary drive reductions in the infant. She is always present when the baby's needs are reduced. On this basis then, mother should be a secondarily reinforcing stimulus of the first magnitude. We have discussed poker chips not in possession of the chimpanzee. Mother not in possession should be a potent condition of secondary motivation for the child. We know that in most homes the child is firmly attached to mother and is disturbed when removed from her. The observed facts are not questionable. The issue is whether this attachment of the infant to mother is based on the close association with the reduction of drive stimuli. It is easy to be critical of such a naïve or superficial view, but it does represent a consistent theoretical position. And more, it is difficult to find more reasonable and equally consistent ones to supplant it. You might try to design an experiment to show that the child's attachment to his parents is not based upon secondary reinforcement.

Secondary reinforcements can be formed by an association with the primary reinforcements or motives, or they can be formed by association with other previously developed secondary reinforcements or motives. For example, words associated with mother's approval come to take on their own reinforcing properties. "Good-boy," "that's right," "nice going" are examples of stimuli which have reinforcing properties derived from their association with previously established secondary reinforcers. "Bad boy," "oh-oh," "that's wrong" can be considered as motivational and acquired on the basis of association with secondary or primary motivators. As an example, consider a situation when a child has done something wrong and the mother becomes angry, says, "Bad boy," and *leaves the room.* We saw earlier that mother's absence could be a secondarily motivating condition. The words, "bad boy," are now associated with conditions of secondary motivation and may come to have motivational properties themselves.

The adequacy of the theory Are the concepts of secondary reinforcement and secondary motivation adequate to explain all of those stimuli which act to foster and consolidate new learning for us? Probably not. For one thing, we know that when a secondary reinforcer is no longer associated with the primary reinforcement it quickly loses its reinforcing quality. Yet secondary reinforcing stimuli such as our parents' approval retains its effectiveness for years after the time when they were related to the reduction of our primary drives. Experimental studies of Zimmerman [12] have demonstrated that under appropriate conditions secondary reinforcements can continue

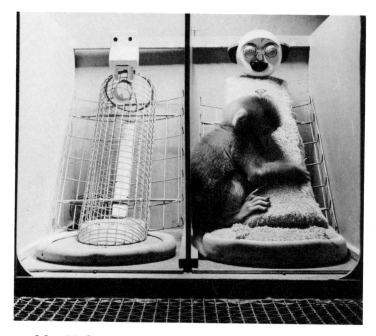

FIG. 6.9. *Mother surrogates used by Harlow. Infant monkey is clinging to surrogate which has more acceptable "skin" qualities. Courtesy of H. F. Harlow.*

to be effective for considerable periods of time. These studies are discussed in Chapter 8, (pp. 348–350).

Another line of work which indicates that traditional views of secondary reinforcement can not entirely account for an offspring's attachment for its mother is found in the work of Harlow [11]. In his study various mother substitutes or surrogates were offered to baby monkeys. The behavior of the baby monkeys could be studied as the stimulus configuration of the mother surrogates was changed. In addition, schedules of feeding (and subsequent reinforcement qualities) could be altered. It was found that there were tactual stimulus patterns (temperature and texture of the surrogate) which influenced the infants' responses to the mother surrogates over and above its need-reducing qualities. A picture of one of the mother surrogates is presented in Fig. 6.9.

Other problems of the traditional views of secondary reinforcement and motivation arise from the definitions themselves. These problems are of a highly technical nature and concern the question of whether the onset or the termination of an unpleasant stimulus has the greatest motivational effects. (You will note that in our definition of secondary motivation the stimulus which was to come to have secondary motivating qualities had to be paired with a sudden increase and a *subsequent decrease in stimulation.*) This controversy has led to many interesting experiments and the development of an alternate theory of secondary reinforcement proposed by Mowrer. (See Chapter 8, pp. 345–348 for his views and other aspects of learning theories as they relate to motivation.)

EXPECTANCY THEORY   So far we have presented the theories of men who have viewed behavior as connections between stimuli and responses. Not all learning theorists look at learning from this same vantage point. For example, Edward Tolman argued that we learn the *relation between the stimuli* around us. Tolman's name has long been associated with "expectancy theories of behavior." For him, learning consists of mastering relations between stimuli in our environment. We learn *cognitive maps* of our surroundings. In these maps we learn various routes. These routes lead to further stimuli which have different values to the person or animal. In Tolman's theory our responses are determined by expectancies that given routes found in our cognitive maps will lead to differentially valuable stimuli.

In this view people follow the routes which will take them to goals which are important and desirable for them at any instant in time. The actual movements involved in getting to the goals are not in and of themselves essential to Tolman.

Do we learn responses?   In his emphasis upon cognitive learning we find the positive aspect of Tolman's work. Viewed from the other side of the fence, however, expectancy theories are an attack upon the foundations of *S-R* association theories. The *S-R* association is the heart of the theories propounded by Guthrie, Thorndike, and Hull, as well as by other behaviorists. Tolman suggests that theories should deal with learned associations *between stimuli*, or *S-S* associations. Which view should we hold? One in which associations are between stimuli and responses or one in which the associations are only among stimuli? Presumably the problem is amenable to experimental resolution. The following experiment has been offered as support for Tolman's *S-S* position.

Rats learned the solution to a maze problem for a food reward [13]. After the animals had learned the desired response, lesions were made in their cerebellums which produced gross impairments in motor performance. The question was, could animals with such severe motor debilities still find their way to the goal compartment? They did. The Tolmanian argument is that the rats could not have learned the maze problem in the first place as *a series of motor responses*, since the mechanisms they would have used to learn these responses were severely damaged by the lesions. Thus, superficially at least, the animals seem to have learned a cognitive map of the environment rather than to make specific responses. The *S-R* theorists, however, could maintain that since many of the muscle movements required to run the maze were common to both the pre- and post-operative phases of the experiment, the results do not provide a conclusive contradiction to their position.

Is reinforcement necessary? The expectancy theory of Tolman differs from the theories of Thorndike and Hull on the question of the need for reinforcing events in learning. Tolman argues that *S-S* associations are learned through contiguity alone and do not depend on reinforcements. For instance, we *know* the drinking fountain is out the classroom door to the left and down the hall about 15 feet. We may know this even though we have never had occasion to drink from it. However, this learning will never become evidenced through performance unless we are motivated to drink. One way to test whether a person has learned where the drinking fountain is located would be to make him thirsty. We observe the subject's reactions when motivated to obtain water. Does he go out the door, turn left, and make a beeline for the fountain? Or does he go out and begin searching in a trial-and-error fashion to find a fountain? Tolman's idea is that motivation acts to select which route is followed, and, therefore, what behavioral act occurs.

Tolman and Honzik performed an experiment with rats which attempted to illustrate that reinforcement was not necessary for learning [14]. Three groups of animals were given experience in a complex maze. The animals were deprived of food during training. One group of animals was always rewarded with food when they reached the goal box (*HR* group). Another group, equally hungry was never fed in the goal box (*HNR* group). The third and crucial group was equally hungry and was not rewarded with food in the goal box until the eleventh day of training (*HNR-R* group). The question was this: Would the performance of the critical group (*HNR-R*) suddenly improve to the level being exhibited by the *HR* group? Tolman and Honzik believed Hull would have predicted a slow learning curve to be exhibited by the *HNR-R* group with the addition to food reward, while Tolman expected the animals to show a sudden improvement because at this point the animals would start to *use* the map of the maze they had built up by their previous aimless wanderings.

On the day following the introduction of food the animals of the *HNR-R* group showed performance at least equal to that of the group that had always been reinforced by food at the goal box. In other words learning became apparent to the observers only when the animals were motivated to show what they had learned (see Fig. 6.10). Tolman believes that this is

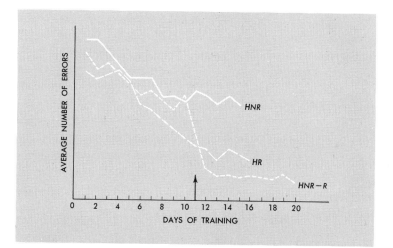

FIG. **6.10.** *Graphic representation of performances of three groups of animals in Tolman and Honzik experiment.* HNR: *animals hungry but never given food in maze;* HR: *animals hungry and always given food in goal box.* HNR-R: *equally hungry animals not given food in goal box until eleventh day and thereafter.* Adapted from E. C. Tolman and C. H. Honzik. *Introduction and removal of reward and maze performance of rats. Univer. Calif. Publ. Psychol.,* 1930, **4,** 257–275.

the *paradigm* for all learning. We learn sensory (*S-S*) associations, and when the situation makes one goal desirable we get there by the shortest route. If this short route is blocked or altered, we still can find the goal by following alternate routes developed in our cognitive maps.

The formal theory   The behavior of a rat at a choice point in a maze, Tolman believes, could be used as an example of the important determinants of all behavior in rat and man. In 1937 he confessed the following belief:

> . . . everything important in psychology (except perhaps such matters as the building up of the superego, that is everything save such matters as involve society and words) can be investigated in essence through the continued experimental and theoretical analysis of the determiners of rat behavior at a choice point in a maze [15, p. 172].

Tolman's analysis of the behavior of the rat at a choice point enabled him to formulate a list of concepts relevant to all behavior. He postulated two general kinds of variables: (1) those concerned with the environmental aspects of choice and (2) those concerned with the differences between organisms as they make their choices. The specific variables are presented below.

1. Environmental variables

M	Maintenance schedule
G	Appropriateness of goal object
S	Types and modes of stimuli provided
R	Types of motor response required
$\Sigma(OBO)$	Cumulative nature and number of trials
P	Pattern of preceding and succeeding maze units

2. Individual difference variables

H Heredity
A Age
T Previous training
E Special endocrine, drug, or vitamin conditions

The first category of variables are those which experimenters usually manipulate. Some researchers, for example, investigate the effect of the length of time an animal has been deprived of food or water on performance (M). Others might be curious about the effect of different incentives (G) on behavior. Tolman suggested the use of the term *independent variable* for those variables which are manipulated in experimentation [16]. Generally speaking, environmental variables are those *most often* manipulated in psychological experiments, although today we find a great number of experiments in which the H, A, T, E variables are the independent variables. In addition he suggested the use of the term, *intervening variable* to describe theoretical terms only indirectly tied to actual experimental operations. In fact, for each of the environmental variables he suggests a related intervening variable.

Tolman presents a third category: *dependent variables.* These represent the performance of the behaving organism. Let us examine a modification of a Tolman diagram which presents all three kinds of variables:

Independent variables (Environmental manipulations)	*Intervening variables* (Theoretical terms)	*Dependent variables*
M	Demand, motivation, persistence	
G	Appetite, taste, preference	
S	Sensory differentiation of situation, sensory capacities	Performance measures
R	Motor skills and capacities	
$\Sigma(OBO)$	The learning of sign Gestalts	
P	Biases toward one choice or another, perseveration, or emotional stability	

To predict behavior, we need to know two sets of relationships with this kind of formulation: (1) how each of the intervening variables is related to environmental manipulations, and (2) how the intervening variables combine to allow prediction of the dependent variables. At this time, we can say very little about this, however. Tolman's contribution remains one of an analytic scheme for future development. Tolman's organization of the behavior of the rat has influenced psychology, but no final plan has been worked out to explicate these intervening variables, nor have the rules of relationship between independent, intervening, and dependent variables been spelled out.

Additional comments The extent to which our cognitive maps range over a great number of environmental stimuli is an important attribute of our personal development. The greater the number of such associations, the wider will be our perspective. As children, our cognitive maps are limited. As we grow older, go to school, meet new people and situations, our range of hypotheses about the world become extended. In general, we tend to value the person who has a broad range of associations. Today, one prominent definition of the creative person is defined in terms of the range of associations a person makes to a set of words or concepts presented to him. As we grow old, we sometimes find the range growing narrower again. This narrowing of the cognitive map is often identified with senility. But there are other times when our maps become restricted too. Under terrific stress we can observe a constriction of our cognitive maps. When a person returns (regresses) to a mode of behavior that is more appropriate of an earlier age, we find a similar reduction in range of associations. When a person adopts a very limited set of behaviors (fixation), can this be identified with a correspondingly limited map? Tolman has suggested that the cognitive map concept might be valuable in understanding these behavior patterns.

The ideas presented by Tolman foreshadowed the theories advanced by Hebb (see Chapter 5). The similarity between the two theories stems from their respective dependence upon expectancies. Hebb goes a step or two further by means of assumptions about the neural mechanisms underlying expectancies. Certain phase sequences lead to others, and synaptic facilitation bears the explanatory burden in his theory. Hebb tries to explain what *expectancy* means physiologically, whereas Tolman merely accepts it as a psychological fact.

All the learning theories discussed have been influential in shaping our concepts in other areas of psychology, and they have altered man's view of himself. These theories are not the only ways in which the professional students of behavior have attempted to understand the learning processes. Some have made models of behavior, or at least certain kinds of behavior, in the hope that these will help with the prodigious task of *understanding* man's behavior.

Machines and Models

Since the beginning of recorded time man has made images of himself. However, until this century these efforts have been aimed at producing images of the external appearances. Even the elaborate creations of the Swiss watchmakers were attempts to create *moving images* in the likeness of men or animals. Recently scientifically minded craftsmen have attempted to produce models that mimicked the psychological functions presumed to exist in man and animals. Reproduction of appearance has taken a poor second place to reproduction of function.

THE SCHEMATIC SOWBUG   Tolman designed a schematic animal called a *sowbug*, to help him understand the properties of rats as they made decisions at the choice points in mazes [17]. Presumably, when forced to design a model, even though a schematic model, one must be explicit about the intervening variables which will be built into the machine. Translating one's

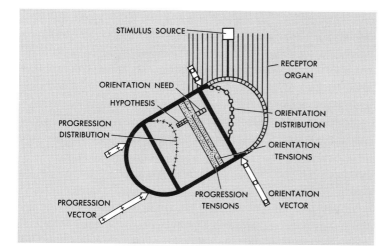

FIG. 6.11.   *Schematic "sowbug" described by Tolman. Adapted from E. C. Tolman. The determiners of behavior at a choice point. Psychol. Rev., 1939, 46, 318–336.*

theory into a model that works is a way of testing one's theoretical precision and may provide fresh insights into behavioral problems as well.

Tolman's sowbug incorporated many of the variables described in the preceding section. The sowbug represents a simple variety of "animal," with one receptor organ at the head and four symmetrically placed motor appendages (see Fig. 6.11). The animal would be sensitive to the direction of light falling on the receptor organ, and, in general, the left-hand appendages would be aroused by receptor cells at the right portion of the head. Correspondingly, right-hand motor appendages would be activated by light falling on the left portion of the receptor organ. This simple mechanism would produce a movement in which the sowbug would orient itself toward any illuminating light. The amount of demand for orientation, a function of maintenance schedule, is an internal variable which would create orienting movements toward the light on some occasions but not others. The effects of previous situations ($\Sigma(OBO)$) is represented in the *hypothesis area* of the bug.

The *progression distribution* represents the motor tendencies of the bug dependent on the orienting distribution and the hypothesis. Tolman suggests that with a few more assumptions and further complications of design we would have a valuable model of simple animal behavior.

MODELS FROM NEUROPHYSIOLOGY Whereas Tolman proceeded to build his model on the basis of observable data obtained from his research with rats and his theory of behavior, other men have developed models based on data and theory in neurophysiology.

Probably the neurophysiological observation most widely used in connection with model building is the *all-or-none law*. This law asserts that if a neuron fires, it does so to its maximum potentiality. This is seen as analogous to a simple electric circuit which is either open or closed. If this analogy is valid, could we not build a complete electronic model of a brain and study it as it learns, behaves, and even becomes emotional?

W. Grey Walter discussed the difficulties involved in building a model of the nervous system proceeding from the all-or-none law [18]. After presenting the problems involved in manufacturing even a single artificial nerve fiber, he goes on to say:

> Supposing a sufficient number of these simplest of imitation nerve fibers were constructed, [more] millions of cubic feet of warehousing would be required. . . .
> At this point we might have to consider cost. A cell with one fiber conceivably made for a dime—in all, say \$1,000,000,-000. Wiring connection 10^{20} of them, at about two cents each, say \$2,000,000,000,000,000,000. Power required would be at least a million kilowatts, even if the transistor crystal were used instead of the prodigal thermionic tube; the human brain runs on 25 watts. The cost would be incalculable. And the comparable cost of producing a first-class living brain? Twenty thousand dollars? [18, p. 117].

Walter estimates the warehouse space necessary for the 10,000,000,000 artificial brain cells at 1½ million cubic feet!

For these and other reasons, Walter sees the road to producing a working electronic model with anything like a similar number of units as closed. On the other hand he suggests that an understanding of the functions of the brain may be based not on the number of units involved but in the richness of interconnections between units.

Machines built by Walter support his view that the richness of interconnections must be one of the more important structural characteristics of the nervous systems of man and animals. Figure 6.12 shows his *Speculatrix* on its way "home." Let us reflect upon some of the characteristics Walter built into this disturbingly alive machine [adapted from 18, pp. 126–128]:

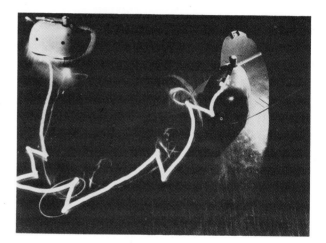

FIG. 6.12. *Speculatrix returning to its hutch. Reprinted from* The Living Brain *by W. Grey Walter. By permission of W. W. Norton & Company, Inc. Copyright © 1963, 1953 by W. W. Norton & Company, Inc., and Gerald Duckworth & Co., Ltd.*

1. *Parsimony.* The machine is very simple in construction. Two cells function as nerve cells. There are only two receptors: a photoelectric cell and an electrical contact serving as a touch receptor.

2. *Speculation.* It is always active, never at rest unless recharging batteries. Since it is always on the move it appears to be exploring. "Like the restless creatures in a drop of pond water, it bustles around in a sense of swooping curves, so that in an hour it will investigate several square feet of ground."

3. *Tropisms, Positive and Negative.* Speculatrix moves toward lights of moderate intensities. When an adequate light signal is presented it stops its exploratory operations and moves toward the light source. The photoelectric-cell eye at the front of the machine is continually scanning the horizon for light signals. Obstacles and very bright lights are repellent to this device.

4. *Discernment.* When an obstacle is met during the pursuit of an attractive light, the light temporarily loses its attractiveness. After the obstacle has been dealt with, the light becomes attractive again.

5. *Optima.* The machine seeks optimal conditions, not maximal. For example, it seeks only moderate intensity lights.

6. *Self- and Mutual Recognition.* The "animal" will be attracted to its own lead light reflected from a mirror. It will approach this light, but a circuit of the machine then extinguishes the light. The "animal" then is no longer attracted to the mirror. But since the photoelectric cell is no longer receiving the reflected input, it turns the head lamp back on. Then the machine is attracted again to the mirror. "The creature therefore, lingers before a mirror, flickering, twittering and jigging like a clumsy Narcissus" [18, p. 128]. The machines tend to group together by their tropic reactions to each other's head lamps, unless disturbed by external stimulation. In such a group the individual becomes alternately a positive or negative stimulus for others. It acts as an approachable head lamp at one time, but an obstacle at the next.

7. *Internal Stability.* In Fig. 6.12 we saw Speculatrix returning to the "hutch." The machines are built in such a way that the light of the hutch is *too* bright when its batteries are fully charged, but becomes attractive when the batteries are run down. Thus, the search for moderation in light stimulation "gives way to appetites" when the energy of the Speculatrix system is depleted.

Walter planned many but not all of the behaviors exhibited by his mechanical prodigies. The headlights were added to inform observers when the steering mechanism was on. Yet these pilot lights made possible the behaviors which could be interpreted as self-recognition and social behavior on the part of a group of the machines.

Furthermore, Walter was able to build a *black box* which has many of the same properties of real animals during learning. He called it the *conditioned reflex analogue,* or CORA for short. This machine was primarily a way of storing information so that it could be used in the future. When CORA was grafted on to Speculatrix, Walter produced a machine that could learn; he called it Docilis.

By having a whistle precede a moderate intensity light for several trials the new creature came to approach the whistle.

Used in another way the whistle could come to mean punishment-will-follow by pairing the whistle with a kick to the shell. Soon, Docilis came to avoid the area of a room associated in the past with a whistle.

In watching these "nut-and-bolt beasts" during the whistle-means-dodge training, Walter noticed an unplanned electronic phenomena. The memory circuits in the machine became reactivated with every presentation of the whistle, something that had not occurred when the machine had been trained under the whistle-means-light program. As a result, the avoidance behavior caused by the kick remained almost perfectly intact despite lack of further kicks! The whistle-means-light response disappeared in a relatively few trials after the light was no longer presented following the whistle. The persistence of the whistle-punishment behavior was unpredicted but very much like the results obtained with dogs trained to make responses to avoid high-intensity electrical shocks. These real animals continued to make responses for a considerable period of time without additional shocks [19].

The dodge response reactivated the memory trace in Docilis and this was responsible for the perpetuation of the learned response. Does an analogous mechanism exist in animals? Unfortunately we do not know enough about the physiological bases of learning or memory to decide, but certainly the findings of the reactivated memory trace in Docilis are suggestive of lines for future research.

Many other modifications of the basic machines have been and will be made with the result of greater and greater approximation to animal reactions. These may result in new ideas of how man behaves. Is Walter only investigating what happens in various kinds of models or what *may* be happening in the living brain? As Walter put it: "Of course we are considering both, hoping that the explicit clarity of the first will illuminate the implicit obscurity of the second" [8, p. 150].

MODELS AND THEORIES Models like Docilis and the schematic sowbug are, after all, merely a mechanical demonstration of an implemented theory of behavior. In current usage the term *model* is merely a synonym for *theory* [20]. For example, Hull's theory can, at least in part, be translated into a mechanical model as he showed in his presidential address to the American Psychological Association in the 1930s. Today, the types of models (theories) of behavior being constructed are more elaborate and sophisticated than ever before. They make use primarily of mathematical language, which is less ambiguous in the definition of terms and in syntactic structure than are natural languages, and more suited for use in modern calculating machines (computers). All scientists are becoming more and more aware of the power of mathematics in their fields. It is no surprise that modern theories of the learning process are formulated in mathematical languages.

Spence   In a sense, Hull's model belongs at the head of any list of mathematic models of learning. Given his list of symbolic terms ($_sH_R$, D, K, etc.) and his rules for combined terms ($_sE_R = {}_sH_R \times D \times K \times V \times J$, etc.), one can know the nature of his theory. The theory or model is completely described. To use the theory one need only interpret the terms. Again, rules for this are provided. For example, the value of $_sH_R$ can be derived knowing only the number of reinforced trials in the training situations. Newer formulations of the Hull type of model have been presented by Spence [21].

Spence's recasting of learning theory have eliminated many inadequacies of Hull's theory. Through the years it was found that many facts of behavior were not predictable from the earlier formulas. The result of Spence's work is two models of learning. One is to be applied in classical conditioning situations, where the animal is trained to make a conditioned defensive response like lifting a paw when it is shocked, when a *CS* is presented. In such situations learning to respond to the *CS* is determined by the variables given in this formula:

$$R = D \times H - I_n$$

where D = function of the strength of the painful stimulus (shock)
  H = joint function of strength of the shock and number of training trials where shock has been used
  I_n = function of number of training trials on which *CS* was presented but animal was not shocked

On the other hand, learning to make a specific response for a positive incentive is supposed to follow quite different rules. The formula governing this kind of learning is

$$R = f(D + K) \times H - I_n$$

where H = function of number of training trials received by individual whether reinforced or not

D = function of time of deprivation

K = joint function of magnitude of reinforcement and number of reinforcements

I_n = function of number of times response has not been followed by a reinforcement, given a number of reinforcement trials

If this formula is compared with Hull's, a number of differences can be observed. Principally, these have to do with the additive rather than multiplicative relationships between drives and incentives, and the nature of the inhibitory variable I_n. Inhibition of a response is thought to occur when an animal has received reinforcements in a goal area but does not find it there. This produces a frustration effect which acts to inhibit the response.

The improvements made by Spence are important since they allow much greater accuracy in the prediction of behavior. On the other hand, this line of theory building is but one of many possible methods of formulating the learning processes. Other methods have been developed and offer promise of even greater usefulness in understanding behavior.

Stimulus-sampling models An increasing number of psychologists are working to develop theorems and formulas which relate changes in responses produced by reinforcement or non-reinforcement. The complete elaboration of such theories are beyond the scope of this book. However, in the next few paragraphs we will attempt to provide a general discussion of the nature of these new directions in learning theories.

The mathematically formulated learning theories deal with three types of events: *responses, stimuli, reinforcing events.*

RESPONSES. All behavior which can be made by the subject in the experimental situation is classified into mutually exclusive and exhaustive categories. In so far as the theory is concerned this means that all the varieties of behavior which can be exhibited by the subject are brought under one of the classifications and that there is no overlap in the classifications. Since the experimental situations used by theorists must be capable of straightforward interpretation, response categories such as "a turn into right alley" or "a turn into left alley" of a T maze are used. In other words only simple learning situations are used where the response categories represent "either-or" types of behavior. The classes of available responses are considered to represent a mathematic collection or set.

STIMULI. An organism's stimulus condition is determined by the nature of its environment and its internal characteristics. All the stimulating conditions, or the environment, may arouse a large number of stimulus-conditions and the collection of all of these constitute a set. The elements of this mathematic set are often called stimulus elements.

REINFORCING EVENTS. It is well known that the probability of a response can be changed by presenting the individual with certain stimuli (for example, food given to a hungry animal). These stimuli are called reinforcements, as we know. For the present purposes, the nature of reinforcement is not important. Reinforcements are presumed to effect the probabilities of elements of the response set given the occurrance of elements from the stimulus set. Once again, the types of reinforcements are presumed susceptible to classification into a set of all such conditions.

Learning is defined as the changes in the probabilities of elements of the response set which come from the training trials of the individual in the situation. Every trial begins with the introduction of specific (and constant) changes in the environment, a response of the individual, and ends with one of the reinforcement outcomes. If other things are constant, the changes in response probabilities are believed to be determined by the reinforcement conditions.

In most models the changes in response probabilities are presumed to be a linear function of the probabilities existing on the proceding trial. By this we mean only that the probability of a response, X, is changed by a mathematically linear transformation by the reinforcement conditions. In other words, if the probability of response. X is P_x on trial 17, and if the response is reinforced, the probability of the response occurring on trial 18 will be increased by an amount predictable from a linear equation.

$$y = ax + b \text{ (basic model of linear equation)}$$

If y is used to represent Px on trial 18, it would be predicted as the sum of a constant factor, b, plus a multiplication operation a upon P_x of trial 17, x. The actual form of the equation depends upon specific assumptions of the mathematical model being used.

RULES OF LEARNING. One form of linear learning models involves the assumption of random sampling of stimulus elements on every trial [22, 23]. The environmental circumstances are assumed to supply a set of stimulus elements, but only a portion of this set are available for conditioning on any given trial. This portion is called the stimulus sample. They are those stimulus elements which are "available" to become completely associated with any response made with them if it is followed by a reinforcement. The learning, or association, formed on any one trial is complete and absolute. (In the theory of Bush and Mosteller [24] the conditioning of stimulus elements to the response is not assumed to be of an all-or-nothing character, but to proceed by gradual increments.)

The performance of the organism depends upon the extent to which the elements of the stimulus set become conditioned to a response. On every trial on which the reinforced response occurs in the experimental circumstances, more stimulus elements become associated with the response. In some models the number of stimulus elements sampled on each trial is assumed to be constant, while in other models different numbers of stimulus elements can be sampled.

Thus, the performance of the individual will show gradual increases in the probability of occurrence of the reinforced response, owing to the increasing number of stimulus elements associated with the response even though the mathematical theory asserts one-trial conditioning between individual stimulus elements and the response.

The stimulus elements sampled on any given trial are likely to be different from those sampled on any other trial. In Fig. 6.13 the elements sampled on trial 17 contain a combination of elements previously associated with the response A_1 (filled circles) and those associated with the response A_2 (open circles). Assuming the response A_1 was made and reinforced, all elements sampled on that trial would be associated with this response. Therefore, on trial 18 there would be more stimulus elements available for sampling which have been conditioned to response A_1 than previously. However, fluctuations in the elements selected for sampling, presumably by a random process, would make for fluctuations in the actual response produced by the animal, even though response A_1 was associated with more stimulus elements through the previous reinforcement. Thus in Fig. 6.13 two possible sampling outcomes are

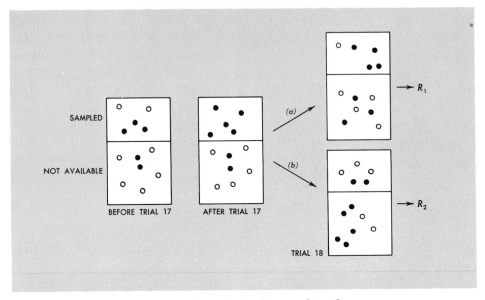

SAMPLED

NOT AVAILABLE

BEFORE TRIAL 17

AFTER TRIAL 17

(a)

(b)

R_1

R_2

TRIAL 18

FIG. **6.13.** *Schematic representation of stimulus-sampling theory. Total set of stimulus elements are represented by rectangles.*

shown. In one case response A_1 would occur, and in the other response A_2 on trial 18. This aspect of the theory provides an explanation of the inconsistent behavior of animals during training.

The development of mathematical theories of learning is in an early stage. Interest is growing in this area of psychology, however, and ever-increasing interest can be expected. At present, several interesting contributions in this area are readily available to interested and mathematically prepared students, for example, papers by W. K. Estes, C. J. Burke, and R. C. Atkinson [25].

Reservations about the use of models Despite the enchanting lures of model building, whether mathematical or mechanical, there are dangers inherent in embracing them unqualifiedly. Chapanis [26] has pointed out some of these dangers for us. A brief list of a few dangers would include the following:

Models lead us to over generalize about behavior. We tend to accept the theory offered as a model of the entire realm of behavior. Models are analogies restricted to a small segment of life, and their limitations should always be kept in mind.

Models lead us to make logical fallacies. If the consequence is confirmed, we tend to accept the premise. If a model predicts a given behavioral event, and it happens, this does not establish the truth value of the theory.

Model building may divert potential useful energy into non-productive directions. Chapanis suggests that the inherent "fun" in model building can take people away from the work of accumulating sound behavioral data, through experimentation. Furthermore, models may be constructed for trivial events. One might ask whether or not a toylike model, like some described earlier, actually helps us to understand behavior.

There is no doubt that model building, testing, and refinement will be major activities of many psychologists for a long time to come. Whether the current work is premature cannot be decided except by history. The enthusiasm for formal theory construction is not shared by all psychologists, even those working in the area of learning. Major contributions in the area of learning have been made by many individuals, for example, B. F. Skinner of Harvard, whose work is of a much different sort than that which has been so far discussed.

The Contributions of B. F. Skinner

Skinner is convinced that psychology should concentrate its efforts upon the accumulation of knowledge through experimentation rather than in the construction of theories. Theories are often justified by the fact that they lead protagonists and antagonists to do experiments to support their positions. But Skinner believes that experiments designed to test predictions from a specific theory are wasteful. He would prefer to explore the changes in responses which result from changes made in the situation.

TWO TYPES OF LEARNING SITUATIONS Since for Skinner the appropriate study by psychologists is the relation between situational change and response change, it is important to study the characteristics of learning situations. In general, Skinner distinguishes two types of learning. One is represented by the classical conditioning situation of Pavlov. Typically, a stimulus to which a response would be conditioned (*CS*) was paired with a stimulus which always *elicited* a response. We call this innately effective stimulus the *US* and the associated response the *UR*.

Pavlov argued that the *US-UR* association was *reflexive* in that the *US* always affected the organism in such a way as to evoke the response. These responses are termed *elicited responses*. As a general rule, he believed the study of elicited responses to be less important for understanding complex behavior than the study of responses which are not reflexively evoked.

One paramount feature of naturally occurring behavior is the large number of responses for which there seems to be no eliciting stimulus. The responses which an animal or person produces which are not unequivocally tied to certain stimuli are called *emitted responses* or *operant behaviors*. They constitute a second type of learning. The essential observation about operant behavior (emitted behavior) is that it can be made more likely to occur in the situation by appropriate use of reinforcement.

It is possible for an experimenter to watch an animal and reinforce certain behavior through devices controlled by a pushbutton or other switch. The button could be connected to a food-releasing mechanism in the box which delivers a food pellet to the animal. With experimenter-operated devices Skinner can train a pigeon in what would appear as marvelously complex behavior in a matter of minutes. Behavior is shaped toward the desired response by a process called successive approximation. To train a pigeon to turn around, a reinforcement is given when the first small turning movement is emitted. This response usually will occur again soon. This time the reinforcement is applied after the animal has turned a little further. After a while, the reinforcing stimulus is presented only after a half or three-quarter turn is made. A few minutes later reinforcement is given only when a full turn is made. The whole training process takes but a few minutes and testifies to the efficacy of properly controlled reinforcements for learning.

REINFORCEMENT EMPIRICALLY DEFINED Earlier we emphasized the distinction between Thorndike and Hull in their use of the word *reinforcement*. Thorndike spoke of a "satisfying state of affairs" whereas Hull referred to a reduction of S_D (drive stimuli). To this date there has been no substantial agreement in definitions of reinforcement which try to explain the nature of reinforcement. Many learning specialists have settled for a rather restricted definition of reinforcement which we may call the *empirical definition*. This restricted definition merely says that a reinforcement is a stimulus which when presented after a response will make the response more likely to occur the next time the person or animal is in the same situation. Reinforcement is defined as the increase in probability that the reinforced response will occur in the future, such as we found in the stimulus-sampling theories. This type of definition presents us with the difficult job of identifying which stimuli will act as reinforcers in a complex situation. It will surprise no one to learn that food can serve as a potent reinforcement to the hungry organism.

Reinforcements are used to guide, or shape, emitted behavior. The operation is simple. The experimenter waits until the response to be studied is emitted. Then a reinforcement is given promptly. The response tends to occur more and more frequently as reinforcements continue. Thus, the behavior of the organism is shaped by the experimenter through his distribution of reinforcements. One of the prime considerations of Skinner's view is that the experimenter must be passive until the response is produced by the subject. When the particular response does occur, the experimenter becomes active and produces the reinforcing stimulus as quickly as possible following the response.

A PROBLEM IN EXPERIMENTS Many of the tasks assigned to subjects in learning experiments produce data which must be examined in terms of what a group (of animals or people) does. The experimental results are reported as statistical descriptions of all the animals in the group. Many times the data coming from such group descriptions look regular and "smooth," whereas the behavior of the individual is neither regular nor smooth. To focus this problem consider the artificial data presented in Fig. 6.14.

In this figure the hypothetical data obtained from four animals learning a complex maze are illustrated at the left. Each animal makes a large number of errors getting to the goal in the maze early in training, but as the trials progress there occurs a point at which there is a sudden drop in the time required to navigate the maze. Furthermore, each animal shows fluctuations in speeds of maze running from trial to trial, before and after the rapid improvement in performance.

The curve on the right side is merely the average performance of the subjects. For each trial the number of errors made by all animals were added and divided by 4. The result is a curve showing gradual rather than abrupt improvement.

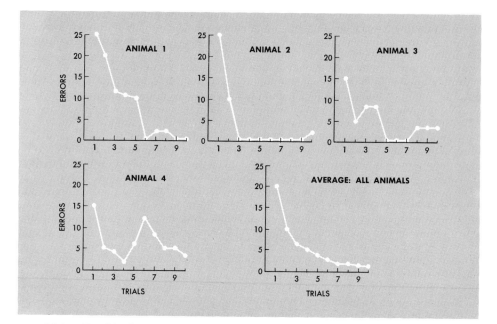

FIG. 6.14. *Graphic demonstration of the possibility that average behavior derived from a group of animals may not describe the behavior of any of the individuals in the group (based on hypothetical data). Errors in maze learning are plotted on the y axis, and the number of trials on the x axis.*

The trial-to-trial fluctuation has been eliminated. The graph of the group data does not typify the behavior of any animal in this hypothetical experiment. This example illustrates some of the possible misinterpretations of data when they are combined from all members of a group of subjects. This should not be taken to indicate that one should never use grouped data, but rather that one should be sure that the grouped data reflect what the individual subjects were doing.

THE OPERANT CONDITIONING BOX Skinner feels strongly that statistical reports of group behavior are too often misleading and that behavioral measures should be regular and reliable reports of the activities of individuals. The data obtained from *operant conditioning boxes* (sometimes called *Skinner boxes*) seem to fit his requirements best. The basic requirement of any operant box is there must be a lever that can be depressed. This depression activates mechanisms which deliver food or other reinforcements. Naturally, the bar or lever in the box does not elicit an immediate pressing response, but through acci-

dental contact with the bar it will be depressed and a reinforcement given to the animal. Then this bar-pressing response will
become shaped by subsequent reinforcements administered by
the subject without interference of the experimenter. A photograph of a typical operant conditioning box is presented in Fig.
6.15. Animals are usually trained while under a food or water
deprivation schedule with food pellets or small amounts of water
as incentives or reinforcers. Automatic response-recording devices are connected to the box so that a continuous recording
of the depressions of the lever can be made. The recording device moves a pen or writing instrument across paper at a constant rate. As the bar is depressed, the pen moves higher on the
paper. If no responses are being made, the pen will make a horizontal line. The more responses made, the faster the line will
ascend. A record obtained from an animal in an operant conditioning box is presented in Fig. 6.16.

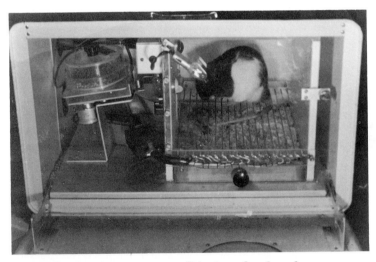

FIG. 6.15. *Rat in operant conditioning chamber depresses
short bar in wall which activates feeding mechanism and
causes food pellet to drop into receptacle in chamber.*

For Skinner, there are two sufficiently reliable measures of
behavior and both of these can be represented in cumulative recordings. One measure is the rate of responding, which is indicated by the slope of the line as it ascends swiftly or slowly.
The other is the number of responses which will be produced
by the subject after no more reinforcements are applied. This
is usually referred to as the number of responses from the last

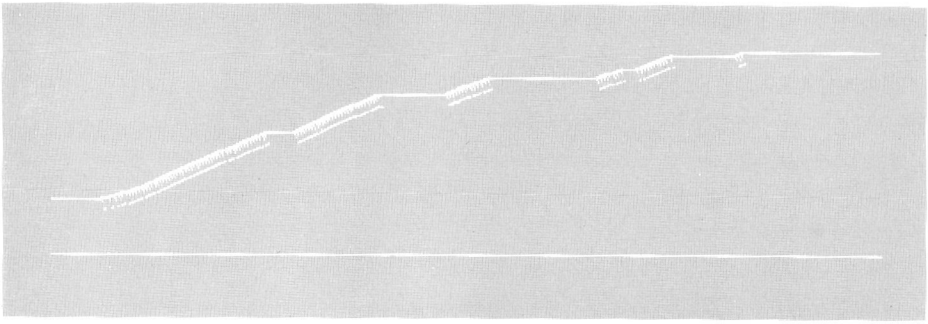

FIG. 6.16. *Sample record of animal under continuous reinforcement in conditioning chamber. Each time bar is depressed, recording mark is made slightly higher on the paper. The faster the rate of bar pressing, the steeper will be the slope of the record.*

reinforced response to that time when the animal fails to respond.

SCHEDULES OF REINFORCEMENT In training an animal, we can reinforce it every time it makes the response we wish it to learn. On the other hand, we can ask what would be the effect of not reinforcing *every* response but reinforcing some fraction of the responses? Would the animal just make fewer responses? Would it take longer to train the animal? What would happen if we stopped reinforcing the animal entirely after training it on a schedule where we have only rewarded the response at periodic intervals?

Given Skinner's use of an empirical definition of a reinforcer, we can investigate the effects upon behavior of applying a reinforcer after each and *every* response, *continuous reinforcement,* or after only some of the responses, *intermittent reinforcement.* There are, of course, many ways we could apply reinforcements; for example, we could reinforce alternate responses or reinforce the bar-press response every four minutes. However, there are four main intermittent schedules of reinforcements that have been studied.

1. *Fixed ratio (FR).* A response is reinforced upon completion of a fixed number of responses counted from the preceding reinforcement. The word *ratio* refers to the ratio of responses to reinforcement.
2. *Variable ratio (VR).* Similar to fixed ratio except that reinforcements are scheduled according to a random series of ratios having a given mean and lying between arbitrary values.

3. *Fixed interval (FI).* The first response occurring after a given interval of time, measured from preceding reinforcement, is reinforced.

4. *Variable interval (VI).* Similar to a fixed interval except that reinforcements are scheduled according to a random series of intervals having a given mean and lying between arbitrary values [27, p. 5].

Combinations of these basic types could be made too. All of these intermittent or partial reinforcement techniques are in contrast to the two continuous schedules of reinforcement: reinforcing every response and reinforcing no responses (extinction training).

Fixed-ratio schedules In the fixed-ratio schedule we find an almost astounding fact. As the ratio of responses to reinforcements increases, the rate of responding also *increases*. An animal can be trained so that it makes more and more responses with fewer and fewer reinforcements.

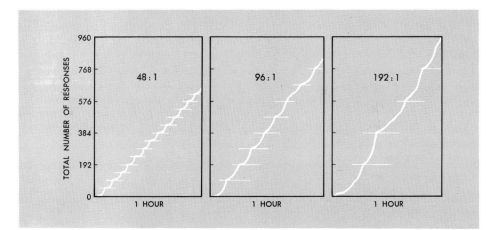

FIG. **6.17.** *Rates of rat response on three fixed-interval schedules.*
Adapted from B. F. Skinner, The Behavior of Organisms, *New York: Appleton-Century-Crofts. Copyright © 1938 by Appleton-Century-Crofts, Inc. All rights reserved.*

Training an animal under an intermittent fixed-ratio schedule results in a more rapidly ascending response record than training with continuous reinforcement. Under this type of schedule the animal must produce *n* number of responses before a reinforcement will occur. As the animal moves to higher and higher rates from original training with continuous reinforcement, the *rate* of responding increases. Figure 6.17 [27, p. 152] shows rates of responding for three different fixed-ratio schedules. The rate of responding is greatest in the ratio of 1 reinforcement for every 192 responses.

After each reinforcement (represented by a horizontal line on the curve) response rate slows down. This results in a scalloplike section of the curve between reinforcements. In part, this represents the time taken by the subject to ingest and chew the food but something else is going on too. For example, it should take no longer for the animal to ingest the food on one schedule rather than another. The food is the same size. At the

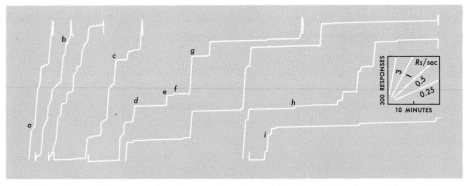

FIG. 6.18. *Cumulative records of rat undergoing extinction following training with fixed-ratio (60:1) schedule. Top of left records are continuous with bottom of right records. Note that periods when no responses are made are longer during extinction, but that otherwise rate of response remains high. From C. B. Ferster and B. F. Skinner,* Schedules of Reinforcement, *New York: Appleton-Century-Crofts. Copyright © 1957 by Appleton-Century-Crofts, Inc. All rights reserved.*

greater ratios the period between the reinforcement and the beginning of the new response period is greatest.

When the response acquired with a fixed-ratio schedule is no longer reinforced, the curves reveal that the decrease of the response rate comes about through progressive lengthening of these plateaus of no responding. When the animal responds it responds at a high rate but the periods of responding do not last long. This is illustrated in records obtained from pigeon research with the Skinner box as presented in Fig. 6.18 [28, p. 152].

One of the reasons for the high response rates obtained by the use of fixed-ratio reinforcement schedules may be that the rate of response itself is being reinforced. During the fixed-ratio schedules the animals tend to be responding at a high rate when the reinforcement occurs.

Fixed-interval schedules   Fixed-interval reinforcement refers to the administration of the reinforcing stimulus following a response occurring after some definite period following the last reinforcement. For example, a reinforcement might follow the first response to occur after a period of one minute from the preceding reinforcement. A minimum period of time must have elapsed and a response must be made by the animal. Generally, lower rates of responding are found with the fixed-interval than with the fixed-ratio schedule, and the longer the period of time between reinforcements the lower will be the rate of response. As with the fixed-ratio schedules there are also lapses in the response rate following each reinforcement, producing a scalloplike effect in the recorded records.

Variable-Interval and ratio schedules   These two more complicated schedules can change the response rates. The exact effects of the variable interval and ratio programs of reinforcement depend to a great extent on the past training histories and prior number of reinforcements given under different schedules. Generally, we may say that some of these manipulations result in response rates which do not show the pauses following reinforcement of the fixed schedules. High rates can be maintained throughout the training of the subjects.

Resistance to extinction   The number of responses which are emitted by subjects after all reinforcements have been stopped is the subject's *resistance to extinction*. The greater number of responses emitted the stronger the resistance.

An animal's resistance to extinction can be increased through intermittent, or partial, reinforcement schedules beyond that which can be obtained through training with continuous reinforcement.

Why do the partial reinforcement schedules affect the subjects so that they emit much greater numbers of responses when reinforcements are eliminated? Skinner is satisfied to report that they do. His interest is in determining the effect of various training procedures and manipulations on his two measures (response rate and number of responses to response cessation). We have only scratched the surface of the ways in which he has manipulated the many possible variables. For example, what are the effects of novel stimuli placed in the box? What is the effect of creating an emotional disturbance in the subject? What is the effect of giving the animal a "clock" to use in gearing itself to the fixed-interval procedures? All these and many more are discussed by Ferster and Skinner in their compendium of research [28].

A general summary of the findings in experiments using various schedules of reinforcement would look something like this:

Acquisition: Continuous reinforcement creates faster learning of the response than intermittent reinforcement.

Response rate: Faster rates with fixed-ratio schedules than fixed-interval schedules. Rate of fixed-interval schedules dependent on frequency of reinforcement.

Resistance to extinction: Intermittent schedules produce greater numbers of responses during extinction.

Possible explanations of extinction effects One explanation of the greater resistance to extinction of the animals trained under partial reinforcement schedules is that the subjects have a more difficult task in recognizing just when reinforcements are eliminated. If animals are trained with continuous reinforcement the transition is abrupt when depression of the lever fails to produce a reinforcement. When trained under an intermittent schedule the animals have had experience with situations when the depression of the lever would not result in the appearance of food. If the animal is on a large fixed-ratio schedule (e.g., 48 to 1), it would take longer for the animal to discover the change in conditions. This type of explanation has been generally referred to as the *discrimination-failure* explanation. The animals fail to discriminate between acquisition and extinction phases of the experiment.

While acceptable at a common-sense level, this explanation is vulnerable to the objection that it depends too much on thinking or cognition. Some psychologists believe this kind of explanation brings back mentalistic, nonbehavioristic terms to psychology. Many people who do not object to the use of mentalistic concepts in the human are not willing to be quite so mentalistic with the rat or pigeon.

Other psychologists are of the opinion that the results of intermittent reinforcement in prolonging the period of responding during extinction training can be explained if we view the "response" differently. They say we should look at the response trained under a fixed-ratio schedule as the total series of *n* responses animals must make between reinforcements. Then during extinction, the total responses should be counted in terms of the number of packages of *n* responses emitted.

Still another way of explaining the intermittent-reinforcement results is through the use of the concept of secondary reinforcement. If the bar-press response has acquired secondary reinforcing properties, then each bar depression adds to the habit strength of the bar-press response. Because of the high response rates, animals under the intermittent schedules have built up greater habit strengths than the animals which receive primary reinforcements less often. Greater habit strength should lead to greater resistance to extinction.

There are data to support and refute all of these interpretations. We cannot say which explanation will be best in the long run. At this time it is best to side with Skinner who simply reports the data and leaves the interpretation to the future.

RELATION OF PARTIAL REINFORCEMENT TO HUMAN BEHAVIOR

One of the reasons intermittent reinforcement is a lively area of psychological research is that outside the laboratory reinforcements are usually provided in an intermittent fashion. Continuous reinforcement is more the rule of the laboratory than of society. Mother's reactions to a child's behavior are seldom consistent time after time. Sometimes other things are going on in the household that make a reinforcement, positive or negative, impossible to provide. The soup may be boiling over or the phone ringing as junior emits the given response. If the behavior is undesirable, it may be that negative reinforcement is withheld because another one of "mother's angels" is doing something even worse. In any case, whether we deal with reinforcements of a positive or negative nature, whether we conceive them as physical or verbal, we can easily see that they are usually applied on less than a continuous basis. From our discussion we know that any response learned or performed on an intermittent basis is difficult to extinguish.

Punishment Reflection on the usual patterns of social learning leads us to recognize the emphasis placed on attempts to "stamp out" undesirable acts through punishment. When a child does something undesirable, we sometimes resort to a slap, spank, or yell. We previously discussed the law of effect made famous by Thorndike. Originally he thought of positive rewards as stamping-in *S-R* connections and negative rewards as stamping-out *S-R* connections. Later, on the basis of studies using negative verbal stimuli (rather weak punishments), he concluded that punishment had little effect on eliminating undesirable behavior. Hull's theory asserts that responses are learned on the basis of a reduction of drive stimuli (S_D). Drive stimuli are produced by punishment. According to Hull's view, responses most closely and consistently associated with the *reduction of aversive drive stimuli* become learned. Skinner's definition of negative reinforcers is much the same. For him, responses can be learned by their association with the termination of negative reinforcers, which are defined as stimuli that adversely affect the rate of responding.

Many things may act to reduce response rates. The presentation of novel stimuli in the responding situation, motives and emotions of certain kinds, and punishment can act to depress response rates. When a response rate is depressed by punishment, the organism can be trained to emit another type of response. This is the important effect of punishment in the Skinner analysis of behavior. If we use punishment at all, we should be careful to train the person or animal in another way of responding while the rate of emission of the objectionable response is lowered.

Through the number of reinforcement and training schedules a certain *operant strength* is built up in the organism. Skinner would define this concept behaviorally as the number of responses emitted during the extinction period. Punishment only acts upon the response rate, *not* the operant strength. Therefore, even though we punish a response, we would expect the same *total number of responses to be emitted* ultimately. This would lead to the punished animal's responding *longer* than an animal not punished following the removal of the positive reinforcement. To eliminate responses, we must have the subject emit all of the responses which constitute the operant strength without reinforcement. The faster they are emitted during extinction, the sooner the animal will stop making the response entirely. As mentioned above, if we depress the rate by punishment, it will take longer for the animal to reduce the operant strength of the response. In Fig. 6.19 we see data from an experiment by Estes in which this prolongation of response is demonstrated [29].

The group of animals punished early in the extinction period show a depression in rate which does not last long. When the punishment is no longer applied (days 2 and 3), we observe the nonpunished animals producing fewer responses than the animals in the punished groups. This in a way summarizes many of the conclusions about the effect of punishment. Punishment can depress the rate of response, but it does not effect the total number of responses that will be emitted during the extinction training. This should serve as a warning to us. *By punishment it is possible to perpetuate those very responses we wish to eliminate.*

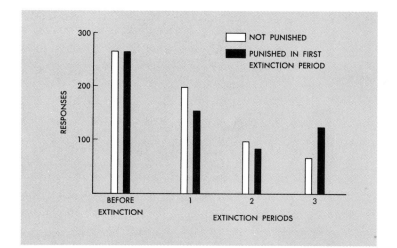

FIG. 6.19. *Effects of punishment on extinction. Note that group receiving punishment shows earlier decline in response rate, but maintains a higher rate in third extinction period. Adapted from F. R. Hilgard.* Theories of Learning. *New York, Appleton-Century-Crofts, 1953. Data from W. K. Estes. An experimental study of punishment.* Psychol. Monogr., *1944, 57. By permission of E. R. Hilgard, W. K. Estes, Appleton-Century-Crofts, and The American Psychological Association.*

Through the problem of punishment and the effects of intermittent reinforcements we have been moving very close to areas far removed from necessary restrictions of laboratory work. Skinner's interests range widely, and his work upon the basic learning processes has fathered one of the more remarkable educational supports developed in recent years.

The teaching machine   One fascinating and important educational innovation which stemmed from the work of Skinner, his colleagues, and students is the teaching machine. It is based on the belief that rapid learning depends upon having the student produce a large number of correct responses. The teaching machine was designed to present many short questions, one at a time. The student writes his answers in a space provided near the question. The material used in the machines is written in a way that makes it difficult for the student to answer incorrectly. A correct response serves as a reinforcement. If there is no reinforcement, there will be no change in the student's responses. From Skinner's point of view responses are acquired through positive reinforcement, and we know that this reinforcement must occur almost immediately following the response. Since asquisition is the important dimension of learning, a continuous schedule of reinforcement is used.

It is too early to make any definite conclusion about teaching machines even though most of the preliminary studies and reports have been favorable. Generally, students using the machines learn factual material faster than students working with traditional methods. It is likely that certain kinds of materials are more amenable to presentation by teaching machines than others. Areas of learning in which a student must master a considerable amount of factual material will undoubtedly be placed into teaching-machine forms early. Areas in which conceptual frameworks must be learned and in which there are alternate interpretations may turn out to be resistant to machine instruction.

Utopia Watson, the early exponent of behaviorism in the United States, argued that all behavior is acquired. He believed that given enough power to control a person's development he could make him into almost any kind of person: a doctor, lawyer, beggar, or thief. This may be too extreme a position, yet Skinner believes that appropriately applied reinforcements are so potent that they could shape our lives in many important ways, and he suggests a possible "utopia" that could be produced with our current knowledge of the effects of positive reinforcement [30].

In summary: In the learning theories and models we have studied in this chapter, one finds the main American tradition in psychology. They have influenced all domains of psychological activity both theoretical and applied; they have fostered controversies, and, more important, they have led to careful examination of the behavior of men and animals in many situations. Perhaps Skinner is right, perhaps the same number of exploratory experiments conducted without theoretical basis would have produced more information about behavior; but on the other hand, without the incentive of personal commitment to a certain theory, experimenters would probably not have conducted as many experiments.

Furthermore, learning theories represent the attempts of man to understand the "why" of behavior. They represent attempts to explain—even though the explanations are not complete and will likely be judged as feeble attempts by history. Yet for most psychologists, it is creative theory building and testing which represent the exciting and absorbing facets of psychology as a basic science.

References

1. Underwood, B. J. *Experimental Psychology.* New York: Appleton-Century-Crofts, Inc., 1949.

2. Boring, E. G. *The History of Experimental Psychology.* New York: The Century Co., 1929.

3. Heidbreder, Edna. *Seven Psychologies.* New York: Appleton-Century-Crofts, Inc., 1933.

4. Pavlov, I. P. *Conditioned Reflexes* (Trans. G. V. Anrep.). New York: Dover Publications, Inc., 1960.

5. Guthrie, E. R. *The Psychology of Learning.* New York: Harper & Row, Publishers, Inc., 1935.

6. Rock, I., & Heimer, W. Further evidence of one-trial associative learning. *Amer. J. Psychol.,* 1959, **72,** 1–16.

7. Hull, C. L. *A Behavior System.* New Haven: Yale Univer. Press, 1952 (published posthumously).

8. Beck, E. C., & Doty, R. W. Conditioned flexion reflexes acquired during combined catalepsy and de-efferentation. *J. comp. physiol. Psychol.,* 1957, **50,** 211–216.

9. Karsten, A. Psychische Sättigung. *Psych. Forsch.,* 1928, **10,** 142–254. (Reported in Koffka, K. *Principles of Gestalt Psychology.* New York: Harcourt, Brace & World, Inc., 1935.)

10. Wolfle, J. B. Effectiveness of token rewards for chimpanzees. *Comp. psychol. Monogr.,* 1936, **12,** 1–72.

11. Harlow, H. F. The nature of love. *Amer. Psychol.,* 1958, **13,** 673–685.

12. Zimmerman, D. W. Durable secondary reinforcement. *Psychol. Rev.,* 1957, **64,** 373–383.

13. Lashley, K. S., & McCarthy, D. A. The survival of the maze habit after cerebellar injuries. *J. comp. Psychol.,* 1926, **6,** 423–433.

14. Tolman, E. C., & Honzik, C. H. Introduction and removal of reward and maze performance of rats. *Univer. Calif. Publ. Psychol.,* 1930, **4,** 257–275.

15. Tolman, E. C. The determiners of behavior at a choice point. In *Behavior and Psychological Man.* Berkeley: Univer. of California Press, 1958. (Originally published in *Psychol. Rev.,* 1938, **45,** 1–41.)

16. Tolman, E. G. Psychology versus immediate experience. *Phil. Sci.,* 1935, **2,** 356–380. Also in *Behavior and Psychological Man, op. cit.*

17. Tolman, E. C. Prediction of vicarious trial and error by means of the schematic sowbug. *Psychol. Rev.,* 1939, **46,** 318–336. Also in *Behavior and Psychological Man, op. cit.*

18. Walter, W. G. *The Living Brain.* New York: W. W. Norton & Company, Inc., 1953.

19. Solomon, R. L., & Wynne, L. C. Traumatic avoidance learning: acquisition in normal dogs. *Psychol. Monogr.,* 1953, **67,** 1–19.

20. Simon, H. A., & Newell, A. The uses and limitations of models. In L. D. White (Ed.), *The State of the Social Sciences.* Univer. Chicago Press, 1956.

21. Spence, K. W. The roles of reinforcement and non-reinforcement in simple learning. In K. W. Spence, *Behavior Theory and Learning.* Englewood Cliffs, N.J.: Prentice-Hall, Inc., 1960.

22. Estes, W. K. Toward a statistical theory of learning. *Psychol. Rev.,* 1950, **57,** 94–107.

23. Estes, W. K., & Burke, C. J. A theory of stimulus variability in learning. *Psychol. Rev.,* 1953, **60,** 276–86.

24. Bush, R. R., & Mosteller, F. *Stochastic Models for Learning.* New York: John Wiley & Sons, Inc., 1955.

25. Marx, M. H. (Ed.). *Theories in Contemporary Psychology.* New York: The Macmillan Company, 1963.

26. Chapanis, A. Men, machines, and models. *Amer. Psychologist,* 1961, **16,** 113–131.

27. Skinner, B. F. *The Behavior of Organisms.* New York: Appleton-Century-Crofts, 1938.

28. Ferster, C. B. and Skinner, B. F. *Schedules of Reinforcement.* New York: Appleton-Century-Crofts, Inc., 1958.

29. Estes, W. K. An experimental study of punishment. *Psychol. Monogr.,* 1944, **57,** 40 pp.

30. Skinner, B. F. *Walden Two.* New York: The Macmillan Company, 1948.

SEVEN VERBAL LEARNING AND HIGHER COGNITIVE FUNCTIONS

weak   rough   small   cold   fresh
strong smooth   large   hot   stale

A most distinctive characteristic of man is his use of language. Therefore, it is essential that the student of psychology know the relationships and factors entering into verbal learning. Such knowledge is rather basic and fundamental in understanding the nature of man, himself.

In the preceding chapter, we reviewed some of the prominent theories of learning and behavior. As noted, they are based upon the associationistic doctrine which stems, in part, from the school of philosophy called British Associationism. We shall find that the theories of verbal learning and retention, as well as the experiments generated by them, are also dominated by associationistic theories. First, we shall learn some of the basic features of verbal behavior. In the sections to follow we shall study adult verbal learning and the related explanations of forgetting, based on the assumption of an interference between verbal responses. Finally, we shall consider some of the newer approaches to the higher mental processes which have developed from work in the field of communications.

Development of Speech

We are all aware that learning to speak precedes learning to write. A baby takes a long time to master vocal communication, and we communicate with spoken sounds long before we master the art of communication through written symbols. Written communications probably came long after man had learned how to depict objects symbolically through primitive art forms.

A baby begins learning vocal communications at birth. The birth cry is a reflexive response to a sudden increase in the carbon dioxide level in the blood occurring when the umbilical cord is cut. There is a momentary lag before the lungs begin to act. Many of the early vocal acts, such as crying, are presumed to be reflexive responses to bodily changes.

In the first four to five months the infant produces just about all of the speech sounds which have been found in the known languages. The infant must learn to reduce the number of speech sounds to those used in his culture. Over a period of time, the repertory of sounds a person can make becomes narrowed to the number found in his native language.

When a baby is being fed, held, or cuddled, he tends to produce sounds which are softer (e.g., open vowels) than those he makes when he is deprived of the bottle or support (e.g., explosive sounds and grunts). Thus, from early in life we note a relationship between the type of sound produced and the state of the organism.

Before six months of age the infant has begun to learn how to control his vocalizations. This means that the muscles of the diaphragm, tongue, and jaws and the parts of the nervous system controlling them have developed to the point where fine discriminative movements are possible.

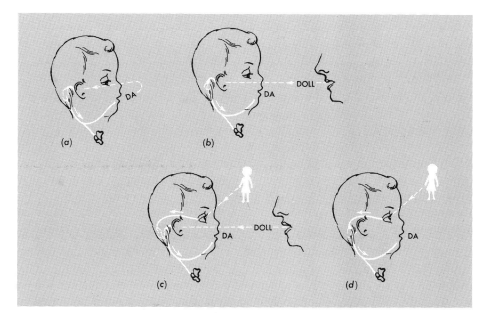

FIG. 7.1. *Stages in development of speech in infant: (1) random articulation of syllables, (2) evocation of same elements by speech sounds of others, (3) conditioning of sounds produced by others to object (doll), and (4) sight of doll produces sounds approximating "doll."* From F. H. Allport. Social Psychology. *Boston, Houghton Mifflin Company, 1924.*

Babbling and imitation   After the fifth month, babies generally can be heard babbling. This refers to sounds like "uggle-uggle," "erdah-erdah," "bup-bup-bup," and other repetitive noises [1]. Babies babble when alone as well as when with others and tend to practice one sound sequence before moving on to another. Perhaps babbling affords the opportunity to master sets of muscle responses which will comprise the building blocks of later speech.

Babies learn to mimic the patterns of sounds they hear. After sufficient muscular and neural development, speech sounds created by others can be duplicated by the infant. The next step for the baby is to be able to create a pattern of sounds which he has heard in conjunction with a perceptual object. The object becomes associated with the sound created by someone else in its presence. This association provides the basis for the child's vocalization of the sound when the object alone is presented. An illustration of this phase of language learning is presented in Fig. 7.1. Here we find the behavioral origins of the verbal acts called labeling. When we label an object, we attach a vocal or other specific response to a particular stimulus.

In all likelihood, labeling and many other varieties of verbal behavior are determined through timely reinforcements. Many psychologists agree that verbal behavior can be explained through the same kind of learning principles used to account for learning in animals. When an animal is placed for the first time in a experimental chamber (see pp. 260–262) in which a bar must be depressed to obtain a reinforcement, the behavior which depresses the bar can be readily inculcated through shaping. Behavior is shaped by means of judicial use of reinforcements. At first, slight movements toward the bar are reinforced. Next, only greater movements toward the bar are reinforced. Gradually, only the behaviors directly concerned with depressing the bar are reinforced. The experimenter is using a method of rewarding approximations to the final response.

Since children emit many kinds of sounds, the parents' job is to shape the child's verbal behavior so that only those responses remain which are significant in the culture. Watching parents with their children, one notices the shaping of sounds. The child's emitted response which is even a rough approximation to "Da-Da" in the presence of his father is subjected to a good bit of intensive shaping effort. Slowly, the rewarding behavior of the mother and father are withheld until "daddy" is a clear response.

Skinner believes that verbal behavior can be explained by extrapolations from his work with the empirical effects of reinforcements [2]. Whether or not all of the richness of human verbal behavior can be explained in terms of simple rules of reinforcement is a question which can not be answered at the present. Yet there is evidence that the rate of occurrence of specific verbal responses can be increased or decreased by rewarding behaviors on the part of others. In fact, the changes in verbal behavior induced by social rewards may occur without the individuals being aware of any such change [3]. The change in the rate of uttering words or word classes on the basis of reinforcing effects produced by others is called the *Greenspoon effect* after the experimenter reporting the result. The Greenspoon effect may be more complex than originally thought and the social rewards may act indirectly by inducing new sets of verbal habits [4].

Grammar   Once the ability to use labels and symbols is attained in childhood, vocabularies rapidly increase in size. We learn labels and symbols at a prodigious rate. However, even with a large vocabulary, language has not been mastered. Vocabulary is only part of language. The other part is the grammar of the language. To use or understand a language, we must know both the vocabulary and the grammatical rules. Only recently has there been much study of how the child develops knowledge of grammar, and much remains to be done [5]. It is interesting to note that most people can create perfectly good sentences in their language without being able to explicitly state the grammatical rules to which the sentences conform.

Spoken communication   The goal of speech is communication of a message from one person to another. We send vocal messages by patterns of sound waves generated by the expulsion of air across the vocal cords and through the oral cavity. No one knows just how many speech sounds the human can make. The set of sounds which are equivalent and can be used interchangeably to transmit meaning are called phonemes, and these can be thought of as the units of spoken languages. Phonemes differ from one language to another. They are the sounds which differentiate words or phrases of a language. In English we may consider them to be approximated by the sound of each consonant or vowel. Not all the different speech sounds are phonemes. There are many more distinguishable speech sounds than there are English phonemes.

We make speech sounds at a great rate. We can produce about 12.5 speech sounds every second when talking. Not all of these sounds carry information of significance for our messages, but they are units which could be used to transmit information. Information is transmitted through the use of sounds, signs and symbols, which have meaning or which elicit special kinds of responses within the perceiver.

The Sign and the Symbol

Most learning theories attempt to explain signs and symbols through the use of familiar concepts found in the study of stimulus-response learning. One could say that when Pavlov trained dogs to salivate to the sound of a metronome, the metronome acted as a signal for the introduction of food powder into the mouth. A red traffic light is a signal to stop, a green traffic light a signal to go. Animals and man both can learn to use signals.

SIGNALS FOR ANIMALS With proper training animals can be taught to make responses which seem to involve the use of symbols. Even simple avoidance learning in a shuttle box can be interpreted as requiring symbolic activity. In the shuttle box a stimulus (*CS*) is presented some number of seconds (e.g., five seconds) before the floor of the box is electrified. If the animal runs to the other side of the box within five seconds after the stimulus is presented, it is not shocked. Why shouldn't we interpret the *CS* signal as a sign or a symbolic event? The sign in this illustration is that if a given behavior is not performed the subject will be subjected to a painful situation. If the animals can be trained to respond to signs such as this *CS* in a shuttle-box experiment then the use of signs is not a characteristic which distinguishes *man* from the rest of the animal world.

It can be argued that animals can learn to respond to signs, but only man can manipulate symbols. But what is the distinction between a sign and a symbol? As a basis for distinction we might consider that stimuli which function as signs have only one or a few associated responses. Symbols, on the other hand, are stimuli which elicit many responses in the perceiving organism. This suggests a distinction between signs and symbols which is of quantity rather than quality. This may be appropriate in as much as the chimpanzees who worked for the poker chips in Wolfe's experiment (pp. 238–239) acted as though they were manipulated objects which had symbolic value.

Psychologists have not agreed on how the words, *sign* and *symbol* are to be used. Some have used the two words as synonyms. Others have used the word *symbol* to refer to a sign which stands for other signs. The use of these words is defined by convention and theory. They are meaningful only by convention.

We may find a useful distinction between symbolic behavior and sign behavior in the observation that some stimuli can produce effects in many situations other than the original learning situation. Symbols can be used in new places and at new times. In addition they do not always act to produce one standard behavioral response. Signs merely represent learned

S-R connections manifested in behavior, symbols are something more than this.

At one time secondary reinforcements were described as symbolic incentives. Secondary reinforcers came to have the ability to change response rates in situations other than that of the original training because of their association with primary reinforcements. In fact in the experiment with the chimpanzees and poker chips we observed that the secondary reinforcing poker chips could elicit distress reactions when they were out of the animal's reach. Owing to their transituational effectiveness, the poker chips acted like symbols.

Many times it is difficult to decide whether or not stimuli are acting as signs, signals, or plain "old-fashioned" stimuli. Let us use this to underline the most important part of this problem: *A given stimulus can be a signal, sign, or symbol, depending on the theoretical position under consideration.* Again we must underscore that the evaluation of any definition of these terms must depend on the success of the whole theory and not a single definition in isolation.

STIMULUS GENERALIZATION *"Stimulus generalization"* describes the fact that stimuli other than the ones used in training can often elicit the same response. If we train a dog to salivate to a 1000 cycle tone and after conditioning is well established present a 1200 cycle tone, we are sure to obtain some saliva flow. Is this odd? In one way, we have not trained the dog on this new tone at all, and yet there has been some generalization of the salivary response to the 1200 cycle tone. The two tones are somewhat alike. Both are auditory stimuli and both are about the same loudness. Furthermore, they "sound" somewhat the same, although dogs can discriminate between the two tones.

Figure 7.2 shows curves of generalization of a learned response along a visual continuum. Visual stimuli nearest the wavelength used in establishing the response evoke the largest number of responses when tests for generalization are made. However, problems exist for any simple technique used for specifying the extent of physical similarities. For example, it has been shown that the slope of a pitch generalization curve is not uniform. Tones representing octave steps from the tone used for conditioning produce greater responsiveness than intermediate tones [7]. This implies that a tone one octave away from the original conditioning tone has "more similarity" to it than many tones which are in fact closer to it along a frequency dimension. *Primary* stimulus generalization refers to a generalization of responses to new stimuli based on *physical similarity*.

Stimulus generalization can be either a handicap or an asset. When a husband coming home late at night elicits the same responses as would a burglar breaking and entering, this may be maladaptive for the husband if the wife is armed with a shotgun.

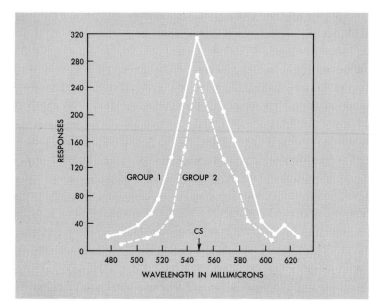

FIG. 7.2. *Stimulus generalization along visual-wavelength dimension in two groups of pigeons. Birds were trained to peck key illuminated by wavelength indicated on the x axis; and later tested by illuminating key with different wavelengths. Extent of generalization is reflected in height of response curves at different wavelengths. Adapted from N. Guttman. The pigeon and the spectrum and other perplexities. Psychol. Repts., 1956, 2, 451–460.*

At first glance one might equate stimulus generalization with some kind of failure in discrimination. Perhaps our dog which salivated to the 1200 cycle tone for some reason failed to discriminate between it and the 1000 cycle tone. Yet, while there are instances when a failure of discrimination can explain some of the experimental results, Gibson [8] has shown that this can not be the entire explanation. She found that subjects who were best able to discriminate between stimuli in an early phase of her experiment were the very same ones who showed the greater amount of stimulus generalization later in the experiment.

It should be stressed that primary stimulus generalization is a phenomena which is found without specific training. It occurs on the basis of some prior similarity between the training stimuli and the stimuli to which the training generalizes.

Let us consider the following experiment. We train subjects to salivate when a red light is presented. We could do this by pairing the red light with the injection of a mildly acidic solution into the mouth. More humanely we might inject some food substance in the mouth. In either way we could achieve a conditioned response to the red light. Now we are in a position to perform our generalization experiment. As a test, we now say "red" or present the written words *red light,* to the subjects. Will this cause them to secrete saliva in the same way as flashing the red light did? Will this verbal symbol which stands for the light be effective through some kind of generalization? From a number of studies in the Russian and American literature the answer is that generalization will occur! [9]

Mediated generalization   What kind of explanation can we provide for generalization of a response from a physical stimulus to a verbal symbol standing for the stimulus? To understand the current directions of research on this problem we must retrace some of the historical steps which lead to the present position. John B. Watson, the great popularizer of behaviorism, argued that thinking was merely vocal movements too small to be easily observed. To test this theory people have tried to record muscle potentials in the arm when thinking of throwing a baseball. Some of these attempts to record muscle movements associated with mental acts have been rewarded with some degree of success. Yet, we know that these minute tensions sometimes found in the muscle systems can not account for the range of mental phenomena in thinking. People without arms can still think of throwing a ball. Thinking and verbal behavior generally were identified with responses occuring in the individual. Today, many learning theorists conceive of verbal behavior in terms of specific *S-R* connections although the responses are now far removed from possible detection or observation. They are postulated to exist, perhaps only *in theory,* although some psychologists propose that their neural correlates may exist in the brain.

These *S-R* connections are thought to account for the learned associations which underlie the verbal symbol's elicitation of the response conditioned to the physical stimulus. They are called *representational,* or *mediational,* responses. The generalization from the actual red light to the words *red light* is mediated generalization. That is to say, generalization based on learned associations between the light and the words. If primary stimulus generalization is a concept used to summarize the fact that people and animals respond in the same way to *physically* similar things, mediated generalization refers to the fact that on certain occasions people and animals respond in the same way to things that are psychologically similar. Mediated generalization must be based on acquired connections arising from the language habits and customs of the society. A Frenchman would not generalize a conditioned response to the word *red* but rather the word *rouge* after conditioning with a red light as the *CS.*

In language we find both similarity of sound and similarity of meaning. Will a person conditioned to respond to a word such as *style* generalize to words that sound like style more than to words that mean the same thing? Razran [10] has tested the amount of generalization of a conditioned salivation response to synonyms and homonyms. More generalization occurred to the synonyms than the homonyms. Thus, subjects responded more to the word *fashion* than to the word *stile* after original conditioning to *style.*

Experimentally created generalization The theoretical foundations for mediated generalization have been laid in our previous discussions. It may be easier to recall them if we review the work of Shipley and the subsequent experiment by Lumsdaine [11].

In these experiments subjects were first conditioned to make an eye-blink response whenever a light was presented. Shipley did this by pairing a light with a tap to the cheek. This tap elicited an eye blink. After this response was established, the subjects were trained to retract a finger from an electric shock when the cheek was tapped. The question is, after this training program, what will happen when the light is presented? Shipley found that the light would now cause the retraction of the finger. The conditioning in the Shipley experiment might have developed as follows:

Light→tap→blink
Tap→blink→finger withdrawal (shock)
Test: light→(blink)→finger withdrawal

The eye blink and the tap to the cheek were both associated with the development of the new response of finger withdrawal. Thus both should have become conditioned to the finger movement. When the light was presented after training, it elicited the eye blink which now was conditioned to the finger withdrawal. It is as though the subjects had built a link-like chain of conditioning.

The Lumsdaine experiment was important because it approached the question of whether it was actually necessary for the eye-blink response to occur. In the early stages of behavioristic theory it would have been presumed to be necessary. In present day learning theory this is not the case. The mediating eye blink may be represented by changes in the central nervous system that never become expressed in observable behavior. Lumsdaine, as reported by Hilgard and Marquis [12, pp. 230 ff.] found that while the eye blink sometimes intervened between the light and the finger withdrawal, it often did not. Many times the eye blink occurred *after* the finger movement. It is because of the evidence from experiments like Lumsdaine's that the modern learning theories have moved toward *central mediational processes*. The actual movement of the eye blink is not thought to be essential to the mediational system, but some nervous system representation of the eye blink is. This central nervous system representation of the eye blink is conceptualized as a *response disposition* or *tendency* that need not reach its fulfillment in the muscle contractions which produce actual movements.

Mediational response Although different workers have proposed different terms and mechanisms of mediational processes, we shall follow the lead of Osgood and use the symbol r_m to refer to mediational responses [13]. Let us assume that every stimulus object produces two kinds of reactions within a person: (1) responses which are closely tied to the stimulus conditions and rarely could be elicited without the presence of the particular stimulus object and (2) responses which can be detached from the actual presence of the stimulus object. When stimuli other than the stimulus object are presented along with it, they tend to be conditioned to the detachable portion of the reaction to the stimulus object. It must be emphasized that only a portion of the total reaction to a stimulus object can be conditioned to another stimulus, namely, the detachable responses. It is some part of the detachable reaction of the total response to a red light that becomes conditioned to the words *red light*. This part would be the r_m which produces the behavioral response to the words *red light* following training to an actual red light in our earlier example. See Fig. 7.3 for an illustration of this process.

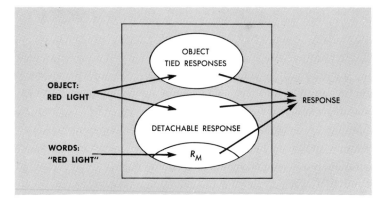

FIG. 7.3. *Physical stimuli elicit both object-tied and detachable responses. If the words "red light" have accompanied presence of a red light during the conditioning of a behavioral response, they alone can elicit the conditioned or detachable response* (r_m).

MEDIATION AND MEANING: THE SEMANTIC DIFFERENTIAL. Osgood has used the mediational response as a way to attack the difficult problem of "meaning." After our discussion of the mediating response we are now in a position to use it to gain greater definition and precision in a discussion of the relationship between words and things.

Osgood and Suci [14] have reasoned that if words have meaning because of the elicitation of mediating responses it might be possible to discover the nature of the different kinds of mediational processes elicited by a word through special statistical techniques. Their procedure calls for many people to rate words on a number of verbal scales. The data are then analyzed to determine the number of different independent dimensions needed to account for the ratings of the test words. Using this technique, Osgood and Suci have been able to find a limited number of independent scales needed to describe most of the words tested.

In Fig. 7.4 we present a sample of the semantic differential scale used to evaluate words. The dimension with the extremes labeled *good* and *bad* is what we might call the *evaluative dimension*. This dimension is the most important one for the evaluation of words. Much of the way we react to words seems to be explained on their "goodness" or "badness." In the figure we find a possible pattern of responses to the word *polite*. The differential patterns of ratings between words on these scales can be used as a very neat and precise method of investigating meaning.

OTHER VIEWS OF MEANING: CONDITIONED IMAGES. Critics of Osgood and Suci have pointed out that their technique gets at only a part of what we usually understand as meaning. Some critics have argued that this technique is only well suited to get at the evaluative aspects of meaning (goodness or badness), or perhaps even the emotional reactions to the test words, but does not attack the problem of the cognitive meaning of words. We should keep in mind that while the good-bad evaluative dimension acounts for a good deal of our reactions to words, it does not account for all. Any word which acts as a label may have an evaluative aspect (its goodness or badness), but it certainly implies other things as well.

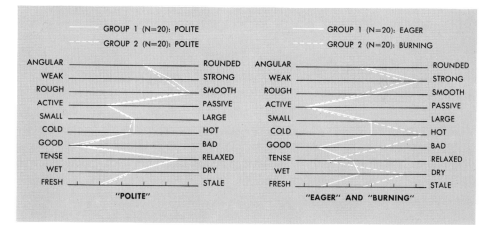

FIG. 7.4. *Preliminary forms of the semantic differential for measuring connotative meanings of adjectives. Based on median profiles of two test groups* (n = 20). *Adapted from C. E. Osgood. The nature and measurement of meaning.* Psychol. Bull., 1952, **49**, 197–237.

Mowrer favors a theory which uses *conditioned images* to account for meaning. Images would be a kind of conditioned sensation (specific sensory attributes in Fig. 7.3) in the organism [16]. These conditioned perceptual responses represent the demonstrative or information-laden aspect of meaning. According to Mowrer's view, the semantic differential is suitable for obtaining information about the emotional but not the informational meaning of a word.

ASSOCIATION VALUE. Some of the most active research specialists in the area of verbal learning identify the degree to which a word has meaning with its *association value* [15]. Through various procedures many investigators have attempted to determine the number of associations which occur to subjects following presentation of a target word or set of letters. The more associations which are reported by subjects after the presentation of a verbal unit, the greater is its association value and, if association value is taken as a measure of meaning, the greater the meaning of the verbal unit.

It is interesting to note that association value can also be measured by other means than the number of associations elicited by a particular word. Measures of how many subjects "get" an association at all (in a limited period of time) or how fast they think they could learn lists of different verbal units all show high correlations with the number of associations produced in a specified amount of time. The association value of verbal units, even assessed by several different methods, provides a useful measure of something related to meaningfulness. As might be expected, association value is related to the familiarity of the verbal units and to the ease with which they can be pronounced. As an example, NEGLAN has less association value than does ORDEAL; ordeal is more familiar and easier to pronounce. In general the less a word is familiar and the harder it is to pronounce the less is its association value. Association value may not encompass all of the needs of people who wish to measure meaning, but, as we shall see later on it is useful as a research device.

DISPOSITIONS. Brown has argued effectively for a different sort of explanation of meaning [17]. For him words have meaning in so far as they tend to occur in connection with other words or in certain parts of sentences. This is sometimes referred to as a *dispositional* theory. Words have meaning to the extent we are disposed to use them in conjunction with other words in sentences or statements. The word *man* has meaning because we would tend to use it in front of specific kinds of verbs and behind other sorts of words. This is a somewhat mechanical approach to the subject of meaning. It leaves out a lot of the romance associated with language, to be sure. However, it may be that this kind of a definition of meaning can be scientifically useful.

As with the approach of Osgood and Suci, the dispositional theory is still in its formative stages. As previously mentioned, many think that the semantic differential can never measure more than some of the evaluative dimensions on which we categorize words. The conditioned image of Mowrer may be able to deal effectively with the informational aspect of the meaning of words. The procedure for understanding the meaning of words by understanding the verbal contexts in which they are found may provide a fresh start from which greater progress toward understanding the nature of meaning may begin.

Acquisition and Retention of Verbal Material

Even though there is a lack of agreement regarding what meaning really is, it is still possible to study and to determine degrees of meaningfulness in verbal material. For example, the word *love* has more meaning for us than the same four letters arranged as VEOL. It is obvious that words, phrases, and sentences vary in meaningfulness, and psychologists have been able to study the effect of this attribute, as well as many others, upon the time required to learn verbal material [18]. In verbal research, the effects of situational factors, the arrangement of learning sessions and materials to be learned, and factors specific to certain individuals have been studied by psychologists who expect that their findings will lead to further understanding of the organization of man.

EBBINGHAUS AND THE NONSENSE SYLLABLE Hermann Ebbinghaus was the pioneer in the study of memorizing verbal materials by rote practice. He really was a one-man research team. For the most part he was his only subject. Picture him at his desk memorizing lists of words and testing himself for retention. He found familiarity of material one very important condition which effected his ability to memorize and he sought to discover the effect of trying to memorize totally unfamiliar material. Since it was difficult to find verbal material which was unfamiliar, he created *nonsense syllables* of consonant and vowel combinations that are pronounceable but yet not words, for example, GOK, MEJ. Such nonsense syllables can be modified and, depending on the requirements of the experiment, can be long or short and can include only consonants or numbers as well. Generally speaking, a nonsense syllable such as TAL has less meaning for a typical subject in a verbal learning experiment than a three-letter word such as BOY.

Many people, however, may have unique associations formed to unusual letter combinations. A person named Terry A. Lane would have rather strong associations built around TAL, and if it was presented to him during a learning experiment, it would act more like a meaningful word than a nonsense syllable. It was found that most nonsense syllables are not free from preexperimental associations [19]. Therefore, the nonsense syllable is an artificial verbal unit which is not totally meaningless but rather has less meaning than do most naturally occurring verbal units. Nonsense syllables are useful because they can be constructed in large numbers to have greater or less meaning (higher or lower association values) for the subjects who attempt to learn and remember them.

MEANINGFULNESS AND LEARNING   It is to be expected that meaningful material can be learned more readily than nonsense material. This expectation has been confirmed many times. For instance, the times required for subjects to learn 200 items of nonsense syllables, digits, words of prose, or words of poetry, were 93, 85, 24, and 10 minutes, respectively [20]. It took over nine times as long to learn 200 nonsense syllables as 200 words of poetry! One might ask why poetry seems easier to learn than prose? The answer may be that in poetry there are additional cues of rhyme and meter which aid recall. Other studies have indicated that nonsense syllables which tend to evoke more associations in subjects are easier to master than those which evoke fewer associations [15].

One of the most satisfactory methods of explaining these results is the very reasonable assumption that subjects come into experiments knowing more about the meaningful materials. Part of their learning has already been accomplished before the experiments start.

METHODS OF STUDYING VERBAL LEARNING   Probably the most common method used to learn verbal materials is the *whole method.* You use it when you memorize an entire section of prose or poetry at once. You study the entire selection. In a verbal learning experiment using the whole method the subject is presented with an entire passage to memorize. He can be tested on how many words he has learned in a given period of time or on how many minutes it takes him to commit the passage to memory. For example, it was reported that it took subjects 93 minutes to learn 200 items of nonsense syllables and only 10 minutes to learn 200 words of poetry using the whole method.

When the whole method is used, there is very little that can be done to isolate specific variables which can help us understand the nature of the verbal learning process. For example, we cannot control the effects of the rate of presentation of the stimulus units, the effect of uncontrolled rehearsal of responses, or the effect of learning earlier or later words upon the acquisition of a particular word in the passage. Since these factors make a difference in the rate of verbal learning, it is necessary to use other techniques in which these factors can be systematically controlled and isolated for independent study.

Another technique used in studying acquisition of verbal material is called the *serial anticipation method*. It is somewhat similar to the whole method except that greater control is achieved over the presentation of the stimuli and when the responses are made. The subject must learn a list of words or nonsense syllables *in the order they are presented to him*. Usually the verbal units to be learned are presented to the subject one at a time in the small window of a *memory drum*. The memory drum is built to expose verbal items for varied durations, and it controls the length of time between presentations. Usually the list is presented at a rapid rate to reduce the possibility that the subject can rehearse one unit while waiting for the next to appear. A sketch of a memory drum is presented in Fig. 7.5.

One other common technique presents the learner with the task of learning a specific verbal response to a specific verbal stimulus. The subject learns pairs of verbal items. This method is called the *paired associates technique*. At the beginning of training, the subject is presented with a list of stimulus and response words, one pair at a time. On subsequent trials only the stimulus words are presented and the subject makes a response. For example, a subject may be asked to learn the following pairs of words:

Stimulus Words	Response Words
Apple	Canary
Blue	Table
Wide	Church
Parlor	Milk
Friend	Verb
Curse	Finger
Fly	Motion

On any given trial the subject is presented with one of the stimulus words and must try to respond with the appropriate response word. If the subject's answer is incorrect, he is informed of the appropriate response. Each time the experimenter procedes through all of the stimulus words, it is counted as a single trial. It is important to remember that the experimenter does not merely go down the stimulus list, from top to bottom, on every trial, or the subject would have only to memorize

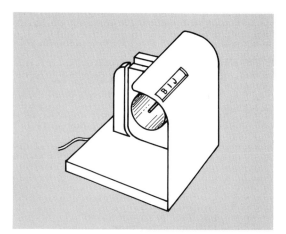

FIG. 7.5. *Memory drum used in studies of verbal learning and retention.*

their order and not pay any attention to the stimulus words at all. By skipping about in the list of stimulus words on each trial, the subject must remember which stimulus word is to be associated with which response word.

Measuring retention Recently, another technique has been developed in which verbal units are presented only once and then subjects are asked to recall them after varying periods of time [21]. This technique has not been given any widely accepted name, so let us call it merely the *Peterson technique,* after its originators. Essentially, the subject is presented with a verbal unit followed by a number. The subject is instructed to count backwards from this number, giving one number each second, until a signal is given for him to recall the verbal unit. Then the subject must try to respond with that verbal item which was given just before the number. The delay between the presentation of the verbal unit and its recall can easily be varied by the experimenter. The subject counts backward so that he is occupied during the presentation-response interval and cannot mentally rehearse the verbal response. The Peterson method has shown itself to be a highly sensitive indicator of short-term retention. The retention of verbal materials is shown to drop drastically even a few seconds after presentation when the subject is prevented from rehearsing in this way.

Measures of learning and retention   Given these representative methods of presenting verbal materials, we are confronted with a number of possible ways to measure both acquisition and retention. We can, of course, measure the time it takes for a subject to memorize the whole passage of verbal units or measure the number of trials required for a subject to master all the paired associates given to him in an experiment. These methods require that the subject produce the correct responses on his own; yet if the subject cannot produce all the correct responses without help, does this mean he has learned nothing at all? Think of the case of a student who can not remember the answer to this examination question (see pp. 87–88): *What kind of positive ions move into the neuron when it "fires" from their position on the outside of the cell during its resting state?* Could this student pick the correct answer if he were given a group of possible responses?

    (a) Na ions   (c) K ions
    (b) Cl ions   (d) Mg ions

It is more than likely that he could. The fact that it is often possible to choose a correct answer from a set of possible answers when it is not possible to recall the answer in unaided fashion must indicate that learning and retention of multiple verbal units are not all-or-none phenomena, but exist in degrees.

It is often useful for the psychologist to direct his attention to two facets of learning. One is the process of acquisition of responses, whether verbal or nonverbal. The other is the process of retention. Retention refers to the subject's maintenance of his ability to perform the acquired responses. While it is easy to talk of two distinct processes, it must be emphasized that they are both inventions of the psychologist seeking the most apt ways to describe and explain behavior. They certainly are not independent processes. In an extreme instance, one can not retain that which has not been acquired. More generally, however, the lower the level of acquisition of responses, the poorer will be the retention. Acquisition and retention represent two sides of the changes in performance induced by suitable changes in environmental conditions. All we can ever observe is the performance of subjects. Despite these qualifications it may prove worthwhile to separate acquisition processes from retention processes and seek measures of each. Several measures of retention have been used:

1. *Recall.* With this technique the subject is asked to recall material previously learned. The recall score represents the percentage of the original material recalled at a later date.
2. *Recognition.* When using this method, the subject is asked to identify material previously learned. A common example would be the student picking out the correct answer in a multiple choice question on an examination.
3. *Relearning.* With this technique the subject relearns material previously studied. The savings score represents the difference in time or number of errors between the first and second learning sessions.
4. *Reconstruction.* Here the subject is presented with all of the verbal materials and asked to place the items in the order in which they were originally learned.

Retention and memory   We should point out that these four techniques are used to measure what psychologists call retention. However, they may also be referred to as measures of memory. This brings up an interesting problem. If the four retention measures are used to assess how much a subject has remembered of his original learning, four scores could result. The different results obtained by different techniques are differentially sensitive indicators of retention. Material that is forgotten as measured in one way may not be forgotten if another technique is used. Think of a speech or poem you once memorized but cannot now recall. It is possible, and indeed likely, that it would take you less time to relearn it now than it took you to learn it originally. The results of a study by Luh [22] are usually considered to be representative of the differences in retention as measured by different techniques. His results, shown graphically in Fig. 7.6, present differences in the methods used to measure differential retention rates of forgetting over a period of time [23].

How often do we say we have forgotten something when we can not recall it? How often do we feel that because we can not recall it we have no *memory* of it? Must we assume a memory is gone when we can not recall it? Does the fact that our previous learning makes it easier to relearn the task mean that the memories exist at some unconscious level within us all the time? Just what do we mean by the word memory?

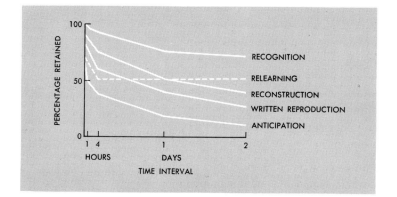

FIG. 7.6 *Percent of verbal materials retained as measured by five different techniques, over periods of one and four hours; one and four days. Adapted from C. W. Luh. The conditions of retention. Psychol. Monogr. No. 142, 1922, 31, 1–87.*

Memory, like perception, is susceptible to many interpretations. Some psychologists think of memory as a process of retention which operates to store, or recover from storage, past experiences. Others may think of memory as composed of those things which reach conscious awareness but are not present in the person's environment at the moment. We must keep in mind, however, that memory is a theoretical concept which we infer from the observation of behavior. Our four measures of retention are measures of behavior. Our concept of memory depends on our theoretical position, and some theories seem to get along quite well without any memory concepts. The very point of studying verbal performance under various conditions is to be able to make more valuable inferences about the kind of view we should hold about the nature of memory. Through the use of the different methods for presenting verbal stimuli and measuring retention, many factors have been found which are related to the speed of acquisition and the degree of retention of verbal materials. Let us consider some examples.

AMOUNT OF MATERIAL TO BE LEARNED. When you came into the introductory course in psychology, you knew from common sense that it takes more time to learn a long list than a short list of things. When you leave the course you *may* remember that as the amount of material increases the time required to learn a *unit* of material increases as well. As the amount of material increases, the time required to learn it grows disproportionately [20]. This is true both for syllables and for prose. It took 1.5 minutes to learn 12 syllables, but it took 6.0 minutes to learn 24 syllables. Doubling the amount to be learned resulted in more than doubling the time required for learning. Thus, the time required to learn a unit (single syllable) was increased by lengthening the amount to be learned.

METHODS OF STUDY: WHOLE VERSUS PART. Given a passage of verbal materials to be learned, would it be better to break it down into small pieces to be learned separately, and then combine the pieces, or to tackle the whole passage at once? The answer is contingent upon a number of conditions (see pp. 296 ff.). Generally speaking, the greater the mental development of the learner, the better it is to study the entire passage. Also, one must consider the length of the passage and the pieces into which it can be subdivided. As we learned in the preceding paragraph the amount of time necessary to learn a passage is related to the length of the passage. Consideration of the length of the passage and possible subdivisions of it can help in deciding which technique should be followed.

MASSED VERSUS DISTRIBUTED PRACTICE. If you only have so much time which can be devoted to studying a verbal passage is it better to distribute this time into separate study sessions or to mass your study in one solid interval? While there must be some qualifications, the best procedure would seem to be mass your studying [25]. To obtain *efficiency* in studying, massed practice on verbal materials will avoid costly warm-up periods and also the time required to get your materials ready for use. In learning motor performances where muscular skills are involved, however, distributed practice results in so much greater acquisition that it overshadows the inefficient side effects. Distributed practice only seems to be advantageous when the learner must master new or unfamiliar responses [26].

In most adult verbal learning the response materials are well-practiced verbal units. The conclusions about the superior *efficiency* of massed versus distributed practice for verbal materials run counter to much professional folklore about these two approaches to studying verbal materials, but the conclusion is based upon solid experimental work.

THE EFFECT OF SERIAL POSITION. When verbal materials are to be learned in a given order, the position in which verbal units occur is an important factor. Items at the beginning or the end of the list will be recalled better than items in the middle. This serial position effect is illustrated in Fig. 7.7, where we can see that the items in the middle of the list were correctly recalled much later than items at the extremes of the list [27].

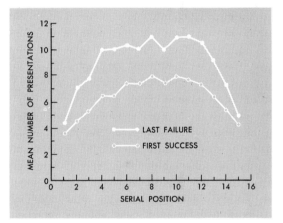

FIG. 7.7. *Effects of serial position on number of presentations necessary for learning. Learning was measured by subject's first correct response and his last error. Humps near center reflect the greater difficulty of learning verbal items in middle positions. Adapted from C. L. Hull, et al. Mathematico-Deductive Theory of Rote Learning. New Haven, Yale University Press, 1940.*

The favorable effect of coming early in the list is the *primacy effect* and the beneficial effect of being near the end of the list is the *recency effect*. These names have no deep significance in themselves and are only descriptive terms. Learning theorists want to explain both primacy and recency effects.

Many theoretical interpretations of this phenomena have been presented. Most of them have one feature in common: the concept of interference of associative connections between the different items in the list. Maximum interference would occur in the middle of the list because these units would have both forward and backward associations to items occurring earlier and later in the list. Items at the beginning or the end of a list would only have associations in one direction [24].

It is possible to overcome the detrimental effects of the middle position. If one, or even a few, of the middle items of the list are made *different* from the rest of the list the rate of learning will be comparable to that of early and late items. We could do this by printing the selected middle items in a different color or by including a set of numerals in a list of syllables. As the number of special items increases, the effect becomes less apparent. Even so, this effect of perceptually emphasizing items can still be observed when 50 percent of the list is differentiated in the ways we have suggested [28].

In summary: We have outlined a few of the variables which influence the acquisition and retention of verbal materials. Many others have been studied by psychologists interested in the processes underlying learning in men. Most studies use one of the methods of presenting verbal material and one of the measures of retention described earlier. These methods allow for a precise determination of the relationships between the variables under study. In a sense, however, they may be overprecise. We all know that it is easier to recall the substance of what we have read than to quote it verbatim. Even though it is more difficult, we must, as students of behavior, investigate learning phenomena related to substance as well as exact duplication of materials. We may find the principles of retention for ideas and concepts will be different from those of rote material.

TRANSFER OF TRAINING   Many people report that they find French easier after having had Latin. If the study of Latin does assist the student in acquiring French, this represents what psychologists call a positive transfer of training. If, on the other hand, Latin hindered a person attempting to learn French this would be negative transfer effect. Of course, Latin may have no effect upon learning French, that is, there may be no transfer effect between them. Transfer of training refers to an effect upon learning a task, *B,* caused by prior learning of another task, *A*. The effect may be helpful (positive transfer) or harmful (negative transfer).

Transfer in verbal studies   One common technique used to study the conditions responsible for positive and negative transfer of training involves changing the stimulus or the response words in a set of paired verbal associates. Experimenters can then study the effect of these manipulations in terms of the effects of different degrees of similarity of the substituted stimulus or response words to the original ones.

From the results of several experiments the following summary statement would seem appropriate: Learning to make old responses to new stimuli produces positive transfer, whereas learning to make new responses to old stimuli is a condition usually producing negative transfer. When one makes old responses to new stimuli, the extent to which the new stimuli are similar to the original stimuli helps produce greater amounts of positive transfer.

Let us assume a subject learns a list of paired associates similar to the one given below. The letters in the examples are used to symbolize verbal units, such as nonsense syllables:

Task 1

Stimulus Word		Response Word
A	—	W
B	—	X
C	—	Y
D	—	Z

We should expect *positive transfer* when in a second task the subject was called upon to learn pairs which kept the same response terms but had new stimulus associates:

Task 2

Stimulus Word		Response Word
E	—	W
F	—	X
C	—	Y
D	—	Z

However, if we asked the subject to learn a list like the following, he should show negative transfer because in this he must learn to make new responses to old stimuli:

Task 3

Stimulus Word		Response Word
A	—	R
B	—	S
C	—	T
D	—	U

This generalization about transfer of training was investigated by Bruce [29]. From recent work we believe that positive transfer in instances where the responses are the same is due to the subjects' learning the response items in the first learning session and having them more readily available for future use. It should be mentioned that Bruce's generalization oversimplifies the rather complex nature of transfer between learning tasks. Positive or negative transfer effects depend upon the degree of learning of task 1, the conditions of presentation of the stimulus items, and the nature of the verbal units employed.

Transfer of principles   To this point we have considered only an elementary type of transfer situation. Another type of transfer which acts to facilitate performances in situations similar to those described above is a kind of learning to learn, in which subjects learn strategems helpful to all situations of a certain kind. Using a different variety of tasks, two groups of grade-school boys learned to throw darts at a target submerged in 12 inches of water. Subjects were then divided into two groups. One group was taught the principle of optical refraction through water, the other was not. After this instruction phase the two groups were tested once more, only this time the target was submerged in only 4 inches of water. The group of boys learning the principle of refraction of the light rays showed positive transfer of training by their quick adaptation to the new conditions. The group that had not been trained on the principle of refraction did not show as much transfer [30].

This study and others indicate more transfer when the subjects know the principle behind the task. Usually this means that one group of subjects has been told certain rules related to their performances or activities. How do the verbal principles of a task come to effect motor performances? What do we mean when we say that one group understands the principle of refraction while the other group does not? (For the present we must stay close to common sense in using words such as *knowledge* and *principle*.) We don't know, but in general it is safe to say that transfer of training is facilitated if the principles of the situation can be verbalized by the subjects. At the same time we should recognize the possibility that principles need not transfer, even though they often do. Principles must be learned in a way which makes transfer to new situations seem appropriate.

Identical elements   Early in the history of psychology, some psychologists held the view that man's mental skills were divisible into several categories, units, or processes. Each division was called a *faculty*. Each of us had a faculty for intellection (thinking), emotion, and so on. Because of this view of man, early leaders in education held that the proper aim of education was to exercise the faculties of the mind, particularly intellection, with the expected result that the mental faculty would grow stronger in the same way a muscle will grow stronger with exercise. Thinking about anything would develop the power to think. It was argued that studying Greek exercises the intellect and should therefore facilitate the learning of mathematics.

Shortly after the turn of the century, this kind of educational philosophy was changed largely because of Thorndike's work on transfer of training. Thorndike found only very limited kinds of transfer. It had been *assumed* that positive transfer would occur between subject matter areas in primary and secondary educational settings. It had been *assumed* that training in any mental or intellectual skill would result in superior performance on any other intellectual skill. The mind would be strengthened. Thorndike's findings were that transfer only occurs between two situations when they are quite similar. He postulated a theory of transfer of training based on the number of *identical elements* in the two situations. He believed that if there were a large number of similar elements (stimulus-response pairs) in two situations we would expect positive transfer. If there were few, or no, identical elements, then one could not expect transfer. His views caused a change in educational philosophy. It was found that courses like Latin and Greek will be beneficial to students only in specific situations. Even training with the use of principles must be of a kind that facilitates transfer to other situations.

Thorndike's identical elements in the transfer of training spring from basic *S-R* association philosophy. No one is sure just what an element should be considered to be. In general, one can say that whether or not performance on task B will be improved or hindered by prior experience with task A can only be predicted by a detailed analysis of the tasks, and this should include the consideration of the number of identical discrete performances found in them. In the final analysis empirical investigators of transfer among situations are essential.

299

Indirect transfer effects   Probably many readers of this book have noted that learning one or another type of academic material requires the development of a special orientation to it. Generally, we approach the study of a foreign language in a different manner from that of the study of mathematics. We orient ourselves differently to these two kinds of tasks. This affects both our preparation for study and what we do while studying. Whatever we do, we have learned to do it through our earlier experiences with the subject matter. We hope they represent rather optimal adjustments of our abilities to the tasks themselves. If we do better in later tasks, say advanced mathematics courses, than in earlier ones, this could be due to the learning of an effective orientation to the subject matter as much as to the gain in knowledge of mathematics.

Harlow [31] has shown that monkeys solve discrimination problems much faster when they have solved similar problems in the past. The monkeys learn to learn. Just what this ability or learning set is, is another problem. This learning to learn represents acquiring an approach to problems. On the other hand, merely assigning the effect to a descriptive category does not help us a great deal. Perhaps, the monkeys have learned to pay attention to certain aspects of the situation which are crucial for the solution of the problem and to disregard distracting influences. On the other hand, they may have learned strategies different from those followed by monkeys without a history of training. Still, they may have learned postural responses which are effective in assisting them in solving the problem. Similar findings exist in laboratory experiments at the human level. Greater speed in learning new verbal materials following previous learning of similar types of materials have been reported [32]. We call the effects of learning to learn *indirect* because they do not seem to be susceptible to explanation in terms of factors prominent in most theories of learning. This is not to belittle either the magnitude of their effects or the significance of theory for research. Rather, the word *indirect* suggests effects of a general strategic sort and not those of specific or direct effect upon the associations formed.

RETROACTIVE INHIBITION   Two of the most important concepts underlying the acquisition and retention of verbal materials are retroactive and proactive inhibition. These terms describe two sources of a decrement or attenuation of retention of verbal materials. Properly speaking, retroactive inhibition refers to a negative effect on the *retention* of a verbal task, learned earlier, by other verbal material imposed between acquisition and the test for retention. The basic outline of experiments used to study retroactive inhibition is as follows:

	Time 1	Time 2	Time 3
Group I	Learn task A	Learn task B	Test task A
Group II	Learn task A	Nothing	Test task A

In this ideal situation the extent to which the retention of task A was less for group I than for group II would reflect the debilitating effects of learning the interpolated material of task B. Several things must be noted about this model experimental situation. First, it is impossible for group II to do "nothing" in time interval 2. They could be rehearsing task A. They could be rehearsing other materials unrelated to task A. Any living animal is more or less active and the nature of the activities exhibited by group II, in time 2, is bound to be influential in determining later retention. If we do not have a time 2 for group II, but test them for retention immediately, then we have given them the advantage of a shorter period of time required for retention. Group I would then have both interpolated activity *and* a longer time before interval 3. In an ideal experiment on retroactive inhibition we would want to study only the effects of one variable: the interpolated activity.

The disruptive effects of interpolated activity on the retention of verbal materials has been intensively studied. In general the amount of retroactive inhibition (the interruptive effects on retention of task A) increases with the amount of practice on the interpolated material provided by task B. This result might be expected on a common-sense basis, of course. However, further investigations of retroactive inhibition have brought to light new facts about the interruptive effects.

Interlist intrusions and unlearning As an example of one factor influencing retroactive inhibition, it has been found that there is no consistent relationship between the number of responses from task B produced by the subject when he is being tested for retention of task A and the total degree of negative effects produced by retroactive inhibition [33]. Intrusions of words from task B account only in part for the total errors made in task A. These interlist intrusions become greatest with intermediate amounts of interpolated practice (task B).

When task B was practiced longer, the number of intrusions from task B into the retest for task A became fewer despite the fact that the over-all performance of the subjects was becoming progressively poorer. In the same study the experimenters observed that the retroactive inhibition effects persisted longest when the interpolated practice was of intermediate length. When the practice on task B was long, this effect did not last as long as when it was in an intermediate range. These results suggest that the verbal responses originally learned in task A become unavailable to the subject, extinguished or unlearned, during the learning of task B. However, with the passage of time, this lack of availability disappears and the original responses are spontaneously reactivated. We should note that this concept of spontaneous recovery of extinguished, or unlearned, responses is similar to the view proposed by Pavlov. For him, no conditioned reflex was ever permanently lost. Even after prolonged extinction training there could be a spontaneous recovery of the reflex. Furthermore, in Hull's theory the learning *variable* ($_sH_R$) can never be diminished. Other variables might act to suppress behavioral expression of the response, but learning itself was supposed to be a variable which did not diminish.

The lack of a relationship between interlist intrusions and the total amount of retroactive inhibition can be explained in other ways. Some authors have argued that the subject in a retroactive inhibition experiment becomes better able to differentiate or discriminate responses appropriate to the two lists as the amount of interpolated training increases [34]. This discrimination hypothesis receives some of its strongest support from studies of proactive inhibition.

PROACTIVE INHIBITION   The learning of one task can effect the subsequent learning of another task. Proactive inhibition refers to the negative effects on a task by prior learning of another task. Diagrammatically this can be represented as follows:

	Time 1	*Time 2*	*Time 3*
Group I (proactive)	Task C	Task D	Retest test for D
Group II (control)	Nothing	Task D	Retest for D

The superiority of Group II over Group I in acquiring task D would reflect the negative effects of proactive inhibition. As with the retroactive-inhibition model, the time interval labeled "nothing" must be considered as qualified to the extent that the living organism never does "nothing."

Underwood [35] has shown that subjects who have participated in a number of verbal learning experiments tend to forget new verbal material of a similar sort more rapidly than those

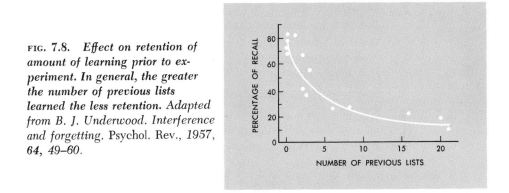

FIG. 7.8. *Effect on retention of amount of learning prior to experiment. In general, the greater the number of previous lists learned the less retention. Adapted from B. J. Underwood. Interference and forgetting. Psychol. Rev., 1957, 64, 49–60.*

who have not done so. Figure 7.8 shows this effect in graphic form. The percentage of verbal material recalled by subjects who had learned only a few prior lists of verbal units was much greater than those who had learned five or more lists of a similar kind. The effect of learning prior lists is a proactive effect since the tasks producing it come before the learning and the test for retention of the task being studied.

	Time 1	Time 2	Time 3
Proactive groups	Some number of lists similar to Task D	Task D	Retest for D
Control groups	Nothing	Task D	Retest for D

At first, these proactive effects may seem antagonistic to the principle of learning to learn. Actually, they are not. Learning to learn refers to an effect upon the acquisition of a new problem, whereas proactive inhibition effects refer to a decrease in retention. Subjects who have learned a number of verbal lists actually *learn* new lists (of similar material) faster than do less-practiced subjects. They just retain them less well.

Intrusions between tasks In studying proactive inhibition experimenters have found that the frequency of intrusions of task C responses into responses made while learning task D is greatest with intermediate training in task C. If C is practiced longer, the number of interlist intrusions declines while the total interruptive effects of the interpolated activity increases. This suggests that two factors may be operating to produce the effects ascribed to proactive inhibition. One has to do with the subjects' ability to discriminate the two tasks and the other acts to suppress recall in a different manner.

EXPLANATIONS OF FORGETTING Experimental psychologists involved in exploring the acquisition and retention of verbal material have been torn between interference theories and unlearning theories of forgetting. According to interference theories, decline in memory comes about through factors interfering with the associations making up the to-be-remembered material. For example, associations presumed to connect stimulus and response elements in paired associate learning never decline, but they may not be demonstrated in behavior due to competition from other responses for the stimulus components. The unlearning hypothesis predicts an actual decline in associative strength between the *S-R* units. This decline is thought to occur as a function of time alone, although other factors could hasten the attenuation of the associative bonds. The battle between these two views of memory is not over. Some psychologists believe that forgetting can be adequately explained by the interference hypothesis alone and others believe that both unlearning and interference hypotheses are required.

As far as the effects of retroactive inhibition on forgetting are concerned, Barnes and Underwood [36] have provided evidence which seems to make it necessary to accept unlearning as a vital concept to explain forgetting. Decrements in performance found in the research on retroactive inhibition comes from two factors: (1) the unlearning of the original responses (task A) during practice on task B and (2) the competition between task A and task B responses. The competition of responses learned in the two tasks is increased when there is less differentiation, or discrimination, between lists. This should occur at intermediate levels of practice on the interpolated learning materials (task B). The contributions of the two components jointly produce the total amount of retroactive inhibition, and the effects of the two components vary over the time given to the subject to recall task A. Of course with the proactive inhibition situation there is no chance for unlearning of the original list since it is only presented after the other verbal materials.

General Views of Memory

Up to this point in the chapter we have emphasized interference theories of forgetting. As we have seen, interference between competing responses and unlearning represents the major analytic concepts of psychologists following in the tradition of Ebbinghaus. The success of recent refinements in interference theories in stimulating research and helping elucidate phenomena of memory can not be doubted. In the next sections we shall present brief discussions of some of the other approaches which have been made to forgetting and memory.

GESTALT PSYCHOLOGY AND MEMORY When discussing perceptual phenomena (Chapter 5), we pointed out that Gestalt psychologists attempted to explain perceptual phenomena on the basis of electrical fields located in the brain. Memories of past sensory events would be related to the reestablishment of particular brain fields by new conditions [37, 38]. There was strong appeal in their argument from basic perceptual phenomena. When a stimulus is presented only briefly and the subject looks away at a neutral field, there is a procession of after-images. These after-images resemble the prior stimulating conditions, although there usually are a series of both positive and negative after-images. (In a negative after-image the colors and light-dark relationships are reversed.) In any case the perceptual effects of the preceding stimulus conditions have effected the person so that their effects remain when the stimulus conditions have been altered. This lingering effect is often termed the *trace* of the stimulus. All memories can be thought of as traces of neural events occurring earlier. Just as perception is altered by forces operating in the electrical brain fields to cause illusions, so memory traces are subject to the same influences. Thus, our memories are represented as subject to all of the distorting influences of field phenomena, generally. The problem has always been that it is difficult to specify precisely what the distortions of the brain field will be in any but very simple perceptual or memory situations.

LEWIN'S FORCES Kurt Lewin was a social psychologist deeply influenced by Gestalt Psychology. (His contributions to motivation are discussed in the next chapter.) He postulated that our actions, both mental and behavioral, are caused by forces operating within us. These forces are produced by the joint effects of the person and the situation in which he finds himself. Memory, for Lewin, was a product of ongoing cognitive activity. To the extent that forces in the person were directed toward past events or objects' they would be remembered. When the forces directed toward maintaining the memory were reduced, the event or object would not be available for recall. One of Lewin's examples was taken from a coffee house in Germany. The waiters did not write down orders or the amounts each customer owed. These waiters were able to remember everything customers were served, even though hours went by, *up to the point the waiter was paid*. Since the waiter would be responsible for the bill if the customers did not pay, this maintained the force necessary for memory. After the customers paid the bill, this force was diminished.

On the other hand, Lewin postulated that strong forces away from events or objects would act to induce forgetting. Examples of this purposeful forgetting could be illustrated by the fact that the name of a "date" with whom you had an unpleasant time is often hard to recall. The frequency with which dental appointments are missed also testifies to the effects of anticipated discomfort upon memory.

FREUD AND REPRESSION Even though Sigmund Freud, the founder of psychoanalysis, and Kurt Lewin were contemporaries, each developed independently his own theory of purposeful forgetting. There seems to have been little communication between them. Freud developed a theory of personality based upon his study of people with behavioral problems. Through his method of psychoanalysis, he came to believe that most personality problems stemmed from anxiety. One of the theoretical mechanisms through which anxiety is minimized in the individual is called repression. Repression is a personality mechanism unknown to the person which keeps anxiety-laden memories from reaching conscious awareness. However, Freud believed that memories hidden from conscious view by repression could still influence behavior. They could be general or specific memories of previous events or situations. Specific repression would account for the loss of a given fact, for example the name of a person or an appointment. General repression could occur to such an extent that a person may have an amnesia for an entire period of his life.

FRAMES OF REFERENCE—ADAPTATION LEVELS No memory exists independently of other memories. For instance, all of our past experiences with teachers combine to some extent to influence our perception of all our current teachers. Our judgments of any stimulus depends upon our past history with similar stimuli. It has been argued that the effect of past experiences is to provide us with an *adaptation level* for particular stimuli. New stimuli will be judged using the past experiences as a *neutral point*. Judgments about immediate sensory input are based on some neutral point determined by past experiences. If the temperature of 80° F seems hot to us, it is because we have had more experiences with lower temperatures. If 80° F seems cold, it is because we have a neutral point higher than 80° F, as might occur when living in the tropics. Just how the nervous system operates to maintain some level of adaptation to all kinds of stimulating conditions is not well understood, although it is likely that the efferent sensory system is involved.

In one sense the adaptation level which we have for any stimulus condition provides a frame of reference against which future stimuli will be evaluated. Frames of reference, however, are often used in other contexts. For illustration, we might hear someone criticize a president. The critic may interpret evidence differently from the way we do, particularly if he belongs to a different political party from that of our choice. Each person, the critic and the observer, has interpreted the same evidence from different frames of reference. New stimuli of all kinds fit into frames of reference which have been learned and which exert continuing influences on behavior. These frames of reference may be so well established that they are unknown to the person. To the extent that they maintain behavioral effects on the individual they must be classified as aspects of memory, and it is often possible to "see" a person's frame of reference influencing the things which are recalled. It is possible that the memory effects produced by such global frames of reference as political identification may some day be explained through use of competing associations or perhaps selective attention to certain stimuli. In any case the frames of reference of a person act to influence his memories and selective forgetting or retention.

PHYSIOLOGICAL BASIS OF MEMORY   Gestalt psychologists proposed that memories be considered as particular kinds of electrical fields in the brain. Little has been done to further an acceptance of this view. Today, the most popular view of the neural substrate of memory is that provided by Hebb [39].

Reverberation and interneuronal growth   In Chapter 5 we learned that Hebb proposed a distinction between neural reverberating and synaptic kinds of growth (pp. 182–190). If we change terminology slightly, we could say learning must be associated with two kinds of memory systems: a memory system related to a period immediately following sensory stimulation, in which traces of the stimulation reverberate through neural circuits in the brain; and a later period in which the reverberations have resulted in changed synaptic connections between neurons. The latter would be the basis of permanent memory, whereas the reverberatory stage would represent a transient stage of short-term memory storage. Thus, interneuronal growth is the basis for the neural changes which represent memory, and these in turn are dependent upon preliminary reverberatory activity.

In Hebb's theory any neural input from sensory systems produces reverberatory activity. This activity may consist of loops of neurons which activate each other in turn. The activity of cells in these reverberatory loops does not last indefinitely; rather this activity tends to die out after some period of time, which is most likely measurable in seconds or minutes. If this reverberatory activity lasts long enough it will produce interneuronal growth. The distinction between the activities in reverberatory loops and interneuronal growth provides a neural distinction between the behavioral concepts of long-term and short-term memories.

Long- and short-term memories   If a person receives a strenuous blow on the head, amnesia may follow. Any traumatic event, expecially involving the head, can produce effects upon memories, although these are often of a special kind. Only rarely is the person's entire memory destroyed by traumatic events. Usually the amnesia extends back to only a short period, say a few minutes, before the accident. Even if the original amnesia extends back further than this before the accident, it is often possible to recover the memories up to this critical period just before the trauma.

Let us assume that reverberatory loop activity must persist

for some interval before sufficient interneuronal growth occurs to lay down a more permanent memory pattern. The evidence of short-term amnesia resulting from traumatic accidents could be explained on the basis that the accident interrupted the reverberatory activity before sufficient interneuronal growth had taken place. Furthermore, the fact that the condition of amnesia does not extend back to earlier times would suggest that interneuronal growth itself was insensitive to traumatic events. The conclusion which this evidence suggests is that short-term memories of events stretching from *now* to a few minutes ago are represented by reverberatory loops of neural activity whereas longer-term memories are represented by some kind of chemical or physical growth between neurons.

Electroconvulsive shock   In certain cases of mental illness, patients are given electroconvulsive shock therapy. Usually an electrical current is passed between electrodes attached to the sides of the head. After such treatment, patients often show a marked improvement in their behavior despite an amnesia for events just prior to the treatment. This amnesia is remarkably like that occurring in cases of traumatic accidents.

Duncan sought to determine the effect of electroconvulsive shock on the performance of learned responses in animals [40]. He found that the effects of the shock depended upon the amount of time after learning that the shock was administered. Electroconvulsive shocks administered shortly after responses in a learning task tended to preclude the formation of permanent memories. If shock was administered an hour or longer after training the effect was greatly reduced. Although there have been questions raised about the adequacy of experimental controls for the unpleasant effects of electroconvulsive shocks [41], the same kind of results have been obtained in situations in which the unpleasantness of the electroconvulsion could not be prejudicial to the outcome of the experiment [42]. The basic finding that electroconvulsive shock administered within a certain period following training interferes with learning stand in support of a reverberatory basis of short-term memory.

Brain lesions   At times, it becomes necessary for a neurosurgeon to remove portions of the brain. The reasons for such surgery must be compelling, of course, and the number of patients is not large. Brain removal of the temporal lobes has been done by several surgeons for epileptic conditions found localized in these areas through analysis of brain waves (using the electroencephalograph). Lesions in these temporal-lobe regions produce abnormalities in the recent memories of the patients [43]. Published reports of these patients' behavior suggest that the recall of events occurring since the operation and almost to the present is adversely effected. These difficulties of recent memory can be alleviated to some extent through the prolific use of notes and other devices to assist recall. It should be noted that the interval of impaired recall labeled *recent memory* (operation to present) is not the same as *short-term memory* (present to a few minutes ago). The involvement of the temporal lobes of the brain in memory is further supported by studies in which these areas are electrically stimulated in the awake and alert patient. When temporal lobe areas are stimulated, the patient often reports the immediate awareness of older memories [44]. While it is reasonable to implicate the temporal lobes in memory processes, we should not consider memories to be stored in neuronal packages in these areas. We do not know, as yet, the nature of the brain's techniques for storing its wealth of information and tapping it for adjustments to present situations.

MEMORY AND VERBAL BEHAVIOR William James once likened both the future and the past to canvases upon which we create scenes amenable to present circumstances. To be sure, memories are not infallible and projections into the future can not be. But memories are more than expressions of present needs, demands, or desires, and they are usually fairly reliable. Part of this reliability stems from the fact that we encode information with verbal symbols. Verbal labels increase memory capacities and exactness in discriminatory tasks. Therefore, to understand memory capacities, we must study, at the same time, learning and the use of words.

There are many different approaches to language and memory. We have by no means tapped all of the approaches to these two related phenomena. And, as in other sections of the book, not all of the approaches we have discussed relate intimately to one another. The work of the interference theorists does not mesh well with the work of those psychologists more interested with the physiological substrates of memory. Each group is following what it believes to be the most promising lead to understanding.

Furthermore, the principles of language may offer important

suggestions for scientists concerned with the organization of the nervous systems of man and animals. Karl Lashley, one of the pioneers in the study of behavior and the nervous system saw a close connection between the serial orders in production of verbal utterances and in all complicated behavioral patterns. He believed the hierachicial organization of verbal behavior resembled the hierarchial organization found in all behavior. In fact all behavior is patterned in serial manner, one movement closely following another, and in units of activity which help the organism attain the goals of life necessary for its existence [45]. Language acts as a bridge between memory phenomena on the one hand, and, on the other, the other attributes of the higher mental processes.

Cognitive Functions

Psychology aims at understanding all important characteristics of man's behavior. Higher processes, cognitive functions, intellection, and thinking are activities which we count as our highest capabilities, that is, those responsible for our personal accomplishments and the accomplishments of the human race. At the same time, we recognize that the ability to think and reason can be a tool for those ends we consider most reprehensible: hate, war, and destruction. Whether applied toward laudable or tragic ends, these higher mental functions can be studied for what they are.

Unquestionably there is a connection between verbal behavior and the higher mental processes. The degree of association, however, has not been clearly established and it is possible to witness behavior which seems to reflect the activity of higher mental processes without simultaneously witnessing signs of the use of verbal behavior. Since it is possible to be engaged in higher mental functions while being silent, it is possible to experimentally dissociate this activity from verbal activities which can not be silent when studied.

Is there a useful definition of what psychologists mean by higher mental processes? Many definitions have been proposed, but each derives its usefulness from the theoretical context in which it is embedded. Generally speaking, however, higher mental processes are inferred from behavior which is not readily predicted on the basis of the environmental (stimulus) conditions presented to the individual or on the basis of the individual's past reactions in similar situations. In other words if a person reacts immediately and with great regularity to a situation, it is likely that this reaction is one which can be explained on the basis of a previously acquired stimulus-response connection. If behavior is regular and swift in a given social situation, the reaction might be one which has become routine and does not require the use of the higher mental processes. On the other hand, if a response does not occur promptly, we tend to suspect that the response, when it does occur, has been produced by higher mental functions. If one is asked to solve the following mathematical problems, the time required for each will be quite different:

$$2 + 2 =$$
$$718 + 496 + 219 =$$
$$\sqrt{61} + \sqrt{23} =$$

The simple answer of $2 + 2$ requires very little time and probably does not require much in the way of higher mental functioning. The response "4" has assumed the character of a simple conditioned response to the stimulus "$2 + 2 =$."

On the other hand the longer time required to complete the other sums suggests that their solutions involve the use of cognitive functions, even though the final response may be quite uniform among subjects.

Responses may be a product of higher mental functions at one time and become, through practice, representative of the simpler *S-R* types of response. For example, when one is learning a foreign language, simple responses to questions in that language may require relatively long periods of time. After practice, the responses may become quite automatic. After more practice, quite complicated interchanges in the newly acquired language may occur without delay.

In these examples, delay in response time is used as an indicator of higher mental processes. Another indicator, of course, is variability in responses among persons, coupled with a delay in response. When we try to solve many kinds of problems, there is no one correct answer, and considerable variability can be found. The strategies devised to meet the demands of the day vary from person to person. One way of organizing our daily activities may not be superior to another, but the techniques we use undoubtedly reflect our individual approaches to problems.

Higher mental processes are inferred when there is a considerable amount of time between the presentation of the problem and the response or when there is variability between people in situations or where it is difficult to determine the single correctness of a given solution. We assume that the time lag between the presentation of a problem and the response represents the time required for the higher mental processes to occur. These processes are thought to be internal activities occurring in the person. Psychologists who believe in association learning theories think of the internal processes as series of *S-R* associations (mediational processes), whereas those disposed to accept the theories of Hebb might conceive of the internal processes as a series of phase sequences. In any case higher mental processes are based upon some kind of sequential activity in the nervous system. Furthermore, the time delay between the presentation of the stimulus conditions and the response is thought to reflect the time required for the neural events to run their course.

In the past the approaches to cognitive function have been based on personality, learning, or perceptual theories. Personality theorists, generally, see higher mental processes as one type of adjustment of the individual to his needs and desires. Learning theorists consider them to be merely another example of mediating responses. A perceptual theorist would look upon such processes in the same way as they would any perceptual situation. They would account for mental activities using the principles derived from the Gestalt psychologists (pp. 175–182). However, with the increasing interaction between mathematics, psychology, and engineering, approaches have been developed which promise new insights into cognition and a means by which most of our lives can be interpreted in a broader cognitive framework.

ORGANIZATION OF COGNITIVE FUNCTIONS The distinguishing characteristic of living systems, from the single cell to the complete individual, is its organization. Every system along this continuum can be divided into subparts on biochemical, functional, or morphological bases. Yet each system, be it a single cell or an entire person, represents a total organization of the subparts into one integrated functional unit. The organization of functions of the body into a total meaningful pattern is the most apparent characteristic of a man's life.

One approach to formalizing this organization is to think of behavior in terms of hierarchies. This is an important consideration because otherwise we have to develop separate explanations of the various levels of observable functions and behavior. We can look at behavior in terms of isolated muscle contractions, isolated movements of limbs, bodily movements of short durations, small verbal units, sentences, or other fragments of total behavior. At the same time, we can recognize that any organized sequence of behavior is organized into a hierarchial structure. Goal-directed activities are comprised of sequences of bodily reactions, which in turn are made up of limb movements, and these in turn are made up of isolated muscular contractions. In language, meaningful verbal utterances are made up of isolated phonemes, these in turn are combined by morpheme units into phrases, and phrases combined into sentences. Meaningful communication depends upon an organized set of sentences. Using either movements or verbal actions, the principle of hierarchical organization seems to be a useful conceptual device.

By *hierarchy processes,* we mean both a set of incorporative parts and a sequential pattern involved in the production of the parts. For example, the operation of hammering a nail consists of such subparts as lifting and striking. Within these categories are various groups of muscle contractions involving the arm and also other parts of the body. Miller, Galanter, and Pribram, in discussing the cognitive processes of man, have developed the role of hierarchical processes [46]. Much of the following discussion on plans and their role in behavior as well as the general perspective stems from their provocative contributions.

Feedback from the environment   The operations of hammering a nail are controlled to a considerable extent by the results of the operation upon the environment. Hammering is begun when the nail is sticking up and usually continues until the head of the nail is flush with the surface into which the nail is being pounded. The hammering operation is dependent upon the sensory information about the effects of the operation upon the environment. This information about the effects of the operations is *feedback.* For every operation undertaken and for every level of it, the activities of the operation are governed to a great degree by the feedback from the environment.

Feedback can exert various effects on the behavior of machines and men. Two broad types of effects should be distinguished: positive and negative. Feedback which results in increasing the particular ongoing operation of the man or the machine is positive feedback, whereas the results which act to decrease the particular ongoing operation are negative feedback. Positive or negative feedback refers to the effect upon the operation of a man or machine of essentially neutral information, itself neither favorable, unfavorable, good, nor bad.

In a furnace-thermostat system designed to heat a home, the thermostat provides feedback from the effects of heat produced by the furnace which is regarded as negative feedback. When the room temperature reaches a determined level, the feedback from the thermostat acts to decrease the heat production of the furnace.

It would be possible to wire a thermostat backwards so that the hotter the room became the more the furnace would produce heat. In this case the information from the thermostat would increase heat production and thus be a positive feedback system. Of course, a furnace-thermostat system operating on such a positive feedback system would be unstable in that the furnace or home would be burned. This typifies the instability of most positive feedback systems. A moth which flies toward a flame until it is consumed represents an unstable and maladaptive positive feedback system of biology. The withdrawal of a finger from a flame, on the other hand, is an example of a negative feedback system since sensory information acts to decrease the movements involved in approaching the flame.

Many of our most familiar actions depend on similar feedback. The use of our muscles at any given moment depends on the kind of sensory information the brain receives from the muscular region concerning its previous movement; in fact, complete, flaccid paralysis results in an area of the body in which the sensory fibers have been severed. In a large sense, feedback from our actions makes it possible to evaluate the degree of success or failure of these actions in executing our plans or for reaching our goals; it can tell us when to initiate an activity or when to cease it; and it can provide clues as to the qualitative or quantitative alteration of an action for the achievement of the action goal.

Feedback and plans   The importance of feedback for human behavior can hardly be overemphasized. Imagine the troubles we would encounter without it. Think of trying to strike a nail, tie our shoelaces, ski, or even walk without immediate feedback from the muscles as each action of these sequences is completed. Each of these skills represents a complicated order of movements. We have learned to expect different kinds of feedback from each behavioral component of the series. If feedback which is not anticipated results from our actions, then we try to alter our plans. We continually evaluate the effects of our behavior on the basis of whether or not our actions produce the feedback we intend or desire.

The examples of the preceding paragraph all involved motor skills, and the feedback discussed was limited to information arising from the body as a result of movements. However, it is important to understand that the concept of feedback is more broad and generalized. More completely, feedback is that which carries information about the effects of our actions upon things, upon other people, and upon society.

A girl going out on a special date may do certain things which she expects will produce a desired change in her boyfriend. Her behavior is organized about a plan. This plan may have several components: one course of action at a party before the dance, a different course of action at the dance, and yet another on the way home. Through each phase of her plan, she is very much aware of effects of these programs upon her partner. This feedback allows her to adjust her tactics according to the extent to which each part of her plan achieves its intended goal, that is, whether or not the feedback from her actions is what she expects or desires it to be. When it isn't, she can change her tactics —or in extreme cases she may drop the course of action or the total plan entirely.

Plans are organizational rules which determine the sequence of behavioral operations undertaken by an individual. The operations themselves present sequences of behaviors which have intended results. The actual feedback from the operations is matched against the expected or intended feedback as a method of evaluating its usefulness.

Psychologists interested in using plans as tools in understanding behavior must know where they come from. Since plans govern the order of behavioral operations, they must represent a higher-level process. Are we born with an innate ability to formulate plans, or must we learn how to construct plans? Given the ability to organize our activity for a functional purpose, what determines the substance and arrangement of our plans?

While each of us has his own individual plans for reaching his own individual goals, what are the determinants of the planning process which are common to all men? The answers to these questions are being sought through research. High-speed digital computors and other similar mechanisms intended to simulate human performances provide one avenue of approach.

SIMULATION OF COGNITIVE BEHAVIOR Man has always been delighted by machines that appear to copy familiar human forms. European clockmakers designed elaborate mechanisms in the shapes of people which were the wonder of their age. These models, however, copied the external aspects far more successfully than the functional. Today, psychologists, mathematicians, and others are seeking to find ways to use the giant electronic computors as models of man.

Of course, a computor does not resemble a man. The similarity between a man and a computor is determined by how well such a machine can generate the psychologist's data obtained from people. If a computor can learn to provide data like those generated by an individual learning a maze, then in some way at least the computor has simulated the person. We don't expect the computor to walk through the maze, but the computer has produced a data sheet indistinguishable from that created by a human subject.

Data from human subjects in experiments are nothing more than systematized descriptions of the behavior. If a computor is programmed to simulate data from a human experimental session, the entire project is only worthwhile in so far as the descriptions of human behavior are useful and meaningful. Despite the romance of electronics, computors themselves are limited creations. A computor must be provided with operational instructions in order to operate at all. When referring to computor simulation of behavior, we must qualify this by emphasizing the fact that it is a computor *plus a program of instructions* which is actually responsible for the operations of the machine.

Interest in the use of computors in simulating higher functions was aroused by a theorem proposed by the mathematician Turing in 1937. This theorem stated that a machine could be built to produce any unambiguous description of the behavior of organisms. Computors have been programmed which will prove theorems in plane geometry and even draw simple drawings as a student might [47]. This is not only a demonstration of what can be done by clever design, but it also shows that many operations of a complicated nature can be accomplished by machines which do not have consciousness. More interesting to the psychologist are machines that can learn. It is possible, for example, to build a machine which can learn to play chess. More fascinating still are the self-instructional machines which are becoming increasingly possible to construct. What goes on within such a machine as it acquires knowledge that was not planned by its own builders and programmers provides an important area for psychological study. By examining the mechanical simulation of cognitive behavior it is possible to learn what changes occurred within the model as its learning progressed.

Types of problem solving Since computors make calculations with lightning speed, they can be programmed to find solutions requiring exhaustive, humanly impossible calculations. For some kinds of problems, one can devise a program so that a solution must be obtained if one exists. Frequently, this kind of program involves making calculations of all possible outcomes and then picking the one most desired. This type of solution is called an *algorithm*. An example of a simple algorithm would be the opening of a three-number lock by simply trying all possible combinations. There are many kinds of algorithms. Some we learn informally while some we learn by formal education.

However, many problems are not amenable to solution by algorithm. Often problems are solved by use of a *heuristic,* a method which offers hope of aiding in the solution, but does not guarantee it. Polya [48] has reported many heuristics used by high school students in mathematics problems. Probably all of us have used some of these methods, such as trying to work back from the solution and trying to make a simpler problem similar to the one assigned which can be solved.

Heuristic approaches are necessary even for computors. In playing chess, for example, a computor would have arrived at an algorithmic solution if the move it decided upon at a given point in the game had been based on a consideration of all moves logically possible for each player at that point, all logically possible outcomes of those moves, all moves possible to each player as a result of those outcomes—and so forth to all check-mate situations that could possibly occur from the given point in the game. Although each move actually made diminishes the number of possible choices open to the future, it has been estimated that even if players worked at the speed of electronic computors, one game could not be completed in a lifetime. Therefore, the chess-playing computors have been programmed to play following certain kinds of heuristic rules, such as protecting the king, controlling the center of the board, developing the pawns, material balance [49]. The computor compares the situation against heuristic rules programmed into it in an order of importance. First, it evaluates its king's position. If it is not safe, it moves to protect it. If it is safe, it considers the board in terms of possible exchanges of pieces and places at which further protection is necessary. Then the machine moves on to consideration of development of control over the center of the board, and so on.

While it has proved possible to develop chess-playing machines which approach perfection, the most important direction would be the development of machines and programs which closely simulate man as *he* plays chess. If this is accomplished, we can study the characteristics of the programs in order to obtain insight into the characteristics of man.

Mathematics is contributing new ideas and approaches to psychology in this area of simulation of behavior. Earlier, we saw another contribution of mathematics in the development of mathematical models of learning and in the application of decision theory to sensory detection experiments. Developments in mathematics shape our view of behavioral problems and the techniques used to study them.

References

1. Shirley, M. *The First Two Years: III Personality Manifestations.* Minneapolis: Univer. of Minnesota Press, 1933.
2. Skinner, B. F. *Verbal Behavior.* New York: Appleton-Century-Crofts, Inc., 1957.
3. Greenspoon, J. The effect of verbal and non-verbal stimuli on the frequency of members of two verbal response classes. Unpublished doctoral dissertation, Univer. of Indiana, 1950.
4. Dulany, D. C., Jr. Hypotheses and habits in verbal "operant conditioning." *J. abnorm. soc. Psychol.,* 1961, **63,** 251–263.
5. Brown, R., & Fraser, C. The acquisition of syntax. In C. N.

Cofer (Ed.), *Verbal Behavior and Learning: Problems and Processes.* New York: McGraw-Hill Book Company, Inc., 1963.

6. Guttman, N., & Kalish, H. I. Experiments in discrimination. *Sci. Amer.,* 1958, **198,** 77–82.

7. Blackwell, H. R., & Schlosberg, H. Octave generalization, pitch discrimination, and loudness thresholds in the white rat. *J. exp. Psychol.,* 1943, **33,** 407–419.

8. Gibson, E. J. A systematic application of the concepts of generalization and differentiation to verbal learning. Unpublished doctoral dissertation, Yale Univer., 1938.

9. Razran, G. The observable unconscious and the inferable conscious in current Soviet psychophysiology: Interoceptive conditioning, semanatic conditioning, and orienting reflex. *Psychol. Rev.,* 1961, **68,** 81–147.

10. Razran, G. A quantitative study of meaning by a conditioned salivary technique. *Science,* 1939, **90,** 89–90.

11. Lumsdaine, A. A. Conditioned eyelid responses as mediating generalized finger reaction. *Psychol. Bull.,* 1939, **36,** 650.

12. Hilgard, E. R., & Marquis, D. G. *Conditioning and Learning.* New York: Appleton-Century-Crofts, Inc., 1940.

13. Osgood, C. E. *Method and Theory in Experimental Psychology.* New York: Oxford Univer. Press, 1953.

14. Osgood, C. E., & Suci, G. J. Factor analysis of meaning. *J. exp. Psychol.,* 1955, **50,** 325–338.

15. Underwood, B. J., & Schulz, R. W. *Meaningfulness and Verbal Learning.* Chicago: J. B. Lippincott Company, 1960.

16. Mowrer, O. H. *Learning Theory and the Symbolic Processes.* New York: John Wiley & Sons, Inc., 1960.

17. Brown, R. *Words and Things.* New York: the Free Press of Glencoe, 1958.

18. Noble, C. E. Meaningfulness and familiarity. In C. N. Cofer and Barbara S. Musgrave (Eds.), *op. cit.*

19. Glaze, J. A. The association value of nonsense syllables. *J. genet. Psychol.,* 1928, **35,** 255–267.

20. Lyon, D. O. The relation of length of material to time taken for learning and the optimum distribution of time. *J. educ. Psychol.,* 1914, **5,** 1–9, 85–91, 155–163.

21. Peterson, L. R., & Peterson, M. J. Short-term retention of individual verbal items. *J. exp. Psychol.,* 1959, **58,** 193–198.

22. Luh, C. W. The conditions of retention. *Psychol. Monogr.,* No. 142, 1922, **31,** 1–87.

23. Postman, L., & Rau, L. Retention as a function of the

method of measurement. *Univer. Calif. Publ. Psychol.,* 1957, **8**, 217–270.

24. McGeoch, J. A., & Irion, A. L. *The Psychology of Human Learning.* New York: David McKay Company, Inc., 1952.

25. Underwood, B. J. Ten years of massed practice on distributed practice. *Psychol. Rev.,* 1961, **68**, 229–247.

26. Underwood, B. J., & Schulz, R. W. Studies of distributed practice: XX. Sources of interference associated with differences in learning and retention. *J. exp. Psychol.,* 1961, **61**, 228–235.

27. Hull, C. L., Hovland, C. I., Ross, R. T., Hall, M., Perkins, D. T. & Fitch, F. B. *Mathematico-Deductive Theory of Rate Learning.* New Haven: Yale Univer. Press, 1940.

28. Pillsbury, W. B., & Raush, H. L. An extension of the Köhler-Restorff inhibition phenomenon. *Amer. J. Psychol.,* 1943, **56**, 293–298.

29. Bruce, R. W. Conditions of transfer of training. *J. exp. Psychol.,* 1933, **16**, 343–361.

30. Judd, C. H. The relation of special training to general intelligence. *Educ. Rev.,* 1908, **36**, 28–42.

31. Harlow, H. F. The formation of learning sets. *Psychol. Rev.,* 1949, **56**, 51–65.

32. Melton, A. W., & Von Lackum, W. J. Retroactive and proactive inhibition in retention: evidence for a two-factor theory of retroactive inhibition. *Amer. J. Psychol.,* 1941, **54**, 157–173.

33. Melton, A. W., & Irwin, J. McQ. The influence of degree of interpolated learning on retroactive inhibition and the overt transfer of specific responses. *Amer. J. Psychol.,* 1940, **53**, 173–203.

34. Thune, L. E., & Underwood, B. J. Retroactive inhibition as a function of degree of interpolated learning. *J. exp. Psychol.,* 1943, **32**, 185–200.

35. Underwood, B. J. Interference and forgetting. *Psychol. Rev.,* 1957, **64**, 49–60.

36. Barnes, J. M., & Underwood, B. J. "Fate" of first-list associations in transfer theory. *J. exp. Psychol.,* 1959, **58**, 97–105.

37. Koffka, K. *Principles of Gestalt Psychology.* New York: Harcourt, Brace & World, Inc., 1935.

38. Köhler, W. *Gestalt Psychology.* New York: Liveright Publishing Corporation, 1929.

39. Hebb, D. O. *The Organization of Behavior.* New York: John Wiley & Sons, Inc., 1949.

40. Duncan, C. P. The retroactive effect of electro-shock on learning. *J. comp. physiol. Psychol.,* 1949, **42**, 32–44.

41. Coons, E. E., & Miller, N. E. Conflict versus consolidation of memory traces to explain "retrograde amnesia" produced by ECS. *J. comp. physiol. Psychol.*, 1960, **53**, 524–531.

42. Madsen, M. C., & McGaugh, J. L. The effect of electroshock on one-trial avoidance learning. *J. comp. physiol. Psychol.*, 1961, **54**, 522–523.

43. Penfield, W., & Milner, B. Memory deficit produced by bilateral lesions in the hippocampal zone. *Arch. Neurol. Psychiat. (Chicago)*, 1958, **79**, 475–497.

44. Penfield, W., & Roberts, L. *Speech and Brain Mechanisms.* Princeton, N.J.: Princeton Univer. Press, 1959.

45. Lashley, K. S. The problem of serial order in behavior. In L. A. Jeffress (Ed.), *Cerebral Mechanisms in Behavior, the Hixon Symposium.* New York: John Wiley & Sons, Inc., 1951.

46. Miller, G. A., Galanter, E., & Pribram, K. H. *Plans and the Structure of Behavior.* New York: Holt, Rinehart and Winston, Inc., 1960.

47. Gelernter, H. L., & Rochester, N. Intelligent behavior in problem-solving machines. *IBM. J. Res. Developm.*, 1958, **2**, 336–345.

48. Polya, G. *How to Solve It.* Princeton, N.J.: Princeton Univer. Press, 1945.

49. Newell, A., Shae, J. C., & Simon, H. A. Chess-playing problems and the problem of complexity. *IBM. J. Res. Developm.*, 1958, **2**, 320–335.

EIGHT MOTIVATION: VIEWS AND THEORIES ➡

Every human being wants food, drink, shelter, comfort, security, love, understanding, and so on. The subjective feelings which are described as wanting, desiring, or needing reflect the fact that sometimes we seem to be aware of the goals toward which our behavior is directed. There are times when we ascribe the cause of our desires to special internal conditions. For example, "I *need* a drink" or "I *need* a cigarette." At times, we are even more emphatic. "That candy bar saved my life, I was famished." Comments such as these suggest a belief that we seek objects because they fulfill a *need* within us. We must rec-

ognize that such statements as "I really needed that _____,"
and "that _____ saved my life" are overstatements and are
quite different from true cases of drastic and immediate biological deficits. Most of our desired objects are not ones that
function as life preservers.

We generally accept the idea that goals concerned with comfort and luxury must be sought secondarily to those related to
survival. A similar belief is that people can be motivated toward the loftier goals of art, religion and political freedom only
after their bodily needs have been satisfied. There are exceptions to these views and some people actually do sacrifice
their lives for idealistic objectives; in fact, many such people
have come to be highly revered by large segments of the
human society. Thus, in some individuals ideational goals can
overcome the basic biological needs as motivating factors.

This chapter presents an overview of some of the ways in
which psychologists study the motivational aspects of behavior.
It does not attempt to present the key to a complete understanding of what makes people "tick." We will be content to
select from various theories the problems that arise in the study
of motivation. After a definition of motivation, we shall outline
what is known about the body's sensitivity to changes within
itself in order to provide a basis for evaluating motivational
theories that are based on biological needs. We shall next relate motives to learning theories in an effort to point out how
theories of learning alone leave much to be desired in the explanation of behavior. In the last section of the chapter, we
shall show how the motivational theories which account for
man's social behavior provide a still further dimension in understanding human behavior.

It will be helpful for the reader to bear in mind the restricted
aims of most motivational theorists. Few would claim their
schemes account for all the motivated behavior exhibited by
man. None would assert any claim on having the one absolutely
valid approach to motivation. Rather, most would contend they
believe their approach to have some ability to increase low
knowledge of man's behavior.

Toward a Definition of Motive

Psychologists tend to use the word *motive* differently depending
upon their theoretical bias and orientation. There is no universal

psychological standard that can be used to find the meaning of the word for all psychologists. Furthermore, the forces which are presumed to be responsible for a person's choices among different objects are complex, and this complexity itself makes it difficult to formulate any single accurate statement of what motives are. One recent attempt to incorporate all that psychologists mean when they use the word *motive* ran to 244 words [1]. However, as a first approximation, we might say that *motives are theoretical concepts used to explain the direction, intensity, and persistence of behavioral patterns.*

Motives are entities inferred from observation of behavior. The statement "a hungry man will seek food and eat" implies a considerable number of assumptions; e.g., one must assume that the motive hunger *directs* the person toward certain environmental stimuli, that this action will *persist* for some finite period of time, that there will be certain *consumatory responses* when the appropriate objects are found, and usually we must stipulate something like, "all other things being equal." By "other things" we mean that this behavioral sequence (seek food, eat) would occur if there were no other more imperative motives functioning at the time. Still, we would be a long way from predicting actual behavior. The patterns of a man's food-seeking acts depend upon learned techniques for food attainment. The ways in which we make consumatory responses vary too. The time of day and many other significant variables are influential in predicting what patterns of behavior will occur.

In many cases of simple biological motives this general framework of assumptions is understood and not stated expressly, but it is nonetheless present. In predicting food-getting behavior on the basis of hunger, we have directed our attention to only one of the determining factors in an implicit, more general theory.

Biological Motives

The biological motive of hunger can be inferred from observations of behavior directed toward food, from verbal reports of hunger made by others, from what we know about a person's immediate past, and from things we can learn about certain neural or physiological conditions in the body. We may wish to accept verbal statements as a measure of hunger. They may represent a conscious awareness of a desire for food. These then are some of the ways in which presence of motives generally may be indicated.

Using one of these methods of inferring the presence of a biological motive, it is possible to study many different aspects of the motives. Some psychologists study the physiological basis of our awareness of motives, others study the brain areas concerned with the initiation and cessation of eating and drinking, and some study the mechanisms underlying other motivated behavior patterns.

THE AWARENESS OF HUNGER   It is in some ways remarkable to believe that a person can be aware of changes in the condition of his stomach. We have learned about the functions of sensory nerves. There are sensory nerves from the stomach which project to several areas of the brain. But knowledge of the anatomical presence of nerves running from the stomach to the brain does not imply that activity in them signals conscious awareness of hunger.

Undoubtedly, Cannon and Washburn [2] were excited when they found that a subject's report of hunger pangs correlated with the contractions of his stomach. In their experiments subjects swallowed a balloon which could be inflated in the stomach. Pneumatic equipment was arranged to record each contraction of the stomach. Since reports of hunger followed the stomach contractions, it was inferred that contractions had *caused* the conscious experiences.

This correlation does not tell the whole story, however. In some diseases it becomes necessary for a surgeon to remove the entire stomach. Many reports have indicated the removal of the stomach does not reduce the awareness of desire for food, nor does it eliminate appropriate food-seeking responses. Experimentally, Tsang [3] reported no loss in the effectiveness of food incentives for stomachless rats. We can only say that stomach contractions may be a sufficient condition for conscious feelings of hunger or of hunger-motivated behavior in otherwise intact animals. Certainly, awareness of hunger must result from other causes too.

BLOOD SUGAR AND HUNGER   There is a great deal of evidence to the effect that the blood of a hungry animal is different from that of a satiated animal. However, the absolute blood sugar level in arteries and veins has not been found to correlate with behavioral indices of hunger. Recently, it has been discovered that the *ratio* of blood sugar in the arteries to blood sugar in the veins is related to hunger. Stunkard obtained measures of the glucose levels in the arteries and veins of human subjects while the human subjects had swallowed balloons in their stomachs. When the difference in glucose levels between the arteries and veins was small, the subjects showed stomach contractions and reported sensations of hunger. When there was a good deal more sugar in the arteries, the subjects did not show these characteristics. These differences between glucose levels in arteries and veins have been interpreted [4] as reflecting degrees of utilization and availability of body sugar. When the artery-vein glucose ratio is low (*S*s hungry), there would seem to be less sugar available for the body's cells. When the ratio is high (*S*s sated) this is believed to reflect a greater amount of available body sugar.

However, even with this relationship between blood sugar and "hunger" we should be careful not to attribute all sensations of hunger to these artery-vein sugar differences. Most likely it is but one of many factors contributing to our awareness of a need for food.

We should also recognize the need for a mechanism by which we become cognizant of these differences in artery-vein sugar levels. It is not enough to know of these blood differences, we must find how the central nervous system becomes aware of them. We must find receptor mechanisms sensitive to these changes in the composition of the blood.

It is likely that such cells are located in the hypothalamus. Mayer and his co-workers have shown that cells in this brain area of the mouse are most likely to be the ones which pick up gold-thioglucose (glucose with a sulfur link to gold). This compound is taken into cells in much the same manner as plain glucose. Once in a cell, however, the cell dies and it is possible to examine the brain of the mouse *post mortem* to find maximum areas of glucose absorption and subsequent cell mortality. Destruction seems to be centered in the ventromedial nucleus of the hypothalamus. If we observe the mouse after an injection of gold-thioglucose which destroys this hypothalamic area, we find the animal becoming more and more obese. A picture of one of these extremely obese, but otherwise normal, animals (called hyperphagic) is presented in Fig. 8.1. The hyperphagic effects caused by the gold-thioglucose is but one of the bits of evidence relating the hypothalamus with the biological motives.

FIG. 8.1. *Comparison of normal rat (left) with one made hyperphagic by lesions in the hypothalamus (right). From Fig. 6, A. W. Hetherington & S. W. Ranson. Hypothalamic lesions and adiposity in the rat.* Anat. Rec., *1940, 78: 155.*

HYPOTHALAMIC CENTERS FOR BIOLOGICAL MOTIVES   Earlier in the book (p. 110) we indicated the existence in the hypothalamus of centers controlling the initiation and cessation of eating and the initiation of drinking. Studies of the hypothalamus have usually been accomplished through evaluating the effects of lesions in, or electrical stimulation of, certain hypothalamic areas. For many years it has been possible to make reasonably small lesions in the brains of experimental animals to evaluate their effects upon behavior. But only recently have techniques been evolved to allow the implantation of tiny electrodes into various areas of the brain and pass minute amounts of electrical current through these electrodes while the animal is awake and moving about naturally postoperatively. The electrical current passed through the implanted electrodes stimulates nerve cells and fibers in the region of the electrodes.

With these two methods, lesions and stimulation, investigators have established the existence of *centers* for some of the biological motives in various hypothalamic regions. When the center in or near the ventromedial hypothalamus is destroyed, the animals will not stop eating [5]. It is as though a mechanism which normally acts to stop the ingestion of food is removed. The ventromedial region is thought to be a satiety center. Lesions placed more laterally in the hypothalamus produce animals which do not eat, and which will starve to death unless special retraining in eating is instituted [6]. This more lateral hypothalamic area can be thought of as a center acting to modulate the initiation of eating: a feeding center.

Teitelbaum has found changes in food appetites which go along with the marked increase in obesity found in animals with ventromedial hypothalamic lesions [7]. The hyperphagic animals are more sensitive to both favorable and unfavorable adulterations of their food. They will eat more or less, as the case may be, even when the amount of adulteration is so small as not to affect food consumption of normal animals.

Hypothalamic centers which seem to regulate the body's water balance have been discovered. Two types have been discovered to date. These are not exactly analogous to those for food regulation. One region in the anterior hypothalamus exerts an influence on the pituitary hormones regulating water excretion thus regulating the body's *need* for water. Another center in the lateral aspects of the hypothalamus seems to initiate the onset of drinking. By implanting electrodes into these lateral hypothalamic areas of goats, it is possible to control their drinking behavior [8]. When these centers are electrically stimulated, the animal drinks immediately and continues to drink, although the goat may have just finished drinking more than it needs.

Many other centers for behavior which are related to biologically motivated activities have been demonstrated in the hypothalamus. Once again we find that there are areas which will alter the animals' biologically directed behavior in one way or another when damaged or electrically stimulated. For example, it is possible to produce an animal that will not sleep at all, or will sleep all of the time, depending on the location of the damage or stimulation. The existence of these centers led Stellar to propose a general model for the phenomena of motivated behavior.

STELLAR'S THEORY Stellar [9] proposed that the amount of motivated behavior (used here in the sense of goal-directed behavior) is a function of the level of neural activity or excitation in appropriate "motivational" hypothalamic centers. The amount of food-directed activity exhibited by an animal reflects the state of the hypothalamic centers related to eating. Every hypothalamic center receives input from a variety of neural and chemical sources. First, as in the case of the food centers, impulses from the peripheral portions of the body (stomach) help regulate the activity in the food centers. Sensory information from all of the receptor organs is fed into these centers. The limbic system and the neocortex act to help regulate the activity in hypothalamic centers too. Finally, the center's state of excitation can be regulated by the amounts of various hormones and the artery-vein glucose ratios of the blood.

Stellar's model suggests a compensatory relationship between these various regulatory influences. Appropriate goal-oriented behavior can be elicited by combinations of the various types of controlling factors. For example, we could become hungry, from stomach contractions, from sensory input (picture or smell of steak), or from cortical influences (thinking of food). These influences could act jointly or independently or in various combinations. The hypothalamic centers are proposed as the point of summation of these several influences. Stellar's model provides us with a useful scheme for conceptualizing the roles of these different physiological factors in determining goal-directed behavior patterns. The amount of biologically motivated behavior exhibited by an animal at any moment was postulated to be a function of the excitation level of specific hypothalamic centers.

At present we had best regard Stellar's work as an admirable beginning for a neurophysiological theory of motivation. Perhaps its greatest fault lies in the fact that it does not help us understand the learned motives which are most characteristic of man. When we learn more about the subcortical and neocortical mechanisms responsible for learning it may be possible to build a suitable extension onto Stellar's basic framework. With this extension the model may have greater applicability to problems of human motivation, although it is by no means certain that the model, as it is, is sufficient to account for all of the biological motives found in animals [10, p. 1507].

Stellar's model was based specifically on experimental analysis of hypothalamic activities. However, another considerably older basis for a physiological model of motivation is based on observations of the body's activities which result in its maintaining itself in the face of changing conditions in the environment.

HOMEOSTASIS The principle of homeostasis can be traced historically to Claude Bernard, the great French physiologist. Its greatest proponent in America was Walter B. Cannon, who receives most of the credit for its popularity. Simply stated, homeostasis refers to the body's tendency to maintain a relatively constant internal environment in the face of external changes. Fortunately, the relative invariability of the internal environment is usually a favorable one for survival of the organism. For example, when the body's supply of blood sugars becomes depleted, more blood sugars are secreted from the liver and other sources to resupply the internal environment. This tendency to maintain a relatively constant internal environment can occur through changes in the internal organs, but it can occur by means of changes in the somatic muscles too. For example, when we become cold we huddle and shiver as our internal organs make appropriate adjustments.

The concept of homeostasis provided psychologists with a philosophic perspective from which they could view behavior. Many early psychologists believed the homeostatic principle underlies all of man's behavior. Freud and Hull developed quite different theories of behavior, but both views are based on the assumption that our actions can best be considered as attempts at the restoration and maintenance of favorable internal states.

However, should we view our own eating habits as fulfilling homeostatic demands? To be sure, eating acts to provide us with the substances needed to maintain the internal conditions necessary for life. But we have already learned something of the actual physiological mechanisms responsible for hunger and eating, i.e., artery-vein glucose levels, stomach contractions, hypothalamic centers. The label of homeostatic mechanism adds little to what we already know. The word *homeostasis* is rather like the word *instinct* in that it is only descriptive and does not provide us with an explanation of the behavior under study.

THE CONCEPT OF NEED   Given the biological orientation provided by the homeostatic principle, the concept of *need* soon developed in American psychology. Needs are presumed to derive from deficits. When we are deprived of food, we *need* it. When we are deprived of water, we *need* it. Experimentally, when we deprive an organism of material necessary for survival, we have created a need for that material. This descriptive use of the term is relatively unambiguous: *deprivation produces need.*

Once needs were defined they could be used as explanations of behavior. Some psychologists began to use the word *need* to explain direction of behavior: a person ate because he needed food. In the same way a need for food was used to explain *persistence* or *intensity* of food-directed behavior. Thus, the simple word *need* began to be used as an explanation of behavior.

However, two types of problems arose almost immediately. First, it became clear that not all deprivations of essential substances alter behavior. If animals are deprived for example, of vitamin A or D, we can find no evidence of any special change in their behavior directed toward meeting this need. Secondly, sexual and maternal behavior patterns are not essential to the survival of the individual organism and not based on deprivation. Yet they are based in part upon internal physiological changes. Thus we are faced with these two types of problems for our definition of *needs*. Should we change our descriptive definition to say that only certain biological deprivations result in *needs* which are capable of directing behavior? Should we also say that any physiological change in the organism can become a *need* even though it may not stem from an internal deficit?

But these problems of definition have been further aggravated by the adoption of the word *need* by theorists dealing with social motives. Motives such as *need for achievement, need for affiliation, need for power* (see pp. 362–368) are defined by operations far removed from the original biological emphasis. The result is that today some psychologists argue that the concept of need is superfluous and should be dropped from current psychological usage [10].

While this suggestion may have considerable merit, it is unlikely to be adopted by any large number of psychologists. Rather, we must be alert to the several meanings and uses of the word *need*. In addition, experiments based on the concept of need have produced important knowledge about behavior. In particular, experiments investigating the relation between biological needs and behavioral preferences have proved fruitful.

NEEDS, PREFERENCES, AND SPECIFIC APPETITES Considered from a homeostatic position, we might expect organisms suffering from biological needs to become more directed toward foods which contain the materials required by the body. In many circumstances rats will tend to choose a balanced dietary fare from cafeteria-style offerings of many foods. With animals some, but not all, bodily deficiencies alter the preferences exhibited for various foods in ways which tend to restore the body's supplies of missing substances. The needs imposed on the animals resulted in specific hunger for the missing substances. Casein is a protein very low in the order of preference for rats. However, if the rats are deprived of this protein for a prolonged period of time, they will come to choose casein in preference to other foods [11].

While some changes in the kind of food sought can be produced by biological need, not all food preferences can be explained on this basis. We want to explain how it is that different people have different tastes in foods. One explanation for taste preferences might be their past association with the fulfillment of the hunger motive and the subsequent homeostatic restoration of the body's food supplies and that people and animals prefer tastes that have been associated with nourishment in their past. Thus, we like the sweet taste of saccharine (which has no nutritive value) because sweet tastes generally have been associated with actual nourishment in the past. We should notice that this explanation attempts to account for preferences on the basis of biological needs and the stimuli associated with them. The general principle is that of secondary reinforcement that was discussed in Chapter 6.

A study which poses a difficulty for this theory has been reported [12]. Shortly after birth a group of guinea pigs was fed a steady diet of food adulterated with a bitter substance. With nothing better to eat, these guinea pigs learned to associate the unpleasant taste with hunger reduction. Later in life these experimental animals were tested against a control group of normally fed guinea pigs and given a choice between food with and without this bitter substance. Despite their exclusive experience with the bitter food, the test group did *not* show any greater preference for the unpleasant taste than did the control animals. Thus, the secondary reinforcement hypothesis failed to be confirmed.

Perhaps the best way to conceptualize food or taste preferences is to assume a basic pattern of preferences to be genetically provided for each species. Sweet tastes might be one of these genetically determined preferred tastes. Transient biological needs and more stable patterns of cultural or individual learning could act to modify these basic biological preferences.

When we talk of *preferences,* we are describing behavioral choices, i.e., a person or an animal selects object A and not object B. To measure preferences we might adopt several techniques but all would use some observable and measurable behavior to indicate the preference of the individual under study. A homeostatic theory attempts to explain preferences on the basis of needs, and we have already discovered some of the difficulties of such theories. Some psychologists explain preference behavior on the basis of an inferred activity or process within the individual called *pleasure.* When we prefer object A to any other, these psychologists infer that the individual expects object A to produce more pleasure, or less unpleasantness, than the other possible choices. This kind of psychological theory has been with us for centuries and is generally called *hedonism.*

HEDONISM As mentioned above, the doctrine of hedonism refers to a proposed general tendency for organisms to attain pleasure and/or to avoid pain or unpleasantness. Let us examine this doctrine as it is related to food preferences.

For hedonists, the affective processes are the prime movers of behavior. Many psychologists believe that the affective quality of the various sensations is innately determined. Any association of these sensations with present or past reactions with need reduction is therefore inconsequential. According to this point of view we eat candy because it tastes sweet and this is a pleasant taste for us. Certain types of stimulation are pleasant, others are unpleasant or painful, and others are neutral.

Those types of stimuli which are affectively neutral can assume secondary reinforcing or motivating properties through association with other stimuli. The issue is whether or not any stimulus can have positive qualities without any association with a reduction in biological need.

In one experiment dogs were raised from birth on a diet of milk. They did not have any experience with the sight or smell of any other kind of food. When meat was first presented to the animals, the smell of it did not produce any salivation. The animals readily ate the meat, however, and after a few experiences of smell, followed by meat, the animals salivated profusely to the odor. Looking at the salivation as a conditioned response in the Pavlovian sense, the smell of meat was an unusually effective *CS*. The establishment of a salivary response to other truly neutral stimuli would have taken much longer to develop. Thus there was something special about the smell of meat which enabled it to become an effective stimulus for the salivary response with great ease [13].

We have already found that raising guinea pigs with adulterated food while they were very young did not give them an appreciable adult preference for the taste. Thus it would appear that there are preferences for certain kinds of stimulation which occur without prior learning, and also certain aversions which are hard to modify through experience.

Other studies indicate that the acts of eating and drinking have reinforcing effects over and above their physiological benefits. The reward value of eating is related to the amount of eating behavior necessary to ingest a given amount of food [14]. Several studies have compared the effectiveness of drinking milk versus having it deposited directly into the stomach through an artificially created fistula [15, 16]. The results from such experiments indicate that tasting the milk provides a more effective reinforcement condition than does the stomach injection of it. At the moment, it is impossible to decide whether the taste of the milk or the consumatory response of drinking it holds priority as the reinforcer.

An interesting experiment shows the efficacy of the sexual consumatory response as a reinforcement to animals. Sheffield, Wulff, and Backer [17] trained sexually naïve male animals to run a maze. They were rewarded by being allowed to start copulating with a female in heat. The animals were always parted before the male reached orgasm (and therefore presumably before a reduction of physiological need occurred). Nonetheless this introductory copulatory activity served as an effective incentive for maze learning. A hedonistic theory might attribute the reinforcing effects of the consumatory responses to an innate pleasurable reaction within the organism resulting from the stimuli arising from sexual act even without orgasm.

When we speak of the effects of the consummatory response on the animal, we refer to the feedback to the central nervous system from the response. In other words, it is the sensory results of the response that will have the reinforcing or affective properties. Which word is chosen to describe the behavior depends to a large extent upon one's theoretical orientation toward behavior.

To this point we have only talked of *affect* as a theoretical concept inferred from behavior. But we do know something about physiological activities more or less closely associated with the hedonistic qualities of pleasure.

PHYSIOLOGICAL CORRELATES OF AFFECT   Some of the results found by Olds have been discussed earlier (Chapter 3, pp. 110–113). The locating of various zones of positive, negative, and neutral affective, or reinforcement effects, in the brain was a major neurophysiological breakthrough, and at the same time a major problem to theories which asserted that affect must be related to reductions of biological need. In the work of Olds and others working with brain stimulation, we find that reinforcing effects are produced without any reduction of biological need. The electrical stimulation is such that it could not have been paired with need reduction in the past. How do the advocates of the homeostatically based theories interpret these results from stimulation of the brain?

First and foremost, the fact that animals prefer intracranial stimulation to other forms of reinforcement does not mean this produces pleasure in the animal. We can never fully know the subjective experiences of animals or people. One type of explanation tried to show that intracranial stimulation produced compulsive, automatic behavior patterns, only superficially appearing to have positive affect for the animal. However, the great number and variety of tasks on which animals have exhibited preferences for stimulation of certain brain areas makes this alternative explanation seem doubtful. But we can not dismiss so easily the arguments that stimulation obliterates ongoing unpleasant neural activities or that the stimulation activates the same neural systems aroused naturally when needs are reduced.

What about pain? Consider the seemingly prodigious effects of this experience upon behavior. There are few impelling motivational conditions which approximate the effects of pain. But the physiological basis of pain is still relatively uncertain despite the considerable research activities devoted to understanding it.

Olds has found areas of the brain of the rat which appear to have punishing or unpleasant effects when stimulated. Areas producing behavior indicative of positive or negative effects are shown in Fig. 8.2 [18]. If depression of a bar acts to produce electrical stimulation in a negative affect area, animals will make special efforts to remain clear of the bar. Other tests indicate that animals will do nothing to produce and actively strive to prevent stimulation of these areas.

Neuroanatomically, pain tracts can be located within the spinal cord and followed to the thalamus. However, at this point the trail ends, and no higher representation of pain has been found in the brain. Stimulation of the neocortical surface of the brain in the human produces no painful sensations [20]. It is for this reason that neurosurgery on man can be performed when necessary with only local anesthetics.

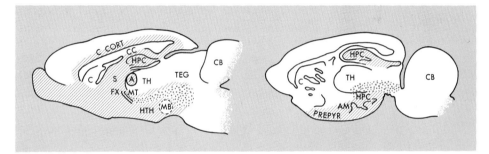

FIG. 8.2. *Locations of brain areas which produce positive (lined areas) and negative (stipple) effects when stimulated electrically. Adapted from J. Olds. Positive emotional systems studied by techniques of self-stimulation.* Psychiat. Res. Rep., *1960,* 12, *238–257.*

In some cases where patients suffer from relentless pain, neurosurgeons have severed certain neural tracts connecting the extreme forward portions of the frontal lobes (called the prefrontal lobes) with other portions of the brain. This operation seems to produce an interesting and, at present, inexplicable result. The patients on whom the operation was performed still report pain existing with the same severity as before the operation, but this pain no longer "bothers them" [19]. The operation seems to free them from domination by the sensation of pain. These results have yet to be satisfactorily incorporated into any theory of behavior.

Another fact about pain which remains unexplained is that a hypnotized subject, given appropriate instructions by the hypnotist, can inhibit pain responses and the memory of pain. Hypnotized subjects have reported no painful sensations from burning or puncture wounds which actually cause tissue damage. The mechanisms underlying these phenomena are unknown.

Finally, evidence from dogs reared under conditions where they were deprived of the normal pains and stresses of puppy life react as though their perception of pain was missing or reduced in adult testing [20]. Time and again these dogs would approach a burning match and extinguish it with their noses without a trace of any painful response and without a lessening of approach tendencies to the match. The suggestion is that certain kinds of early experiences may play a crucial role in development of our sensations of pain, but the mechanisms responsible for development of pain and pleasure are not really understood.

HEBB'S THEORY RELATED TO MOTIVATION Only a few behavioristic theories attempt *to explain* the phenomena of pleasure and unpleasantness. Many theories use pleasure and pain as conceptual tools to explain behavior, but only Hebb has undertaken to explain these tools themselves, in a way acceptable to many psychologists, using reasonable assumptions about the operation of the nervous system. In Chapter 5 we discussed the major features of Hebb's theory, including the basic unit of neural functioning, the cell assembly. Cell assemblies become related to each other through past sequential associations to form phase sequences. Phase sequences can be facilitated by environmental stimuli or by previous phase sequences. This facilitation of phase sequences was related to behavioral expectancies. One individual in a given social group builds expectancies, or phase-sequence chains, differently from an individual in another social group. An animal raised in one background will have different expectancies from one raised in a different setting. Thus far, we can account for the different cell assemblies and phase sequences; but why should we prefer one set of phase sequences over another, or one set of neural conditions to another?

This problem is resolved by postulating a principle of optimal conditions for growth in the nervous system. Let us assume that the optimal nervous system condition is one in which some small phase-sequence growth is possible. Hebb assumes this small growth to be a result of conditions where the sensory input from the receptors is *almost* what is expected, *almost* the phase sequence which has been facilitated, but not quite. A small amount of disparity between expected and obtained allows a dominant phase sequence to continue without disruption and allows some few new cell assemblies to be incorporated into the ongoing phase sequence. This condition of small disparity is assumed to be desirable for the preservation of the organism and *is the physiological correlate of pleasure.*

On the other hand when the disparity between the expected and the obtained is too large, there is insufficient sensory support for the dominant phase sequences. The ongoing sequences are disrupted. This disruption is defined as unpleasantness or

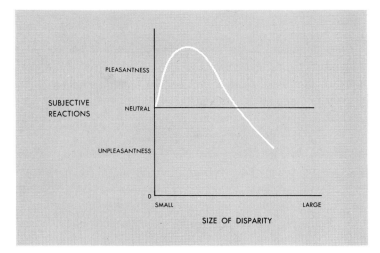

FIG. 8.3. *Presumed relationship between disparity in expected vs. obtained sensory experiences and affective reaction. Note that greatest positive affects occur with small disparities; negative affects occur with large disparity.*

subjective pain. When there is an exact matching of expected and obtained, Hebb assumes that no affect is involved. Figure 8.3 presents this theory in diagrammatic form.

We should note that this theory predicts that as the sensory stimulation deviates from our expectancies, we first experience positive affect or pleasure. This diminishes as the discrepancy between the expected and obtained becomes larger until a disruptive amount of discrepancy is reached. At this point and beyond, greater discrepancies are perceived as unpleasant.

The discrepancy between expected and obtained simuli is predicated, of course, on the basic theory of cell assemblies and phase sequences. The expectancies are the facilitations produced by the dominant phase sequences, and these account for

339

the direction of behavior. Since dominant phase sequences determine the direction of behavior, they are motivational in nature.

In 1949 Hebb believed that the direction of behavior was the only aspect of motivated activity that needed explanation. He argued that we need not explain the initiation of behavior because all living organisms are constantly active. Later modifications of this type of theory have recognized the need to account for levels of activation or arousal, presumably mediated by diffusely projecting systems [21, 22]. At least in his original theory the most important motivational concept was the ongoing phase sequence. He believed that an organism is food-oriented when food-related phase sequences are dominant. The same organism is sex-oriented when sex-related phase sequences predominate the central nervous system activities. Because of the nature of the phase sequences activated, different expectancies for certain kinds of stimuli are activated in each case. When sex-related phase sequences are dominant, the presentation of food stimuli may produce large discrepancies.

What is widely divergent from what is expected, would therefore be unpleasant. When food-related phase sequences dominate, the presentation of sexual objects may be unexpected and irksome. Of course, these new stimuli may trigger off new phase sequences appropriate to the new type of object. If the object remains in the presence of the organism, it may soon present only a slight discrepancy from the altered phase sequences and might tend to become an object of pleasure.

What are the conditions which are responsible for ongoing phase sequences at any moment? First of all we must recognize the importance of stimuli from the receptors. Sights, sounds, tastes, and smells may trigger phase sequences which dominate the central nervous system activities. For example, how often have you suddenly become hungry while looking at a picture of a sizzling steak? Another source of phase-sequence control consists of stimuli arising within the body; for example, stomach contractions or certain patterns of activity in cells located in the hypothalamus may initiate new phase sequences. Perhaps, the hormones in the blood facilitate certain phase sequences while inhibiting others. According to Hebb's views, any or all of these factors could initiate food-related phase sequences.

The similarity of these regulating factors to those postulated by Stellar (pp. 329–330) should be apparent. The differences between Hebb's and Stellar's position is in the mechanisms controlled by these factors. In Stellar's model each factor contributes to the excitation in specific hypothalamic centers. The amount of excitation in them is correlated with the amount of appropriate motivated behavior. In Hebb's theory each factor facilitates one or more types of phase sequences which may actually exist in many areas of the central nervous system. The two theories could prove to be complementary in explaining motivated behavior.

While disruption and unpleasantness most often occur from large discrepancies, Hebb also has postulated that activity in some of the peripheral nerves which reach the brain through the cord have the inherent ability to disrupt ongoing neural activities. These nerve fibers are what we call the pain fibers. In Hebb's views these neurons are painful *because they disrupt the ongoing phase sequences,* not because of any mysterious perceptual quality received or elaborated in the brain.

It is too early to tell if the motivational aspects of Hebb's theory will stand the test of time and research. We do know that there are times when sensory experiences, widely divergent from our expectancies, do produce unpleasantness, and there are occasions when small discrepancies produce pleasantness. Yet we can find exceptions to the predictions based on the discrepancy hypothesis. If someone were to promise you 50 cents for doing a job and gave you $5000, this should be a large discrepancy; but there is some question of whether unpleasantness would be associated with it. In the more prosaic world of research, subjects report that small discrepancies between new salt solutions and salt solutions to which they have adapted (and have come to expect?) are pleasant and greater ones unpleasant, but the same relation is not found for sugar solutions (see Fig. 8.4). Why should the discrepancy hypothesis work for one type of solution and not for others?

It is difficult to accept the simple discrepancy hypothesis as the entire explanation of pleasure and pain. On the other hand we should recognize its merit as one of the few attempts to explain the subjective affective states. Further, Hebb's theory provides a rather different approach to the direction and persistence of behavior. This approach relates direction and persistence in behavior to direction and persistence of phase sequences in the brain which are initiated, supported, or disrupted by sensory experiences.

341

In Chapters 6 and 7 we discussed theories of learning which did not postulate anything about neural events or physiological events between stimuli and responses. These theories, generally, do not attempt to deal with subjective experiences of any kind, including affective experiences. Yet these theories do attempt to explain the direction and persistence of a person's behavior, and in this manner may be said to be motivational

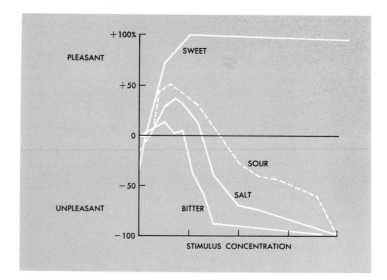

FIG. 8.4 *Pleasantness and unpleasantness of various tastes as a function of stimulus intensity. Based on data obtained by R. Engle, adapted from R. S. Woodworth.* Experimental Psychology. *New York, Holt, Rinehart and Winston, 1938.*

theories. In the next section we shall discuss some of the concepts in learning theories which are most invoked to account for motivational aspects of behavior.

Motives in Learning Theory

Earlier, we suggested that motivational concepts were those which were related to the direction, intensity, and persistence of behavior. To begin, let us examine the learning theory proposed by Hull (pp. 223–232) to determine those concepts with motivational properties.

HULL'S THEORY In Hull's theory, behavior is predicted from a formula which considers the following factors:

1. Past learning, or number of stimulus-response $(S\text{-}R)$ pairings that have been followed by a reinforcing stimulus, which contribute to habit strength $(_sH_R)$.
2. The amount of biological need experienced by the animal. This is called *drive* and is the sum of all deficits (D).
3. The incentives at the goal region experienced by the animal in the past (K).
4. The intensity of the stimulus eliciting the response (V).
5. The interval between the response and the presentation of the reinforcing stimulus (J).

In the chapter on learning (Chapter 6), we discussed the additional postulates regarding secondary reinforcement and secondary motivation, as well as the role of the drive stimuli (S_D) in performance.

It is hard to decide which of Hull's many terms should be called motivational. Each plays a part in directing and maintaining behavior. Drive, for example, is one of the most frequently occurring words in the motivational literature. Certainly, its nondirective energizing characteristics qualify it for inclusion in a list of motive terms. What about $_sH_R$? It provides the direction of behavior in any stimulus context, yet it is seldom used as a motivational term. Perhaps, it is because the value of $_sH_R$ is in part a result of other concepts more directly related to the direction of behavior

The drive stimuli (S_D) have properties which are important for the analysis of motivational phenomena. For example, we can think of S_D as those stimuli which occur whenever a drive is activated by deprivation or by pain. Thus S_D are those stimuli uniquely associated with a specific need. Of course, the S_D are a component of the s variable in $_sH_R$. If learning to navigate a maze depends upon the learning of a series of $_sH_R$'s (habits) which will lead to the goal, then S_D, being a component of each $_sH_R$ in the series, can act as a common link uniting the whole series. If a hungry rat is learning to reach a food goal through a complicated maze, each response it acquires will be made in the general context of "hunger stimuli." Hunger stimuli, the S_D, occur in the animal at the beginning, the middle, and the end of the behavioral sequence. Each response is learned to the specific cues of the maze *and* the hunger stimuli arising inside the animal. To understand Hull's learning theory analysis of sequential acts (like learning a maze), we must consider other theoretical concepts as yet un-introduced, the r_g-s_g mechanism.

In Chapter 6 we introduced the concept of a goal response (R_G). Hull's theory asserts that a portion of the response at the goal becomes conditioned to stimuli present at the goal and is generalized to cues earlier in the sequence. After a few trials, as an animal enters the maze a portion of the actual goal response occurs. It is not the entire goal response but fractions of it which do not interfere with successful navigation of the maze. This fractional and anticipatory goal response, r_g, in turn elicits its own unique pattern of stimuli, s_g. The r_g and s_g usually occur together and may be considered inseparable; therefore they are joined with a hyphen, r_g-s_g, in theoretical symbols. The r_g component is learned as any response is learned in Hull's theory and the s_g component acts in the same way as any stimulus in the theory.

The persistence of any behavioral sequence stems in part from the drive stimuli (S_D), and the direction of behavior is a joint function of the environmental stimuli (S), the anticipatory goal reactions (r_g-s_g) and the drive stimuli (S_D). These variables are used to account for both the direction and persistence of behavioral sequences.

Now let us examine the variables which have the function of energizing behavior. We tend to think of the variables of drive (D), the amount of incentive (K), the stimulus intensity (V), and the reciprocal of the delay in reinforcement (J), in this way. Each acts as a multiplier of $_sH_R$ to obtain *excitatory potential*, $_sE_R$.

$$_sE_R = {_sH_R} \times D \times K \times J \times V$$

We should pause to note that the relation between all of the variables is the same. Each variable acts as a multiplier of behavior and each thus acts to influence the amount of excitatory potential. Because behavior at any moment is determined by the excitatory potential having the greatest numerical value at that time, each can contribute to the observed direction of behavior.

Where we have two possible responses leading to different incentives, the response which occurs will be the one whose components multiply together to obtain the greatest $_sE_R$.

$$_sE_{R_1} = {_sH_{R_1}} \times D \times K_1 \times J_1 \times V_1$$

and

$$_sE_{R_2} = {_sH_{R_2}} \times D \times K_2 \times J_2 \times V_2$$

According to Hull's theory, D is constant for all excitatory potentials. Let us arbitrarily assume the delays in reinforcement and stimulus intensities identical in the two equations. The equations then hinge upon $_sH_R$ and K. Then if the habit strengths

$$_sE_{R_1} = _sH_{R_1} \times K_1 \times \text{(constant terms)}$$
$$_sE_{R_2} = _sH_{R_2} \times K_2 \times \text{(constant terms)}$$

of the two habits ($_sH_R$'s) are nearly the same, the response which will occur is dependent upon only the incentives. In the same fashion, delays in reinforcements or stimulus intensities could exert directional influences.

Inasmuch as drive level (D) is identical for all behavioral potentials evoked at any time, we can consider it as a general concept. Some psychologists think of drive (D) as an activating or arousing concept. As such, it is a concept which is related to the intensity of behavior exhibited by an individual. Drive level is sometimes identified with the level of physiological arousal, although this is not assumed by most theories of learning. Drive is most clearly defined by strictly behavioral operations, like hours of deprivation.

Perhaps learning theory's important contribution to our understanding of motivation has come through the elaboration of the ideas of secondary motives and secondary reinforcements. We have discussed the traditional aspects of these concepts earlier (Chapter 6), but at this point we shall extend our treatment of acquired motives and reinforcements by presenting some of the contributions of Mowrer.

MOWRER'S ANALYSIS OF SECONDARY REINFORCEMENT It will facilitate our discussion if first we note a difference in the meaning of terms used by Hull and Mowrer [23]. Hull used the terms *secondary motive* and *secondary reinforcer*. He argued (see Chapter 6) that the term *secondary motive* should be applied to stimuli associated in the past with a rapid *increase in drive* (and its subsequent diminution), whereas *secondary reinforcement* should be applied to stimuli which have been associated in the past with a *reduction of drive*. When stimuli with these different associational histories are presented, secondary motives should act to raise drive level and secondary reinforcements should act to lower drive level. In Mowrer's terminology we use only secondary reinforcements. However, he postulates two kinds of secondary reinforcements. One is associated with drive increments and the other with drive decrements. Thus, the distinction between the effects of stimuli associated with drive increases and drive decreases is maintained.

Basically, Mowrer is an advocate of drive theory in psychology. All behavior stems from drives which are produced by biological needs. He believes that two kinds of drive conditions are of central importance for behavior: (1) *incremental reinforcement,* in which drive is increasing; (2) *decremental reinforcement,* in which drive is decreasing.

Four types of secondary reinforcements can be produced on the basis of the association of neutral stimuli with these changes in drive:

1. Stimuli associated with incremental reinforcements which act as danger signals. These produce an emotional response which can be called *fear.*
2. Stimuli associated with the termination of incremental reinforcement which act as safety signals. These produce an emotional response which can be called *hope.*
3. Stimuli which are associated with termination of safety signals. These produce an emotional response which can be called *disappointment.*
4. Stimuli associated with the termination of danger signals. These produce an emotional response which can be called *relief.*

The association between stimuli and the increments and decrements in drive requires only the simple association of the stimuli with alterations in drive. These primary drives and secondary reinforcements are presumed to be the basis of all behavior. They represent primary and secondary emotional reactions which are acquired by simple association. Mowrer assumes that an individual will act to seek decrements in primary drives and to avoid increments in them. Similarly, an individual should react positively to secondary reinforcements of types 2 and 4, hope and relief, and react negatively to reinforcements types 1 and 3, fear and disappointment. Responses which lead to reinforcements of types 1 and 3 will be dropped, whereas responses leading to reinforcements of types 2 and 4 will be enhanced.

For Mowrer, emotional reactions are conditioned by contiguity alone. Fear is his most popular example. A fear reaction is learned when a neutral stimulus is paired with a primary incremental drive, some noxious stimulation or drive, usually electrical shock. Reduction of drive provides a suitable condition for response learning (habits), as well as for the learning of secondary reinforcers, type 1. In a typical laboratory experiment a rat learns to avoid an electric shock by crossing to the opposite side of a shuttle box within a certain time interval after the onset of a buzzer or bell (*CS*). Both types of learning take place. The animal learns to *fear* the bell, through its contiguous appearance with shock, and responses which terminate the buzzer are learned because they reduce this learned fear response. Avoidance responses are difficult to extinguish in the sense that they persist for many trials even when the animal is no longer shocked if it fails to respond. Of course, the animal must fail to respond to find this out. But one reason the response is so persistent may be that the response is *always* useful in reducing the conditioned fear response to the *CS*.

Mowrer believes that both fear and pain are produced by noxious stimulation, and the fear component is conditionable to neutral stimuli. Animals will work to terminate or otherwise eliminate this fear-producing stimulation. When the fear-evoking stimulus is eliminated the animal experiences *relief* (type-1 secondary reinforcement). However, if one were to present a neutral stimulus with the termination of a painful stimulus, this neutral stimulus should evoke *hope* (type-2 secondary reinforcement).

Some of Mowrer's examples are informative. In one of them he imagines the relief of desert weary travelers who see a mirage in the distance. Although their thirst is not reduced, they feel better. For Mowrer, this would represent the effect of conditioned hope, or type-2 secondary reinforcement. To take another of Mowrer's examples, think of the relief we usually feel after a temporary sickness has been diagnosed by a physician. His presence and reassurance that we soon will be well again provide another example of type-2 secondary reinforcement. Yet another example comes to mind when we think of common experiences in the office of a dentist. As we arrive, we become fearful (conditioned fear). When the dentist begins to drill a cavity, the fear mounts—fear of both an unconditioned portion of the slight pain and of an indefinite continuation of the slight pain. Fear of fear, itself! When the dentist tells us, "just one more minute," or some action of his signals the imminent end of the drilling, we feel better, even though he might still be drilling (type-2 secondary reinforcement). And, when he stops at last, we experience relief (type-1 secondary reinforcement).

There is a similarity between the effects of type-2 secondary reinforcement and those of "suggestion." Mowrer states this is one of the few instances in which a learning theory has attempted to deal with phenomena like suggestion. How often do we attribute the effects of the reassurances of a physician to some mysterious concept like suggestion? It may be possible to equate positive suggestion with secondary reinforcement, type-2, and negative suggestion with conditioned fear. Mowrer's elaborate analyses of secondary reinforcement make this concept a much more influential one. However, many psychologists believe that it is impossible to explain all behavior on as simple a basis as secondary reinforcement.

A GENERAL PROBLEM OF SECONDARY REINFORCEMENT
Critics of secondary reinforcement explanations of adult human behavior have dwelt on one major problem in any such explanation: many experimental studies have shown secondary reinforcers to be ephemeral in nature. In short, the experimental evidence from animal studies indicates that secondary reinforcing stimuli have to be continually associated with primary drives to maintain their potency for any length of time. Since men tend to seek goals which are not primary reinforcements year after year, these critics claim that these goals can not be explained through secondary reinforcement theory.

Zimmerman [24, 25] has shown that one *can* establish secondary reinforcers that retain their effectiveness for considerable periods of time after they are dissociated from changes in primary drives. Zimmerman's technique involves the use of what is called *double intermittent reinforcement*. For some while we have known that reinforcing responses on every other trial or every third or tenth trial will make the response more difficult to extinguish than reinforcing it on each trial. It remained for Zimmerman to demonstrate that by (1) *intermittently* associating the neutral stimulus with primary reinforcement and (2) using this new secondary reinforcer only intermittently following a response, the response will become much more difficult to extinguish.

Let us examine one of Zimmerman's procedures in greater detail to clarify this method. Laboratory rats were placed in a small box which opened into a runway. A few seconds after the animal was placed in the box, a door opened and the rat could go into the runway. The rats were moderately hungry and food could be found in the goal box at the end of the runway. Soon the animals ran directly to the goal box when the door was opened. After some fifteen to twenty trials, the animals were running swiftly to the goal box. Additional trials did not improve their running speeds. At this point food was not placed in the goal box on every trial, but rather only on every other trial. Then, after a few more trials, food was placed in the goal box more rarely, until it was found there on only one trial in every eight, on the average. Actually, whether or not the food was placed in the goal box was decided randomly, with the probability that it would be there one time in eight. This did not mean every eighth trial is reinforced. There was no regular pattern of reinforcement. Remember that on each trial the door separating the starting area from the runway had been opened a few seconds after the animal was placed in it. It had been a neutral stimulus associated with primary drive reduction and should have come, therefore, to have secondary reinforcing properties itself.

Now the entrance situation is changed so that the animal has a bar in the starting box which will open the door leading to the runway if it is depressed. *From this point on food is never again placed in the goal box.* The animal begins to press the bar, opening the door. After five or six trials, the experimenter changes the situation so that it takes many depressions of the bar to open the door. The door will be opened once every eight bar depressions, on the average. The effectiveness of the bar-press response is placed on an intermittent schedule. Because both the reinforcement and the door operation have been learned on intermittent schedules, the procedure is called *double intermittent* reinforcement. If we were to watch an animal in the final stages of the experiment, we would see a rat pressing a bar in the starting box over and over again until the gate lifts, allowing it to run to an empty goal box. Then the animal is returned to the starting box, and the whole sequence repeated.

Using this technique an animal will press the bar about 2000 times to enter the continuously empty goal box. This is a great many more responses than has previously been obtained with only secondary reinforcements. While this double intermittent technique does not produce entirely permanent behavior, Zimmerman's results show that secondary reinforcers can be quite effective even when no longer associated with primary drives. Perhaps, they would be even stronger if further intermittencies were incorporated in the training procedure. For many years it seemed unlikely that secondary reinforcers could account for the persistence of human goals and incentives because of the transient nature of their potency once they are no longer associated with primary reinforcers. Since secondary reinforcement was the main conceptual link between laboratory research based on learning theories and human behavior, this tended to limit learning theories to explanations of animal behavior. However, the persistence of behavior based on secondary reinforcements illustrated by Zimmerman's work tends to strengthen the position of all learning theories in so far as they may be applicable to adult behavior.

Drive and Anxiety

For Hull, as well as for many other learning theorists, drive is a general concept. All biological needs contribute to drive (D). Drive increases as biological need becomes more and more acute. Tissue damage resulting from electrical shock, or other noxious stimulation, can also produce an increase in drive level; and, as we have seen, Mowrer's incremental reinforcement refers to situations where the drive level of the animal or person is increasing. Hull's concept of secondary motivation also refers to situations in which D increases. But, which way D is caused to increase is unimportant to these theories. The effects of hunger, thirst, and pain (and other sources) all add together to achieve the resultant D level.

One factor related to the D level of an individual is his own individual characteristic responsiveness to emotional situations. In general one can say that D is a joint product of the situation and the way in which the person reacts to it. How can we measure this variable in the human being?

Janet Taylor developed a self-report questionnaire which was designed to determine the number of clinical symptoms of anxiety evidenced by subjects. Questions were selected by clinical psychologists so that the answers to them reflected internal anxiety levels. It was assumed that anxiety test scores indicate the individual's emotional responsiveness, and a person with a higher anxiety score will have generally a greater D than subjects with low anxiety test scores. If this assumption is justified, it should be able to predict the differential behaviors of groups of people with high and low test anxiety on the basis of different drive levels.

Both Hull and Spence have models with a multiplicative relationship between habit strength and drive:

$$_sE_R = f(_sH_R \times D)$$

In a simple situation which involves only one response (or habit strength, $_sH_R$) the greater the level of drive (D) the

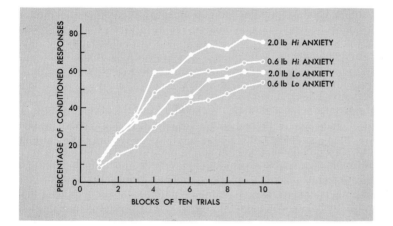

FIG. 8.5. *Performance in eyelid response conditioning as a function of US intensity (in pressures) and position of subjects on anxiety scale.* Adapted from K. W. Spençe & Janet A. Taylor. Anxiety and strength of the UCS as determiners of the amount of eyelid conditioning. J. exp. Psychol., 1951, 42, 183–188.

greater the response should be. In one experiment [26] subjects were trained in an eyeblink conditioning experiment. A puff of air to the eye (*US*) was paired with a previously neutral stimulus (*CS*). As training progresses we can observe the increased tendency for the *CS* to elicit the eye-blink response. The data are presented in Fig. 8.5. We observe the subjects with high anxiety scores to show a greater percentage of conditioned responses than those with low anxiety scores *for a given pressure of air puff*. We observe also two factors influencing

351

drive and operating to increase the conditioned response: the anxiety levels of the subjects and the strength of the puff of air used to condition the response.

In this experiment highly anxious subjects, as measured by an anxiety scale, showed faster conditioning than did the less anxious subjects. What would we expect in a more complex situation? To predict an answer from our theory of drive, we must consider the significance of the multiplicative relationship between drive and habits. Because drive multiplies habit strength to form (with other factors) the response tendency, it acts to magnify the differences between response tendencies. Suppose there are only two responses which can be made in a given situation. Let us assign a strength of .60 to one of them $(_sH_{R_1})$ and a strength of .70 to the other $(_sH_{R_2})$ for a given subject. If we can place the subject into the situation at different drive levels, it is possible to calculate the effects of these levels on performance. If we assign values of 1, 2, and 3 to three drive levels and multiply these values with the two habit strengths, we would obtain the following results:

Under drive level 1:

	Drive	×	habit strength	=	response tendency
Response 1	1	×	.6	=	.6
Response 2	1	×	.7	=	.7

Under drive level 2:

	Drive	×	habit strength	=	response tendency
Response 1	2	×	.6	=	1.2
Response 2	2	×	.7	=	1.4

Under drive level 3:

	Drive	×	habit strength	=	response tendency
Response 1	3	×	.6	=	1.8
Response 2	3	×	.7	=	2.1

At increasing drive levels the differences between response tendencies become larger. This means that the probability of R_2 becomes greater as drive increases. If R_2 is the response which is the one which the experimenter desires, this condition is advantageous. In the eye-blink experiment just reported there was only one response involved and increased drive acted to accelerate the growth of the response tendency. However, if the desire was to increase the weaker habit strength, higher drive would interfere with learning.

Spence, Farber, and McFann [27] tested this type of reasoning in an experiment in which subjects had to learn two kinds of lists of paired associates. One list was prepared so that the responses were readily available and had relatively high habit strength before the experiment. For this list, high drive helped acquisition of the list. The other list was constructed so that the correct responses were of lower habit strength than incorrect responses. On this list subjects with high anxiety (drive) were poorer in acquisition. Therefore, the effect of drive upon performance depends upon place of the response to be learned, relative to other possible responses in the situation. When this response is already nearly dominant in the situation, drive will facilitate performance. When this response is less dominant than other responses, high drive will interfere with performance.

Since everyone's drive level is, to some extent at least, a unique property of the individual, it is difficult to formulate any general statement of whether a person should take steps to increase or decrease his drive level before an examination. For individuals with normally high drive or anxiety levels, it would probably be best to try to reduce anxiety by going to a motion picture the night before the examination and trying to relax and not to think of it. For individuals with normally low drive or anxiety levels, steps should be taken to raise the drive level. Black coffee and jangling nerves may actually improve the performance of a person with a normally low drive level. We should remember that this discussion of drive level and examination performance has assumed learning to be constant for all individuals; but we should recognize that examination performances are jointly determined by drive and learning.

Other Views of Anxiety

Behavioristic theories have been developed by people who view anxiety somewhat differently from the way Taylor and Spence do. Some psychologists believe that it may be best to consider anxiety as a response to specific conditions. A situation that is anxiety producing in one person may not be anxiety producing in another [28]. A questionnaire that attempts to measure anxiety symptoms specifically occurring in testing situations has been developed [29]. These authors believe that anxiety interferes with performance through elicitation of responses which

353

are aimed at reducing anxiety rather than at the task at hand. This view of the effects of anxiety is based on the assumption that anxiety fosters task-irrelevant responses.

Anxiety is a conceptual term in these behavioristic theories, defined on the basis of a test score. A score on an anxiety scale is presumed to be an indicator of individual drive level, as defined by the theory behind the scale, and not an indicator of *real anxiety*, whatever it may be.

FRUSTRATION BEHAVIOR   It seems likely that some behavior can not be explained on the basis of goal-directedness. Maier [30] believes that some behavior is not goal-directed at all;

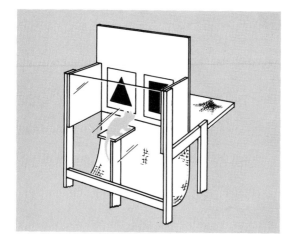

FIG. 8.6.   *One form of the Lashley jumping stand.*

rather, he believes some responses become *fixated* through frustrating circumstances. Once a response becomes fixated, it will occur again and again quite apart from any beneficial or detrimental effects produced by the responses. Only through special retraining procedures can this fixation be altered, according to Maier.

In a typical experiment rats are trained to jump to a given pattern in a window of a Lashley jumping apparatus which is illustrated in Fig. 8.6. Cards are *placed in the two windows of the jumping stand*. There are different figures on each card. The animal is forced to jump from the stand to the platform behind the windows. The windows can be fixed so that a card can be locked in place or just lightly held so that the rat's jump will knock it down and allow entry to the platform. If the animal jumps and strikes a window with a card locked in place, it falls into a net below. If the animal jumps at a window which is blocked by a card, lightly held, it lands easily on the platform behind. Usually the animals are trained while on mild food-deprivation schedules and food is available on the platform behind the windows.

Let us assume that the card with a circle painted on it is always locked in place and a card with a square painted on it is only held in place lightly. The cards are placed in the right or left windows on a random basis. The animals soon learn to jump to the card with the square on it. By doing so, they gain entry to the platform and do not bump their noses and fall into the net below as happens when jumping to the card with the circle.

The next step is to change the situation by randomly locking the cards in place so that there is *no solution* to the problem. Now a jump to either card may or may not pay off. Half the time a jump will result in bumped nose and a fall. What happens to the behavior of the animals? Quickly the animals adopt an invariant position response. For example, an animal will jump toward the right window on all trials. This is the *fixation* of a response. It occurs on every trial and in a stereotyped fashion. If an animal has fixated a jumping response toward the right window, and the left window is completely open, the rat will lean out toward the open window, sniff at it, then jump at the closed right window on trial after trial. Maier's argument is that frustration (in this case the insoluble problem) leads to response fixation, and this fixation serves no goal. When an individual's frustration toleration has been exceeded there is a complete loss of adaptivity as stereotyped behavior is initiated.

Many things may lead to the frustration-instigated fixation of responses. In the jumping-stand experiment above it was the introduction of an insoluble problem. In other instances frustration-instigated fixation could be caused by punishment, anxiety, a series of business failures, disappointments in love, in short any frustration. Maier uses the term *frustration* somewhat more broadly than many psychologists who restrict the term to instances where an individual is thwarted in attaining a specific goal.

The fixated responses discussed by Maier are similar to those exhibited by mentally disturbed individuals who exhibit compulsive behavior. Any one may show fixated behavior when frustrations have temporarily exceeded tolerances; but the compulsive person evidences fixated, stereotyped responses day in and day out, relentlessly. Both temporary and permanent fixation responses are a phenomenon which we cannot deny. They exist in animals and in man. Whether they will best be explained in terms of anxiety-reduction, frustration, or more elaborate personality dynamics is an empirical problem which future research must decide.

Behavior in Society

To this point in our discussion of motivation we have concentrated our attention on the physiological and behavioristic analysis of motivation. We have, it is true, discussed the concepts of hedonism and anxiety, but restricted our discussion to approaches to these problems which are very close to the behavioristic learning theories. Next, we shall attempt to explore other kinds of motivational theories that have been developed to account for man's behavior in the society in which he lives.

LEWIN'S AHISTORICAL APPROACH   One of Kurt Lewin's more widely quoted statements is that behavior is a joint function of the person and of his environment [31]. This means we cannot

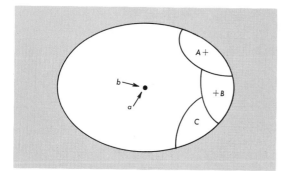

FIG. 8.7. *Simplified drawing of life space as used by Lewin. Regions A, B, and C are differentiated by the individual; A and B have positive valence and forces "push" subject toward these regions.*

understand why a person behaves knowing only one of these factors. More important, we must know the environment as the person perceives it. As we already know, our perception of the world may correspond to a greater or lesser degree with others' perceptions of the world. Behavior is a joint function of the person and *his* perceived environment. Lewin expressed this relation as

$$B = f(P,E)$$

Lewin incorporated this assertion into his conceptual term, *the life space*. The life space is a psychological space representing the person in his perceived environment and describes relationships between its various subspaces, forces, and valences. A simplified example of a drawing of the life space is presented in Fig. 8.7. The life space is the entire enclosed region. The enclosed subareas *A, B,* and *C* are regions of the life space. The regions may be objects, other people, institutions, or ways of behaving. The arrows *a* and *b* represent forces in the life space

FIG. 8.8 *Vector summation.* z *represents sum of vectors* x *and* y. *Lewin believed that all behavioral choices represented the summation of all motives (forces) acting upon an individual at a given moment, which could be represented as vectors in the geometry of life space.*

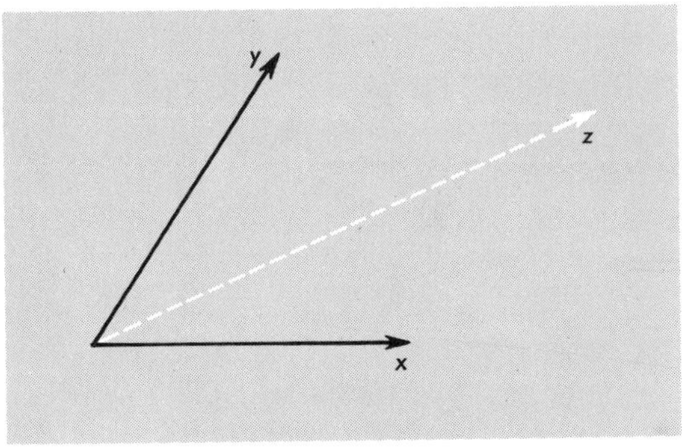

directed toward regions *A* and *B*. The plus signs indicate regions that have a positive valence for the individual who is represented by the point. Region *C* is discriminated by the individual but has no valence for him. Since there is no valence, there is no force toward or away from this region. If the valences in regions *A* and *B* were negative, the forces in the life space would be acting to push the person away from these regions. In most situations we should recognize that our conceptual life spaces would be very complex with numerous subareas more or less clearly differentiated from each other. Many different forces act upon us, many valences appeal to us. Each varies in quality (positive or negative valence) and quantity. How do we reach decisions when faced with these complex situations where many competing forces place us in situations of conflict?

Lewin conceived of the forces operating in the life space as vectors. The resolution of conflicting forces is made by the mathematical rules governing addition of vectors (a vector is a quantity with a direction). Vector addition can be represented rather easily. Consulting Fig. 8.8 we see two vectors, *x* and *y*. The dashed line, vector *z,* is simply the addition of vectors *x* and *y*.

The same principle can be applied when adding a great number of vectors. According to Lewin's position all of our decisions are made this way. Therefore, our behavior is influenced by all the forces and objects with valence operating on the individual at any moment in time. Any force operative in one's life space will have some effect, however slight, on behavior.

This analysis serves to introduce the concept of *overdetermination of behavior*. If some of the forces acting on the person are known, Lewin's rule (vector addition) enables us to combine the forces. Suppose we use the word motive in place of force. Then we would say behavior is the result of many motives and seldom reflects the operation of any single motive. In general it is wise to recognize this as a useful principle: any given behavior is usually determined by more than one motive.

Lewin's terminology also allows us to illustrate a possible danger in interpretation of behavior. It is impossible to safely infer similar underlying motives from similar behavior patterns. If we were to observe two students working hard in a high school study hall, we might be impressed with the great similarity of their behavior and be *mislead* into concluding that their actions were produced by similar motives. This is not necessarily true. One student's behavior could be produced by the motives for academic achievement and for power over others. This student might believe success in high school will lead to these goals. The other student's behavior may be a result of motives for affiliation with the teacher and to avoid failure in an impending examination. Both students might believe that studying hard will help them fulfill these differing underlying motives. The issue at hand is whether motives represent hidden determinants of behavior which can or cannot be inferred directly from behavior. Two individuals may exhibit identical actions resulting from widely divergent motive patterns. Along the same line, we can imagine two people with similar motive patterns who exhibit different behavior because each believes divergent courses of action will be instrumental in motive fulfillment.

Lewin believed the life space to exist on both conscious and unconscious levels. There can be different subregions and valences in the various possible levels of awareness. Behavior can be a result of forces on the conscious or unconscious level, or on both. In any case behavior is only determined by forces operating at the moment of the behavior; about this, Lewin was emphatic. If the forces do not exist *now,* they do not influence present behavior. It would be important to know about an individual's past only if we knew just how the past influences the present life space. Since we know little of the relation between past and present, Lewin pressed the point that psychologists should seek to understand the present psychological environment. Surely forces and valences of the present have origins in the past, but the best we can do is to assess the present representation of the past. Similarly, we can not be influenced by events yet to happen in the future, but we can assess how an individual anticipates the future. Our anticipations or expectations of the future can and do influence our actions.

Lewin's emphasis on understanding the present life space can be thought of as a *cross-sectional* approach to understanding behavior. He would advise us to take a cross-section of a person's life space and use this segment, containing perceived objects, valences, and forces, to understand the individual. Compare this approach with that of a learning theorist who studies the development of behavior patterns over some period of time or of a personality theorist who studies the effects of different early childhood experiences on later characteristics. In these cases the psychologist takes a *longitudinal view,* studying the changes in behavior over a period of time. Lewin's belief that we must concentrate on the current make-up of the individual foreshadowed much of the recent investigations into modern theories of motivation where attempts are made to assess the current motive structure of the individual.

MURRAY'S VIEW Murray collaborated with others in an interdisciplinary study [32]. The investigators were from varied professions and included psychiatrists, psychoanalysts, psychologists, physicists, and anthropologists. They undertook to study in depth a large number of "normal" individuals, in the hope of arriving at a conceptual scheme that all of the experimenters could use and understand. This goal was not reached completely, of course, but a novel framework of analysis of personality stemmed from their efforts. Many of the important variables in this framework can be regarded as motivational because they represent attempts to explain energizing and goal-directing aspects of personality. Murray called certain of these concepts *needs,* defined much more broadly than a physiological deficit. Needs, for Murray, refer to some hypothetical brain activity which disposes an individual to respond in certain ways in certain specific situations. The reference to hypothetical activities in the brain indicates a hope that needs can someday be related to physiological activities and a belief that they *must* depend upon neural activity in some fashion yet to be determined.

Needs are described in terms of the effects produced by behavior. When people do things or say things which produce similar behavioral effects, Murray believed the actions to be motivated by the same or similar needs. The normal individuals at the Harvard Clinic who served as subjects were exhaustively studied to find the common behavioral effects and, consequently, the pattern of common needs. The results of the study were interpreted to reveal two broad categories of common needs: the biological needs of the body (viscerogenic needs) and needs unrelated to the biological urges (psychogenic needs). Some of the viscerogenic needs are similar to those studied earlier in this chapter, for example, need for food and need for water (symbolized *n* food, *n* water). Other needs related to our physiological well-being were added, for example, need to avoid cold (*n* coldavoidance) and need to avoid harm (*n* harmavoidance).

The list of psychogenic needs was a product of the analysis of common behavioral episodes found in the subjects. While Murray makes passing comment that the psychogenic needs "are presumably dependent upon and derived from the viscerogenic needs" [32, p. 80], this is not an important feature of his system. The important aspect is that the list of psychogenic needs was to represent the motive systems apparent in the majority of subjects.

To give the flavor of Murray's analysis, some brief descriptions of some of the secondary or psychogenic needs are presented below:

1. *n* Acquisition (acquisitive attitude). To gain possession and property. To grasp, snatch or steal things. To bargain or gamble, to work for money or goods.
2. *n* Conservance (conserving attitude). To collect, repair, clean and preserve things. To protect against damage.
3. *n* Order (orderly attitude). To arrange, organize, put away objects. To be tidy and clean. To be scrupulously precise.

4. *n* Retention (retentive attitude). To retain possession of things. To refuse to give or lend. To hoard. To be frugal, economical, and miserly.

5. *n* Construction (constructive attitude). To organize and build.

6. *n* Superiority (ambitious attitude). This has been broken into two needs: *n* achievement (will to power over things, people, and ideas) and *n* recognition (efforts to gain approval and high social status).

7. *n* Achievement (achievement attitude). To overcome obstacles, to exercise power, to strive to do something difficult as well and as quickly as possible. (This is an elementary ego need which alone may prompt any action or be fused with any other need.)

8. *n* recognition (self-forwarding attitude). To excite praise and commendation. To demand respect. To boast and exhibit one's accomplishments. To seek distinction, social prestige, honors, or high office [32 pp. 80–81].

These are but a few of the social, or psychogenic needs listed by Murray. As the thinking of Murray and the group developed, four observable indices became most prominent for evaluation of needs:

1. Statements by individuals of their desires or wishes for certain end situations.

2. Behaviors which tended directly to bring about a specific end result.

3. The occurrence of special amounts or kinds of affect with special types of behaviors. For example, anger may be used as a sign of aggression. When a behavior sequence is blocked and anger or aggression results, we can infer there was some underlying need being blocked.

4. Some motor patterns are more or less stable indicators of underlying needs. Movements of striking out or hitting represent aggression; crying represents the need for succor; smiling, the need for affiliating with others.

In effect, Murray suggested that we can view motives or needs in terms of end states resulting from behavior and from some other reliable indicators. The origin of these motives was not a paramount interest to Murray; rather, attention was focused upon determining what motives are found in normal individuals. Most important, perhaps, is the conceptualization of human behavior as motivated by urges toward such abstract goals as achievement, affiliation, and recognition. Motives are assumed to be socially acquired, and transmitted through our culture. Furthermore, this conception of motives makes them the prime, dynamic movers of behavior rather than merely passive traits or habitual modes of behavior.

McCLELLAND AND THE ACHIEVEMENT MOTIVE Both the types of common needs found by Murray and the methods used to establish the presence of motives served as useful background for McClelland and Atkinson in their work on the motive for achievement. McClelland *et al.* published [33] an extensive elaboration of one of the motives suggested by Murray in which a new theory of motivation was delineated, based in part on the theory of hedonism.

Certainly, on a subjective level it would seem that much of our behavior is determined by our expectations of future pleasures or pains. In fact one might inquire why hedonism has not been accepted as a general principle, or even *the* general principle underlying behavior. Probably the reason why hedonism was virtually ignored in American psychology for its first fifty years stems from the emphasis on measurement and objectivity that marked the behavioristic movement in general. For many years a behavioristic point of view was identified with a scientific one. However, the current work on hedonism (discussed earlier) along with a growing discontent with motivational explanations of *S-R* learning theories have caused workers to return to hedonism as an important principle in the explanation of behavior. However, the behavioristic influence can still be seen in the newer brands of hedonism. Today, psychologists tend to define pleasure and pain as theoretical concepts defined in terms of behavioral or environmental changes. McClelland et al. believe that motives are learned through the association of affective states with stimulus conditions, and they define affect in a manner somewhat similar to the discrepancy hypothesis mentioned earlier (pp. 338–342 ff.). For our current purposes, let us use *affective qualities* to define the term *motive*. McClelland and his co-workers define motive as follows: "a reintegration of a change in affect by a cue and an anticipation of future change in affect contingent upon certain actions." [This definition, condensed from several, captures three important features of the McClelland model: the motivated individual (1) is experiencing affect, (2) anticipates a further change in affect, and (3) expects these further changes to be contingent on certain of his behaviors.]

According to this view, an individual is motivated when a cue in the environment elicits an affective response in him, and the individual anticipates a further change in affect depending upon some subsequent behavior. A person is motivated by hunger when a cue produces a part of the pleasure experienced in the past through eating and expects that doing something, like heading to a restaurant or dormitory, will produce even more pleasure. A person high in *n* achievement is one in whom a competitive situation elicits some of the positive affect which has been experienced in the past in competitive situations and at the same time expects that some action on his part, such as studying long and hard, will lead to even more pleasure. *n* Achievement refers to a positive motive to attain success in competition with a standard of excellence. Other people might be motivated in a negative or aversive fashion by competitive situations. For these people, cues of competition suggest some of the unpleasantness experienced in past failures and even offer the possibility of greater pain through yet another failure.

The person who experiences positive affect from competitive situations has a need for achievement (*n* achievement), whereas the person who experiences negative affect is motivated by a fear of failure (*f* failure). A person for whom competitive situations elicit positive affect will act so as to continue and enhance the situation; whereas a person motivated to avoid failure would try to leave the competitive situation or at least to terminate it as soon as possible.

The types of motives which dominate an individual's life develop as a function of an individual's past experiences. The motivation model of McClelland postulates that affect is conditioned to stimuli by mere association. The more frequently pleasure or unpleasantness is associated with neutral stimuli, the stronger will be the association formed and the more likely it is that this formerly neutral stimulus will evoke affect in the future.

If one's parents provide pleasure for the child as a reward for engaging in competitive activities, or if the child is often successful and wins the pleasures of victory, then we would expect the child to develop strong achievement motivation. If a child has learned to expect the worst from competitive activities, one would expect him to have more fear of failure.

Individual patterns of rewards will determine the extent to which one is motivated by achievement, failure, power, affiliation, or by any of the other motives discussed by Murray. At the moment, most research in this area has centered on the achievement motive. Even a cursory view of our culture would suggest that everyone is motivated to some extent by needs for achievement, failure, and affiliation. The job of the motivation specialist then is to establish an order or *relationship* among a group of individuals for a given motive.

McClelland's *n* achievement is currently assessed through a written test given in one of several forms. Subjects are asked to write creative stories based on stimuli which are sufficiently ambiguous to allow many possible interpretations After the stories are written, they are scored on the basis of the amount of "achievement imagery" in the stories. It is assumed that the stories reflect the motives of the writers.

Projective technique is the generic term for tests which result in subjects revealing things of theoretical interest about themselves through stories created as a result of ambiguous or unstructured stimuli allowing various interpretations. The McClelland system for measuring motivation is objectified to allow a minimum of subjective evaluation. One of the techniques used by the McClelland group to measure motivation stems from the earlier work of Murray.

Murray developed a method for evaluating various aspects of personality. The subject would be shown several different kinds of pictures and would be asked to tell the experimenter what he believed the individuals in the pictures were doing. The experimenter might ask the subject about the outcome of the activities, intentions, or emotions of the person in the picture. This general procedure and the set of pictures is known as the *Thematic Apperception Test* (TAT). The name comes from Murray's interest in the over-all nature of the stories (thema). As with most projective instruments the information obtained from the TAT is evaluated in relation to all that is known about the subject (or patient, in a clinical setting).

For many reasons, for example, different theoretical approaches of the interpreters and different previous experiences with the person being examined, the interpretations of TAT stories are known to vary among interpreters. Another difficulty is that the training of those who interpret TAT stories is long and intensive. These difficulties led McClelland and his colleagues to search for new techniques to assess human motives that would be more amenable to research purposes.

The method McClelland developed as an attempt to find a more objective way to score imaginative stories for motives was as follows. The scorer for a particular motive, say need achievement, would examine the stories for their themes. A significant portion of a story had to concern attempts to reach achievement goals in order for it to be scored for *n* achievement at all. A passing mention of achievement behavior is not sufficient to represent *n* achievement in the protocol. The determination of whether or not a character of a story was trying for achievement ends was made using at least one of several objective criteria.

Once it has been determined that the story contains achievement imagery, other categories of possible behaviors which indicate strength of interest in success may be scored. For example, the scorer scans the story for statements indicating that the character(s) is anticipating possible outcomes of the activity and is experiencing emotions related to his possible success. For every type of behavior exhibited which is related to the act of achieving, the person writing the story is given another point; having started with a point for a story containing achievement imagery in the first place. In review: The scorer (1) judges whether it is an achievement theme and then (2) looks for certain specific types of activities in the stories postulated as represented indicating strength of motivation.

This scoring system attempts to approximate a counting procedure. Ideally, the scorer should only have to search the story for certain statements, emotions, activities, etc., and enumerate their frequencies. However, some interpretation is still required of the scorer, although much less than required for an interpreter of a traditional TAT or a Rorschach test. Instructions for scoring stories have been published [34]. With practice scorers can reach high levels of agreement in their scoring in a relatively short period of time—a week or so. Thus one of the aims of McClelland has been accomplished, at least in part: a system for evaluating projective tests with a vastly reduced subjective component. But even if scorers can agree, on what are they agreeing? Does the score which is the total of the achievement points have anything to do with motivation for achievement?

Atkinson and McClelland [35] showed that responses to ambiguous stimuli could reflect the arousal of a biological motive. Stories written in a projective test situation by adult human beings under food deprivation contained more references to food deprivation and food-related objects than did stories written by subjects not food deprived. The number of direct responses concerning food did not increase with increased deprivation, however. Would it be possible to arouse experimentally the motive for achievement and show corresponding increase in achievement imagery?

It is worthwhile to note a difference between the arousal of hunger and the arousal of *n* achievement in the McClelland system. Hunger was elicited by deprivation of food in the Atkinson and McClelland experiment; but deprivation of achievement (or failure) would not be an appropriate condition to arouse the achievement motive. The McClelland view sees *n* achievement as an affective response in the person aroused by hopes for success. In broad scope it is a fulfillment theory; success feeds on itself.

One type of experiment has effectively demonstrated the effect of situational stimuli in arousing achievement imagery. Imaginative stories written after prior experiences with success and failure contained more achievement imagery than stories written by comparable students at other times [36]. Presumably, the examination provided cues which raised the hope of successful competition with a standard of excellence. While both environmental circumstances and the cues of the TAT pictures can contribute to the achievement imagery produced in creative stories, the most important factor for evaluating *n* achievement is the contribution of the individual. The theory assumes each person to be differently disposed to produce achievement imagery. The standard practice is to use the achievement-imagery score obtained under what are defined as *neutral conditions* (using certain pictures) as the measure of an individual's *n* achievement.

The next logical step would be to show that people attaining high achievement scores will work intensely to obtain success in situations where doing so would likely result in reaching achievement goals. Rather than go into the many experiments which have been done to demonstrate the ability of *n* achievement scores to predict behavior [e.g., 37], we shall discuss an experiment in which n achievement scores predict behavior only under certain conditions.

Atkinson and Reitman [38] performed an experiment in which two tasks were given to two groups of subjects under different conditions. In all conditions the instructions asked the subjects to do their best on the tasks. In one group they were told these tests were ones which in the past had been useful in predicting those who would "do well in life." The subjects in this group worked at the tasks alone in private rooms. The subjects in the other group were told the same thing but in addition they were told cash prizes were to be given to students doing best. The subjects in the latter group worked on their tasks in a group situation in which the experimenters walked around more or less proctoring their work. It could be presumed that the group situation and the experimenters' actions increased the motivation of the subjects to affiliate with the other students and to favorably impress the experimenters.

The results of this experiment indicate that people who were measured as having high achievement scores performed better than those with low achievement scores only in the first group. When the additional sources of motivation were added (money, affiliation) the performance of the high and low achievement groups was indistinguishable. This experiment shows that differences in behavior can be predicted on the basis of the achievement motive only when the situational cues elicit achievement cues and little else. Atkinson and Reitman recognized the principle that almost all of our behavior is overdetermined, i.e., it serves many motives. Typically, we measure only one motive, the others left uncontrolled and unassessed. In their group situation they purposely introduced situational cues for money and affiliation motives. True to their prediction, the introduction of cues for these other motives obscured the predictive ability of the achievement scores. This experiment serves to bring to our attention the point made before that it is only possible to observe the effect of a motive when the person perceives that an activity can serve as a means to fulfillment of that motive.

Progress has been less rapid in the research in other motives stemming from Murray's theoretical contributions. Scoring systems have been developed for n power, n affiliation, and f failure by workers of the McClelland orientation [37]. While such

367

primary efforts are, by and large, encouraging, there remains much to be accomplished in regard to all of these motives.

Perhaps the most urgent need is to develop measurement devices for these needs which are even more objective than the McClelland system. While trained scorers correlate highly with each other in the McClelland technique, there are other practical measurement problems in the system. This may indicate one administration of the test is all that can be used profitably. The measure can be made only once. Correlations between *n* achievement scores on different stories in a set are low, and sometimes show a cyclic effect from story to story. Does this mean achievement is not as general a motive as we have thought? Should the *n* achievement score be considered as a sum of scores representing similar yet different motives?

As with many areas in psychology, a great deal has been learned about motives, but a great deal remains to be learned. This chapter has presented a variety of theories and frameworks to stimulate thinking. It remains for the student of psychology to evaluate the work and points of view represented by Stellar, Hebb, Hull, Mowrer, Lewin, Murray, and others and to continue the exploration of behavior so that new and more effective theories may be developed. It is today's student who will be tomorrow's researcher in man's never-ending attempt to understand himself.

References

1. Littman, R. A. Motives, history, and causes. In M. R. Jones (Ed.), *Nebraska Symposium on Motivation.* Lincoln: Univer. Nebraska Press, 1958.

2. Cannon, W. B., & Washburn, L. An explanation of hunger. *Amer. J. Physiol.,* 1912, **29,** 441–454.

3. Tsang, Y. C. Hunger motivation in gastrectomized rats. *J. comp. Psychol.,* 1938, **26,** 1–17.

4. Mayer, J. Regulation of energy intake and the body weight: the glucostatic theory and the lipostatic hypothesis. *Ann. N.Y. Acad. Sci.,* 1955, **63,** 14–53.

5. Hetherington, A. W., & Ranson, S. W. Hypothalamic lesions and adiposity in the rat. *Anat. Rec.,* 1942, **78,** 149–172.

6. Anand, B. K., & Brobeck, J. R. Localization of a "feeding center" in the hypothalamus of the rat. *Proc. Soc. exp. biol. Med.,* 1951, **77,** 323–324.

7. Teitelbaum, P. Sensory control of hypothalamic hyper-phagia. *J. comp. physiol Psychol.,* 1955, **48,** 156–163.

8. Andersson, B., & McCann, S. M. A further study of polydipsia evoked by hypothalamic stimulation in the goat. *Acta physiol. Scand.,* 1955, **33,** 333–346.

9. Stellar, E. The physiology of motivation. *Psychol. Rev.,* 1954, **61,** 5–22.

10. Stellar, E. Drive and motivation. In J. Field (Ed.), *Handbook of Physiology.* Washington: Amer. Physiol. Soc., 1960.

11. T. Tomita, data reported by P. T. Young. The role of hedonic processes in motivation. In M. R. Jones (Ed.), *op. cit.,* 1955.

12. Warren, R. P., & Pfaffman, C. J. Early experience and taste aversion. *J. comp. physiol. Psychol.,* 1959, **52,** 263–266.

13. Cytovich, I. S. Dissertation, Petersburg, 1911. Reported in J. Konorski, *Conditioned Reflexes and Neuron Organization* (Trans. S. Garry). England: Cambridge Univer. Press, 1948.

14. Wolfe, J. B., & Kaplon, M. D. The effect of amount of reward and consummative activity on learning in chickens. *J. comp. Psychol.,* 1941, **31,** 353–361.

15. Berkun, K. J., Kessen, M. L., & Miller, N. E. Hunger-reducing effects of food by stomach fistula vs. food by mouth measured by a consummatory response. *J. comp. physiol. Psychol.,* 1952, **45,** 550–554.

16. Miller, N. E., & Kessen, M. L. Reward effects of food via stomach fistula compared with those of food by mouth. *J. comp. physiol. Psychol.,* 1952, **45,** 555–564.

17. Sheffield, F. D., Wulff, J. J., & Backer, R. Reward value of copulation without sex drive reduction. *J. comp. physiol. Psychol.,* 1951, **44,** 3–8.

18. Olds, J. Positive emotional systems studied by techniques of self-stimulation. *Psychiat. Res. Rept.,* 1960, **12,** 238–257.

19. Freeman, W., & Watts, J. W. *Psychosurgery in the Treatment of Mental Disorders and Intractable Pain.* (2nd ed.) Springfield, Ill., Charles C Thomas, Publisher, 1950.

20. Clark, R. S., Heron, W., Fetherstonhaugh, M. L., Forgays, D. G., & Hebb, D. O. Individual differences in dogs: preliminary report on the effects of early experience. *Canad. J. Psychol.,* 1951, **5,** 150–156.

21. Hebb, D. O. *A Textbook of Psychology.* Philadelphia: W. B. Saunders Company, 1958.

22. Milner, P. M. The cell assembly: Mark II. *Psychol. Rev.,* 1957, **64,** 242–252.

23. Mowrer, O. H. *Learning Theory and Behavior*. New York: John Wiley & Sons, Inc., 1960.

24. Zimmerman, D. W. Durable secondary reinforcement: method and theory. *Psychol. Rev.,* 1957, **64,** 373–383.

25. Zimmerman, D. W. Sustained performance in rats based on secondary reinforcement. *J. comp. physiol. Psychol.,* 1959, **52,** 353–358.

26. Spence, K. W., & Taylor, Janet A. Anxiety and strength of the US as determiners of the amount of eyelid conditioning. *J. exp. Psychol.,* 1951, **42,** 183–188.

27. Spence, K. W., Farber, I. E., & McFann, H. H. The relation of anxiety (drive) level to performance in competitional and noncompetitional paired associates learning. *J. exp. Psychol.,* 1956, **52,** 296–305.

28. Sarason, I. G. Empirical findings and theoretical problems in the use of anxiety scales. *Psychol. Bull.,* 1960, **57,** 403–415.

29. Mandler, G., & Sarason, S. B. A study of anxiety and learning. *J. abnorm. soc. Psychol.,* 1952, **47,** 166–173.

30. Maier, N. R. F. *Frustration: The Study of Behavior without a Goal*. New York: McGraw-Hill Book Company, Inc., 1949.

31. Lewin, K. In D. Cartwright (Ed.), *Field Theory in Social Science*. New York: Harper & Row, Publishers, Inc., 1951.

32. Murray, H. A. *Explorations in Personality*. New York: Oxford Univer. Press, 1938.

33. McClelland, D. C., Atkinson, J. W., Clark, R. A., & Lowell, E. L. *The Achievement Motive*. New York: Appleton-Century-Crofts, Inc., 1953.

34. Smith, C. P., & Feld, Sheila. How to learn the method of content analysis for *n* Achievement, *n* Affiliation, and *n* Power. Appendix I in J. W. Atkinson (Ed.), *Motives in Fantasy, Action, and Society*. Princeton, N.J.: D. Van Nostrand Company, Inc., 1958.

35. McClelland, D. C., & Atkinson, J. W. The projective expression of needs: I. The effect of different intensities of the hunger upon perception. *J. Psychol.,* 1948, **25,** 205–222.

36. McClelland, D. C., Clark, R. A., Roby, T. B., & Atkinson, J. W. The effect of the need for achievement on thematic apperception. *J. exp. Psychol.,* 1949, **37,** 242–255.

37. Atkinson, J. W. (Ed.), *Motives in Fantasy, Action, and Society*. Princeton, N.J.: D. Von Nostrand Company, Inc., 1958.

38. Atkinson, J. W., & Reitman, W. R. Performance as a function of motive strength expectancy of goal attainment. *J. abnorm. soc. Psychol.,* 1956, **53,** 361–366.

INDEX

371